Scaling Oracle8i™

Scaling Oracle8i™

Building Highly Scalable OLTP System Architectures

James Morle

ADDISON–WESLEY

An Imprint of Addison Wesley Longman, Inc.

Reading, Massachusetts • Harlow, England • Menlo Park, California
Berkeley, California • Don Mills, Ontario • Sydney
Bonn • Amsterdam • Tokyo • Mexico City

Many of the designations used by manufacturers and sellers to distinguish their products are claimed as trademarks. Where those designations appear in this book, and Addison Wesley Longman, Inc. was aware of a trademark claim, the designations have been printed with initial capital letters or in all capitals.

The author and publisher have taken care in the preparation of this book, but make no expressed or implied warranty of any kind and assume no responsibility for errors or omissions. No liability is assumed for incidental or consequential damages in connection with or arising out of the use of the information or programs contained herein.

The publisher offers discounts on this book when ordered in quantity for special sales. For more information, please contact

AWL Direct Sales
Addison Wesley Longman, Inc.
One Jacob Way
Reading, Massachusetts 01867
(781) 944-3700

Visit AW on the Web: www.awl.com/cseng/

Library of Congress Cataloging-in-Publication Data

Morle, James, 1970–
    Scaling Oracle8i : building highly scalable OLTP system architectures / James Morle.
        p. cm.
    Includes bibliographical references and index.
    ISBN 0-201-32574-8
    1. Oracle (Computer file) 2. Relational databases. I. Title.
QA76.9.D3 m658   2000
005.75'85—dc21
                                                                99–051334
                                                                CIP

ISBN 0-201-32574-8
Text printed on recycled paper
1 2 3 4 5 6 7 8 9 10—MA—0302010099
First printing, December 1999

Contents

Figure List

Preface

This is a book about getting the most out of Oracle8i on UNIX systems. While many people understand how to administrate Oracle and UNIX, far fewer understand the issues and workings of the software and hardware, thus limiting the scalability of the system. This book aims to open up this essential information, enabling the reader to build faster, larger, and more scalable systems than ever before.

The purpose of this book is to provide grounding in all the areas required for large systems implementation using UNIX and Oracle8i. Some of the information in this text is available elsewhere, scattered throughout a large number of specialized volumes, while other information, taken from experience in implementing such systems, is previously undocumented.

Unlike many Oracle books, this book avoids the "one size fits all," cookbook approach to improving the skillset of the reader. In my opinion, such books do little to improve foundation skills and serve only to confuse readers when their circumstances deviate from those of the author. Rather, the intent of this book is to communicate a distillation of many years of experience in building very large Oracle database systems. The information presented here allows the reader to make informed decisions, based on real facts, that directly apply to the actual case at hand.

Where appropriate, this book will make recommendations to the reader, mostly from an approach standpoint. These recommendations are intended to guide the reader past some of the common pitfalls often encountered during the building of large systems. In addition to technical information, the book also makes organizational and procedural recommendations intended to help the reader avoid dead ends and other sources of aggravation.

Although the focus of this book is on Oracle8i, the principles presented also apply to other database software. UNIX is the premier platform for very large Oracle systems and is therefore presented as the underlying operating system, although many of the hardware and theoretical discussions also apply to other operating systems, such as Windows NT. Large, custom-written applications are the main target of this book, but all of the concepts presented here also apply in varying degrees to smaller systems and packaged applications.

Who Should Read This Book

This book is primarily aimed at the following audiences.

- System architects
- Database engineers wanting to expand their knowledge
- System administrators working on UNIX/Oracle systems
- Senior application developers

In addition, this book will be of value to the following audiences.

- Technology managers
- Computer science students

Credits

Sincere thanks need to be made at this point. I want to thank the following people for their help, reviews, support, and sanity throughout the writing of this book (in no special order): Jeff Needham, Jan-Simon Pendry, John McGarva, Brian Best, Mike McNall, John Mashey, Doug Rady, Russell

Green, Daniel Semler, Kevin Closson, Bob Robinson, Juan Loaiza, Greg Doherty, Graham Wood, and Richard Sarwal, plus the many that I am sure to have forgotten.

Feedback

If you have any questions or comments regarding this book, please feel free to contact me at *BookFeedback@Morle.com.*

James Morle, 1999

Introduction

Database systems are growing at an enormous rate. Both connection volume and data volume have grown exponentially since the large-scale adoption of open systems and of commodity database server software such as Oracle. These systems are now matching and exceeding the capabilities previously demonstrated only by mainframe systems.

Database systems can be separated into two broad categories:

- Online transaction processing (OLTP) system

- Decision support systems (DSS) such as data warehouses, data mining, reporting and so on

Both types of systems present unique challenges in implementing systems of large scale. The challenge of large transactional systems involves the management of many small operations occurring at once, while DSS systems need to process vast amounts of data. Consequently, transactional systems need low latencies, and DSS systems need high throughput.

This book is focused mainly on *transactional systems*, with references to DSS systems where appropriate.

In the mainframe world, scaling and robustness are often heavily ingrained in the cultures of all involved; system programmers, DBAs, application programmers, and the vendors themselves conform to rigorous standards and methodologies that are practically set in stone. The net result of this enforced conformance is a greater probability that scalable, robust business systems will be produced.

In the open systems world, no such constraints are set on any of the personnel who build the system; any method can be used as long as it achieves the required result. This flexibility is the catalyst behind the proliferation of open systems, allowing very rapid development and inclusion of more powerful functionality within the application. Unfortunately, this flexibility results in the following costs:

1. Unscalable applications are the default product.

2. Reliable systems are difficult to obtain.

Both of these costs bear down hard on a business. Although the business has been able to develop the application and implement the hardware for a fraction of the cost of a comparable mainframe system, this advantage is overshadowed by potentially long, unscheduled downtime and by difficulties in scaling the system in line with business growth.

In order to mitigate these disadvantages, it has become increasingly important for builders of open systems solutions to change the way these systems are built. This involves two fundamental changes in the default, anarchic method of open systems development:

1. A return to some of the ground rules introduced by the mainframe, particularly multitier architectures

2. A much greater level of technical knowledge within the teams

The first change involves taking the "good" aspects of the mainframe development sandbox and adopting them in the open systems arena. Multitier application architectures are prime among these aspects, moving away from the single points of failure, poor scalability, low reusability, and often proprietary, two-tier solutions.

The second change requires open systems teams to have a far greater understanding of how the systems work than they ever had before. Mainframe developers have historically had to deal with two contrasting levels of complexity during development. On one hand, the segmentation of function within mainframe systems meant that the developer did not need to be concerned about portions of system operation. On the other hand, the development of applications in low-level languages meant that application developers were *forced* to be concerned about performance and "doing the right thing."

In open systems, applications are typically developed using high-level or object-based languages, which means that the separation between the application developer and the underlying systems is far greater than when procedural, third-generation languages are used. The effect of this is that application developers are often too far removed from the system, and the only individuals on the team who can see the whole picture are the database engineers. It is important, therefore, that the database engineer be able to understand all the issues, and that the application developer also be aware of the necessary considerations.

How To Read This Book

The book is divided into several parts, each of which can mostly be read independently of the others. It is recommended, however, that the book be read sequentially from front to back. The reason for this is that, although all the parts overlap somewhat, the book has been written from front to back. For this reason, some assumption of knowledge of prior chapters is made.

The order of presentation (hardware before software) may initially appear to be exactly reversed, as the greatest impact can be made in the software. This is true, but it is my opinion that software cannot be understood or responsibly architected without prior knowledge of how it relates to the actual execution on the hardware. Therefore, we take the journey from the ground up.

Part I: Concepts and Architecture
Chapter 1: Scaling Concepts

What is scaling? Why do I need to be concerned with scalability? What are the common concepts used to provide scalability? This chapter presents the basic concepts of computer science that are required in order to understand some of the later chapters.

Chapter 2: Hardware Architectures and I/O Subsystems

This chapter describes the many different hardware architectures on the market today, all of which have significantly different operational profiles.

Understanding the differences among the platforms and how those differences relate to the operation of Oracle are critical during platform selection and subsequent configuration and tuning.

The chapter goes on to discuss I/O, a core part of any database system. A thorough understanding of the mechanics of the physical disk, and of the various RAID options, should be considered a prerequisite to building a database.

Part II: Building Support Software
Chapter 3: Benchmark Concepts and Design

Large systems cannot be simply rolled into production. At least some element of initial testing must be performed in order to certify both the performance and the stability of the platform. This chapter shows how a simple benchmark can be produced using simple Oracle trace files. Also presented is the Oracle-based scripting tool, dbaman.

Chapter 4: System/Database Monitoring

This chapter explores how a large Oracle database server can be monitored using low-intrusion techniques. Included in this chapter is an introduction on how to interrogate the Oracle fixed tables to derive operational data, and how to present that data using standard PC tools.

Part III: How Oracle Works
Chapter 5: Physical Oracle

This chapter concentrates on the physical attributes of Oracle, including the initialization file, the different types of objects, the internals of those objects, and how consistent read is implemented.

Chapter 6: Oracle8 in Operation

The other side of Oracle is the "living" side of it, the Oracle instance. This chapter describes the various caches used by Oracle and the measures that have been taken within the product to allow it to scale effectively. An introduction to Oracle Parallel Server is included, along with some more details on the v$ views.

Part IV: How UNIX Works
Chapter 7: Introduction to UNIX

A knowledge of the UNIX kernel often becomes important when one is trying to determine why a database server behaves the way it does. This chapter describes the UNIX kernel and the virtual memory system, and how they relate to an Oracle database server.

Chapter 8: Oracle User's Guide to UNIX

Oracle relies heavily on the underlying operating system. This chapter describes how Oracle interfaces with the operating system, using the virtual operating system abstraction. An introduction to a selection of the invaluable UNIX tools is provided.

Part V: Implementing Oracle
Chapter 9: Scalable Transaction Processing

This chapter provides guidelines on how to develop applications that scale, and how to tune the database to execute the requests most effectively. Included in this chapter are sections on writing scalable SQL, the purpose of a transaction processing (TP) monitor, and an approach to tuning for the desired result.

Chapter 10: Pulling It All Together: A Case Study

The proof of the pudding is in the eating. This chapter gives an overview of a real-life, large-scale Oracle system, along with pointers to the lessons learned during implementation.

Part VI: Further Considerations

Chapter 11: Building a Successful Team

This small but important chapter introduces some techniques for building a good team to do this kind of work.

Chapter 12: Pitfalls

This chapter concentrates on software problems—bugs. It is inevitable that large systems will be impacted in some way by bugs, and dealing with them effectively is important in maintaining a stable system.

Chapter 13: Internet Applications and the Future

The final chapter looks at the direction of application engineering and the future direction of Oracle.

PART I

Concepts and Architecture

Chapter 1

Scaling Concepts

In order to build a large system of any kind, it is important to have a good understanding of some basic scaling principles. By understanding these basic principles, it becomes much easier to interpret the requirements for building a large-scale Oracle-based system, and to address performance issues in existing systems that are not scaling satisfactorily. This chapter does not aim to cover all aspects of a system that affect scaling, but does intend to cover the more important aspects, giving examples that highlight situations in which they are found in real systems.

1.1   What Is Scaling?

scaling *n .... 2: act of measuring or arranging or adjusting according to a scale.*
—Webster's Revised Unabridged Dictionary (1913)

To make this old-fashioned and generic-sounding definition a little more explicit, here are a few examples of scaling in action.

- Increasing the processor count on the system
- Increasing the number of active users on the system
- Increasing the number of records your batch job processes in a given time

The word "increasing" appears in each listed item: that's the scaling that we are interested in for this book—increasing the system capability, whether "system" is defined as hardware, software, or, more typically, both. Indeed, the most common view of scaling is that of hardware scaling, even though scaling has at least as much to do with the software components as with the hardware. Nevertheless, it serves as a useful (if overused) example of what we mean by scaling.

If we were to double the number of processors in a system, would we achieve twice the processing capability? The answer is probably "no." Scaling, like most things, can be classified in either of two ways: good (*efficient*) scaling and poor (*inefficient*) scaling.

Good Scaling. Good scaling is observed as a highly linear increase in capability as the system grows. Using the tired old hardware example, this means that the system would demonstrate a near-linear gain in capacity when additional resource is applied (see Figure 1.1).

In Figure 1.1 the capacity of the system is increasing at almost the same rate as the resource being added. This means that, as long as the software scales equally well, the system will be able to process almost *n times* the data within a given amount of time if *n times* the resource is available.

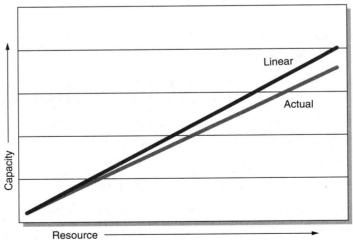

Figure 1.1 Good scaling

Poor Scaling.   Poor scaling demonstrates a negative deviation from linear when a system grows. This means that the system capacity diverges farther away from linear when additional resource is applied (see Figure 1.2).

The poor scaling illustrated in Figure 1.2 shows that there is actually *less* system capacity available when all of the resource is applied than when the system had less than one-half of the total resource. This is an example of what can happen when a system scales badly: performance goes down, not up. This is true of both software and hardware scaling, and is of particular concern when a large system is being built. Good scaling is a function of both hardware and software, and unless both are optimized to scale, overall system throughput will be considerably less than expected.

Scaling can be viewed from two different perspectives: a *speedup* of tasks within the system; and an increase in concurrency in the system, sometimes referred to as *scaleup*. Both speedup and scaleup use the same principles, applied in slightly different manners.

1.1.1   Speedup

If a job takes *n* seconds to run under normal circumstances, and it is desired that the job should run in *n*/2 seconds, then a twofold *speedup*

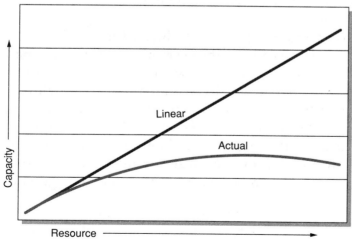

Figure 1.2   Poor scaling

is required. This speedup can be gained in either of two different ways:

- Doubling the execution capacity of existing components
- Breaking the job into two parts, and assigning twice as much hardware to the job[1]

Doubling the execution capacity of the existing components is great if it is possible: it allows the required speedup to be achieved with no increase in complexity and with few concerns as to the required scalability. In fact, speedups gained in this way are not really subject to any scalability concerns at all, assuming that the entire system is doubled in execution capacity (including processor speed, cache sizes, communications latencies, clock speeds of all components, and so on). Unfortunately, this is rarely an option, because speedups are frequently needed immediately after the initial rollout period or are required to be many times the speedup offered by faster parts. If the system has just been installed, it's probably already using the fastest components available, because vendors rarely sell parts that are not at the highest specification available for their system architecture. On the other hand, another vendor may have dramatically faster hardware, and a reassessment of the platform may need to be made; this, however, is an expensive option and is potentially unnecessary when other techniques, such as parallelization, are available.

The most common option is to break the job down into smaller "bite-sized" pieces and have the system process them in parallel. This technique, known as *job partitioning*, allows the system to be added to where necessary to increase the overall system bandwidth. This has a scalability implication for the system and makes the speedup element dependent on the *concurrency* available within the system. Parallelization of tasks is the common scalability requirement for decision support systems. One of the most common parallel activities in a decision support system is *parallel query*, which is a good example of speedup.

---

1. Assuming that perfect linear scaling of the system is achievable.

Example

In a DSS system, there is a query that requires a full table scan of a very large table (1 billion rows). This table is spread over many disks and many controllers, and the system has many processors available for the execution of this query. Now, if this query were to be executed without any partitioning of the workload (see Figure 1.3), it would simply take a long time for a single processor to read and validate every row in the table against the predicate in the query. No number of additional processor boards would make this query faster, and faster processors would probably limit the speedup to two to three times, even if you were lucky and were not bound by the serial disk access anyway.

Using Oracle Parallel Query, this job can be made many times faster, potentially providing a speedup of an order of magnitude or greater. This is achieved by logically breaking the large monolithic table into several smaller logical ranges. Once this has been done, additional slave processes can be used to scan each of the logical ranges in parallel, thus scaling the query across several processors (see Figure 1.4).

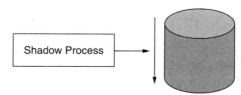

Figure 1.3 Nonparallel query

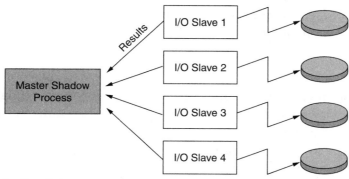

Figure 1.4 Parallel query

1.1.2   Concurrency (Scaleup)

Good scalability in this context could be defined as "achieving maximum useful concurrency from a shared system." This is the major area of concern for transaction processing systems.

In multiuser systems, the system must share out all of its resource to all the users of the system. It must do this in a fair-share manner, prevent sessions from corrupting others, and not consume excessive resource or impose artificial bottlenecks in the process. In order to achieve this desirable state of *concurrency*, the system must *scale* effectively.

Achieving concurrency is one of the greatest challenges when building a system, whether you are the hardware designer, the RDBMS vendor, or the end user. In the building of large-scale systems, it is the concurrency that must be considered at all times.

Strangely enough, concurrency is made possible through the use of enforced *serialization*. Through serialization, we achieve the necessary *synchronization* required to process tasks concurrently.

Synchronization needs to occur on any concurrent system and is most commonly handled through the use of latches and locks. The specifics of how these structures are used will be covered in more detail later in this chapter.

Latches themselves also need serialization support, in this case from the hardware itself. In order to take out a latch, a bus transaction must be performed in order to write to the memory location that contains the latch. On a multiprocessor system, many processors could be attempting to write to the same location concurrently, and therefore the bus transactions need to be arbitrated in order to allow them access one at a time. This will be discussed in more detail in Chapter 2.

Digression

In fact, synchronization sometimes also needs to occur for straight performance reasons between cooperating programs on the same or different systems, and this needs to be carefully designed if maximum concurrency is to be maintained. A good example of this is two batch jobs operating in parallel against the same data set. Oracle will automatically prevent the sessions from corrupting each other at the transactional level, and will take out implicit locks to enforce this. If these jobs collide on their respective data sets, they will get caught up in serious contention between each other as a result of Oracle protecting the data from transaction level corruption. This is especially true with Oracle Parallel Server, because Oracle needs to use locks to protect both the transaction layer and the cache layer.

If these sessions partition their data access and cooperate with each other before Oracle enforces it, they will be able to process a good deal more data. This results from the developer of the batch jobs having more knowledge of the actual data itself, and therefore knowing how to synchronize more intelligently. Either way, the synchronization has been performed in order to allow the two jobs to run concurrently without corrupting data.

1.2   Latches and Locks

> **latch** *n .... the catch which holds a door or gate when closed, though it be not bolted.*
>
> —Webster's Revised Unabridged Dictionary (1913)

Latches and locks can be viewed as very similar entities, and in many software engineering circles there is no difference between the two terms. However, in an Oracle environment, there are apparent differences between them. The basic differences are

- *Duration.* Latches are normally very transient, whereas locks are typically a longer-term prospect.

- *Degree.* Latches are switches, whereas locks have levels (or degrees) of severity.

- *Scope.* In Oracle, latches are instance-specific, whereas locks are mostly database-wide.

Their function remains identical—to prevent other sessions on the system from modifying the critical resource that they are protecting. The *Webster's* definition almost describes a modern software latch accurately, in that it captures the spirit of the transient operation. However, the door is most certainly bolted when a latch is taken out—it's just faster to unbolt after use.

1.2.1 Why Lock?

As we started to explain in the description of concurrency, it is inherently necessary to serialize some operations on a concurrent system in order to protect different tasks from corrupting each other. This applies only to access to shared resources. Let's run through a couple of examples to help get the real point across.

Example: Memory Protection Using Latches

Let's take a complex memory update as an example in order to add substance to the explanation. This kind of operation is typical in large transactional systems, in order to update several memory blocks atomically (i.e., as a single, indivisible operation). Figure 1.5 shows a region of memory that is protected by a latch.

The diagram in Figure 1.5 shows a memory buffer that is used to batch together many physical I/O requests before issuing a write for all of them at some later stage. Many user sessions on the system write a few hundred bytes of data into this buffer, and then update a structure at another location to reflect the new address to which other sessions can write. In this scenario, there are could be many thousands of sessions on the system that would potentially need to write into this buffer at any one time, and it is clear that some kind of serialization is required in order to prevent a *race condition*[2] from occurring (see Table 1.1).

In the example shown in Table 1.1, the buffer is corrupted through a race occurring between the respective tasks. Not only were the 50 bytes written by user 2 overwritten, but the 300 bytes written by user 1 were effectively truncated due to user 2 setting the "next" pointer incorrectly as a result of a race condition.

It can be seen that this operation must be protected from other sessions while it is in progress. This is where latches come in. Using the same example, Table 1.2 should make it clear why latches are required.

---

2. A race condition is any situation in which multiple sessions are able to corrupt each other through a lack of synchronization between the sessions. Many system crashes that are caused by software error are attributable to race conditions.

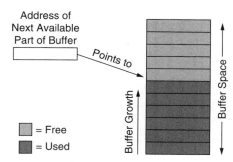

Address of
Next Available
Part of Buffer

Points to

Buffer Growth

Buffer Space

☐ = Free
■ = Used

Figure 1.5 Multiuser memory buffer

Table 1.1 Race Condition Caused by Nonatomic Memory Updates Without Latch
Protection

User 1 Action	User 2 Action	Value of "next" Pointer
Idle	Write 50 bytes to buffer, starting at location pointed to by "next" pointer.	0
Write 300 bytes to buffer, starting at location pointed to by "next" pointer.	Idle <Preempted by O/S>	0
Update "next" pointer to point to location after write.	Idle	300
Idle <Complete>	Update "next" pointer to point to location after write.	50

In this situation, a latch is taken before the copy, and thus the area is protected from other sessions until the copy and subsequent pointer update are complete. It is obviously important to keep the period during which the latch is held as short as possible, and also to minimize the contention for the latch. This means that this necessary serialization of the latch is of the lowest possible impact. However, as can be seen in the example, it is not uncommon for the operating system to intervene, and to context switch the latch holder off the processor and back onto the run queue. This can happen for several reasons, including standard process scheduling and receipt of an interrupt on the processor in use.

Table 1.2 Prevention of Race Conditions Using Latches

Latch Holder	User 1 Action	User 2 Action	Value of "next" Pointer
None	Idle	Data ready to write into buffer; request latch to perform write.	0
User 2	Data ready to write into buffer; request latch to perform write.	Write 50 bytes to buffer, starting at location pointed to by "next" pointer.	0
User 2	Wait for latch to become available.	Idle <Preempted by O/S>	0
User 2	Still waiting for latch.	In processor run-queue	0
User 2	Still waiting for latch.	Update "next" pointer to point to location after write.	50
User 1	Take out latch.	Release latch.	50
User 1	Write 300 bytes to buffer, starting at location pointed to by "next" pointer.	Idle <complete>	50
User 1	Update "next" pointer to point to location after write.	Idle <complete>	350
None	Release latch.	Idle <complete>	350

Despite user 2's process being switched off the processor, a race condition is prevented in the situation shown in Table 1.2. This kind of protection is vital in multiprocessor systems, because there are many ways in which race conditions can occur.

Data Protection Using Locks

As stated earlier, the term *latch* is normally associated with memory locks that are held for short periods. The term *lock* is frequently used as a catchall for all types of locking, using the word as an adjective. When we are dealing with Oracle databases, however, it is correct to use the word in terms of *data locking*. These are longer-duration locks that are used to protect the integrity of changes made to the database, such as user transactions and system (recursive) transactions. In the case of a user transaction, the durations of these locks are sometimes controlled by the users themselves, as follows:

```
SQL> SELECT pkey FROM SOME_TABLE WHERE jref = 123456789 FOR UPDATE OF
status;

1 row selected.
```

(1 Row now also locked under a TX lock)

```
SQL> UPDATE SOME_TABLE SET status='INVALID WHERE jref = 123456789;

1 row updated.

SQL> commit;
```

(also releases TX lock)

No other user can update or delete the row with jref = 123456789 while this lock is held. This example is very simplistic, and it is hard to see why you would need this facility. The truth is, however, that some transactions are so complex that the individual pieces of the transaction need to be protected in order to ensure that the entire transaction can be completed in a consistent, atomic fashion.

It is also worth noting that, in the example above, we explicitly lock the row that we need to update prior to updating it. This is not actually required for most types of operations, because the update statement will implicitly lock the row before the update is performed. This kind of explicit row-level locking can cause serious problems in a large-scale system and should be reserved for situations in which an atomic transaction is absolutely required and cannot be performed in any way other than SELECT ... FOR UPDATE. In fact, a recommendation will be made against the widespread use of overzealous locking in "Maintaining Concurrency" in Section 9.1.1.

An important difference between a lock and a latch within Oracle is that a lock is typically *database-wide* whereas a latch is typically local to the *instance* that is managing it. As it is database-wide, a lock affects all instances of a Parallel Server environment, not just the one executing on the local node. There are some exceptions to this rule, but in general it holds true.

Another difference is in the way that sessions wait on the locks. See Section 1.2.3 for more information on lock waits.

1.2.2   Things That Need Locking/Latching

Table 1.3 presents some real-world examples of locking and latching. To make the concept clearer,

Table 1.3   Latching and Locking Examples

Object	Latch or Lock	Description
Redo log buffer	Latch	In order to prevent multiple users from allocating space in the redo buffer concurrently (leading to corruption), allocation of space in the redo buffer can be performed only after obtaining the single `redo allocation latch`.
Shared pool	Latch	The various caches in the shared pool grow and shrink dynamically as required within the static boundary of `shared_pool_size`. The internal boundaries within the shared pool therefore need adjusting, and this is performed one session at a time while holding the `SHARED POOL LATCH`.
Buffer cache	Latch	There are many latches covering the buffer cache. One of these latches is the `CACHE BUFFER LRU CHAINS LATCH`. This latch (which now actually exists as several child latches from release 7.3 onward) is taken while buffers are heated and the LRU chain is manipulated. See Section 1.3.1 for more information on chains.
User data	Lock	There are a whole bunch of locks that relate to the protection of user (or application) data. These locks can be held longer than a latch protecting memory because of their frequent dependence on user actions.
Space transaction	Lock	This is displayed in `V$LOCK` as an ST lock. An ST lock is taken out when Oracle needs to allocate or deallocate extents for an object. It is commonly

Table 1.3   Continued

Object	Latch or Lock	Description
		seen when temporary space is allocated for an on-disk sort. It is implemented in a lock because Oracle needs to perform a recursive transaction on internal tables (`sys.fet$` and `sys.uet$`) in order to provide access to the space. Taking out this lock prevents other sessions from updating the same information concurrently, leading to corruption. It is also important to note that because this is a lock, ALL INSTANCES of Parallel Server will be affected.
Sort segment	Latch	This is a good example of the difference between a lock and a latch within Oracle. In Oracle7 release 7.3, a performance enhancement was made called Sort Segments. This means that once a temporary sort segment has been allocated, it will not be deallocated for that instance. Instead, the sort segment is now managed by a latch local to that instance. Other instances cannot allocate this particular segment, and therefore the ST lock does not need to be allocated until an instance has no more sort segments available.
Process table	Latch	The UNIX Operating System uses latches to protect many internal data structures. One of these is the process table, which is maintained as a linked list. Latches are used to protect the table from concurrent updates from multiple processors in a multiprocessor system.

1.2.3   Waiting on Latches and Locks

If something (such as a memory structure, data, or an entire program flow) requires protection with latches or locks, then it follows that other sessions, processes, or types of execution context must have some way of waiting on those latches or locks. These waits fall into two categories: active and passive.

An *active wait* is the method most commonly used for latch allocation. When a session cannot acquire a latch on the resource that it requires, it goes into an active wait on that latch. In active wait, the session repeatedly attempts to acquire the latch until it is successful—that is, waiting impatiently. The reasons for this are that (a) it is unlikely that the latch will be held for very long and (b) it is normally too expensive to set up any kind of queue for the resource.

Sessions that cannot acquire a latch immediately will *spin* until they get the latch. Spinning involves locking into a tight loop testing the latch and trying to acquire it. Spinning uses significant CPU resource but typically results in acquisition of the latch in a shorter time than it would take to establish any kind of formal queue. These types of latches are also referred to as *spinlocks*, owing to the nature in which they are waited on. The active wait is frequently implemented using the host's *test-and-set* functionality—a hardware-level serialization instruction (see "Test and Set" in Section 2.1.2).

The actual algorithms used for waiting on latches/spinlocks varies between implementations. In the Oracle kernel, for example, a process will spin on a latch for *spin_count* (`init.ora` parameter) iterations before backing off and sleeping. The process will then spin again before going to sleep once more; the actual sleep time between spins increases exponentially. The reason for the incremental backoff is to reduce the likelihood that the system will disappear off the map as a result of all the processes locking into infinite spin loops.

The alternative method of waiting on a serial resource is to perform a *passive wait*. Typically, these waits are used on less timing-critical components, of which a TX (row-level lock) is a good example. Such a lock is known within Oracle as an *enqueue*.

Enqueue is a strange word that has an opposite sibling called *dequeue*. Once the two are put side by side, their meanings become more apparent. They are both operations on a queue: one enqueues requests (puts them onto the queue) and the other dequeues the requests (takes them off the queue).

Oracle uses enqueue functionality to manage locks within the database. This includes the TX lock, as stated above, and the ST lock, which are more correctly termed the TX enqueues and the ST enqueue, respectively. In comparison with latches, none of these enqueues need to respond quickly to multiple requests. Several milliseconds or even several seconds would be easily fast enough for higher-level serialization such as this.

When a user takes out a row lock, a TX enqueue is created for that user. If another user subsequently attempts to update that same row, that user's session will block (wait on) the enqueue that the initial user created. If a third user tries the same update, he or she will also be blocked on the same enqueue. This is visible to the database administrator as multiple entries in V$LOCK with the same TYPE, ID1 and ID2. The first session will have an LMODE (lock mode) of 6, indicating an exclusive lock gained on that enqueue resource. All the other sessions will report an LMODE of 0 (no lock gained) and a REQUEST of 6 (exclusive lock).

At this point, all the waiters on the enqueue are using zero processor capacity on the database server—they are blocked. This is the nature of a passive wait. However, if the sessions are not actively trying to allocate the lock, how do they ever get it? The answer lies in the dequeue part of the equation, and this occurs once the first lock is cleared.

The first user will issue a commit or rollback against the updated row data protected by the TX enqueue. Once this occurs, the second user session is unblocked and is granted the LMODE of 6 on the enqueue. When that user commits or rolls back, the third session will get a piece of the action, and so on. This is the enqueue/dequeue function in operation.

Not all enqueues work in a FIFO (first in, first out) manner like the TX enqueue. The other example given, the ST enqueue, operates in a LIFO (last in, first out) mode, apparently as an optimization in its sharing algorithm.

1.2.4   Design Considerations to Reduce Lock Contention

When operating systems and relational database engines are designed, special attention is given to minimizing contention for locks on shared resources. This is of obvious importance for the scalability of these systems and merits a good deal of attention from the designers. However, we have already established that locking is *necessary* within these shared systems, so what can the system designers do to alleviate this contention?

There are several things that can be done where appropriate. Sometimes a good deal of reworking of the logic is necessary to implement some of these techniques, but the engineering impact can be enormous, and so these techniques are often considered as last-resort measures. We'll go through some of the more common methods of reducing lock contention in turn.

Locking Degrees

The first thing that can be affected is implementation of locks/latches with different degrees of exclusion. This is done in order to provide as much concurrency as possible even though it is necessary to lock things. In simplistic terms, there are three different states that a lock can be in:

- NULL. No lock is acquired for this type.

- Acquired Shared Exclusive. Otherwise known as a *multireader lock*, this lock allows any number of readers, but no session can acquire an exclusive lock in order to perform a write.

- Acquired Exclusive. This lock is acquired to write to the region protected by the lock.

The use of multireader locks allows the system to process read-only workloads while maintaining the data integrity of the system. It is frequently the case that a process may only need to prevent the resource from being updated while it performs some other task, and the use of multireader locks allows many processes to share access to the resource concurrently in read-only mode. If a process needs to modify the resource that the lock is protecting, the lock must be upgraded to an Exclusive mode before this is permitted. This would then prevent any readers or writers from accessing the region.

These three degrees of locking are used throughout both the UNIX kernel and the Oracle Server. Oracle actually defines even more locking degrees than this, in order to provide even more control over the required degree of locking. These locking degrees are described in detail in the Oracle documentation.

A large performance benefit results from maintaining different locking degrees, and this forms a fundamental part of the internal locking mechanisms used in modern systems.

Fine-Grained Locking

A more complex technique is to provide *fine-grained locking* within the system. This involves reducing the sizes of the regions covered by locks in the system, so that many locks can be used independently in the place of a single lock. This allows far greater concurrency within the system. Fine-grained locking for persistent types of locks, such as transaction locks, is good for all systems (uniprocessor and multiprocessor), while fine-grained latching is most useful on multiprocessor platforms where multiple latch acquisitions can be made concurrently by different processors.

Examples of fine-grained locking include

- Row-level locking with the Oracle transaction layer. Only users that need to access the same *row* as another user will contend for this data lock. Other RDBMS systems have relied on page-level locking or, even worse, table-level locking.

- Multiple library cache latches. In the pre-7.2 releases, a single latch enforced serialized updates to the shared SQL cache. In releases 7.2 and above, Oracle allows multiple concurrent updates by providing multiple latches. The latch used is determined by the hash value (see 1.4) of the SQL statement.

- Function locks within the UNIX process table. For example, a separate lock can be used to cover the structure that contains pending signals.

Implementation of fine-grained locking often is very difficult for system engineers and frequently requires redesign work. For this reason, it is common for portions of systems to be left for the users to "suck and see" as to whether the system requires fine-grained locking. Although you may not be able to fix any of these problems personally, it is important that you report them to the responsible party if it can be demonstrated that the lock granularity is causing a performance problem. This is usually easier to do within the Oracle product than within the UNIX kernel, because the latch activity is very well reported through the v$ views.

Algorithmic Enhancements

The best way to eliminate lock contention within a system is to use algorithmic enhancements in the software. By changing the algorithms used within the kernel, it is sometimes possible to eliminate the need to lock at all in certain areas. Many such algorithms have been produced within research circles, and some have been implemented into production software to aid scalability.

For example, assume that in a shared-memory-based application, there is a single writer and many readers of a single record in shared memory. The record is larger than the largest atomic update that is possible on the platform. A bad algorithm for dealing with updates to this record would be to lock the record and prevent the readers from accessing it while it was being updated consistently by the writer.

A better way to code this problem is to maintain a master list of pointers to the actual records. The reader processes will first read the master list and then follow the pointer to the actual record. Using this method, a newly updated record can be written to a private memory address, and the pointer in the master list can be updated atomically to point at the new location when the update is complete. This way, no locks have been taken out at any time, and all reader processes can execute in a contention-free environment.

The example shows a simplistic change that removed the need for locks in that part of an application. However, this example is about as simple as it gets: if there is more than one writer, for instance, this technique becomes more complex. The level of effort required to eliminate locks using different algorithms varies from the implementation of simple hashing algorithms to complete redesign of the software architecture. For some truly shared resources, algorithmic changes are impossible as a result of logic restrictions.

1.3   Linked Lists

1.3.1   What Is a Linked List?

A linked list is simply a programming construct that allows the programmer to traverse a list easily without relying on the physical storage for any specific layout. The reason that linked lists are detailed in this book is because lists are used extensively within the Oracle RDBMS, and it is necessary to understand why they affect performance.

So, what does a linked list look like? In C, a linked list is composed of several simple data structures similar to the following:

```
struct linked_list {
     struct linked_list *prev_item; /* List management */
     char name[80];    /* Data */
     int value;        /* Data */
     struct linked_list *next_item; /* List management */
};
```

So, using the data structure example above, the linked list could be loaded from a file as follows:

```
#include <stdio.h>
#define maxpoints 180

struct linked_list {
      struct linked_list *prev_item; /* List management */
      char name[80];     /* Data */
      int value;         /* Data */
      struct linked_list *next_item; /* List management */
};

void
main() {

      struct linked_list *list_head, *last_item, *curr_item;
      FILE *fp;

      list_head = curr_item = (struct linked_list *)
            malloc(maxpoints*sizeof(struct linked_list));

      if (!(fp=fopen("./data","r"))) {
            perror("fopen");
            exit(2);
      }

      last_item=(struct linked_list *) 0;

      while(fscanf(fp,"%s %d",curr_item->name,&curr_item->value)!=EOF) {
            if (last_item!=(struct linked_list *) 0 )
                  last_item->next_item=curr_item;
            curr_item->prev_item=last_item;
            last_item=curr_item;
            curr_item++;
      }

      curr_item->next_item=(struct linked_list *) 0;
      fclose(fp);

}
```

Once the list has been loaded, it is very simple to manipulate it; inserting or deleting an item is almost as straightforward as adding an item to the end. Equally, shuffling the entire list in a sort operation is very efficient, because only pointers are changed—the data is never relocated.

So, it should be pretty clear by now what a linked list is and why it is found in nearly every program that manipulates data. At the end of the day, that's exactly what Oracle is.

1.3.2   What Are Linked Lists Used For?

Linked lists are used to manage working sets of information, with the classic example being an LRU (least recently used) list as commonly found within Oracle. An example of the use of LRU algorithms can be found in "LRU Algorithms" in Section 1.5.4. They will always be updated in conjunction with latches, because multiple sessions will use the lists concurrently, and without latch protection even simple list manipulations can produce corruption. Using the LRU list example, it can be seen that it is straightforward to add items to both ends of the list, if pointers to the "hot" (most recently used) and "cold" (least recently used) ends are kept in fixed locations.

This is achieved by taking the following actions (based on fixed-length chains).

"Cold" End

Inserting an entry into the cold end of the LRU list is very straightforward. You can already assume that the entry currently on the cold end is ready to be removed from the list, because it is already the "least recently used." Therefore, you simply overwrite the contents of the entry that is currently on the cold end.

"Hot" End

Inserting an entry into the hot end is slightly more complex, but is still straightforward using linked lists, as shown in Figure 1.6.

1. Take out the latch that protects the list. Go to the cold end of the list (element one) and set the "next" item pointer to be NULL, indicating that there are no entries past this point (i.e., this is the hottest end of the LRU). Set the "previous" item pointer to point to the entry that used to be hottest (element four). Put the new contents into element one.

2. Step along one entry to the second-coldest entry (element two).

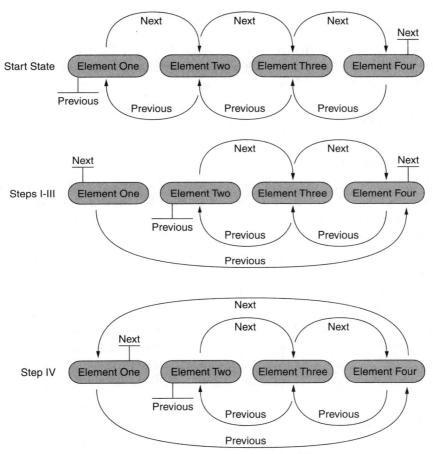

Figure 1.6   Inserting an entry into the hot end of a linked list

3. Update the "previous" item pointer here to be NULL, indicating that there are no more entries (i.e., we now have a new cold end of the list).

4. Go to the item in the list that was previously hottest (element four) and change the "next" item pointer to point to the new hot end.

5. Update the master references to reflect the address of the new cold and hot ends, if applicable.

6. Release the latch.

Using lightweight memory manipulations like those above, lists are one of the most efficient ways of manipulating data in memory. It can be seen, though, why the list needs to be protected from other reads and writes while it is being manipulated. If another session were to start to read the LRU list while the updating process was at step 2, it would get very confused indeed owing to the interim state of the pointers. This would likely result in either data corruption or a system crash.

1.3.3 Optimizing Chain Lengths

As well as inserting entries into the linked list, the list is often scanned to find particular entries. Using the LRU example, the LRU list may be scanned until a block has the correct status, or indeed to *heat* the entry to a higher (more recently used) point in the list. This can prove to be an expensive operation if the lists get too long (especially because you are holding the latch during this period to prevent other sessions from updating it under your nose), and so linked lists should generally be kept as short as possible.

Any linked lists that are managed while a latch is being held are potential bottlenecks in the system. For this reason, it is imperative that high-contention lists be kept as short as possible, unless of course the list is never fully scanned. If this is not ensured, the latches will be held for a longer duration than is desirable, and waits will build up on the latch.

db_block_buffers

The `db_block_buffers` parameter is absolutely typical of this management and is subsequently prone to contention. All the buffers in the cache are split up and managed by separate lists, each of which is governed by a latch. This applies to both the LRU list for the blocks (from release 7.3 onward) and the actual blocks themselves (db block hash buckets).

When the buffer cache gets very large, these lists grow with it. So while you are gaining the extra benefit of running with a larger cache, you are also incurring greater overhead from the management of the chains, and you are probably suffering latch contention from the management of the chains. This was particularly true prior to release 7.3, when there were no multiple chains for the LRU list. This meant that the LRU list did not scale at all well prior to release 7.3, and the only way to manage the contention for the *cache buffer LRU chain* latch was either to decrease the number of blocks in your cache or to tune the database writer. This had an obvious impact on performance if your system was relying on the enhanced cache hit ratio available with the larger cache size.

In this case, it is wise to study the work profile of the system to determine whether the block size is too small for the application. If this were the case, the option would be open to increase the block size of the database, meaning that the cache can be larger than before with no overhead in contention for the LRU chain latch, and no increase in management overhead.

It can be seen that keeping chain lengths to a minimum is a good idea until all the software vendors do it automatically. Many of the chains that are managed are not controllable by the end user and thus are not an option. It is important, however, to keep tight control of the ones that you *do* have control over, an example of which is demonstrated in "Avoiding High-Contention SQL" in Section 9.1.

1.4 Hashing

Hashing is another technique for speeding up the management operations of a system. In particular, hashing is an approach taken to achieve dramatic speedup of searches for data within a list (usually within a cache; see Section 1.5). Hashing is used just about everywhere possible in high-performance systems because of its efficiency and its simplicity.

1.4.1 What Is Hashing?

Hashing is the term given to performing some kind of algorithm on a piece of data in order to determine an index number for those contents, rather than performing value comparison along a potentially long list of entries. That index number can then be used as a reference to either an absolute piece of memory or a smaller list that can be searched further to find specific entries.

Hashing Algorithms

Hashing algorithms range from incredibly simple manipulations, such as those found in a CPU cache, to more complex ones such as those used to manage the Oracle Shared SQL cache (library cache). A simplistic algorithm might be used to split numbers into buckets known as hash buckets in order to keep some statistics up to date:

BucketID=n MOD 7

Using this algorithm, a number can be quickly assigned to the correct hash bucket, where the hash buckets are used as shown in Table 1.4.

It may not be clear to you at this stage *why* you would want to group things together into buckets in this way. The answer is that things are easier to find once they are contained in known places. To see if the number 68 has been stored, one would only have to calculate the bucket number (68 MOD 7) and then compare 68 against the 14 possible entries in that list. This is much faster than comparing it against values in 100 possible locations.

One good example of this is the Oracle buffer cache, which manages the blocks within it using latch-managed linked lists. Rather than have a single list that covers all the cache block entries, the blocks are divided into thousands of buckets, in a way similar to that shown in Table 1.4. When a block address is known, it is hashed to determine the list (bucket number) that could contain it, and then the list is traversed. In this way, any list manipulation can be constrained to a much shorter chain while still gaining fast access to the chain though the use of hashing.

Table 1.4 Hash Buckets Based on Module 7

Bucket Number	Values													
0	7	14	21	28	35	42	49	56	63	70	77	84	91	98
1	1	8	15	22	29	36	43	50	57	64	71	78	85	92	99
2	2	9	16	23	30	37	44	51	58	65	72	79	86	93	100
3	3	10	17	24	31	38	45	52	59	66	73	80	87	94
4	4	11	18	25	32	39	46	53	60	67	74	81	88	95
5	5	12	19	26	33	40	47	54	61	68	75	82	89	96
6	6	13	20	27	34	41	48	55	62	69	76	83	90	97

Hashing Example: CPU Direct Mapped Cache

This will be covered later in this chapter in more detail, but serves as a good example here. Basically, a CPU cache is comprised of several *lines*. A hashing algorithm is a perfect way to identify data lines within the cache, because it is very efficient. In the case of a CPU cache, it needs to be a massively efficient operation, implemented in hardware, in order to keep the latency of a cache lookup as low as possible.

Due to the way the cache lines are organized, the line can be identified by simply hashing the memory address and obtaining the line ID (see Figure 1.7). The hash operation in this case is a simple AND operation to extract a subset of the bits in the address in order to derive the line number. This is a very efficient operation to perform within a CPU cache.

Hashing Example: Oracle Shared SQL

From Oracle7, the Oracle server maintains a cache of SQL that can be used to reduce dramatically the workload required when another session submits the same piece of SQL. In order to implement this cache, Oracle needed a way to speed up the identification of the SQL and to check if it was already cached. It is simply much too expensive to do a text comparison of a submitted piece of SQL against all other SQL requests in the cache.

Oracle adopted a hashing algorithm to speed up the search for identical statements in the library cache. This is essentially an arithmetic operation on the actual text that makes up the piece of SQL in order to derive a single index for that statement. Don't be misled by the term *index*: these

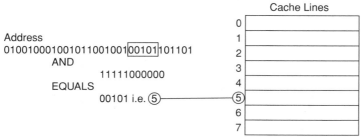

Figure 1.7   Hashing to obtain a cache line identifier

are large numbers, and it is actually very unusual for more than one statement to hash to the same value.[3] The hash value for each new statement is then used as an index, in order to do a fast lookup in the library cache to see if an identical statement has been hard parsed already. If so, a good deal of the parsing work for this statement can be reused, reducing the overhead of parsing the "new" statement.

The alternative methods of locating previously parsed SQL statements are inefficient by comparison. In particular, if a text-based comparison was needed against every piece of cached SQL, the effect would be a greater parsing overhead than running with no cache at all.

1.5   Caching

> cache *n ....hiding place, for concealing and preserving provisions which it is inconvenient to carry.*
>
> —Webster's Revised Unabridged Dictionary (1913)

1.5.1   Cache Fundamentals

A cache is a smaller, higher-speed component that is used to speed up the access to commonly used data stored in a lower-speed, higher-capacity component. There are several different applications of caching, including

- Caching of main memory locations next to the CPU
- Caching of disk blocks in main memory
- Caching of network information on disk

The best known of these is the CPU cache, which is largely a result of the efforts of the Intel marketing machine. However, in order to build a high-

---

3. There was an interesting bug in Oracle7.1.6 that was intended by Oracle to be a performance improvement.This was a change in the SQL text hashing algorithm that used only the first 64 bytes and the last 64 bytes of a piece of SQL. Unfortunately, in many applications (especially Oracle applications, such as Oracle Financials), the `select` list and the `order by` clause were identical, with just the table names and/or the first part of the WHERE clause changing. This meant that many nonidentical statements would hash to the same hash value.

performance, large-scale system, caching needs to be implemented and tuned at every opportunity.

1.5.2 Memory Hierarchies

A cache is one component in a memory hierarchy (see Figure 1.8). The memory hierarchy ranges from the very fast access speeds of a CPU register through cache, memory, disk, and network. It is viewed as a hierarchy because of the relative access speeds of the various components.

The fastest access path to storage on a system is between the CPU registers, and from there on, things slow down mostly in orders of magnitude (see Table 1.5).

Figure 1.8 The memory hierarchy

Table 1.5 Access Times for Key System Components[a]

From	To	Typical Access Time	Approx. Price per MB	Typical Size Ranges
CPU register	CPU register	2 ns	N/A	8–4096 bytes
CPU	Primary cache (on chip)	8 ns	N/A	8KB
CPU	Secondary cache (off chip)	30 ns	$150	1–4MB
CPU	System memory (off CPU board, over system bus)	100 ns	$15	1–16GB
Memory	Local disk (DMA over system bus)	3×10^7 ns	$0.15	200–n0,000GB
Local disk (via memory)	Networked host	1×10^8 ns upward	N/A	15,000,000GB[b]

a. All figures derived from manufacturer specifications for typical parts in 1997.
b. Based on 30,000,000 Internet hosts with an average of 500MB of storage on each.

It can be seen from the table that as the speed of components goes down by orders of magnitude, so too does the cost of the components. It is clearly not reasonable to expect a system to be built entirely from fast SRAM (the RAM technology used in CPU cache memories) running at core CPU speeds, the cost of which would be prohibitive. Therefore, the goal of caching is to give the performance *illusion* of slower components running at the same rate as the fastest component. While this is impossible to achieve in reality, any step toward it gives a huge boost in system performance by reducing the waits on lower-speed components.

Cost, however, is not the only reason for caching. Another reason to keep data as close to the CPU as possible is to reduce the contention on, for example, the system bus. Clearly, if all traffic needs to be passed across a single shared resource such as a bus, limits are going to be hit before they need to be. The system is not going to scale effectively.

1.5.3   Cache Reference Patterns

In order to make a cache as efficient as possible, some knowledge is needed of the access patterns within the device you are caching. In this way, assumptions can be built into the cache design in order to gain the most from the limited amount of cache space.

There are two main patterns of access that directly relate to caching:

- Temporal locality of reference
- Spatial locality of reference

Temporal locality is a time-based reference pattern: if this data was used once recently, it's likely that it will be needed again soon.

Spatial locality is a location based reference pattern: if location *abc* was used, then it's likely that location *def* will be needed sometime soon.

Pretty much all types of caching follow one or both of these patterns. Some devices need to employ very complex techniques in order to achieve spatial locality, owing to limited natural association between their access pattern and spatial locality.[4]

---

4. An example of this is when an EMC storage array "notices," through trend analysis, that a sequential scan is being performed. It can then perform a cached "read ahead" of the drives in question and thus hopefully eliminate transfer stalls resulting from rotational latency (waiting for the disk surface to come back around to the required sector).

Two types of caching will be concentrated on for the remainder of this chapter: I/O caching and CPU caching. I/O caching is very important to understand, because it is directly tunable by the end user. The CPU cache concepts are presented as an interesting piece of background reading to help you further understand the operation of large scalable systems.

1.5.4 I/O Caching

Effective caching of disk I/O is perhaps the biggest single performance improvement that can be made to a database system by the end user. The reason for this can be clearly seen in Table 1.5—disk I/O has the poorest response time of all within a system. In fact, it takes about 100,000 times as long to access a disk block as it takes to access a memory block.

It is obviously not practical to keep the entire database in memory (although there are situations in which it is desirable to force large pieces into memory), so there needs to be a way to control the use of memory to keep the cache as efficient as possible. The most common way of keeping the cache relevant is through the use of a least recently used (LRU) algorithm, in order to benefit from temporal locality of reference.

LRU Algorithms

An LRU algorithm is a very common cache management method that retains data based on frequency of use. The most frequently used blocks will always remain in the cache, while the least recently used blocks will be flushed from the cache and replaced by new entries for more active blocks as they are required.

In order to achieve this, block access is maintained by a list (see Figure 1.9). The list has two ends: the least recently used end, also referred to as the cold end, and the most recently used end, also referred to as the hot end.

When a block is added to the cache, or when a block that is already in the cache is referenced, it is *heated* to the most recently used end of the cache management list, or *LRU chain*. If this block is then unused for a period of time it will be implicitly made colder by the act of heating other blocks. Once the block becomes the coldest block on the list, it is eligible for reuse when an empty block is required. The example in Section 1.3.2 demonstrates how the heating of a buffer is implemented.

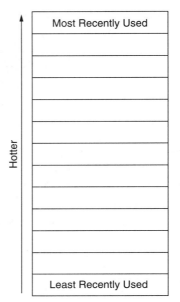

Figure 1.9 Least recently used list

This is the simplistic view of the operation of an LRU managed cache. There are many differences between this model and the real-life model, most notably the introduction of "dirty blocks" handling into the algorithm, but the principle is basically the same.

LRU Managed I/O Caching

The LRU management technique works very well for I/O caching. This is because there is nearly always a great deal of repetitive access to the same blocks on disk (temporal locality). The most prominent example of this is found in B-tree indexes used by Oracle. The root block of the B-tree is the starting point for all accesses to the index, in order to determine on which side of the index the value lies. Then the branch blocks are accessed to home in further on the required leaf block. Oracle maintains very shallow B-trees, making them very efficient within an LRU cache, because a single branch block will hold references to many leaf blocks. This means that the branch block will be used frequently and will always remain in cache and be subsequently available immediately out of cache for other sessions accessing it.

Table 1.6 Effect of I/O Caching on Response Time

Block Gets	Cache Hit Ratio	Blocks Gotten from Cache (No Disk I/O)	Total Time for All Block Gets
1,000,000	0 percent	0	30,000 seconds
1,000,000	95 percent	950,000	1,500.01 seconds

It is not uncommon to achieve cache hit ratios from the Oracle buffer cache that are 95 percent or greater. Table 1.6 demonstrates the effect of the caching in the aggregate response time of the system.

It can be seen that if all the disk I/Os and memory loads are performed in series (one at a time), the cached example takes around 25 minutes, compared with the noncached example, which takes a shade under 21 days. This example used serial access for reasons of clarity, but if parallel access were used, the difference could be potentially far higher: solid state memory is far more concurrent than the physical heads on a hard disk spindle.

1.5.5 CPU Cache Concepts

First, the bad news: there is little that you can do about the efficiency and utilization of the CPU cache. This is the domain of the hardware engineer and very much the speciality of the compiler writer. However, it is very useful to understand how the CPU cache works, as a piece of additional information for your global understanding of system operation. If you are ever called on to assess platforms of completely different architectures, knowledge of processor and associated cache operation will aid you in understanding what actually matters.

The Bad News About MHz

The effectiveness of CPU caching has been well proven and should be considered essential in all high-performance systems from PCs right up to the largest UNIX server. This is attributable to the very nature of the processor's function.

If a processor is running at a clock speed of 500MHz, it is capable of processing *at least* 500 million instructions per second. With techniques such as pipelining, the processor may be capable of processing many times that number of instructions per second.

Pipelining is where the CPU breaks up a sequential stream of instructions into separate components, which it executes in parallel. Part of this may be "speculative execution" of pieces of code, before the result of a preceding conditional test is known.

The bad news: the CPU can perform at this rate only if it is able to get the instructions and data at the same rate.

If the processor is a 64-bit unit, each word is 8 bytes wide. This means that you need to be able to access almost 4GB of memory per second simply to supply the instructions. Even on today's highest-capacity shared bus, the maximum sustainable rate is approximately 2GB/s, and that is shared among several processors. Therefore, the latest processors on the market would spend most of their time *waiting* on main memory—not performing real work—if a cache were not present to provide faster access to memory locations in the system.

CPU Cache Basics

First of all, let's zoom in on our memory hierarchy diagram (see Figure 1.10).

The simplest view of a CPU cache is that of a temporary storage area that resides between a CPU and main memory, where CPU instructions and program data are stored in very fast memory to speed subsequent, repeated access to the same locations. The cache provides much faster access to repeatedly used memory locations by

- Residing physically closer to the processor than main memory and therefore not being subject to the same degree of physical limitation (the speed of an electron)

- Not requiring bus transactions

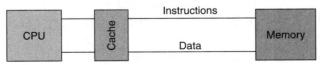

Figure 1.10   Memory hierarchy closeup

- Running with much lower latencies than main system memory
- Allowing parallel access

The basic theory behind CPU caching is the same as for any other caching: if something is used once, it is likely to be used again in the near future. Also, with instruction caching, if something in a particular memory location is used, it is fairly likely that surrounding memory locations will be referenced soon. Therefore, CPU caches are able to deliver both temporal and spatial locality.

Temporal locality within the cache speeds the execution of common coding constructs such as

- Instructions executed within loops
- Frequently called functions
- Frequently referenced variables

Once the instruction or piece of data has been accessed the first time (and therefore is now in cache), all subsequent references can be retrieved from cache as long as the cache entry has not been overwritten by the contents of other memory locations (see Figure 1.14).

Spatial locality within the cache speeds up the access to

- Sequential instructions
- Inlined function calls

This is achieved by loading the cache with several contiguous memory locations when a miss occurs on the first one.

In order to gain the greatest impact from these two types of locality, the mechanism for storing and retrieving data from the cache needs to be both simple and efficient so as to make its access as fast as possible.

Lines and Tags

CPU caches are organized into a fixed number of *lines*, and each line contains a fixed number of bytes that reflect the contents of main memory, as shown in Figure 1.11.

The number of lines and the size of each line varies from processor to processor. For example, the Intel Pentium processor has an 8KB primary cache. This is split into 256 lines of 32 bytes each, totaling 8KB.

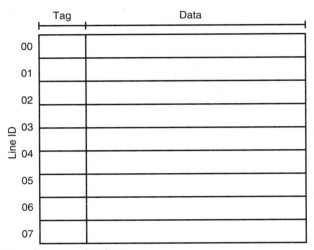

Figure 1.11 CPU cache organization

The way these lines map to physical memory varies from cache to cache. However, when a reference is made to a memory location by the CPU, it first looks in the cache to see if the address is already present. If the address is not present, a request is made over the bus (sometimes referred to as a *bus transaction*) to acquire that memory location and also the surrounding locations required to fill the line. A line cannot be partially filled at any time, because this would lead to corrupt data through lack of information in the tagging infrastructure (used to map cache lines to physical memory location), which will be covered a little later. Anyway, the loading of an entire line at a time is the mechanism that gives us the ability to achieve spatial locality of reference.

As a processor cache is potentially many orders of magnitude smaller in size than the main system memory, the design of the cache allows any single line to be populated with the contents of a finite number of discrete memory addresses.

As an example, we will use a CPU that has 32-bit addressing and therefore can individually address memory addresses from 0 through 4294967295, or 4GB. Any of these regions can be in the CPU cache at any one time. A hashing algorithm is used to take this memory address and locate the cache line from it, as described in "Hashing Example: CPU Direct Mapped Cache" in Section 1.4.1.

For this example, we have 128 cache lines, each of which contains 16 bytes of data. We therefore need to be able to hash uniquely a number from the range 0 to 4294967295 into a range of 0 to 127 in order to assign each memory location to a cache line. This is achieved by hashing bits 10 through 4 of the 32-bit address, as shown in Figure 1.12.

Due to the use of low-order bits for the cache line hashing (the lowest 4 bits, 0–3, are used within each line to identify uniquely the byte), consecutive memory addresses are effectively *striped* across the cache, allowing good locality hits within the cache (i.e., all local memory regions are in cache). This is good for high cache hit ratios with consecutive calls from a program's text (code) segment.

In Figure 1.13, you can see what happens when a hashing algorithm is used as described. Sequential, line-sized memory addresses get loaded into sequential cache lines. In this way, if a piece of code is the same size as the cache or less, then all the instructions will eventually be executed directly out of the cache. Only when addresses beyond the size of the cache are accessed will lines start to be replaced.

When an address is referenced within the CPU, the logic will check the cache to see if it is resident. We have already decided that a good way to select the line should be to use a range of low-order bits, so this means that any one of several different memory locations could be the one currently resident in the cache, as shown in Figure 1.14.

This reuse of cache lines means that we need some mechanism in the cache organization of determining whether or not we have a cache hit. This is where *tags* come in.

A tag is required to identify the contents of the cache, and therefore whether or not a cache hit is achieved. As you have seen, any one cache line could represent one of several memory locations at any one time: in the example above,

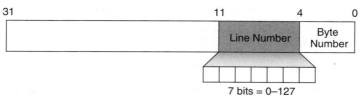

Figure 1.12   Obtaining the line ID through hashing

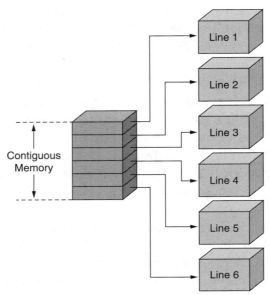

Figure 1.13   Cache line sharing

11110111011010110101101100101000 = 0xF76B5B28
00100101010001001010101100101000 = 0x2544AB28
Line 50

Figure 1.14   Different addresses that share the same cache line

there would be 4294967296/(16*128), or 2,097,152 different 16-byte memory pieces that could be loaded into any location at any one time.

In order to account for this ambiguity, each cache line also stores a tag for the line. This tag is simply the remaining bits of the memory address that were not used to locate the line/byte number. In our example, this would be the remaining 21 bits of the address. These 21 bits allow for 2,097,152 different values for the tag. The tag, therefore, positively identifies for the cache search logic whether or not the correct line is loaded at that time.

CPU Caching in an Oracle Environment

While the kind of locality optimization found in cache architectures works very well for small C programs (including scientific applications), the effects are not so clear-cut for caching within an Oracle database server. The execution of Oracle code holds the following negative attributes that offset the effectiveness of caching:

- Very large binary (20MB is not unusual in Oracle8.0)
- "Callback" architecture
- Virtually random access patterns of shared memory

Each of these attributes goes out of its way to ensure that the cache is challenged fully to provide good locality. The large binary means that even in a perfect world the entire code base is not going to cache resident (cache sizes are typically just getting into the 4MB range). The callback architecture means that the access pattern through the code is difficult to predict for the compiler. Therefore, it is not unusual that the memory requested is not in cache. Finally, the access pattern of the shared memory effectively blows away the data cache within the CPU, because the access pattern is totally unpredictable.

Performance architects often refer to the clock per instruction (CPI) index for a system. This is a measurement of the average number of clock cycles taken by the processor to process a single instruction. The lower the CPI for a given system, the greater the performance, because the system can execute a larger number of instructions per second. The whole reason for a cache's existence is to reduce the CPI for the system.

Because of the way Oracle is architected, Oracle Database Servers are often faced with a high CPI and subsequently a relatively inefficient use of the hardware. The way to improve on this situation is through continuous improvement of compiler technologies.

Compiler writers use knowledge of the physical layout of the cache, including cache line size and number of lines, in order to optimize the generated machine instructions for the specific CPU and cache architecture. In this way, huge efficiency gains can be had just from recompiling the Oracle software using a new release of the compiler. Of course, this needs to be performed by the relevant Oracle porting group and is often transparent to the end user.

Increasingly, the compiler writer will become the king of performance. This will be especially true when the first IA-64 chip (Itanium) is released. While details of the chip are still not in the public domain, it *has* been made public that the chip will rely heavily on explicit direction from the code generator as to how it should execute parallel instruction streams. This differs from the current technology, where the CPU must make pipelining decisions without knowledge of the global code picture. Using explicit compiler directives as to how the code should be executed optimally, more control can be obtained over the most useful parallel execution.

1.6 Chapter Summary

This chapter has introduced several concepts, mostly concentrated on software scaling. While it is unusual to have direct input into such fundamental aspects of the system and RDBMS software, it is important that you be able to understand the techniques and structures used to build scalable software.

If a system is not scaling adequately, knowledge of these principles will allow more accurate hypotheses as to the real cause of the problem. Often, a scaling issue in the system software can be mitigated procedurally or by small changes in the application. In-house changes will always be faster to implement than waiting on the software vendor, and this speed can make the difference between good and bad response times. Where an in-house fix is not possible, information can be passed more efficiently to the software vendor when the problem is well understood.

1.7 Further Reading

Patterson, David, and John Hennessy. *Computer Architecture: A Quantitative Approach, Second Edition*. Burlington, MA: Morgan Kaufmann, 1996.

Schimmel, Curt. *UNIX Systems for Modern Architectures*, Reading, MA: Addison-Wesley, 1994.

Van der Linden, Peter. *Expert C Programming: Deep C Secrets*. Upper Saddle River, NJ: Prentice Hall, 1994.

Chapter 2

Hardware Architectures and I/O Subsystems

This chapter will provide an overview of UNIX server hardware architectures. In the interests of greater scalability and lower price/performance, the architectures available today are not as straightforward as they were even three years ago. It is important to understand the distinctions among these platforms and how to configure them for maximum performance.

2.1   Introduction to Hardware Architectures

Gone are the days of the uniprocessor. Going are the days of the shared-bus symmetric multiprocessor. Building more and more powerful systems at lower and lower cost is very challenging for the hardware architect. Moore's Law[1] has been holding very true from a processor perspective, with virtually no impact on the retail cost of the hardware. The rest of the system, however, has been lagging behind the processor advances. For example, memory speeds are certainly not doubling every 18 months, and

---

1. Gordon Moore, Chairman of Intel in the 1960s, stated that the transistor density (and therefore potential power) of a CPU would double roughly every 18 months.

disk speeds are lagging even farther behind. The traditional method of connecting multiple processors and memory cards together over a shared bus started to hit the practical limits of known physics sometime around 1996 (more on the specifics in "Bus Architecture" in Section 2.1.2).

Mismatches in performance among system components, combined with the economic driving force toward production of ever cheaper hardware, have forced hardware architecture in certain directions. In order to walk our way through these new architectures, it makes sense to sort them by level of complexity, and so our path goes as follows:

1. Single-processor architectures
2. Symmetric multiprocessors, including shared-bus and crossbar switch systems
3. Clustered symmetric multiprocessors
4. Massively parallel architectures
5. Nonuniform memory architectures
6. Hybrid systems

For each of these architectures, we will look at the hardware and software modes that comprise it and at how Oracle is implemented on such a system.

Before we jump in, there are several concepts that you need to understand in order for the descriptions of each architecture to be the most useful.

2.1.1   System Interconnects

Even within the most fundamental modern computer there is some kind of system interconnect. What is an interconnect? It's a communication mechanism shared by several components, designed to allow any-point to any-point communication among the components. By definition, the system interconnect is very much a shared device, so it often becomes the subject of scaling conversations.

There are essentially two different reasons for system interconnects, and all systems have to have at least one of them:

1. Connecting components *within* the system
2. Connecting systems together

When we talk about interconnects connecting systems together, we do not include LAN connections. Interconnects provide more of an intelligent link between the systems than a LAN provides, typically at lower latency and greater bandwidth.

The first type of interconnect, one that connects the components within the system, is the one in which we are primarily interested in this book, although we will address the second type when we discuss of clustered systems (Section 2.5) and massively parallel processor (MPP) systems (Section 2.6).

For many years, the principal method of connecting components together within a system has been the shared system *bus*. A bus is the simplest type of interconnect and is the one on which most high-end UNIX kernels have been engineered to work. Therefore, many of the operations found in modern interconnects are directly synonymous with their old shared bus equivalents. For this reason, we will concentrate on a bus architecture for the concepts, diversifing where necessary to incorporate newer interconnect technology.

2.1.2 Bus Architecture

A bus must support several concurrently connected devices, such as a CPU, memory, and I/O controllers. In order to achieve this, and to allow the devices to communicate without interfering with each other, communication across the bus is handled by means of *bus transactions*. A bus transaction is very similar to a database transaction in that it is an atomic packet of work that is initiated and completed without interruption. All devices on the bus communicate across it in this way.[2] For example, if a CPU on the system needs to load a cache line from main memory, it will initiate a read across the bus. The bus logic will turn this into a bus transaction to perform the read and will send the request over the bus. At this stage, it's safe to think of the bus as being arranged as shown in Figure 2.1.

---

2. Some busses allow the splitting of a bus transaction into a packet-based protocol to achieve greater bandwidth.

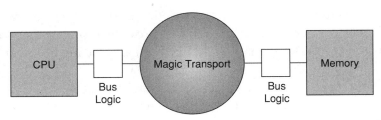

Figure 2.1   Simplistic bus view

The CPU will then wait while the bus logic sends both the request to the memory controller and the data back to the CPU from the appropriate memory locations.

I have used the term "Magic Transport" in Figures 2.1 and 2.2 to allow these illustrations to represent bus-based interconnects or indeed any type of interconnect method. In the case of a bus-based interconnect, the magic is simply a backplane within the system that has all devices connected to it. In this way, any device is connected to all other devices.

This is where the "practical limits of physics" mentioned earlier come into play. A bus is essentially a load of wires, one for each bit of the n-bit width of the bus, plus some extras. These wires (or tracks on a circuit board) all run in straight lines, parallel to each other, with periodic "breakouts" to connectors that allow devices to be connected to the bus.

If we ignore all the other electrical challenges of building such a bus, a limitation still exists. That limitation is the speed of an electron. All electrical flow is made up of electrons passing through a conductor, and the electrons are capable of traveling only up to a fixed maximum speed. Within a bus, all messages (electrical signals) must arrive at all devices within the clock frequency of the bus. Therefore, the electron must be capable of traveling the full distance of the bus in the time window specified by the clock rate of the bus.

To highlight how limiting this is, we will go through an example that, instead of the speed of an electron, uses the fastest known speed—the speed of light (the speeds are similar anyway). Let's assume that we have a "light-based computer," which is identical to today's shared-bus computers but uses light instead of electrons to transport the signals. The light all travels in a vacuum, and there is no overhead introduced anywhere, so the speed of light within the machine is $2.99792458 \times 10^{10}$ cm s^{-1}, or around 300,000 Km per second. If the bus is running at a rate of 200MHz (a mere fraction of today's CPU core speeds), then the maximum width of this bus would be 150 cm, or about 5 feet.

Clearly, we are some way from a light-based computer, and even if we had one, it doesn't look promising for the long-term future of a shared-bus architecture. Five feet is not very wide for an absolute maximum size backplane, especially once you start to reduce it due to the internal signal path length within each card.

Now that we have a simplistic view of a bus from a point-to-point perspective, we can complicate the issue by adding more devices to the bus. The bus now becomes a many-to-many communication device and thus needs some way to manage multiple requests at once, in order to prevent the devices from corrupting each other.

This can be achieved in either of two ways. The first, simplest, cheapest, and least scalable way is to have a single bus master. A bus master is a device capable of initiating reads and writes across the bus. A CPU *has* to be a bus master, and so to limit ourselves to a single bus master is to limit ourselves to a single CPU—clearly not very scalable. In order to get around this restriction, the bus needs to support *bus arbitration*.

Bus arbitration allows multiple bus masters to exist on the bus but allows only one device to perform a transaction at any one time. The arbitration logic within the bus prevents concurrent transactions and shares out the access among the bus masters in a (randomized) fair-share manner. A good way to view the bus at this point is shown in Figure 2.2.

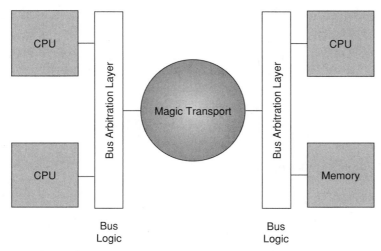

Figure 2.2 Multiple device bus view

Now we have a concurrent, multiple bus master configuration. All access to the bus is now serialized, allowing atomic memory operations. These atomic memory operations are essential for implementing any kind of locking mechanisms in the software layer.

Test and Set

One such locking mechanism uses the test-and-set machine code instruction available on many CPUs[3]. This is an atomic instruction that tests a memory location for a value and, depending on the result, changes the value to something else. This is used as "test to see if the lock is free, and if so, give it to me," and is an implementation specific that allows processes to "spin on a latch" during active waits.

2.1.3   Direct Memory Access (DMA)

In order to increase the concurrency of the system and decrease the load on the CPUs, there is the concept of "intelligent" I/O controllers that do not require intervention from the CPU to do their work. All that the CPU is required to do is to set up the memory required to do the work and initiate a request to the controller to execute the work.

Let's use a SCSI (Small Computer Systems Interface) controller as an example of this. Figure 2.3 shows a non-DMA-based write operation from memory through the I/O controller.

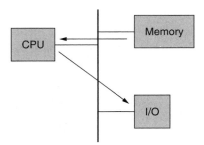

Figure 2.3   Non-DMA I/O operation

---

3. CPUs without test and set use other atomic instructions to achieve the same result. However, the test-and-set operation remains the best view of the concept.

All of the data needs to go through the CPU before being written to disk. The I/O controller is just a dumb controller that waits for data submissions and requests.

The DMA controller eliminates this requirement by building some intelligence into the controller itself. The card is configured with full bus mastering logic and maintains a memory map of the system memory. When the CPU needs to initiate an I/O request, it simply posts the DMA I/O controller with the location of the data and then resumes work on other tasks, as shown in Figure 2.4. Once the I/O is complete, the controller sends a hardware interrupt to the CPU in order to signal completion.

2.1.4 Cache Coherency

Cache coherency is an essential attribute in shared-memory multiprocessors. A system exhibits cache coherency when it is guaranteed that a read of any memory location, from any processor, will always return the most recent value of that location.

The big deal regarding cache coherency is that because of the way most modern processor caches operate, and because there are multiple processors potentially reading and writing from the same physical memory location at any one time, it is very possible to get different values from the same memory location by different processors unless steps are taken.

We have seen that caches form an essential part of all high-performance systems, because they mitigate the differences between the memory

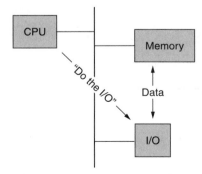

Figure 2.4 DMA I/O operation

speed and the core speed of the CPU. However, when there are multiple caches in the system, each of these caches could potentially have different values for a given memory location. To compound this, caches are typically operated in *write-back* mode to gain the most benefit from the cache. In this mode, when a processor changes the value of a memory location, the cache does not necessarily write the new value back to memory at that time, in order to minimize the wait time on slow memory devices. The main memory is normally updated at a later time by the operating system. So at any one time it could be possible for main memory, and all the caches, to have different values for the same memory location.

To demonstrate the effect of this problem, assume that we have a system with two processors, each with a write-back-based cache, but no measures taken to maintain cache coherency. Running on this system is a single program that increments a counter four times, with an initial value of zero for the counter. Assume that when the program starts, all caches are empty. I have also taken the liberty of making the situation as bad as possible by executing each counter increment on alternate CPUs each time. This is done purely to demonstrate the problem in an exaggerated way for clarity. The result is shown in Table 2.1.

Walking through the example, during the first increment, a cache miss occurs in CPU 1, and the value (0) is loaded from main memory and incremented to become the value 1. The next increment is executed on CPU 2, where a cache miss also occurs. Due to the use of write-back caching, the value in main memory is still 0, and so this is what is loaded into the cache of CPU 2 and incremented to become the value 1. Already the problem is evident: two increments of the counter have yielded a value of 1 in both

Table 2.1 Inconsistent Caches

Correct Value of Counter	Main Memory Value of Counter	CPU Cache 1 Value of Counter	CPU Cache 2 Value of Counter
1	0	1	N/A
2	0	1	1
3	0	2	1
4	0	2	2

the processor caches, and a value of zero in main memory. At this point, the system is in an inconsistent state.

In order to prevent this from happening, the caches on the system must be kept coherent. To achieve this, and to support write-back caching, a fundamental rule must be put in place on the system: the value of main memory location can be stale (old) in relation to caches, but caches cannot contain stale data. Once this rule is in place, the memory and cache consistency can be maintained with some simple rule, normally implemented in hardware.

When a value is changed by a CPU, its cache contains the most recent value of the given memory location. Using the rule presented above, this means that any other caches in the system that contain an old version of this location must either

- Be sent the new value (known as write-update) in order to conform to the rule, or
- Have the cache line invalidated, enforcing a reload on the next use (write-invalidate)

A system designer will adopt one of these methods for exclusive use within the system.

Now that the caches are kept in sync, there is only the main memory that could potentially be out of step as a result of write-back caches.

If the operating system has not yet written back a cache line to main memory when another CPU needs the most recent value, the CPU cache containing the most recent value intervenes and initiates a cache-to-cache transfer of the most recent value from its cache, thus effecting the final piece in the cache consistency resolution.

The hardware can be designed in one of two different ways in order to be "aware" of the load and stores in the system that will require write-updates, write-invalidates, or cache-to-cache transfers. The two methods of achieving this are the called the snoopy bus protocol and the directory protocol.

The snoopy bus protocol (see Figure 2.5) is a broadcast-based method. This is the method used in virtually all bus-based symmetric multiprocesor (SMP) systems and represents the most straightforward technique. It uses the fact that all bus traffic is broadcast-based: all traffic is visible to all

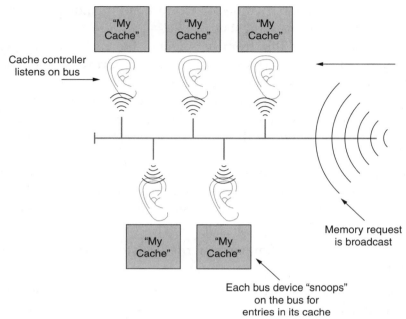

Figure 2.5   "Snoopy" bus

components. This being the case, logic is built into each component to "snoop" on the addresses of the memory loads and updates/invalidates occurring across the bus.

When an address is picked up on a snoop, it is compared with those addresses in cache and appropriate action is taken. In the case of a write-back cache picking up a load request for an address that is still dirty (unwritten to main memory) in its cache, it initiates a cache-to-cache transfer of the most recent value from its cache. In the case of a cache line invalidate, the corresponding cache line is marked invalid in the snooper's cache. As every message is broadcast, the entire bus is unusable during the operation, thus limiting the scalability of the bus as more processors are added.

The directory-based protocol (see Figure 2.6) is normally associated with distributed memory systems. Each "node" maintains a separate directory of which caches contain lines from the memory on that "node." Within this directory, a bit vector is kept for each line of main memory, reflecting which processors in the system have that line in their cache. The

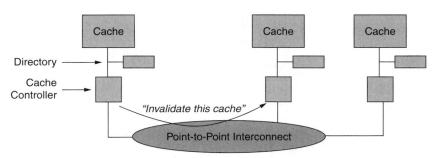

Figure 2.6 Directory protocol

major reason for implementing such a scheme is to remove the need for a broadcast-based protocol, because broadcast-based protocols have been found to be inherently unscalable.

Using the directory protocol, the directory for a node (and thus its memory) is used to determine which caches need to be made consistent (through invalidate or update) in the event of a write. At this point the individual caches can be made consistent, using some kind of point-to-point communication rather than a broadcast, thus allowing other parts of the interconnect to be used concurrently. This is much more efficient than the broadcast protocol, where all traffic exists on all parts of the bus at all times; this is the reason that snoopy bus protocols do not scale very effectively.

2.2　Single Processor Architectures (Uniprocessors)

A uniprocessor machine (see Figure 2.7) has the simplest architecture of all UNIX servers. It includes a single processor plus cache, connected to some memory and I/O controllers through some kind of shared bus. In many implementations, there is a separate bus on the system for connection of I/O controllers and peripheral devices. Devices on this bus communicate with the CPU and memory bus by means of a bridge between the two busses.

2.2.1　Advantages

As there is only one CPU in the system, there are no inter-CPU cache coherency issues to be handled by the operating system. This is not to say

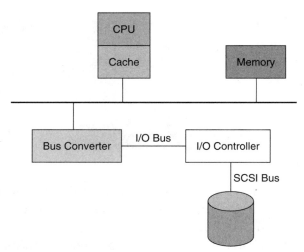

Figure 2.7   Uniprocessor architecture

Examples: Standard PC architectures, most computers more than ten years old

that there is only one bus master in the system—the system still needs to be concerned about the cache coherency issues arising as a result of DMA I/O controllers. This can be handled solely by a bus snooping device to invalidate the CPU cache lines where appropriate when DMA writes take place in main memory. This is much simpler to manage than having multiple processors all writing to shared memory areas and invalidating each other's caches.

In addition, no operating system locking is required and so there is no contention for kernel resources, because the operating system can guarantee that no other processors are executing kernel code. For example, only the single processor in the system could be writing to the process table at the same time.

However, it is still possible within a uniprocessor architecture for a kernel data structure to be corrupted through the processing of *interrupts*. When this happens, it is the same CPU that is corrupting the data structure, only operating in a different context. For example, if the CPU is performing a complex memory update in kernel mode, and a hardware interrupt is received (from an ethernet card, for example), the CPU must stop processing and switch to interrupt handler code and process it. Within this interrupt handler could be a memory update to the same region that is partially completed, and therefore data corruption could be produced.

This eventuality is prevented through the use of *interrrupt priority levels*, which represent the only type of short-term exclusion required on a uniprocessor system. This works by setting the current priority level of the processor to the highest level available on the system, effectively temporarily disabling interrupts. Once the critical update is complete, the interrupts can be reenabled by resetting the interrupt priority level to the prior value. This kind of temporary blocking of interrupts is adequate for kernel data protection in a uniprocessor system.

In reality, many vendors run the same version of the operating system on both uniprocessors and multiprocessors, therefore slightly invalidating this advantage. This also applies only to kernel mode data structures. Oracle must still provide its own user mode locking, because any process could be preempted from the processor before Oracle memory updates are complete.

In addition to the locking that is *required* for safe concurrent operation in a uniprocessor system, there is locking that is *highly desirable* for increased concurrency. Communicating with peripheral devices, for example, takes a comparatively long time. It is clearly not an option simply to ignore interrupts and be nonpreemptable for what could be several milliseconds, and so another method is required to allow the processor to be safely used by another process while the response from the peripheral device is outstanding. This is achieved through the use of *long-term locks*, which protect the data structures from corruption by subsequent processes but allow the kernel to be safely preempted by another process. This allows the overall throughput of the system to be unaffected by access to slower components.

So, in summary, the uniprocessor potentially requires only two types of locks: the interrupt-disabled, short-term exclusion method and the long-term, preemptable method. Both of these methods are considerably simpler to implement than the locking required in a scalable multiprocessor environment.

2.2.2 Oracle on Uniprocessors

Oracle is fundamentally not suited to a uniprocessor architecture. By its very nature as a multiple-process software architecture (DBWR, PMON, shadow processes, etc.), serious compromises in efficiency are made when these multiple processes are run in a uniprocessor environment. This is attributable to the required context switching (see Section 2.2.3) among all the processes in the Oracle RDBMS, even if the work is being submitted by a single process. There have been many different twists in the Oracle architecture that could optimize running on a uniprocessor system, most notably the single-task connection architecture designed to reduce the number of processes for the user connection, and the "single-process Oracle" architecture that combines all the functions into a single process (actually targeted for the MS-DOS platform). However, single-processor UNIX systems simply do not make very good database systems, regardless of what you do to them.

Finally, at the end of the day, a uniprocessor system can perform only one task at a time, however good it is at pretending otherwise. Therefore, only one person can parse an SQL statement, read a block from buffer, execute a PL/SQL package, and so on, at any one time. This inherent lack of concurrency in the uniprocessor makes it less than ideal in a multiuser environment.

2.2.3 Other Disadvantages

Nobody in their right mind would suggest building a large-scale Oracle database server on a uniprocessor server. There are numerous reasons why the day of the uniprocessor in the data center is very much over.

With only one processing engine in the system, high-context switching ties up a larger percentage of available processor time in wait state when compared with an equal workload on a multiprocessor system. For example, if ten processes are executing on a uniprocessor system, each of the ten processes must be switched onto the processor, allowed to execute for the quantum period, and then switched off the process once more. On a five-way multiprocessor system, the same ten processes would generate exactly one-fifth of the context switches as the uniprocessor, because there are only two processes competing for any one processor. Each of the context switches takes a finite amount of time, during which the processor cannot be executing any useful work. The time will be spent preserving and restoring the CPU registers, the stack pointer, the program counter, and the virtual memory mappings.

The increased context switching creates another problem. As all processes run on the same processor, there is therefore only one cache by implication. This means that there are no cache affinity[4] choices available to the operating system. Therefore, all processes are competing directly for the same cache lines, and, for the same number of executing processes, the cache warmth will always be less than that achievable on a multiprocessor system.

With only one processor in the system, it is obviously not scalable beyond the speed of a single CPU. Although the single processor could be upgraded, the system remains only as scalable as the single processor within it. Even with Moore's Law being achieved, this means that the system could only double in performance every 18 months, unlike a multiprocessor system, which may have the option of doubling its capacity every week (for a few weeks, at least).

Finally, the thing that absolutely kills the uniprocessor in the datacenter is the fact that a single CPU failure impacts the entire business by the machine being unavailable until hardware is physically replaced. That is, if a processor board expires, the system cannot be restarted until a hardware engineer has been called, travels to the site, and installs the board. This takes around two hours even under the most comprehensive service contract. It is rare for a business to find this acceptable—especially because the failures always seem to happen during the peak period.

2.2.4 Summary

It can be seen that despite the potential advantages gained through reduced locking administration (which are very slight in comparison with modern lightweight, multithreaded SMP kernels), the disadvantages are severe. This makes a uniprocessor fundamentally unsuitable for high-end enterprise computing. However, there will always be a place for these machines in the low end of the market, in addition to their use as development platforms.

---

4. Cache affinity is discussed in Section 2.3.

2.3 Symmetric Multiprocessors (SMPs)

A symmetric multiprocessor extends the capability of the uniprocessor by increasing the capacity of the system bus and allowing the addition of multiple processors and memory subsystems. All of the memory in the system is directly accessible by all processors as local memory, a configuration known as a *tightly coupled* configuration.

> Examples: Sequent Symmetry, HP T-class, Siemens E600, Sun E6500, SGI Challenge

The most common SMP architecture is that shown in Figure 2.8—the shared global bus architecture, where all components exist on the same, shared bus. While currently the most common, this architecture is increasingly being replaced by either a crossbar-switch-type bus (discussed in Section 2.4) or the NUMA architecture (discussed in Section 2.7). However, we will start off with the shared-bus model, because it represents the most simplistic view.

2.3.1 SMP Advantages

The SMP architecture allows additional scalability to be gained through the addition of processor cards to the system. Each of the processors added can be used by the kernel for the processing of presented work. In

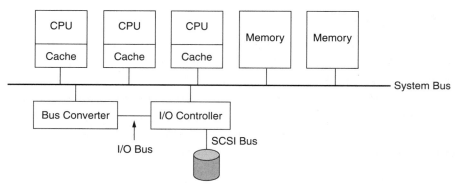

Figure 2.8   Shared global bus SMP architecture

this way, the effective bandwidth of the system is increased each time a processor is added.

The ability to add additional processing capacity to a system at will allows significant flexibility in operating an SMP system. It also allows far greater performance gains to be made than by purely upgrading the processor in the system to a faster one.

One thing needs to be noted here. I have just stated that SMP allows "performance gains to be made." It is important to clarify this point before we get any further into the book. Performance gains will *not* be gained simply by adding more processors to the system. Rather, the processing bandwidth of the system is increased, allowing performance gains to be made.

For example, if a system with a single processor can run a given task in one hour, this task would take exactly the same time to complete on a ten-way SMP system with the same processors. The reason for this is that the task is *serialized* on one processor and the addition of extra processors will not make the serial stream of instructions complete any faster. In fact, it is likely to make it slightly worse, depending on the scalability of the SMP platform.

However, if the same task is split into ten pieces that can be run concurrently, the ten-way SMP system *could* provide close to ten times the "speed" of the single-processor system, if the system scaled efficiently. Likewise, if the single-processor system were running 1,000 processes at any one time, the addition of nine more processors would add significant computational bandwidth to the system and individual processes would wait less time before being scheduled to run. In fact, the run queue for the system would be only 10 percent of the depth of the uniprocessor system, and all of the processes would appear to "run faster," although they are simply being allowed to run more often.

The final advantage of an SMP architecture (whether it has a single shared bus or otherwise) is that the programming model does not change from the user (non-UNIX/Oracle kernel programmer) perspective. The system is described as having a *single system image* or a *single instance of the operating system*. This is a very important point, in that it allowed the SMP architecture to be introduced in a virtually transparent way, because all the existing user code ran without change. It also means that the programming model remains very simplistic and allows easy programming on a multiprocessor system. This contrasts with the massively parallel processor

(MPP) model (see Section 2.6), where the programmer needs to be personally aware of the hardware configuration and is required to assign processing tasks to the processors individually.

2.3.2   Kernel Challenges

In order to make an SMP system scale effectively, the system designer faces several challenges. Ultimately, a large number of these challenges need to be met by the operating system engineer.

The presence of multiple processors in the system automatically gives us multiple bus masters, as discussed at the beginning of this chapter. It also gives us multiple caches that need to be maintained, as discussed in Section 2.1.4. Finally, it opens up a whole bunch of load balancing and affinity options to the process scheduler within the UNIX kernel.

We have already discussed the first two of these issues (multiple bus masters and caches), but what about the last ones (load balancing and affinity)? Really, these two things are fairly closely related. When a process becomes *runnable* on the system, the kernel must associate the process with a processor and enable it to run. With a uniprocessor system, there is only one choice of where this should go, because there is only one processor. On an SMP system, however, the kernel needs to make a choice as to which processor (or engine) is optimum for executing that particular process.

The most important thing that the kernel must do is to ensure that the work on the system is well distributed across the engines. For example, if there is enough work to keep all of the processors busy, then all of the processors, rather than just a subset of them, should be kept busy. This is the load-balancing part of the problem.

Next, the kernel must decide whether it is worth attempting to get the process assigned to any particular processor. This part of the problem may seem a little strange at first, but there is good reason to assign a process back to the last processor on which it ran, provided that there is some benefit to be gained from the residual cache warmth from the last time the process ran. The kernel can make educated guesses as to whether this is the case, based on the number of processes that have executed on that CPU since this one last ran. This kind of processor preference is known as *cache affinity*, because the process has an affinity for one particular cache on the system.

Modern UNIX kernels are very good at managing the administration burden of multiple processors. The ability of the kernel to handle the additional administration directly affects the scalability of the system, and some vendors are better than others at achieving this.

2.3.3   Oracle on SMP Architectures

The Oracle architecture is probably most suited to an SMP-like hardware architecture. This is no accident, because SMP has made Oracle a datacenter reality for large-scale systems. The multiprocess architecture fits perfectly into a system with multiple processors to run these processes on.

The fast, uniform access to main memory found in SMP architectures allows Oracle to use bus primitives for implementing very fast latch operations (i.e., test and set). This is vital for operation of very large single-instance implementations of Oracle, because all operations share common latches. While multi-instance implementations of Oracle (using Oracle Parallel Server) are not subject to the same intense contention for the same latches, they are subject to contention on significantly slower methods of synchronization than those used in a single-instance configuration.

However, for reasons that are separate from any bandwidth issues associated with the bus, SMP still has inherent limitations for scaling Oracle infinitely. For the same reason that SMP architectures are good Oracle platforms, they also have a very definite upper boundary: the speed of latch operations.

For a latch operation to occur, a CPU must use test and set or a similar instruction to attempt to gain control over the latch (a value in shared memory). Only when the control is gained can the processor perform the real work that it is required to do. If the memory location is in the cache of other CPUs, then the processor and/or operating system must ensure that the caches are kept coherent on those other processors.

If a large number of user sessions require a common latch, it becomes more and more likely that all processing engines in the system will be executing test and set against the memory location. Every time the latch value changes, all of these operations need to be serialized by the bus arbiter, and so there is a finite number of latch operations possible on any SMP system. Therein lies the inherent limitation. At the end of the day, it really doesn't matter if the bus has another 10GB/s of bandwidth left unused if the system spends all of its time serializing down the bus on required latch operations.

All this being said, being bound by the speed of a latch is not as big a problem as it used to be, because Oracle has spent considerable time breaking nearly all of the single latches out into multiple latches, thus reducing the actual contention (it's the contention that hurts most). As more and more vendors produce nonuniform memory access (NUMA) architectures (see Section 2.7), Oracle is likely to start making more and more private latch allocations, in addition to implementing algorithmic alternatives to taking out the lock in the first place.

2.3.4   Shared-Bus Limitations

Due to all the system traffic going across a single shared bus, the system is limited by the capacity of the bus, in addition to the rate of arbitration and the capabilities of any bus snooping logic. As discussed earlier, the bus itself is limited by physics, and the upper limit on the number of processors that can be usefully attached is something of a religious war in the SMP industry. Many SMP designers believe that building an SMP of more than eight processors is a waste of time. Others can demonstrate reasonable scalability of SMPs of 16 to 20 processors. The real answer is very dependent on the way the bus is designed, the speed of the individual processors, the effectiveness of the cache, and so on, and there is no simple answer.

The one thing that is certain, however, is that the upper bounds for simplistic SMP scaling using a shared bus are pretty much at an end as of today. This is affirmed by the hardware vendors, who are all converting to some alternative type of SMP-like technology, using either NUMA, which we cover Section 2.7, or some kind of intelligent, point-to-point interconnect fabric to replace the global shared bus.

2.3.5   Summary

The shared-bus SMP architecture is the architecture that really changed the viability of UNIX-based Oracle database servers to deliver world-class, high-performance solutions. Although there are a decreasing number of hardware manufacturers still producing vanilla SMP architectures of this design, virtually all of the current products present that same, or very similar, programming model.

2.4 Point-to-Point SMP

One of the approaches taken to extend the useful life of a pure SMP architecture is to provide greater bandwidth and more interconnect concurrency through the use of some kind of point-to-point interconnect between components (see Figure 2.9).

> Examples: Sun E10000 (a.k.a Starfire), HP V2500

The actual architecture of the interconnect fabric varies slightly among systems, but the common goal of the systems is to allow point-to-point

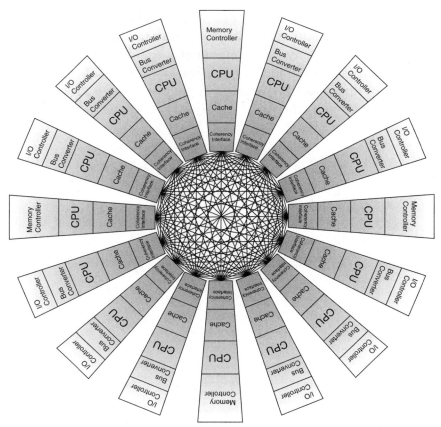

Figure 2.9   Crossbar switch interconnect SMP architecture

communication among all of the processors and memory in the system. This allows for full connection bandwidth between any two points at any time, in addition to increasing the concurrency of the "bus" as a result of multiple connects being active at any one time (remember that the shared global bus allows only one at a time).

The typical sustainable bandwidth for such systems is in the 16GB/s range, with each connection capable of around 2GB/s.

Figure 2.9 shows a schematic view of such a system, with all of the components connected to one another. To my knowledge, there isn't actually a real system out there that looks precisely like the one in this example, but I took interesting features from all of them and made a more useful example.

The first thing to note is that my system is constructed from 16 system boards, all interconnected to one another. The actual method of interconnection demonstrated here is direct point-to-point connection, which was chosen for reasons of path demonstration rather than to show any particular technology. Most likely, the components would be interconnected by some kind of crossbar or other switch fabric (see Figure 2.10).

On each of these boards resides a single processor, a processor cache, cache coherency logic, and either a portion of system memory or a bus

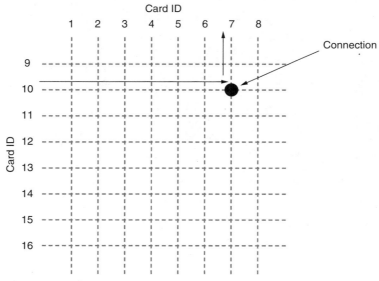

Figure 2.10   Crossbar switch

converter and I/O controllers. The trade-off between the memory controller and the I/O controllers was done on purpose to make the hypothetical system have the same kind of trade-offs as those of a real system.

For the sake of clarity in the illustration, none of the I/O controllers has been connected to any disk. Just assume that half of these controllers are connected to different disks in the disk cabinet and that the other half are providing alternate I/O paths to the same disks for the sake of redundancy. None of the I/O controllers is "private" to the board that it resides on: all I/O controllers are shared among all processors, as is the memory.

2.4.1 Cache Coherency

The important omission from the illustration is that of some kind of cache coherency mechanism. With point-to-point communication within the system, the standard SMP bus snooping method no longer works, because there is no shared bus. There are two main approaches to providing the solution to this requirement: a broadcast-based *address-only* bus with a snoopy bus protocol, and a directory-based coherency protocol designed for point-to-point communication.

By building a global address-only bus, systems such as the Sun E10000 benefit from the simplicity of the snoopy bus protocol. Greater scalability is achieved when compared with a full shared (address-plus-data) bus, because the system does not need to know the details of the activity (the data itself), just the locations. This allows the most appropriate component—be it a memory controller or the cache of another CPU—to service requests for memory, and allows cache lines to be invalidated accordingly when memory locations are changed by another CPU. It is also possible for a system to have multiple address busses in addition to multiple data connections, because an address bus is very readily partitioned by address ranges into any number of subaddress busses.

All access to other components, whether or not they are resident on the same system board, follows the same logic path. This ensures that all the access times to any particular component from anywhere else in the system are the same (*uniform*). This kind of fair sharing of access is critical in the design of these systems, because software changes need to be made as soon as the memory access becomes nonuniform. It is easy to see how a CPU with faster access to a certain piece of memory could "starve" the other CPUs on the system from accessing that component through unfair speed of access—a bit like having a football player on the field who can run ten times faster than all of the other players. This subject will be covered in more detail in Section 2.7, where it will become necessary to worry about such things.

As far as the operating system and Oracle are concerned, a crossbar-type system is a shared-bus system. The changes in operation all occur in the hardware itself and are therefore transparent.[5] Therefore, the introduction of such a system does not impose as great a risk to stability and performance as does a more radical one such as MPP or NUMA.

The increase in bandwidth of the "bus" allows for immediate performance improvements in non-latch-intensive workloads. The increase in concurrency, and the ability to have multiple address busses and therefore arbitration bandwidth, allows for greater performance in latch-intensive workloads.

2.4.2   Summary

This type of SMP system has bought the SMP architecture some time. The introduction of multiple interconnects has significantly increased the performance capability of the SMP software model, and this model probably has some way to go before it is exhausted.

However, scaling of SMP beyond the capabilities of crossbar SMP is a difficult task. For example, if we already have point-to-point data connections that are running as fast as physics will allow, how do we increase the throughput of the system? At some stage, the open system world needs to break out of the SMP mold once and for all, but until the software support is there, this cannot happen.

2.5   Clustered SMP

Clustered SMP configurations extend the capabilities of SMP further by *clustering* multiple SMP nodes together, as shown in Figure 2.11.

---

5. Although this statement is true in theory, it is likely that vendors choose to allow some visibility of the hardware changes to the O/S to allow for further software optimization.

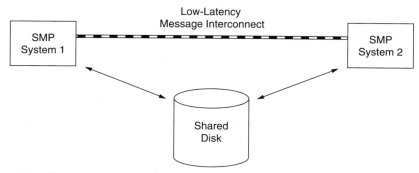

Figure 2.11 Clustered SMP systems

Examples: Sequent ptx/Clusters, Digital Trucluster, HP MC/ServiceGuard, MC/Lockmanager

A cluster is also known as a *loosely coupled* configuration, in that the systems that are clustered have no direct access to each other's memory or CPUs. All the systems run a discrete copy of the operating system and maintain a memory map containing only local memory addresses. The systems are coupled by a low-latency interconnect between all the systems and share only message information, which is why the coupling is termed "loose."

With this coupling, the systems can perform intersystem coordination but not much else because of the limited amount of information that they share. However, when connections are made from each system to a shared disk array, the usefulness of the cluster becomes far greater. Now the systems can share common data and coordinate the sharing through the use of messages passed over the interconnect.

2.5.1 Clustering Types

In the UNIX world, a cluster is currently useful for one or both of the following:

- Provision of high availability
- Oracle Parallel Server (OPS)

A *high availability cluster* is one in which the cluster interconnect is used solely as a "heartbeat" monitor between the systems. When the heartbeat from one of the systems ceases as a result of system failure, another system takes appropriate action to support the workload of the deceased system. This could include mounting of the dead system's file systems (thus the need for a shared disk), a change of IP address to make the system look like its peer, and the start-up of software subsystems.

There is no concurrent sharing of data in a high-availability solution, only sharing of mortality information.

The *Oracle Parallel Server (OPS) cluster* is more complex. In this type of cluster, full access is granted to the shared disk from all systems via the database. Note that it is still only the database that is shared, not file systems or any other UNIX resources. Any system in the cluster can bring up an Oracle instance and use it as required.

Clearly, some kind of synchronization is required to prevent all the Oracle instances from writing all over the same pieces of disk and to maintain the same consistent view of the data. This synchronization is provided by the *Distributed Lock Manager*, or *DLM*.

The DLM is a piece of software that was, for Oracle7, written by the hardware vendor[6] to provide the interface between Oracle and the hardware communications. For Oracle8, the DLM is incorporated into the Oracle product itself, and the vendor-specific lock manager has been retired.

The specifics of the DLM and how it integrates into Oracle will be covered in Chapter 6, but in order to get the basics right here, we can assume that whenever Oracle needs to read a block from disk, it checks in with the DLM. The DLM will send a request to any other Oracle instances that have the block and will ensure that no outstanding writes are pending by flushing the block from cache to disk (this is known as a *ping*). The requesting system will then be notified that the block is safe to read from disk, and normal operations will continue. This is a dramatic simplification of a complex issue, but should suffice to demonstrate the basic operation of an OPS cluster.

The DLM lock management is *not* transparent to the application, whatever people may try to tell you. Actually, it's fair to say that enough

---

6. Most vendors wrote their own DLMs for Oracle7, but some adopted a DLM written by Oracle, known internally as the UNIX DLM, instead. Notable among these were HP and IBM.

people have been severely burned by that claim that it has become a rare and uninformed statement.

A good deal of work is required to alter the design of the application to operate in this type of configuration. Specifically, anything that could cause communication with other nodes in the cluster by means of the DLM should be minimized wherever possible within the application. Examples of this are

- "Hot block" data access between the nodes, causing excessive pinging
- On-disk sorting

Specifically, a successful SMP cluster implementation will demonstrate good partitioning within the application. This could mean different areas of the application getting processed on different nodes or, even better, "private" data access per node through the use of a transaction processing (TP) monitor.

2.5.2 Summary

The implementation of a clustered system is a special requirement. This is not to say that you shouldn't do it—if you are building a very large scalable system, a clustered system of one of the types described above becomes a necessity. It's important, however, that you choose the most suitable method of clustering for your needs.

When deciding which type of clustering to use, you should keep your choice as simple as possible. Unless it is absolutely necessary, an OPS cluster should not be considered. The difference between the two methods of clustering is acute: high-availability clustering is reasonably simple whereas OPS clustering is very complex. This should be prime in your mind when making the decision.

One particularly bad reason for using OPS is for scalability, when the other option is to buy a larger machine. My advice on this is simple: although buying a second, smaller machine may be the most attractive proposition from a cost perspective, just remember that cost comes in many different forms. For example, don't forget to factor in extensive application modification (perhaps a total redesign in extreme cases), a large team of very experienced DBAs, and potentially more unplanned downtime owing to complex, multinode problems.

That having been said, the very best reason for going the OPS route is when you *need* scalability—and I really do mean *need*. When there is no system big enough to house the entire database processing requirement, OPS is the only way to go. Just remember that it will be an expensive ride. Do your homework, and never, ever, underestimate the undertaking.

2.6 Massively Parallel Processors (MPPs)

2.6.1 Definition

A massively parallel processor (MPP) is known as a *shared-nothing* configuration (see Figure 2.12).

> Examples: Siemens RM1000, nCube, IBM SP/2

Despite the grand title, there is nothing very complex about the architecture of an MPP system. Traditionally, the building block of an MPP system has been a uniprocessor node, comprising a single CPU, some memory (16 to 1024MB), a proprietary interconnect, and a finite number of *private* disks.

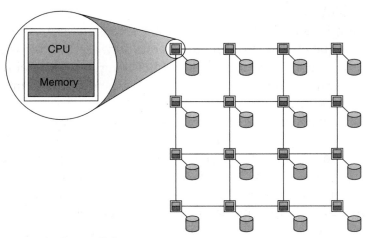

Figure 2.12   Massively parallel processors

Note that all of the disk is private; this is the reason that MPP systems are called "shared-nothing" configurations. Not only does each node run its own instance of the OS, but it does not even physically share any of its disk with other nodes. Think of an MPP system as a bunch of uniprocessors in a network, and you are pretty close to the truth of things.

The sole distinguishing feature of an MPP system (and the only one that makes it more than just "a bunch of uniprocessors in a network") is the proprietary interconnect between the nodes and the software layers that use it.

Each node runs a private copy of the OS, and thus MPP systems are comparatively simple to produce, because there are no cache coherency issues to deal with. Each processor has its own memory, its own disk controllers, and its own bus.

Typically, MPP is considered when high system bandwidth and good scalability up to potentially hundreds of nodes are required. The reason that MPP is well suited to such applications is that the nodes do not interfere with each other's resource and thus can scale very effectively, depending on the type of workload.

Workload is the key: MPP is suited to workloads that can be partitioned among the nodes in a dedicated and static fashion, with only *messages* (as opposed to *data*) traveling across the interconnect among the nodes. In this way, almost 100 percent scalability is possible because there is no data sharing among nodes. Examples of workloads that have been scaled effectively on MPP systems include

- Digital video streams for video on demand

- Complex mathematical problems

- *Some* decision support/data warehouse applications

Only some decision support workloads scale effectively, because they are often prone to data skew, thus breaking the static partitioning rule. For example, if a parallel query is to scale effectively, it is important that all the processors in the system are processing the query. In a shared-nothing environment, this would mean that the pieces of database that are to be scanned should be evenly distributed across all the nodes in the MPP system. As soon as the physical distribution of the data changes, the system is suffering from data skew.

As the data is skewed in this way, the query can be serviced only by a subset of the nodes in the system, because in a 100 percent shared-nothing environment a node can process only data that it is physically storing.

As an example, let's assume that there is a table of historical information that is populated by daily feeds and purged by date range, with the oldest first. When it was first loaded up, there was an even spread of last name values in the table, and so it was decided that the data would be loaded onto the system in "last name" partitions. Each range of names would be stored locally on the respective nodes, as shown in Figure 2.13.

When the first queries are run (full table scans, in parallel), all nodes are busy. However, as time goes on, old data is deleted and new data is added. After a few weeks, the data distribution looks like that shown in Table 2.2.

If the same query were to be run against the new data distribution, node 4 would finish 40 times faster than node 2 and then would sit idle while the other nodes continued processing.

In fact, this particular problem is easy to fix, because the partitioning criterion (last name) was clearly incorrect even from a logical standpoint. However, unlike this very simplistic example, a real data warehouse has many hundreds of tables, or many tables of many billion rows each. This

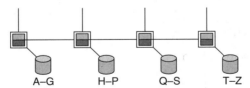

Figure 2.13   Last name partitioning

Table 2.2   MPP Data Skew

Host Node	Partition Row Count
Node 1	1 million
Node 2	2 million
Node 3	500,000
Node 4	50,000

is a very serious problem—a problem that is difficult to resolve without significant periodic downtime.

Examples of workloads that definitely do not scale effectively across MPP systems (no matter what anybody tries to tell you) are

- Transaction processing

- Transaction processing

- Transaction processing

Hopefully this is clear. Transactional workloads do not scale well on an MPP architecture, because it is very unusual to be able to partition the workload beyond a handful of nodes. For the same reason that it is difficult to write scalable applications for clustered SMP systems running Oracle Parallel Server, MPP systems are even more complex. When there are tens or hundreds of nodes out there, it is virtually impossible to make a logical partition in the application that corresponds to the physical partitioning of the system.

2.6.2   Oracle on MPP Systems

You might have been wondering how, on a system that consists of physically private disk, Oracle can be run as a single database. This is a valid question, because one of the clear assumptions that the Oracle architecture makes is that it resides on a system with the entire database accessible through standard I/O system calls. Oracle is often termed a *shared-disk database* for this reason.

The answer is that Oracle can't be run as a single database. Or rather it can, but not without help from the operating system. Without this special help, Oracle would not be able to open many instances across all the nodes, because each node would be able to see only a tiny portion of the database. Most nodes would not even be able to open the SYSTEM tablespace.

The special support that the operating system provides is a Virtual Disk Layer within the kernel. This layer of software traps all I/O destined for remote disk and performs the I/O using remote calls to the node that is physically connected to the required disk. The data is then passed over the interconnect and returned to Oracle as if it had just been read from a local disk. At this point, the system looks like a very large cluster, with shared disk on all nodes.

You might be thinking that this is a terrible, nonscalable thing to do, and you would be correct. Passing data over the interconnect breaks the fundamental rule of MPP scaling: pass only *messages* over the interconnect. In this way, the scenario described above, with the data skew, changes form a little on an Oracle database hosted on an MPP system. Instead of nodes becoming idle in the event of a data skew, Oracle does a fairly good job of keeping them all busy by reassigning the query slaves when they become idle. However, when this is done, it is likely that the "local disk affinity" aspect is then destroyed. The local affinity aspect is where Oracle attempts to execute the query slaves on the nodes with the most preferential disk transfer rates: the local nodes. When Oracle can no longer maintain this affinity because the local nodes are still busy, the data needs to be read over the interconnect. So, the system is kept busy, but the system is potentially more limited than an SMP system, because the interconnect does not have as much bandwidth as an SMP interconnect.

The final requirement for running Oracle on an MPP system is a DLM. The DLM provides exactly the same services as on a clustered SMP system, because the system is effectively a large cluster. However, the cluster software needs to be more robust than ever, because the number of nodes to manage (32 to 1,024) is dramatically larger than a clustered SMP system (typically a maximum of eight).

2.6.3 Summary

The use of MPP architecture has always been a niche piece of even the high-end marketplace. Although many customers have been sold down the river by their salespersons, the word is now getting out that MPP is definitely not the way to go if

- You need fewer than 32 processors of total computing capacity

- You do not have sufficient resource to manage an *n*-node system, where a separate instance of the operating system and a separate instance of Oracle need to be maintained on each node

- You have a transactional system

With the large leaps in SMP bandwidth and, potentially more significantly, with the introduction of NUMA, the MPP is forced even more into a corner. It is my opinion that MPP had a single shot at the DSS goal, as the bus-based SMPs ran out of steam, but failed to make a big impression owing to the management overhead of implementing such a system.

2.7 Cache Coherent Nonuniform Memory Access (ccNUMA)

2.7.1 Definition

ccNUMA (NUMA from now on) could be described as a cross between an SMP and an MPP system, in that it looks like an SMP to the user and to the nonkernel programmer, and yet is constructed of building blocks like an MPP system. In Figure 2.14, the building block comprises four processors, similar to the Sequent NUMA-Q 2000 system.

Examples: Sequent NUMA-Q 2000, Silicon Graphics Origin, Data General ccNUMA

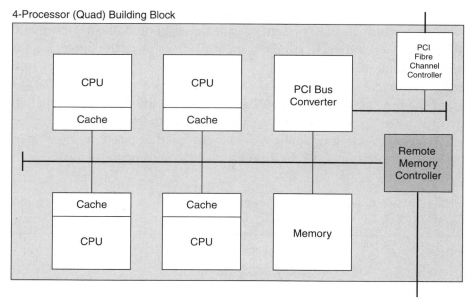

Figure 2.14 Nonuniform memory access building block: Sequent NUMA

These building blocks are *not* nodes—at least not by my definition. My definition of a node is an atomic entity that executes an operating system, and this does not apply to the building blocks of a NUMA system. Different manufacturers use different names for their building blocks (see Table 2.3).

For ease of explanation, I will adopt the Sequent NUMA-Q 2000 system as the primary example for the description, with a breakout later on to describe the key differences between the Sequent approach and the SGI (formerly Silicon Graphics, Inc.) approach found on the Origin platform.

2.7.2   Sequent NUMA-Q 2000

Sequent uses a four-processor Intel Pentium II Xeon board, similar to that shown in Figure 2.14, as the building block for its NUMA-Q system. This component is known as a "quad," and for simplicity's sake I will use this term for the rest of the description.

With a single quad in the system, the remote memory controller in the quad would not be needed for system operation. The system would look and behave (in this case) exactly like a four-processor shared-bus SMP machine.

The difference becomes apparent when multiple quads are linked together through the remote memory controller, as shown in Figure 2.15.

When a multiple-quad system such as this is booted, the presence of the additional quads is detected and the memory from all of the quads is added to the global memory address map. The addition of remote memory to the system introduces a new level to the memory hierarchy (see Figure 2.16).

For the time being, don't worry about the "remote memory cache" that has been introduced as a peer to the local memory. This is a Sequent-specific implementation detail, which will be discussed in more detail when we get into how NUMA delivers cache coherency.

Table 2.3   NUMA Building Block Names by Manufacturer

Vendor	NUMA Building Block
Sequent	Quad (four processors)
Silicon Graphics	Node card (two processors)
Data General	SHV (Standard High Volume) (four processors)

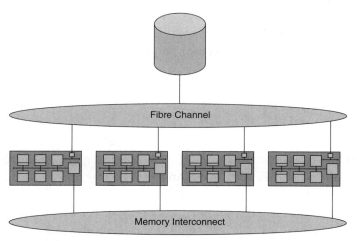

Figure 2.15   Nonuniform memory access system

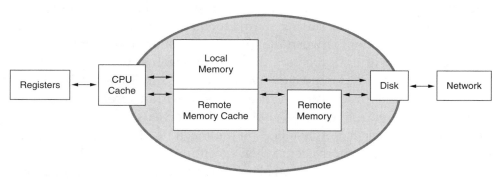

Figure 2.16   Sequent NUMA-Q memory hierarchy

The NUMA-Q handles the references to remote memory locations with the remote memory controller hardware (known as IQ-link), making the circled levels of the hierarchy appear from the software perspective to be one, local memory level. With the hardware hiding the implementation of the remote portion, the system looks a lot like an SMP, even from the operating system perspective.

However, this is only the start of the design of a NUMA system, because without significant software work the system above would perform poorly under high load. Although the IQ-link logic *can* successfully hide the fact that there is remote memory, the operating system still needs to be very intimately aware of this fact. The reason for this is that a load or store (read or write) from/to a remote memory address take longer than a local one,[7] and so it is vital that the operating system take careful action to minimize the remote references within the system.

This difference in latency between local memory and remote memory is the reason for the "nonuniform" part of the NUMA name. It is also the reason that the architecture of these systems is absolutely fascinating, and subsequently why Stanford and MIT have ongoing NUMA projects. It is also the reason why this section is longer than the others in this chapter. Let's get back to the operating system.

The first big gain to be made within the operating system is to ensure that processes have their resident set all located on the same quad and that this same quad is used when scheduling the process for execution. These two simple changes guarantee that all of the code and data associated with the process are local, and therefore fast. The one exception to this occurs when the process is using shared memory segments, because there is no direct correlation between the location of a shared memory segment and the location of the processes that execute against it. This is a major issue in an Oracle environment and will be covered in Section 2.7.4.

With the user processes executing mostly within local memory, the number of remote references is substantially decreased. Assuming for a moment that Oracle is not installed on the machine, the remainder of the remote memory references occur when executing in kernel mode.

In kernel mode, processors on all quads must access common memory structures that comprise the kernel address space. Examples of kernel structures that are shared in a standard SMP kernel include

- Process table
- Run queue
- Streams buffers
- File system buffer cache

---

7. First-generation systems had a *remote:local* latency of around 10:1 (ten times slower for remote access), current systems are around half that (i.e., five times slower), and future systems are likely to be in the 2:1 range.

Potentially more important than the structures themselves are the locks that protect the structures. If read locks are prevalent in the kernel, a good deal of remote memory activity can be felt just by reading some of these structures.

In Chapter 1, we covered some of the issues associated with locks and how they affect scaling. In a NUMA environment, even fine-grained locking can cause problems if the locks in use are not based on the local quad. Therefore, to minimize remote memory references in kernel mode, the OS engineer must implement

- Distributed kernel memory structures
- Quad local kernel locks

In the same way that SMP kernels have taken many years to mature into fine-grained, scalable kernels, it likely to be several generations before the NUMA kernel engineer has located and changed all the significant areas of the kernel that decrease the scalability of NUMA.

In addition to the kernel-induced remote references, DMA-based I/O that occurs on nonlocal I/O controllers also increases the number of remote references, because the data must be passed over the interconnect between the quads. For example, if the SCSI bus with the swap disk on it were hosted by quad-0, the kernel would need to copy pages of memory over the interconnect every time it needed to page out memory on any quad other than quad-0.

For this reason, Sequent adopted fibre channel I/O for the NUMA-Q rollout. With fibre channel, all I/O can then be made quad-local by adding a fibre channel card to each quad. The fibre channel on each card can be configured to "see" all the drives in the disk array, and therefore each quad can perform I/O locally. Again, this is a kernel value add, because the kernel must instruct the card as to which quad to perform the I/O, and is one that is unique to the NUMA architecture.

With the potential for many remote memory references to be always present on a NUMA system, the system needs to provide optimizations to lower the impact of this condition. In the Sequent implementation, the impact is mitigated by the use of the remote cache component within the IQ-link (see Figure 2.17).

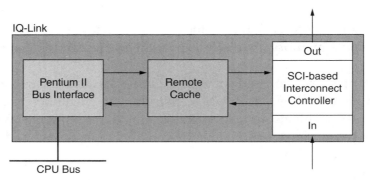

Figure 2.17 Sequent IQ-link

When an address is requested by a processor as a result of a cache miss, the request goes across the bus to the local memory controllers and to the IQ-link card concurrently. If the address is a remote address, the remote cache component acts a little like a CPU cache—it searches its cache for the memory region and, if a hit is found, returns it to the CPU's L2 cache. If no hit is found, a request is issued to the remote cache component of the quad that has the most recent copy of the cache line. When the remote memory is received, it is sent on to the CPU's L2 cache, and a copy is kept in the cache for future reference.

In order to optimize the cache coherency requirement among all the caches in the system, the designers of the NUMA-Q system decided to adopt *both* main types of coherency protocol: snoopy bus and directory. The snoopy bus protocol is used within a quad component, where its broadcast-based approach is very effective because there are a small number of processors within a quad. This snoopy bus protocol ensures cache coherency within each quad, with the IQ-link simply acting as another device on the bus.

To ensure coherency between the quads, a directory-based protocol is used, because the interconnect between the quads is essentially a point-to-point connection, implemented as a unidirectional ring. For example, for quad 1 to communicate with quad 4, the communication will "hop" through quads 2 and 3. Although the traffic is going through quads that are not involved in the communication, the data is simply passed through without incurring any significant latency, because the IQ-link card does not need to be concerned with the content if it is not the intended recipient, and therefore the overhead is kept to a minimum. If the cache coherency protocol used over the interconnect were a broadcast-based protocol, all IQ-link cards would need to look at the content, and therefore a more significant delay would be incurred in forwarding the traffic to the next quad in the ring. This delay would be in addition to any decrease in capacity resulting from the IQ-link controller logic. The directory-based coherency protocol is therefore the most suitable in order to minimize the traffic across the shared interconnect.

The IQ-link card provides the critical link between these two protocols and allows the most suitable protocol to operate in the appropriate area of the system.

2.7.3 SGI Origin 2000

The SGI Origin 2000 more closely resembles the Stanford DASH ccNUMA developed at Stanford University, in that there is no remote cache component within the system. Instead, the designers of the Origin 2000 decided to go for a full directory-based system, with the directory maintaining the states of all blocks (cache lines) of memory in the system. In order to gain greater scalability from a directory-based protocol, the designers also chose to distribute the directory evenly across all the node cards in the system.

The key components of the Origin 2000 include the HUB ASIC and the router to the CrayLink interconnect fabric (see Figure 2.18).

The HUB ASIC is a crossbar switch that handles high-bandwidth point-to-point communications within the node card. The router chip provides a similar function for traffic between cards, but provides multiple paths between any two points.

The directory memory on each node card maintains the status for the local memory only. This is done so that no single part of the interconnect is bearing the burden of directory interrogation.

The Origin 2000 also differs from the Sequent NUMA-Q 2000 in that it offers dynamic memory page relocation based on use. When a page is referenced, a counter is incremented on the basis of where the request came from. If the page is found to be referenced from one particular remote node card at greater frequency than from the local card, the page is relocated to the remote node card.

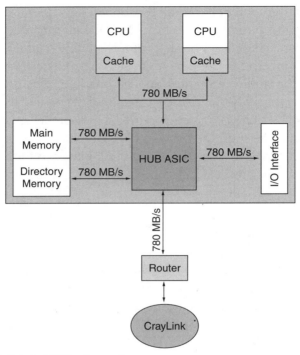

Figure 2.18 SGI Origin 2000 schematic

This relocation occurs at the operating system level in that the page of memory is simply copied to a free page on the remote card and the virtual address map of the mapping process is altered accordingly. That is, the contents of the page are relocated, not the physical address itself.

2.7.4   Oracle on NUMA Systems

During this explanation, the Sequent architecture will be used for examples. Oracle is currently architected to run most efficiently on an SMP architecture. Evidence of this includes the following:

- All disk must be accessible by any process at any time, through standard UNIX system calls.

- Shared memory is central to operation.

- All latches are implemented using atomic test-and-set (or similar) operations on shared memory addresses.

We have already seen that the Oracle architecture can be fairly well adapted to run on MPP, and even better on clustered SMP. However, because of the items listed above, Oracle runs *best* on an SMP architecture.

We know that NUMA is a lot like SMP from a user perspective but not from an operating system standpoint, so into which of these categories does Oracle fit?

Oracle is pretty close to being an operating system. If one views the Oracle System Global Area (SGA) as the kernel memory region and the shadow processes as "user processes executing in kernel mode," then Oracle looks a good deal like an operating system.

It's no coincidence, therefore, that Oracle faces the same kind of scaling challenges that the UNIX kernel faced, except that with Oracle the challenges are heavily compounded by the use of a shared memory buffer cache and by the very nature of database software. The following aspects of Oracle operation cause varying degrees of difficulty on a NUMA system:

- Shared buffer cache

- Shared redo log buffer

- Global (nonquad local) latches

The implication of the shared buffer cache is not much different from that in an SMP system. The very existence of a shared-memory cache means that a significant number of cache misses and cache invalidations are inevitable. The two big differences with a NUMA system are as follows.

1. It is more expensive to miss if you need to do a remote reference to get the buffer.

2. It is important to increase the statistical chance of the buffer being in local memory, not remote memory or even the local remote cache component, when you miss in the L2 cache.

Because of reason 1, reason 2 becomes important—not so much because of access speed as because of cache line turnover. If the SGA were to be created on a single quad of an evenly loaded eight-quad system, there would be seven remote accesses of the SGA for every eight attempts. This means that the remote cache components of the other seven quads would be replacing lines very rapidly to keep the cache updated with the artificially increased remote reference loading. It also means that the quad that owns the SGA is spending a good deal of its resource processing memory requests on behalf of the other quads.

Sequent's approach to this problem was to equally distribute the buffer cache portion of the SGA across all the quads in the system. This ensures, by virtue of the random access patterns of an Oracle buffer cache, that all remote cache components are equally loaded and that every quad has a one in eight chance of getting a local hit.

The redo log buffer is a different animal. All user sessions writing to the database need to write to the redo buffer. Therefore, there is no optimal location for this buffer as far as making it fair for all users. It is already equally unfair to all users, except the ones executing on the quad where it is located. Striping of the redo buffer over the quads is not an option, however, because in this case it is definitely preferable to give priority access of the redo buffer to one process on the system, the LGWR process.

If the redo buffer fills because the LGWR process is unable to keep up (because of long access times to the buffer), the database will prevent any more writes until LGWR flushes some space. Therefore, in a NUMA environment, it is important that the LGWR process be given a larger slice of the pie. Sequent supports this through the use of (a) an initialization parameter that builds the buffer on a quad of choice and (b) run queues that bind the log writer to the same quad.

Global, shared latches are potentially a larger problem factor than anything else in a NUMA environment. This is where the biggest impact of nonuniform memory access times is felt.

Oracle relies on latches to protect nearly every memory structure in the SGA. These latches are physically implemented using padded data structures[8] throughout both the fixed and variable portions of the SGA. The usage profile of these latches is as follows.

1. Get the latch.

2. Do some manipulation within shared memory.

3. Release the latch.

---

8. The structure is padded with unused memory allocations to ensure only one latch per cache line. On systems with very long cache lines, such as Alpha-based systems, this "wastes" a larger proportion of the usable cache size than systems with smaller line sizes.

We know from Chapter 1 that when a latch is allocated, this equates to a memory update. We also know that when memory is updated, all the caches in the system must be made coherent, either by invalidating the lines in the caches of other processors, or by updating the caches of other processors. Combining this information with the knowledge that there is a high probability of both the latch and the protected memory structure being in remote memory, the potential for problems can be seen.

The first problem in this environment is that latch acquisition is no longer fair. Imagine the situation where two processes are spinning, trying to acquire the same latch. Each of these processes is on a different quad, but one of them happens to be on the same quad as the current latch holder. The process that is sharing the quad with the latch holder will always "see" the release of the latch faster than the remote process, due to its locality to the (now dirty after the release) cache line. Therefore, the local process will be able to acquire the latch while the remote request is still in transit.

In a latch-intensive Oracle environment, which is essentially any very-large-scale system, this can lead to false sleeps on the latch as a result of the remote quads failing to acquire the latch within their specified spin periods, causing starvation on the latch. A system with a high proportion of sleeps on a latch will demonstrate poor response time.

This particular issue of latch unfairness is one that can be addressed through special software algorithms. Sequent currently utilizes patent-pending locking algorithms within their operating system and is working with software partners such as Oracle to get such support into their products.

There is still a further challenge with latch allocation in a NUMA environment. Latch throughput for a given latch could be measured as the number of (time to acquire latch plus time spent holding plus time to release latch) quantums per second. Therefore, if the acquire, hold, and release times are all artificially high as a result of all the memory references being remote, the maximum number of latch operations per second is proportionally lower than if all the references were on local memory.

This all assumes that the request has missed in all caches, but this becomes a reasonably likely event when latch contention is evident on the system and the cache lines are frequently invalidated by the latch changing hands.

In fact, the more quads you add, the more likely it becomes that the next latch requester will be a processor on a remote quad. If the next requester is on the same quad, the cache line either will be refreshed by local cache-to-cache transfer or, if requested by the same CPU, will still be valid. If it is on a remote quad, the cache line will be invalid on the quad at that time, removing the beneficial effect of the remote cache, because the line needs to be refreshed from a remote location.

When this occurs on the system, the symptom is likely to be a very high latch sleep count, with the CPUs potentially not busy. Adding additional quads in this situation not only will fail to improve the system performance, but could make it worse.

2.7.5 Summary

The types of latch problems described above mean that despite all the efforts of the system designer, NUMA is still not the incredibly scalable system that it has the potential to be. Although many things have been done to alleviate other types of remote memory reference, this problem eludes all of these optimizations. At the end of the day, shared global latches are absolutely dependent on the latency to memory.

For workloads that do not rely on very frequent updates of shared memory, NUMA already promises to be vastly scalable. This is the key point—the Oracle architecture, as it exists today, is retarding the scaling potential of NUMA systems. Until Oracle provides complete base code support for NUMA, this will continue to be the case. As of Oracle release 8.1, Oracle has started to cater for NUMA in the kernel, and these changes are covered in Chapter 8.

Nevertheless, NUMA systems are competing well with other high-end architectures. By increasing the power of each quad, for example, the number of quads can be reduced for a given load, and the statistical likelihood of memory references being remote is reduced accordingly. Likewise, the latency of remote memory accesses is decreasing as the architectures develop—Sequent has already halved its remote memory latency. This in itself directly raises the system's "Oracle ceiling."

For many, the time for NUMA is already here. Depending on the work profile of the system, NUMA can already beat many of the latest SMP architectures. As time goes on, and Oracle's architecture lends itself more to this architecture, the upper bounds of system performance stand to be dramatically increased.

2.8 Storage Systems

It is a surprising fact, but the truth is that in many large-scale database systems insufficient attention is paid to the I/O subsystem. Plenty of time is spent tuning processor and memory utilization, whereas the impact of potentially badly configured disk is ignored.

For example, a database administrator may closely monitor the wait states from within Oracle and determine that any users waiting for physical reads are doing OK because one has to go to disk sometimes, anyway. This is true, but it should not be assumed that the waits for disk activity are short ones.

To highlight the effect of a relatively slow device such as a disk in a query, let's look at an example. Assume that the example system already has an optimally tuned cache and that no further disk accesses can be prevented from further tuning of the cache. For a given query it is found that a cache hit ratio close to 100 percent is achieved, with only 500 reads necessary from physical disk. The total time spent retrieving buffers from memory is 2 seconds, and so doubling the speed of the system memory and processor will improve the response time by 1 second. In contrast, the 500 reads required from the disk are performed from a single disk, one at a time, adding approximately 8 seconds to the response time of the query. So, even the small amount of I/O still required by the query has an overpowering effect on the response time, accounting for a full 80 percent of the total time. Doubling the speed of the memory and CPU was clearly not the way to improve this system, because it improved the response time of the query by only 10 percent. A further doubling of speed in these components would yield an additional improvement of only 5 percent. A change in the system that would be more effective in improving the response time of the query would be to find a way to double the speed of the physical I/O, thus reducing the query response time by 40 percent. This is something that is easiest to do during the storage design phase, in order to obtain the greatest impact in performance with the least system interruption.

With most databases being many times the size of all the caches combined, it is clear that significant physical disk access is likely, even if everything is optimally tuned. With this certain knowledge, it is of obvious importance that the disk configuration in a database system be designed, built, and maintained as carefully as any other component in the system.

In addition, the disk on the system is the sole form of persistent storage for the data and is therefore the single most critical component. Although a system can typically be rebooted immediately after a processor or memory failure without further problem,[9] a terminal failure in the disk subsystem needs to be repaired before the system can safely be used once again by the business, even though the UNIX system is likely to keep running. If there is no form of redundancy built into the I/O subsystem, this repair is likely to include the dreaded restore from tape.

2.8.1   I/O Busses

We have already touched on the concept of an I/O bus. Owing to the number of connections available on the CPU and memory interconnect, it is not practical to "waste" these specialized connections with potentially tens or hundreds of I/O controllers. While the traffic from the I/O controllers ultimately travels across the system bus, it does not make financial or architectural sense to attach these devices to it directly.

To implement I/O connectivity, most systems have the concept of an I/O or peripheral bus, which is designed to connect several I/O controllers, Ethernet cards, and the like to a single slot on the system bus by means of a bus adaptor. Examples of I/O buses include PCI, S-Bus, VME, and Microchannel.

I/O busses are typically designed for a different goal than that of a processor-memory bus. For an I/O bus, it is more important to be able to have an accessible bus, to ensure that components can be replaced with

---

9. Assuming that the failed component is deconfigured from the system after the initial crash.

minimal interruption of system operation. For this reason, the I/O bus is typically longer, narrower (fewer bits), and subsequently slower than the processor-memory bus.

It is also typical for a system to support multiple I/O busses, in order to allow for connection of many disk controllers, network cards, and so on. Although this has been quite necessary in the past owing to the capacity limitations of SCSI busses, it is getting less important as fibre channel becomes the common form of I/O adapter for high-end systems.

2.8.2   Controllers

Several controllers are available for the connection of disk arrays to a UNIX system. The one used most commonly is some form of *SCSI*, with an increasing trend toward *fibre channel*.

SCSI Controllers

SCSI (pronounced "scuzzy") stands for Small Computer Systems Interface. SCSI has long been the I/O controller of choice for UNIX systems, due to its comparatively low cost and high performance in a highly concurrent, I/O-intensive environment.

The first implementation of SCSI, now known as SCSI-1, is an 8-bit-wide bus operating at a theoretical maximum bandwidth of 5MB/s. The bus protocol allows a maximum of eight *targets* (0 to 7) to be connected to the bus, one of which is always the host adapter/controller itself. The inclusion of the host adapter as a target is because the SCSI protocol is, at least in design, a peer-to-peer protocol, with the host simply existing as a unit on the bus. For all practical purposes, however, the host adapter acts very much as the master, with the other devices acting as slaves.

A target typically is the same thing as a physical device, such as a disk. More accurately, a target is an entity that can be physically selected by the bus protocol. In the case of directly attached devices such as disk drives and tape devices, this means that a maximum of seven disks or tapes can be attached to each SCSI bus.

In the case of RAID-based disk arrays, the RAID controller within the disk array could be the target, with multiple *logical unit numbers* (LUNs) assigned within the array equating to physical disks. The access to the disks within the array is handled by the RAID controller hardware itself.

The limitation of eight targets on the bus comes from the target selection method used in the bus protocol. The target is selected by electrically selecting the physical line (1 to 8) to which the device has been configured on the bus and is therefore limited to the physical width of the bus—in this case, 8 bits. When bus conflicts arise that need to be arbitrated, the highest target number is chosen over the lower ones. For this reason, the highest target ID (ID7) is chosen for the host adapter.

SCSI-2, also known as Fast SCSI, increased the frequency of the bus from 5MHz to 10MHz, increasing the throughput to 10MB/s in synchronous mode. In addition, SCSI-2 introduced the concept of *command queuing*, which gives SCSI-2 devices the ability to process certain SCSI commands in a sequence different from that in which they were received. This allows the drive to optimize certain operations and minimize excessive head movement where possible. The most important of these optimizations is the ability for a device to accept a second write instruction before the prior write instruction is complete. This allows the communication latency of the write instructions to be overlapped/hidden in the actual write phase of another write. With a SCSI-1 protocol, the second write could not be dispatched until the first one had been signaled complete.

SCSI-2 also comes in a Wide SCSI-2 format, more commonly known as Fast/Wide SCSI. This has been the most commonly available SCSI format for high-end systems for several years. The Wide version of SCSI-2 increases the bus width to 16 bits and allows the concentration of up to 15 devices. The doubling of the data path allows the maximum bandwidth of the bus to go up to 20MB/s.

Even with SCSI-2, systems were rapidly becoming full of SCSI controllers to allow for the required throughput from the disk subsystem. The latest version of SCSI is Ultra SCSI, or SCSI-3. Ultra SCSI provides another doubling in the bus clock speed, taking the frequency up to 20MHz and the capacity of a Wide Ultra SCSI bus up to 40MB/s. The SCSI-3 standard also provides an extension in command set, allowing the host to negotiate optimal behavior from the drive.

At the time of this writing, another standard of SCSI is reaching the marketplace—the confusingly named Ultra2 SCSI. This doubles the data rate once again to a maximum of 80MB/s in synchronous mode. Ultra2 SCSI needs to be implemented over *differential SCSI cabling,* as opposed to *single-ended SCSI cabling.* The differential interface has been used for some time in high-end UNIX systems, because it allows longer cables owing to the use of twisted pairs, which eliminates a proportion of electrical noise picked up by the cable.

One of SCSI's most limiting factors for building large systems is the maximum cable length on a SCSI bus. Even using a differential interface to get the maximum distance, the limit for a SCSI-2 implementation is 25 meters. This seems like quite a lot to begin with, but this distance includes all the cables between the drives, the cable between the system and the drives, and a good deal of the circuitry *inside* the drives themselves. Once all this is factored in, it very quickly becomes a major engineering feat to connect a large amount of disk to a system. This is further complicated when the SCSI bus includes more than one host system, as is the case in a shared disk cluster configuration. In this case, it is common for the clustered systems to be *physically* clustered around the shared disk cabinets, because the physical proximity reduces the cable lengths required for the connections.

SCSI Throughput

The real-world throughput of a SCSI bus never actually gets to the theoretical bandwidth of the bus. This is attributable to the overhead incurred from the SCSI protocol. The actual throughput that can be observed varies depending on the access patterns.

For a sequential disk access pattern, the bus can be quickly saturated using a small number of drives, because the drives spend most of the time transferring data rather than waiting for seeks and rotational delays. The actual number of drives that will saturate the bus depends on the size of the I/O units requested. In the case of 2KB reads, the overhead of the bus protocol dominates the bus and the effective bandwidth of the bus drops by as much as 60 percent. For larger reads of 32KB, 64KB, or greater, the SCSI overhead is far less, and a bandwidth closer to the theoretical value will be achieved.

For random access patterns, the bus becomes less of a problem because the drives spend a large proportion of the time waiting for seeks and rotational delays before sending data. Even with a modern drive per-forming 100 reads/s, it would take around 40 drives on a single SCSI bus to saturate the bus with 2KB reads.

In real life, however, it is unusual for a database system to be either sequential or random. Rather, databases tend to use a combination of the two, particularly in transaction-processing environments. The user trans-actions are typically all small, random units of transfer, whereas the batch cycle has a completely different profile, using large, sequential I/O trans-fers to process large amounts of data. For this reason, it is very unusual to find a SCSI bus with 40 or more drives attached to it, because the system must be built to process both types of workloads effectively. Oracle helps out with multiblock reads for full table scans, which batch together several smaller reads into one large request. Typically, this larger unit of I/O is returned by the drive in a comparable time as a single block of its constitu-ent parts, owing to the amount of latency incurred regardless of the I/O size requested. Once Oracle is performing multiblock reads, a bus with too many drives on it will quickly become saturated, and queues will build up and all users of disk on that channel will be adversely affected. For this reason, it is rarely a good idea to economize on the number of channels at the cost of the batch process.

Fibre Channel

Fibre channel is a fiber optic link between the host and the disk subsys-tem. With a theoretical maximum bandwidth of 100MB/s, fibre channel has a large bandwidth advantage over any of the SCSI standards. In addi-tion, the physical attributes of fibre channel make it attractive in the data center:

- Optical transmission ensuring freedom from electrical interference
- Maximum cable length increased to 500 meters
- Thin, flexible cable

These advantages allow far greater flexibility than ever before, including campus-style (in another building) disaster recovery strategies without specialized disk hardware, flexibility over physical disk cabinet place-ment, and a good deal less cable to keep tidy under the raised floor.

There are two main ways of implementing fibre channel I/O subsystems: point-to-point and arbitrated loop. In a point-to-point configuration, a direct connection is made between the host and each individual disk device. This allows for the full bandwidth of the fibre channel connection to be available between the two points, but in reality no single device will be able to realize the full fibre chanel bandwidth, and it is not practical to connect each device in this way.

In an arbitrated loop configuration or Fibre Channel-Arbitrated Loop (FC-AL), disks and hosts are connected together in a full duplex ring, similar to fiber distributed data interface (FDDI). This configuration (see Figure 2.19) allows fully shared access among all "loop nodes," including hosts, disks, and other peripherals.

Although this topology provides a very flexible and simple way of stringing the system together, there are several drawbacks to this approach. First of all, the full bandwidth of the fibre channel has to be shared among all "nodes" in the loop. While 100MB/s is a good starting budget, this is very quickly consumed in a large-scale system. Second, fault diagnosis becomes significantly more difficult, because failures of devices and/or fiber interconnects are more difficult to locate and could affect the entire system.

A preferable alternative to both of these methods is to create a fibre channel fabric using fibre channel switches and/or hubs (see Figure 2.20).

When this kind of topology is used, all devices within the fabric are visible to others, and the bandwidth is scalable as required by the addition of more fiber connections into the fabric from the host. When a failure occurs in the fabric, the fault can be quickly isolated to the relevant part of

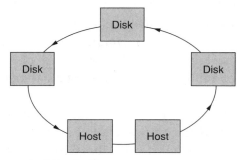

Figure 2.19   Fibre channel arbitrated loop

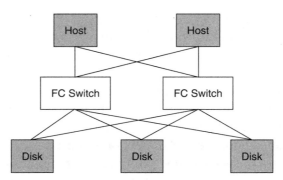

Figure 2.20 Switched fibre channel fabric

the fabric and resolved accordingly. Using multiple switches and alternate paths, a fully redundant I/O system can be built, without the electrical headaches that have long been associated with SCSI.

The switched fibre channel topology is rapidly becoming the preferred method for large systems, despite the higher cost resulting from the use of expensive fibre channel switches. At the time of this writing, native fibre channel disk drives are only just becoming available. As a temporary measure, vendors have been using existing SCSI disks within the fibre channel fabric through the use of fibre channel-to-SCSI bridges.

2.8.3 Disk Drives

At the end of the controller chain lies the individual disk drive. Because the disk drive is the fundamental building block of the system, it's important to have a good understanding of disk drive mechanics in order to build the system most effectively. The disk drive is ultimately the slowest component in the system, and so any gain in disk drive performance will have a significant effect on the performance of the overall system.

A disk drive (see Figure 2.21) is composed of several disk *platters* stacked one on top of another with enough of a gap between them to fit in a read/write *head*.

The data is stored on the platter in a series of concentric rings called *tracks*. Each of the tracks is composed of several *sectors*. In modern SCSI disks, each of these sectors has a capacity of 512 bytes and represents the smallest unit of data transfer that the disk will process. A group of tracks,

Figure 2.21   Disk drive organization

all with the same offset but on a different platter, is known as a *cylinder* because of the shape formed by the stacked tracks.

The platters themselves rotate at a constant speed of 5,400 rpm to 10,000 rpm, while the heads move laterally across the platters in response to commands from the I/O controller.

To access a particular block on disk, the disk head needs to be moved to the track that contains the requested data. This operation is called a *seek*. After the seek is complete, the head waits for the requested block of data to pass underneath it. This wait period is called *rotational delay* or *rotational latency*. Once the data to be read is in position, the head initiates the read, and the data is sent back across the I/O bus to the requesting host. If this were a write operation, the new data would be written to disk instead of being read.

The two aspects described above, seek and rotational delay, constitute the vast majority of most I/O operations and should be the focus of attention in the design of any I/O system.

Seek Times

Several aspects affect how long you spend seeking with your disk drives. The first of these aspects is the usage profile of the disk. At one extreme, if the disk usage pattern is sequential—that is, accessing each block in sequence—then seeking will not be a problem, because the only seeking performed will consist of moving the disk head onto the next track once the current one is fully read. This type of track-to-track seek is typically an order of magnitude lower in latency than a quoted "average seek" time.

The opposite extreme is a random access pattern. Welcome to transaction processing systems. The Oracle buffer cache has already "stolen" any sequentiality out of your disk access (to your benefit, I might add), and the disks are left to supply single rows using rowids gleaned from index lookups. The one thing you can be sure of here is that the block needed will not be on the same track that the head is currently on. Therefore, a certain amount of seeking is guaranteed.

The key here is to control the amount of seeking that is performed. The obvious thing to consider, therefore, is keeping the data on the disk grouped as closely as possible, thus keeping the seek distances minimized. There is one aspect of disk drive mechanics that is essential knowledge when planning your disk placement strategy. Modern disk drives read and write constant bit densities across the entire platter, using a recording format called *zone bit recording*. For any given square centimeter on the disk, the same number of bits can be stored, regardless of location on the disk. What this means is that tracks near the outer edge of a disk are capable of storing more data than tracks near the inner edge, because more of the 512-byte sectors can be fitted onto each track (see Figure 2.22). The implication of this is that more data can be stored within a given number of tracks near the outer edge than can be stored near the center of the disk. It is therefore statistically more likely that if you place your high-activity data at the edges of the disks, fewer and smaller seeks will occur than if you store it near the center of the disk.

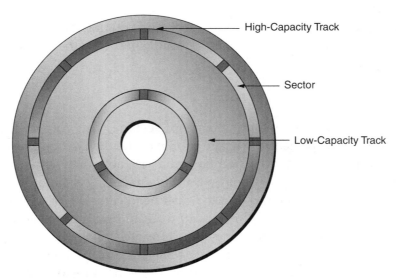

Figure 2.22   Zone bit recording format

In addition to the improved seek times near the outer edge of the disk, the increased density also allows far greater data transfer rates, potentially 50 percent greater or more.

Rotational Delay

Rotational delay is affected by one thing alone—the rotational speed of the drive. If you take a look at a data sheet for a disk drive, the "average latency" statistic is the one describing rotational delay. If this isn't quoted, don't worry: divide 60 seconds by the rotational speed of the drive (in revolutions per minute) and then halve the result. This is the same number— that is, assuming that there is an average of one-half turn of the disk platter on each read. Clearly, the faster the drive spins, the quicker the required sector will arrive under the head.

2.8.4 Disk Drive Sizing

We have seen several disk metrics. As a demonstration of how these disk metrics are employed, let's use a sizing example in which we choose between two drives with the specifications listed in Table 2.4. For this example, we will be using unprotected, plain disk.

The proposed system is believed to exhibit a peak load of 12,500 reads per second on the I/O system, evenly distributed across the 400GB database. A decision needs to be made as to which disk drives to use.

Table 2.4   Disk Drive Performance Evaluation

	Drive 1	Drive 2
Average time to seek	5 ms	3 ms
Spindle speed	5,400 rpm	10,000 rpm
Rotational delay	5.6 ms	3 ms
Time to read 4K data from track	6 ms	3 ms
Storage capacity	4GB	18GB
Price	$2,000	$3,500

Conventional wisdom from the uninformed would dictate a purchase of 22 of the 18GB drives, because this would be the cheapest way to get the required capacity. Herein lies the problem: many people still use the *storage capacity* of a drive to determine how many drives are required. This would be absolutely the worst choice that could be made.

Assuming now that we are buying according to the number of I/Os per second that the drives are needed to perform, which do we choose? First, we need to know how many reads per second each drive is capable of. To determine this, we calculate how long each read request will take, as follows:

$$Disk\ Read\ Time\ =\ Seek\ Time\ +\ Rotational\ Delay\ +\ Transfer\ Time$$

Once we have this time, we can calculate how many reads can be performed per second:

$$Reads\ per\ Second\ =\ \frac{1}{Disk\ Read\ Time}$$

The results of these calculations are shown in Table 2.5.

It can be seen that, although the instinct may be to go with the smaller drive to obtain more spindles, the newer drive is not only faster but also requires fewer controllers and offers a total cost reduction of $64,500. The part of this that most bean counters find hard to swallow is that about 1.5TB of storage space will not be used if drive 2 is chosen. The solution is simple, of course—don't tell them.

Table 2.5 Disk Drive Evaluation Summary

	Drive 1	Drive 2
Average read time	16.6 ms	9 ms
Average reads per second	60	111
Drives required	208	113
SCSI controllers required (at $4,000 each)	26	15
Total cost	$520,000	$455,500
Used capacity per drive	1.9GB	3.5GB
Unused capacity (total)	436.8GB	1,638.5GB

The additional benefit of choosing drive 2 in this situation is that only 19 percent of the drive is needed, as opposed to 48 percent of the 4GB drive. This means that significant performance gains can be achieved by using only the *outer* 19 percent of the drive.

2.8.5   Redundancy

The provision of full redundancy in the storage system rapidly became a hot topic when people started to implement systems with several hundred disk drives. For example, if a system has 500 disk drives in its storage subsystem, each rated at 1,000,000 hours mean time between failures (MTBF), the effective MTBF of all the disks in the system becomes 2,000 hours, or 83 days. It is clearly not acceptable to have the database exposed to a crash every 83 days on average.

The term *redundancy* is used to describe the use of spare, redundant parts that allow the system to keep running in the event of a component failure. For every fan, cable, power supply, and so on in the system, there needs to be redundant capacity from another part to allow the system to run unaffected by the failure of the primary. Examples of this include fans that can speed up to compensate for other failed fans, twin power supplies that are each capable of supplying all required power, and twin power cables each rated at full current capacity and connected to its own power source.

In the I/O world, redundancy is an art form. Almost every component in a modern disk system can sustain at least one failure. This includes the host I/O controllers (and therefore the cables attached to them), the power supplies of the disk cabinet, and the disks themselves. One of the most common ways of providing disk-level redundancy is the use of RAID.

2.8.6   RAID Levels

In 1987, Patterson, Gibson, and Katz of the University of California, Berkeley published a paper entitled "A Case for Redundant Arrays of Inexpensive Disks (RAID)." This paper was written to demonstrate the case for using cheaper, commodity disk drives as an alternative to the very expensive disk drives found in large mainframe and minicomputer systems.

The authors proposed that, by combining several these cheaper devices, the performance and reliability of the combination can match or exceed those of the more expensive devices. At the time the paper was written, the commodity disk drive was a 100MB disk drive costing $1,100, compared with an IBM 3380 disk drive with 7.5GB capacity and a price of more than $100,000.

The real driving force behind the research that went into this paper was that while CPU and memory speeds were increasing dramatically year after year, the speeds of disk systems were not advancing at anything approaching the same rate. As already described earlier in this chapter, any increase in processing speed will ultimately be restricted if the operation has to include a slower device.

The idea behind the research was to configure a large number of comparatively inexpensive SCSI disks to look like one very fast, high-capacity disk, rather like the IBM disk. Once many disks are combined in this way, however, the aggregate MTBF for the disk system is substantially reduced. The example in the paper shows the drop in mean time to failure (MTTF) to 2 weeks for the combined array of 100MB disks. Clearly this is not acceptable, and so the paper goes on to describe different techniques (now known as RAID levels) for increasing the reliability while still retaining the performance.

These RAID levels are identified by number, 0 through 5, and have varying degrees of success in balancing price, performance, and reliability. RAID levels 2, 3, and 4 are not commonly implemented, although some RAID disk arrays use a RAID-3 variant to obtain the results they require. For the sake of simplicity, I will concentrate on RAID levels 0, 1, and 5, because these are the most commonly used levels.

RAID-0

RAID-0 is not formally defined in the Patterson et al. paper. However, it is named as such because it conforms to the spirit of the paper—using multiple disks to achieve higher aggregate performance. In a RAID-0 configuration, multiple disks are configured together as a set, or a "bank," and data from any one datafile is spread, or striped, across all the disks in the bank. For the sake of example, we will use 64KB stripes over a six-disk stripe bank, as shown in Figure 2.23.

= 64KB Block

Figure 2.23 RAID-0 physical organization

This type of organization has made RAID-0 more commonly known as *striping*, because of the way the data exists in stripes across the physical disks. Using striping, a single data partition is physically spread across all the disks in the stripe bank, effectively giving that partition the aggregate performance of all the component disks combined.

The unit of granularity for spreading the data across the drives is called the *stripe size* or *chunk size*. Typical settings for the stripe size are 32K, 64K, and 128K.

If one were to perform a 384KB read from the file in Figure 2.23, starting at zero offset (i.e., at the beginning of the file), this would be translated as six physical reads from the respective disks. Disk 1 supplies bytes 0 to 65,535, disk 2 supplies 65,536 to 131,071, disk 3 supplies 131,072 to 196,607, and so on. The impact of this differs (yet again) depending on the access pattern.

If the disk access is sequential, it is bound by the transfer time of the actual data. That is, most of the time spent servicing the request is spent transferring data rather than waiting for a physical data rendezvous. In a striped configuration, all the disks that compose the stripe can transfer data concurrently, making the transfer rate the aggregate rate of all the drives. For example, if a file on one disk can be sequentially scanned at 3MB/s, then the same file striped across six disks can be sequentially scanned at a rate of 18MB/s. The achievable bandwidth is still subject to other constraints, such as SCSI bandwidth limitations, but, with careful planning, significant gains in throughput can be made using striped disk.

With a random access pattern (a.k.a. transaction processing), the gains are less quantitative, but significant nonetheless. However, if a single user were to make random read requests against a striped file, virtually no difference in performance would be observed. This is because the gains that are made in a random access environment have much more to do with concurrency than with bandwidth.

The first benefit that striping provides in a random access environment is load balancing. In a database environment, some files are always busier than others, and so the I/O load on the system needs to be balanced. Unfortunately, this is never as easy as it would first appear, owing to the way database files are accessed. It is very typical for a file to be busy in just a small portion (maybe 1MB) of its total volume. This is true even if the file contains only one database object. In a nonstriped environment, this will cause a hot spot on the disk and result in poor response times.

Using a striped disk array, the exposure to hot spots is significantly reduced, because each file is very thinly spread across all the disks in the stripe bank. The effect of this spreading of files is random load balancing, which is very effective in practice.

The second advantage of striping in a random access environment is that the overall concurrency of each of the files is increased. If a file were to exist on a single disk, only one read or write could be executed against that file at any one time. The reason for this is physical, becasue the disk drive has only one set of read/write heads. In a RAID-0 configuration, many reads and writes can be active at any one time, up to the number of disks in the stripe set.

The effects of striping in both sequential and random access environments make it very attractive from a performance standpoint. There are very few situations in which striping does not offer a significant performance benefit. The downside of striping, however, is that a striped configuration has no built-in redundancy (thus the name RAID-0) and is highly exposed to failure.

If a single disk in the stripe set fails, the whole stripe set is effectively disabled. What this means is that in our set of six disks, the MTBF for each disk is now divided by 6, and the amount of data that is not available is 6 times that of a single disk. For this reason, RAID-0 is not often found in plain vanilla RAID-0 form, but is combined with RAID-1 to provide the necessary protection against failure.

RAID-1

RAID-1 (see Figure 2.24) is more commonly known as *mirroring*. This was not a new concept in the paper by Patterson et al., but rather a traditional approach to data protection. Mirroring involves taking all writes issued to

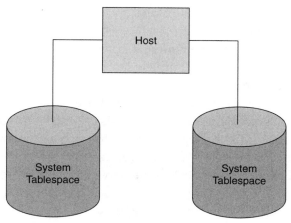

Figure 2.24   Host-based RAID-1 implementation

a given disk and duplicating the write to another disk. In this way, if there is a failure of the first disk, the second disk, or mirror, can take over without any data loss.

RAID-1 can be implemented using volume management software on the host computer or using a dedicated intelligent disk array. The details of the implementation vary slightly depending on the method used, and thus need to be described separately.

A full host-based RAID-1 implementation uses dedicated controllers, cables, and disk drives in order to implement the mirror. This provides two positive benefits to the configuration. First, it protects the mirrored disk from failure of any of the primary components. If a controller, cable, or physical disk fails in the primary disk array, the mirrored disk remains isolated on its own controllers. This type of configuration is a full RAID-1 configuration—all components in the I/O infrastructure are protected by the presence of a redundant peer. The host ensures that both sides of the mirror are consistent by issuing all writes to both disks that comprise the mirror.[10] This does not mean that all

10. It is typical for a mirror to be made up of two "sides"—a primary and a mirror. Most mirroring implementations also support maintenance of three or more sides. This is generally used to implement fast backup solutions, where the third mirror is detached and backed up offline from the online database.

writes take twice as long, because the writes are issued in parallel from the host, as shown in Figure 2.25.

When the write is ready to be issued, it is set up and sent to the first disk. Without waiting for that write to complete (as would be the case in a sequential write), the write to the second disk is initiated. Therefore, the "write penalty" for mirrored disk is significantly less than the expected 100 percent.

When a host needs to *read* a mirrored disk, it takes advantage of the fact that there are two disks. Depending on the implementation, the host will elect either to round-robin all read requests to alternate disks in the mirrored set or to send the request to the drive that has its head closest to the required track.

Either way, a significant benefit is gained by using the disks on an independent basis for reads. If the reads are sent round-robin, a 100 percent gain in read capacity is possible.[11] If they are optimized to minimize head movement, the gain could potentially be greater than 100 percent.

Failure of any component on one side of the mirror will cause the system to start using the other side of the mirror exclusively for all read and write requests. During this period, the read capability of the system is substantially reduced, because only one disk is available for reading.

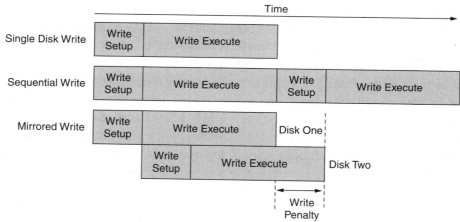

Figure 2.25   RAID-1 write penalty

---

11. This 100 percent gain assumes that no writes are occurring at the same time.

Once a failed side of the mirror is restored, by replacing or repairing the failed component, the contents of the new or repaired disk are considered *stale* in comparison with the active side. The writes that have occurred while one side of the mirror was unavailable have to be applied to the newly restored side in order to bring the mirror back online.

Typically in host-based solutions, bringing a disk back online will involve physically copying of the surviving mirrored disk onto the replaced peer. This is necessary because the system has no record of what has changed since the disk failed and so must take a brute-force approach.

This process is called *resilvering*, to further the mirror analogy, and can take a considerable amount of time when the system is still servicing its normal workload. This can also present response time problems, because the active side of the mirror is servicing all user requests and supplying the data for the full copy. Often, there are options available as to how quickly the resilvering is performed. This is a fine balance, because it is undesirable to be unprotected for any extended period (as you are when the other side of the mirror is stale), but it is also undesirable to resilver too aggressively, because the system will suffer poor response times as a result.

There is another situation that can cause resilvering in a host-based solution. When the host system crashes, there is no guarantee that writes were performed to both disks that constitute the mirror. Therefore, the system cannot rely on the integrity of the data between the two sides of the mirror and must take action to ensure that the data between the two sides is clean. The approach taken to achieve this is simply to designate one side of the mirror as clean and the other side as stale. This forces a resilvering, and the mirrored disk can once again be guaranteed to be consistent with itself. This can be a catastrophic occurrence in a production system, because it is likely that *most* disks in the system will require resilvering, and you must pay this penalty after getting your system restarted after the crash.

Some of the problems associated with host-based mirroring are resolved when the mirroring is performed within an intelligent disk array (see Figure 2.26).

In this configuration, a slightly different approach needs to be taken from the host's perspective. All of the mirroring is taken care of inside the disk array, with the host aware of only a single target to read from and

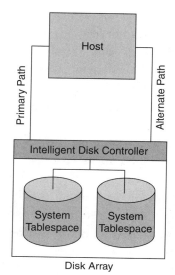

Figure 2.26   RAID-1 hardware implementation

write to. As two connections are no longer necessary between the host and the disk, the failure of the single connection means that *both* the mirrored disks are unavailable.

To get around this problem, the concept of an alternate path is introduced. During normal operation, both of these channels are used to read from and write to the disk. On failure of one of these channels, the other channel takes on the entire workload until the failed channel is restored. In this way, the connections to the disk are once again fully protected, and the full bandwidth of two channels is available once more.

Within the disk array, the read and write operations are converted into discrete requests to the relevant disks, without the host being aware that there is more than one disk. The write activity is still subject to the over-lapped write penalty as the host-based mirroring, unless caching is used within the disk array.

There are essentially two benefits of performing the mirroring within the disk array itself. First, there is no processing overhead incurred by the host to manage the mirrored I/O. Although this is not a very high over-head, in a very-large-scale system it is important to maximize the available processing capacity wherever possible.

Second, the mirror is not exposed to problems resulting from crashing of the host. If the host crashes, the mirror does not become stale, because the state information is not stored on the host and therefore is unaffected by any host operations, including crashes. This single attribute makes disk-array-based (commonly called hardware-based) mirroring very attractive for building a highly available system.

Other advantages of using a hardware-based mirroring policy come into play when the disk array includes a quantity of cache memory. These advantages will be discussed in Section 2.8.8.

The downside of disk mirroring is that the cost of the entire disk infrastructure is exactly 100 percent greater, with no gain in storage capacity. This having been said, in a large-scale database environment, the storage capacity is often a concern secondary to the service capacity of the disk system. Mirroring *does* provide a significant uplift in the read capability of the system and so provides performance improvements in addition to absolute protection of the data.

RAID-0+1

RAID-0+1 is another RAID level that was not described by Patterson et al. Based on the "made up" RAID-0, RAID-0+1 is exactly what its name implies: striped and mirrored disks.

Figure 2.27 shows a RAID-0 implementation comprising a set of six striped disks *mirrored* over discrete SCSI channels to an identically configured mirror of the stripe set. This is the most common configuration used in high-end transaction processing environments, because it presents excellent performance and reliability.

The RAID-0/RAID-1 combination has started to be called RAID-10. This has nothing to do with RAID levels, of course, but with the marketing departments of RAID hardware vendors. Still, it's easier to say than "0+1," so we'll adopt its use in this book.

RAID-10 can be implemented using various combinations of hardware-based RAID and host system software. For the purposes of this book, we will concentrate on the two most common implementations, because they also demonstrate an important operational difference between them.

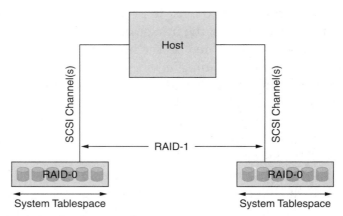

Figure 2.27   RAID-0+1 implementation

The most common environment for the first of these implementations is a 100 percent software solution, with the striping and mirroring both handled by software on the host. In this configuration, the stripe set is first created and then mirrored. In this configuration, it is the entire stripe that is mirrored, and any disk failure in the stripe set will take that entire side of the mirror offline. For example, if any disk in stripe set A in Figure 2.28 fails, the entire A side of the mirror will become unavailable.

If a failure were then to occur anywhere in the remaining side of the mirror (side B), the entirety of side B would also be taken offline. At this stage, all of the data (A and B) is unavailable and logically corrupt.

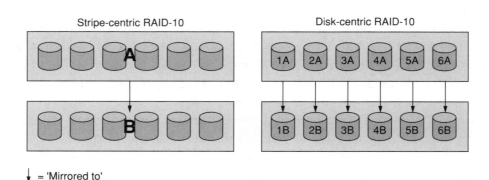

↓ = 'Mirrored to'

Figure 2.28   Stripe-centric versus disk-centric RAID-10

The other common implementation of RAID-10 involves a combination of hardware-based RAID and host software. The RAID-1 component is handled by the hardware, and the RAID-0 striping is taken care of in software on the host. The important difference between this configuration and the 100 percent software solution is that in this configuration it is the disks themselves that are mirrored, not the stripe. What this means is that data loss can occur only if the *corresponding* disk on the other side of the mirror goes bad, not just any disk. For example, in Figure 2.28, if disk 1A fails, it would take a failure in disk 1B for data loss to occur. No disk other than 1B would make any data unavailable.

Obviously, this issue comes into play only in a double failure situation and is therefore not very statistically likely to cause a problem. However, in the stripe-centric configuration, there is an n-fold greater likelihood of data loss if a double failure occurs, where n is the number of disks in the stripe.

2.8.7   RAID-5

The goal of the RAID-5 design was to provide a reliable, high-performance array of disks with the minimum amount of redundant hardware. RAID-5 is based on the use of parity protection across several drives in order to provide protection against disk failure. The RAID-5 configuration (see Figure 2.29) is essentially a striped configuration with an additional disk added to cater to the additional storage needed for the parity information.

With the data striped across the drives in this way, the read performance of RAID-5 is comparable to that of RAID-0. A five-disk RAID-5 configuration will perform practically the same as a four-disk RAID-0 configuration, because no performance is gained from the parity disk.

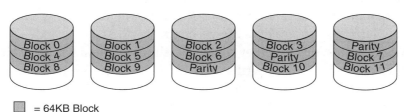

= 64KB Block

Figure 2.29   RAID-5 organization

Parity protection uses the storage of a mathematically derived "check value" for each stripe of actual data. This block of calculated parity information is then stored on one of the disks in the array. The actual disk chosen to store the data is changed on a round-robin basis, so that one disk does not become the bottleneck in a write scenario (see below).

In Figure 2.29, blocks 0, 1, 2, and 3 are used to generate the parity information stored on disk 5. RAID-5 uses an exclusive-OR method of parity generation, which allows any value to be recalculated from the remaining parts. The exclusive-OR operation (XOR or $\oplus$) is a Boolean operator that returns 1 when one and only one of the bits compared is a 1. What this means in real terms is that the following formulas are possible:

$$Parity = Block1 \oplus Block2 \oplus Block3 \oplus Block4$$

and

$$Block3 = Block1 \oplus Block2 \oplus Parity \oplus Block4$$

You can try this reversible operation on any scientific calculator to make sure that you are happy that this "just works." With this ability to recalculate any missing values, RAID-5 can sustain the loss of any single disk in the stripe with no loss of data. However, when this occurs, RAID-5 runs in a "degraded mode." This degradation is significantly worse than, for example, losing one side of the mirror in a RAID-1 configuration.

When a read is issued to a degraded RAID-5 array, the array must rebuild the missing data from the failed disk. To do this, it must read the corresponding blocks of data from *every other disk in the array*. In our example, if the middle disk were to fail, and a read of block 2 were issued, disks 1, 2, 4, and 5 would all need to be read in order to recalculate the missing data from the remaining data plus parity information.

When the disk is replaced, the disk must be rebuilt by using all of the other member drives to recompute the missing data. This can be an extremely lengthy process on a busy system.

RAID-5 writes, on the other hand, are almost legendary for their poor performance. The "RAID-5 write penalty" is well known in most storage circles. When a write occurs on a RAID-5 volume, the block that it replaces must first be read, in addition to the parity block for that stripe. The new parity can then be calculated from this as:

$$newparity = (olddata \oplus newdata) \oplus oldparity$$

The new data and the new parity information must now be written as an atomic operation, because any partial writes will corrupt the data. Therefore, a single write within a single block on a single disk equates to a minimum of two reads and two writes, to keep the array up to date.

The necessary writes of the parity information are the reason that the parity information is spread across all the disks in the array. If all the parity information were stored on a single disk, that disk would ever be capable of executing one read or write concurrently. This implies that only one concurrent write could occur in the entire array of disks, because all writes involve a write to that one parity disk. By spreading the parity over all the disks, depending on the block accessed, the theoretical number of concurrent writes at any one time is the number of disks divided by 2.

It is most common for RAID-5 to be implemented in hardware for several performance-related reasons, the most significant of which is the sheer number of I/O requests that need to be performed in order to operate in RAID-5 mode. For example, one write takes at least four I/Os, assuming that the I/O does not span more than one drive. If the RAID were implemented in software, all of these I/Os would need to be set up by the operating system and sent across the bus. In comparison with the I/O overhead, the task of processing the XOR operations is insignificant.

The final reason that RAID-5 lends itself to hardware implementation is that it benefits greatly from caching the I/O requests, especially for the write requests. For anything that is sensitive to slow response time from the disk (such as redo logs), the use of a write cache is essential.

RAID-5 works well for applications that are mostly read-only, especially very large data warehouses in which the data must be protected with a minimum of redundancy. In large-scale transaction processing environments, a pure RAID-5 solution does not typically provide the performance that is required. If RAID-5 is the only possibility within the budget, a hybrid solution is recommended that stores redo logs, rollback segments, and temporary tablespaces on RAID-1, and the rest on RAID-5. This addresses the most significant problems of RAID-5 in an OLTP environment by keeping the heavy write activity away from RAID-5.

2.8.8 Cached Disk Arrays: EMC Symmetrix

A cached disk array, such as a member of the EMC Symmetrix family, provides several interesting variations on the standard disk technologies presented in this chapter. Although these units can be more expensive than other solutions, the increases in flexibility and performance can often justify the additional cost. The EMC units, in particular, extend beyond the capabilities of raw disk devices and justify this dedicated coverage.

The architecture of the EMC units (see Figure 2.30) is very similar to that of a multiuser computer, only this is a computer that communicates with SCSI commands rather than with keystrokes on a terminal. The "users" of the computer are the database server hosts.

The EMC Symmetrix disk system looks a little different from conventional disk arrays. The fundamental difference is that the cables from the host are never physically connected to the actual disk storage. All commu-

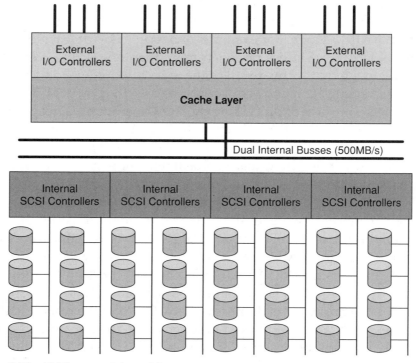

Figure 2.30   EMC symmetrix architecture

nication between the host and the storage goes through the cache. This decoupling of the physical connection allows several enhancements of the functionality of the disk array and provides a large cache to improve the performance of the system.

When a read request comes in, the operating system in the Symmetrix checks to see if the requested data is already in memory. If so, the request is immediately serviced without being subject to seek or rotational delays. If not, a read miss occurs on the cache and a physical I/O is issued to the disk. When the data is returned from the disk, it is loaded into the cache and returned to the host. The software in the system keeps track of these accesses and attempts to determine patterns in the access. For example, in a RAID-1 configuration, the system will try to determine whether it is optimal to read always from one side of the mirror, always round-robin, or a combination of the two based on minimization of head movement. Another pattern that is acted on is that of a sequential read. If a sequential read pattern is determined, the system will go ahead and prefetch several tracks, up to a finite maximum, in order to try to predict the next request.

When a write is issued from the host, the data is written to memory and immediately acknowledged back to the host. The external controllers do not have any concept of the physical storage and are concerned only with reading and writing the cache. The cache buffers that are now dirty are scanned periodically by the internal SCSI controllers, and any dirty blocks are flushed to disk, depending on the activity of the system. If the system is too busy, the writes may be deferred until later.

The EMC system guarantees that the write will eventually make it onto disk, because it has a built-in battery power supply that provides sufficient power to run for a few minutes and fully flush all dirty cache buffers to disk prior to power down. Any reads that occur before the data is written to disk will read the correct data from the cache, and so the data returned will always be valid.

The benefit of the cache will vary from application to application. However, two things are certain:

1. Writes will be significantly faster.

2. The Oracle buffer cache will already have taken care of a good deal of the locality gains in the data access. Don't expect cache hits ratios in the 90 percent range.

In a transaction processing environment, the ability to write out the redo log entries faster will directly benefit the response time of the system.

The EMC Symmetrix supports two levels of RAID: RAID-1 and RAID-S. RAID-1 we have already discussed, but RAID-S is a new concept. Essentially, RAID-S is an optimized implementation of RAID-3, which in turn is virtually identical to RAID-5 but with a dedicated parity disk. The enhancements provided by EMC include

- Faster writes than RAID-5

- Automatic reconfiguration into plain disk on disk failure

The writes have been enhanced by performing the XOR operations at the disk drive level. This eliminates one of the I/O operations, leaving a total of three operations per write. Although this improves the write performance, it is still substantially slower than a RAID-1 configuration. The big improvement in write performance on the EMC unit is the use of the cache to buffer the writes. If the write activity comes only in spikes, the cache will successfully hide the high latency of the actual write.

When a disk in a RAID-S rank fails, the EMC provides the missing data through XOR computation, in the same way as RAID-5. However, when the new value is calculated, it is stored on the parity drive to eliminate any future calculations for that data. Eventually, the entire rank gets converted back to plain (non-RAID) disk in this way.

Another big benefit of the decoupled storage in the EMC is its ability to present *hypervolumes* to the host. A hypervolume is a logical extension of the physical disks, in that one disk can be represented at the external interface as several physical disks, all with different physical identifiers on the bus. Likewise, the disks are not physically connected, and so the identifiers for the storage are configured in software, allowing strong naming conventions.

This flexibility in how the storage is presented to the server can also present problems if not carefully managed. For example, when you carefully split up your most active database files onto two different disks, make sure that the two disks are not in fact the same disk once you get inside the EMC box. Also, despite any assumed gains from the cache layer, it is important always to lay out your database carefully across the physical disks, ignoring the presence of the cache. Treat any caching benefits as a bonus, not something that you can rely on to bail you out of a poor disk layout.

Finally, the Symmetrix units provide some useful value in the form of extensions of the usual services provided by disk arrays. The first of these is Symmetrix Remote Data Facility (SRDF), which provides additional levels of mirroring between cabinets. This facility allows an additional mirror to be set up in a disk array that is remote from the primary, either by ESCON channel within campus or by a WAN link to a very remote unit. There are three different methods for operating the SRDF facility: synchronous, semisynchronous, and adaptive copy.

In synchronous mode, every write must be guaranteed to be written to the caches on both systems before the host receives an acknowledgment. This is the "safest" mode of operation but also the one that could impose the largest latency on the host.

In semisynchronous mode, the write is acknowledged by the host as soon as the local cache has received it. The remote cache is updated asynchronously to the actual write request, and so the performance is the same as that of a non-SRDF-based system. No further writes will be accepted for that particular piece of disk until the remote cache is consistent. The key to this working effectively is the introduction of a track table.

The EMC unit maintains a track table for every track of every disk in the system. This is simply a list in the cache of every track in the system, with a status against it. This status is used to determine whether the version of the track is the same on mirrored peers, whether local or remote. In the case of the semisynchronous writes, the track table stores the status of the track in comparison with the remote track and determines whether the write is complete.

The adaptive copy mode of SRDF is designed for one-time updates from the local volumes to the remote volumes. This mode compares the track tables on both systems to determine which tracks need to be copied to the remote system to bring it up to date. In this way, the amount of data to be copied is kept to a minimum.

An extension of the adaptive copy mode of SRDF is the Business Continuance Volume (BCV), created by the Timefinder product. This is essentially SRDF within the local cabinet and is designed to allow fast backups of the data to be taken.

In an Oracle environment, the database is put into hot backup mode, and a Timefinder copy is made from the primary database volumes to the BCV copy volumes. These are unmirrored volumes that are updated in a way similar to the adaptive copy mode of SRDF—via the track table. Using the track table, the copy can be substantially faster than if the entire data set were copied, because it is typical for only a portion of the datafiles to be written to during the business day.

Once the BCV has been synchronized with the primary volumes, the updates are halted once again (known as *splitting* the BCV), and the database is taken out of backup mode. During the split, it is likely that there will be some impact on the Oracle database. The reason for this is a small implementation difference between the SRDF function and the BCV function.

When SRDF copies a track from one cabinet, the net effect is that there is a clone of the track buffer on the remote cabinet. With this clone present, the SRDF volume can be split from the master volume without flushing anything out to physical disk. Unfortunately, BCV does not have clone buffers, because clone buffers are not applicable for copies within the cabinet. The effect of this is that all dirty buffers must be flushed to physical disk before the BCV volume can be dissociated from the shared, single-track buffer.

Once the split has occurred, the BCV volumes can be archived to tape without any impact on the database operation, provided the shared busses within the cabinet are not saturated. This backup can also be performed from another machine that imports the BCV volumes after the split is complete.

2.9   Chapter Summary

The purpose of this chapter has been to give an overview of the concepts used in modern hardware architectures. While some of this information may remain as background knowledge, it is important to have a good understanding of the concepts and architectures used in order to make educated decisions about purchasing and configuring the right hardware for the job at hand.

Above all, when selecting and configuring hardware for a large system, keep it simple. If you invest the time to lay things out in a logical and consistent manner, it will pay dividends over and over again during the operation of the system.

2.10   Further Reading

Lenoski, D. and W-D. Weber. 1995. *Scalable Shared-Memory Multiprocessing.* Burlington, MA: Morgan Kaufmann.

Patterson, D. and J. Hennessy. 1996. *Computer Architecture: A Quantitative Approach, Second Edition.* Burlington, MA: Morgan Kaufmann.

Schimmel, C. 1994. *UNIX Systems for Modern Architectures.* Reading, MA: Addison-Wesley.

Wong, B. 1997. *Configuration and Capacity Planning for Solaris Servers.* Upper Saddle River, NJ: Prentice Hall.

## PART II

Building
Support Software

Chapter 3

Benchmark Concepts and Design

This chapter covers some of the more critical reasons for benchmarking and highlights why this type of testing is so important. Some ideas are then presented as to how you can go about developing a benchmark suite for your own application, including the provision of some useful software tools for speeding up the process.

3.1 Why Develop a Benchmark?

First of all, we should get some definitions straight. This section discusses *benchmarks*, but this term is used in a very generic way. There are many reasons for running benchmarks, such as:

- Proof of concept
- Capacity planning
- Upgrade testing
- Platform selection/platform changes

Only the last item in this list, and the performance part of capacity planning, could be classed as true benchmarks, because the others do not compare system performance. In order to keep things clear, the term *benchmark* will be used when referring to the testing, whereas *simulator* and *simulation* will be used when referring to the actual test software.

The importance of running benchmarks cannot be overstated. Running Oracle on a UNIX server offers many advantages over mainframe systems, and it is frequently a cost-centric argument that is used to sell the systems. However, the real benefit of this combination comes in the form of rapid evolution. Major releases emerge at intervals of 6 months to 12 months, and the processor and interconnect architectures leapfrog each other every 6 months. With the Oracle tools protecting the application developer from most of the porting effort associated with changing platforms, the price/performance ratio can be progressively lowered during a system's life span. Of course, this actually happens very rarely, because new functionality is always "needed" just as extra headroom is obtained. Either way, the rapid development of software and hardware provides tangible business advantages.

Unfortunately, the rapid change element does not come without occasional problems. Owing to the flexibility of the programming model and the rapid rate of change in the hardware and software, any single system can be exposed to literally millions of different states. Combined with the financial pressures that the vendors are under to get new releases to market, it is not unusual for unexpected problems to slip through their testing programs.

In smaller systems, most software and hardware changes can occur transparently because the demands that the application makes on the system are minimal. Large-scale systems that push the hardware and software in unique and extreme dimensions cannot rely on this kind of plug-and-play approach. In fact, in order to implement any significant changes at all, the target system should be tested as extensively as possible with the real application. This is the only way to eliminate major problems before they occur in a production environment.

3.1.1 Capacity Planning

Capacity planning is a very ambiguous term and yet actually suits this category quite well. Capacity testing should be considered in the following situations:

- Initial platform sizing
- Increased user count or increased transaction rate
- Proposed application/data changes

Initial Platform Sizing

The initial sizing of a platform is potentially the most complex, because little information is available to aid the process. Frequently, such sizing is made far more difficult by the fact that the application development has not even been started at the time the systems need to be purchased, and so no information about the operation of the future system is available. Unfortunately, there is no easy solution to this problem, although some pointers on building a reasonably accurate simulation in these circumstances can be found in Section 3.5.

If the application has already been developed, things are considerably more straightforward. If the application is a well-known package such as Oracle Financials, then it becomes easier still, because most hardware vendors have specialized expertise in these products and extensive experience regarding how they run on their particular platform. The only word of caution here is that most of these packages—particularly financial packages—have to be tailored to the particular business or accounting structure of the company, which can significantly change the operational profile of the application.

Whether the application is brand new or an off-the-shelf package, some kind of testing should be performed as a sanity check for the paper-based sizing exercise. In the case of a new application, extra caution needs to be exercised. It is not unusual for an application "proof of concept" to establish a system sizing that differs by an order of magnitude from the actual requirement.

Increased User Count or Increased Transaction Rate

A change in the size of the user community or an increase in transaction rate is relatively simple compared with the initial sizing exercise. The application profile is well known by this stage, and the footprint of each transaction can be recorded quantitatively—which is a major advantage. However, it should be clear by now that doubling the capacity of the system, for example, does not necessarily allow a doubling of user count.

Increasing the number of users and increasing the transaction rate are both common in an expanding business. Acquisitions can increase user population, and simple increases in business volume resulting from company growth can produce a steady increase in transaction volume. While the former is rarely a surprise, an increase in transaction volume is frequently overlooked and needs to be planned for in advance whenever possible.

The goal of this type of testing is to verify that, for a given release of the application code and a resized system configuration, the new user base or transaction volume will be able to operate within the contracted response times. As long as the right types of metrics are available from both current production and the simulator, this should be a relatively simple exercise. There are basically two metrics that need to be followed:

- *Throughput, a.k.a. transactions per second.* Throughput will be altered in either of these situations. The throughput of the system would be expected to go up with the addition of more users. The estimated increase in transaction rate should be ascertained from business data prior to testing, in order to test the system at the correct load.

- *Response time, or user-perceived response time.* The response times of the system should not exceed the contracted times.

Knowledge of how the existing system runs is essential for this type of testing. In addition, baseline testing should be run with the simulator. During these tests, the benchmark system should be loaded at the same level as the current production system. In this way, the loading imposed by the simulation software can be compared directly against the production system at an identical transaction load. This is an important test to perform, because benchmark workloads are almost always too clinical in profile when compared with the natural randomness encountered in production. Using the baseline test results, more accurate estimations can be determined for production system utilization.

Proposed Application/Data Changes

Can we run yield analysis concurrently with online users during the day? Can we add application-level auditing? If we add three times more products to the portfolio, does this impact the response time of a transaction? These are the types of questions that are frequently asked during the life cycle of an application. They are fairly significant questions with no easy theoretical answers, and there are severe penalties if they are answered incorrectly.

These questions are most accurately answered using the application simulator, particularly if remote terminal emulation is employed (see Section 3.6). Once again, it is important to establish a set of baseline results that show how the simulation software ran prior to the change. The benchmark tool can then be executed in the new configuration, and the results of the simulation can be directly compared with those of the baseline test.

Some application changes, such as the integration of a transaction monitor, are too major for this kind of testing. Changes of such proportions should be considered as new developments, because they change the entire profile of the system.

3.1.2   Upgrades

The types of upgrades discussed here are operating system, Oracle, and hardware upgrades. While maintenance releases, such as an upgrade from Oracle 7.3.3.3 to Oracle 7.3.3.4, typically address only known problems, any release that contains feature code should be viewed suspiciously. With the Oracle RDBMS, any change in the first two fields of the version number denotes the implementation of feature code. Occasionally, "minor" feature code is implemented in maintenance releases. This happens most often shortly after a large implementation of new features, because the developers have missed the freeze date for checking in their new feature code.

With the operating system, the risk associated with each release varies from vendor to vendor. Careful attention should be paid to release notes prior to planning an upgrade. The same is true of Oracle releases, to ensure that the right steps have been taken to minimize the risk of upgrade. With hardware, certain upgrades can be performed without testing. Typically, processor and memory upgrades can be implemented with minimal risk. The things to watch are new I/O subsystems, firmware upgrades, and completely new architectures.

The bottom line of all this is that when you are building or maintaining a large-scale database system, you need to be scared of *bugs*, because they will be evident in any nonmaintenance upgrade. Don't kid yourself:

if you think the new release will go without problems, you are being way too optimistic.

It's a good idea to approach upgrades as follows:

- Don't upgrade until you have to, unless the new release contains fixes of critical outstanding problems that cannot be backported.

- Upgrade one thing at a time. Maximize change control, and increase the chance of keeping at least some of your upgrades in place, should problems occur.

- Bundle testing together. Minimize the time you spend testing releases, and bundle the testing of several products (such as Oracle and O/S) together. As long as you test all the combinations that you will pass through in the upgrade cycle, you should find this a low-risk optimization of your time.

The important point here is to test the new releases. Neither Oracle nor the operating system vendor will have tested the very particular set of dimensions that *your application will test*. Therefore, your system is fairly likely to hold the key to exposing unforeseen race conditions, system states, and so on, and it is your responsibility to find such problems before they hurt you in production. With major Oracle upgrades, such as from Oracle7 to Oracle8, there is little opportunity to reverse the process in the event of a major problem after the upgrade, because data changes occur in the database structure that cannot be undone. This makes the testing process more important than ever.

3.1.3 Platform Changes

Testing a new platform is a common use of a benchmark. This is a really great way to ascertain the *real* potential of a new machine on which you intend to run your system. Although you can study the SPEC numbers for the platform, factor in the latency and bandwidth of the system interconnect, and maybe even take into account the CPI (clocks per instruction) count of the processor, you will probably still achieve, at best, only a ballpark estimate of a new system's potential. Running a quantitative benchmark of the system with the actual application is the only way to ascertain the effectiveness of a new platform. There are too many other variables, not least of which is the scalability of the O/S, that can drastically affect the real capability of the system.

Normally when testing new platforms for a system, you are primarily interested in testing the database server. This, after all, is the component of the system that has to provide the most scalability and is also the most variable in terms of pure workload. Testing of support systems, application servers, and so on is not essential in a platform change benchmark, although it could be argued that such testing is still worthwhile even if only to verify the entire system in operation on the new platform.

3.2 What Are We Simulating?

3.2.1 Defining Application Areas

It is important to have a good understanding of your application when developing a simulator for it. The first part of such an understanding is being able to identify the different types of users accessing the system, how they are using the application, and how many of them are doing so. This is important in order to be able to understand what is going on in the simulation runs and to be able to comment on why things are occurring that may not have been expected.

3.2.2 Defining the Application Split

Once you have a good understanding of the overall application areas, you need to start defining functional areas of the application. In practice, the split is never black and white—the application will, by nature, share data among application areas. That is the whole reason that it accesses a common database in the first place.

However, there will be clear boundaries between the functions defined in the applications, and probably among the day-to-day duties of the users on the system as well. For example, if a hotel had a single system to cater to all of its needs, it would include the following functional areas that can be classified as distinct areas:

- Reservations
- Front desk (guest check-in and check-out operations)
- Billing

- Stock control
- Finance
- Housekeeping
- Maintenance

Although there is a strong link among all of these areas, they can be individually classified as different functional areas.

Once the split has been defined, work can begin on each area. Specifically, the process should look a little like the diagram in Figure 3.1.

3.2.3   Careful with Those Assumptions, Eugene

The "Significant Workload?" decision is a difficult one. It is very easy to make a simulated molehill out of a resource mountain, and this could compromise the entire result set of the benchmark. It's important to remember that one query can destroy a system, so although only a handful of users may be performing this type of transaction, make sure that the function they perform is definitely insignificant before discounting them from the simulation.

In addition, when an application has functional areas that overlap, it is sometimes necessary to build some types of transactions simply to feed other transactions with dependent data. In this case, either the transaction needs to be implemented or the data needs to be prebuilt into the database (see Section 3.6).

Once all the significant application components have been defined, scenarios need to be described for each transaction type. For some transactions, there will be only one way of completing the transaction, and so this will equate to a single scenario for that transaction type. More typically, there will be potentially hundreds of scenarios that could be defined.

In our hotel example, a hotel guest could have a reservation, have no reservation, have any number of frequent flyer cards, and/or select one of many different types of rooms. In such situations, it is not practical to build scenarios for all possible combinations, owing in no small part to the difficulty of providing the data required to execute them. A realistic sample of the scenarios should be adopted in this situation.

The final pieces to be created are the actual simulation and the data required to run it. These pieces will be covered in the next section.

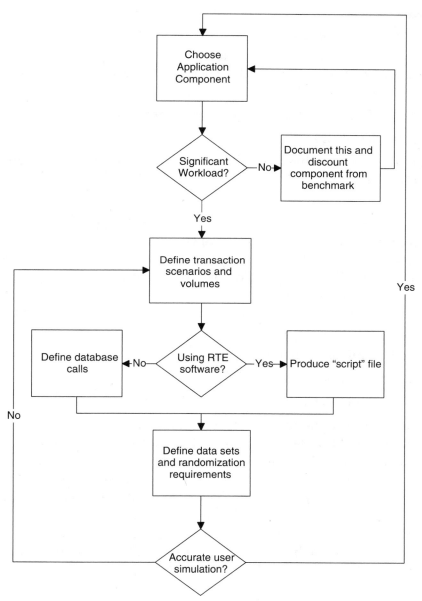

Figure 3.1 Transaction scenario development process

3.3   Selecting a Development Approach

It is important to choose the most suitable development approach for your application and your environment. There are two approaches for building benchmark software:

1. Remote Terminal Emulation (RTE) software

2. Completely custom development

Each of these approaches has its merits, not only in terms of cost but also in terms of useability in different scenarios.

3.3.1   Using Remote Terminal Emulation Software

RTE software is a specialized piece of commercial software such as Performix or preVue from Rational Software. Good results can also be obtained using Expect, a public domain utility[1] that provides many of the same features but uses an interpreter instead of compiled code.

There are several different approaches that can be taken to simulate the load on the database server:

- Dumb terminal emulation

- Client/server network protocol

- HTTP (Hypertext Transfer Protocol) Web simulation

The common attribute of these approaches is that they all simulate real users accessing the system. The correct tool to use depends on your application architecture. Dumb terminal emulation works very well for simulating the use of a character-based application, regardless of how it was written or what happens at the back end of the application. The client/server emulation traps the network communication between the client and the server, and subsequently simulates the load in this way, including three-tier architectures. The HTTP emulation simulates hits on a Web server, which in turn accesses the database.

---

1. Expect can be downloaded for free from http://expect.nist.gov.

This type of software has the following advantages over writing your own simulation of the application:

- Rapid development of simulation scripts owing to supplied tools
- Ability to simulate application servers as well as database server
- Very accurate simulation of load on database server
- Less susceptibility to application code changes when compared to custom simulators

The only disadvantage of RTE software, in fact, is that it costs money.

One thing to bear in mind when looking at RTE software is that it presents the same problem of data generation that you would face in a custom simulation suite. None of the available products has the capability of knowing how your application needs to be driven. Ask your vendor about what kind of infrastructure they provide for the type of data generation you will need to be doing.

3.3.2   Custom Simulation Development

The home-grown approach to simulators involves building the code from scratch, using the Oracle Call Interface (OCI) to gain the most control available over what is executed on the database server. This approach has the following advantages over the RTE approach:

- Zero capital cost
- Does not need a completed application to run

This approach also has several disadvantages:

- Much longer development time
- Needs redeveloping every time the application changes
- Does not test application servers
- Not as accurate as RTE simulations

Despite the certain disadvantages of developing the simulation from scratch, there are occasions where it still makes more sense. If the application does not yet exist, for example, it is the only choice. Also, if the simulation does not have many scenarios or much complexity, it may be more cost-effective to develop it without the aid of RTE software. For these reasons, this type of development cannot be discounted and will be covered in this chapter.

3.4   Building a Simulator Using RTE Software

An important part of the value of using RTE software is the availability of a variety of tools to assist in the process. These tools include

- Transaction capture tools
- Generalized programming interface
- Execution harness
- Statistical analysis tools
- Debugging tools

These tools provide a fast path to a simplistic simulation of your application. In a matter of minutes, a simple simulation of your application can be running and the results analyzed.

The single most important attribute of RTE software, however, is that it simulates the real user, utilizing the same kind of input as the actual production workload. Sometimes the importance of this attribute is not apparent.

Using, for example, Pro*C, which has long been the favorite for benchmark applications, the database server is (mostly) communicated with at a SQL level. This allows SQL to be submitted and answers to be retrieved. Although this simplistic approach seems good in theory, in practice more control is required. SQL*Forms, for example, communicates with the database at the UPI layer a lower lever, Oracle-proprietor communication protocol. This allows more control over the opening and closing of cursors, the steps of execution, and subsequently the way that memory is allocated on the server.

The consequence of this is that a Pro*C emulation of the application will not produce the same work profile of the server as the real application, even if the statements are issued in the same order and with the same bind variable assignments. RTE software provides true emulation of the application's usage of the database server, complete with all its horors and triumphs.

Although RTE software provides an accurate way of simulating the application, it provides no benefit from a data perspective. It is most common for an application to be expecting certain data from the user. This may be as simple as a name, a reference number, or a date, but input is expected nonetheless. During normal use of the application this does not present a problem, because the user of the system is presented with this data from some source such as a customer in the store or paperwork on the desktop. In a simulated environment, this data is not available through these means, and so it needs to be generated in some way. This is the problem that is common to both methods of simulation.

3.5 Building a Custom Benchmark Suite

There are two common starting points in building an application simulator from scratch: situations in which the application (a) has been developed and (b) has not been developed.

3.5.1 Programming Environment

A variety of programming tools are available for use in developing a custom benchmark suite. While these tools have various merits of their own, it is recommended that the Oracle Call Interface (OCI) be used for this type of development. OCI is recommended for any programming exercise in which simple but absolute control is needed over actions requested of the RDBMS, because it is the closest thing to the explicit server instruction set in the UPI interface. OCI has a widespread reputation for being "hard," but this is really not the case. There are two things that make using OCI "hard" in comparison with standard C programming:

1. You need to know the steps involved in SQL processing from the server perspective.

2. You need massive parameter lists for each function that are mostly unused in C.

The truth is, you need to know the steps of SQL processing anyway in order to support a large system, and the parameters list problem can be easily fixed using macro wrappers for each OCI call used to eliminate redundant parameters. Once these obstacles are out of the way, OCI is in many ways more straightforward than Pro*C, because no precompilation is necessary.

3.5.2   When the Application Has Not Been Written

In order to reduce the degree of error in building initial simulations before the application has been developed, it is important to learn from some painfully gained experience. Most of this falls squarely in the "common sense" category, but it is surprising how much of it is frequently missed. When the application has not been written, the use of RTE software is clearly out of the question, and so a call-centric approach needs to be taken instead of an application-centric one.

First of all, it is important to get as close to the final transaction profile as possible, and when the application is not written this can be difficult. However, certain pieces of the application environment must be at least partially complete before it is worth conducting a preliminary benchmark. The specific things to look for are as follows:

- *Final data model.* Unless the data model is virtually complete, the simulation will not be accurate. It does not need to be polished, but the basic structure of the model should be final. A classic stumbling block in this area would be where the data model becomes more normalized than the simulation, thus adding a good deal of complexity to several of the queries in the application. This could result in an undersized system.

- *Query profile.* How many queries are executed within each transaction, and what do they look like (primary key single-row fetches, index-driven range scans, etc.)? Don't neglect "list-of-values" processing either, which can very quickly become a major part of the system.

- *Insert/update/delete profile.* Which tables do we insert/update/delete, and how many rows are processed each time? Where do these activities occur in relation to the query workload and the commits/rollbacks?

- *Stored procedures.* To what extent is application logic handled with database stored procedures? This is really hard to simulate adequately, because it is likely that you will be several months (or years) of development time away from knowing the answer to this question. It is a bad thing to have significant processing within stored procedures, in my opinion, because the primary goal of a stored procedure should be to reduce network round trips between the client and the server by bundling multiple SQL interactions into a single SQL*Net call. In fact, as your application is not written yet, you still have a chance to try to make sure that stored procedures are used for the right reasons.

3.5.3 If the Application Exists: Trap and Emulate All SQL Calls

When the application is in some kind of executable state, it is possible to capture all the calls to the database and replay them in a simulated environment during the benchmark. This is more straightforward in a two-tier environment, where there is a one-to-one relationship between the requests made through the application and the process executing the SQL against the database. In a three-tier environment, there is more complexity, but the same principles apply.

The starting point is to find a person who really knows the application and how it is used in reality. The perfect person to do this is a real-life user of the application, who can show you ways of operating the application that you, the developer, or the instructor could never imagine. This is as close to reality as you can get. If this is not an option that is available to you, then an expert developer is your only option, although the simulation will then take a more clinical, how-it-should-work type of model: try to make sure that you find some way to inject the "wild-card" factor into it.

For each application area that is defined, define the types of transactions that can be performed within it, and run through each of these screens while tracing the calls made by the session, as detailed in the next subsection. It's important to include the following actions when building the list of tasks performed by the system:

- Logging on
- Logging off
- Menu navigation

When running through each of the screens, it is very beneficial to use recognizable values for the fields that will need to be generated by the simulation, rather than using the explicit values used in the walkthrough. Values such as 'RND3HERE','GEN2HERE' and '12345','99999' generally work well and can dramatically speed up later steps.

Tracing Sessions by Setting Events

Most people know of the "alter session set sql_trace=true" technique for tracing the calls made from an application. This is a useful technique, but not as useful as it could be, because it does not contain the bind variable information for each cursor.

In addition to this well-documented approach is an undocumented method of tracing the activity of a session, a considerably more useful one for this type of activity. While useful for determining database access for use in a simulator, this method of tracing also represents one of the most powerful tools available for diagnosis of performance problems as they happen. For this reason, a full user's guide is required for this function, and so we will invest some book space accordingly.

The method for activating the improved tracing is the use of a database *event*. An event is a signal to a database session that alters its behavior according to the definition of the event. The definition of the event is determined within the kernel code of the Oracle RDBMS and is not documented beyond brief descriptions in the message file. The message file is the same file that Oracle uses to look up NLS-specific error messages, such as "`max # extents (50) reached in table SCHEMA.TABLE`" and, in the case of English language systems, this file is `?/rdbms/mesg/oraus.msg`. Embedded in this file are the numbers and descriptions of the events that are defined within that particular Oracle release.

A word of caution, however: many (most) of these events are not for public consumption. For example, event 10066 simulates a file verification error:

```
10066, 00000, "simulate failure to verify file"
// *Cause:
// *Action: level is file number to fail verification
```

These types of events are used internally to Oracle for the simulation of problems. For this reason, it is wise to stick to events that are known to be safe.

The event that we are interested in is 10046:

```
10046, 00000, "enable SQL statement timing"
// *Cause:
// *Action:
```

This event is set with the following syntax:

```
10046 trace name context forever, level <x>
```

The level, or degree, of the tracing is set using numbers 1 through 15 in place of the *x*. The level number corresponds to the setting of particular bits within the range 1 through 12 (Table 3.1).

Table 3.1 10046 Trace Detail Switches

Bit Offset	Detail Level
Any	Same as `sql_trace=true`
3	Values of bind variables reported
4	Wait states reported

For this event, only bits 3 and 4 are used. With the event enabled for any level, the output includes the same attributes as `sql_trace=true`. When bits 3 and 4 are set, additional information is returned that is extremely useful. Try using level 4 for just bind variables, level 8 for just wait states, and level 12 for all of the above.

The event can be set at either the *instance level* or the *session level*, and the event can be set by any one of three distinct methods:

1. `alter session set events "10046 trace name context forever, level x"`
   (personal user session level)

2. `event="10046 trace name context forever, level x"` in the `init.ora`
   (instance level)

3. On a process-by-process basis using `svrmgrl oradebug`
   (other user session level)

Method (1) is the most straightforward method of setting the event on the correct session, but it is useful only if this call can be made by the application session as and when required. It involves the connected session issuing a SQL call, as detailed above, to set the event on itself.

Method (2) is useful when performing tracing en masse, because it operates at the instance level, forcing all sessions to set this event at start-up. This is the most appropriate method to use when performing application capture, because it eliminates the manual activation steps. It requires the event to be set in the `init.ora` so that all sessions are affected by the change.

Method (3) is used to set the event on any process from another session. This method is most useful for reactive problem diagnosis, because it can be set on any user session that is connected to the database and shows a consistent view of the user state, including calls and wait states. A further digression may be useful at this stage to cover the

use of the "svrmgrl oradebug" functionality that is available in releases
7.3 and above.

ORADEBUG. The svrmgrl product that is shipped with the Oracle
RDBMS contains a set of functions that were previously available
only through a tool called oradbx. Oradbx was a binary that was
shipped with prior releases of Oracle and needed to be explicitly built
using the supplied makefile. This binary was not created as part of
any standard installation . For this reason, oradbx was not widely
known in the Oracle community.

Now that the functionality is provided as part of svrmgrl, it is available
on every Oracle system without any manual intervention. The commands
are accessed using the oradebug prefix, as demonstrated below, to gain help
on the facility:

```
SVRMGRL> oradebug help
HELP            [command]                Describe one or all commands
SETMYPID                                 Debug current process
SETOSPID        <ospid>                  Set OS pid of process to debug
SETORAPID       <orapid> ['force']       Set Oracle pid of process to
debug
DUMP            <dump_name> <level>      Invoke named dump
DUMPSGA         [bytes]                  Dump fixed SGA
DUMPLIST                                 Print a list of available dumps
EVENT           <text>                   Set trace event in process
SESSION_EVENT <text>                     Set trace event in session
DUMPVAR         <p|s|uga> <name> [level] Print/dump a fixed PGA/SGA/UGA
variable
SETVAR          <p|s|uga> <name> <value> Modify a fixed PGA/SGA/UGA
variable
PEEK            <addr> <len> [level]     Print/Dump memory
POKE            <addr> <len> <value>     Modify memory
WAKEUP          <orapid>                 Wake up Oracle process
SUSPEND                                  Suspend execution
RESUME                                   Resume execution
FLUSH                                    Flush pending writes to tracefile
TRACEFILE_NAME                           Get name of tracefile
LKDEBUG                                  Invoke lock manager debugger
CORE                                     Dump core without crashing
process
IPC                                      Dump ipc information
UNLIMIT                                  Unlimit the size of the tracefile
PROCSTAT                                 Dump process statistics
CALL            <func> [arg1] ... [argn] Invoke function with arguments
```

Once again, this is a facility that should be used with extreme caution: the database can be corrupted beyond all repair if some of these commands—most notably POKE, SETVAR, and CALL—are used. In addition, requesting one of the background processes to perform an extensive dump will effectively suspend the real function of that process for that period, possibly hanging the database.

The commands in which we are most interested at this stage are

- SETOSPID xxxx
- UNLIMIT
- EVENT "xxxx"

SETOSPID should be the first command issued, as it identifies the Oracle process (UNIX process) on which the tool should operate. This information is available from V$PROCESS, joined to V$SESSION on the PADDR column. Next, the UNLIMIT TRACE directive should be used to remove the limits set within the init.ora for restricting the size of a tracefile. This makes sense, because you will manually turn off the trace when you have all the required information. Finally, the event can be set, as detailed above. From this point forward, a tracefile will be created in user_dump_dest, of the form ora_PID.trc. To be sure of locating the correct file, the TRACEFILE_NAME directive can be used om oradebug.

Whichever method is most appropriate for tracing, it can be turned off again on the session level by using the following command:

```
10046 trace name context off
```

Using this event provides the following advantages over the sql_trace=true method:

- It can be set for a running session without the user being aware of it, using the svrmgrl oradebug facility.
- It shows wait states that the execution of each statement goes through.
- It details binding information for each cursor.

The bind information can be used in generating the simulation code, and the ward states can be used in the tuning of application SQL.

Here's a sample piece of output from a 10046-generated tracefile, using level 12 to get all available information:

```
========================
PARSING IN CURSOR #1 len=50 dep=0 uid=20 oct=3 lid=20 tim=3802520068
hv=650761597 ad='c12dc1f0'
select count(*) from some_table where some_col=:b1
END OF STMT
PARSE #1:c=8,e=10,p=2,cr=29,cu=1,mis=1,r=0,dep=0,og=0,tim=3802520068
BINDS #1:
 bind 0: dty=2 mxl=22(22) mal=00 scl=00 pre=00 oacflg=03
   bfp=400e7700 bln=22 avl=02 flg=05
   value=1
EXEC #1:c=0,e=0,p=0,cr=0,cu=0,mis=0,r=0,dep=0,og=4,tim=3802520068
WAIT #1: nam='SQL*Net message to client' ela= 0 p1=1650815232 p2=1 p3=0
WAIT #1: nam='db file scattered read' ela= 1 p1=1 p2=4752 p3=5
WAIT #1: nam='db file scattered read' ela= 0 p1=1 p2=4882 p3=2
FETCH #1:c=1,e=1,p=7,cr=7,cu=3,mis=0,r=1,dep=0,og=4,tim=3802520069
WAIT #1: nam='SQL*Net message from client' ela= 0 p1=1650815232 p2=1 p3=0
FETCH #1:c=0,e=0,p=0,cr=0,cu=0,mis=0,r=0,dep=0,og=0,tim=3802520069
WAIT #1: nam='SQL*Net message to client' ela= 0 p1=1650815232 p2=1 p3=0
WAIT #1: nam='SQL*Net message from client' ela= 0 p1=1650815232 p2=1 p3=0
STAT #0 id=1 cnt=0 pid=0 pos=0 obj=0 op='SORT AGGREGATE '
STAT #0 id=2 cnt=414 pid=1 pos=1 obj=0 op='FILTER '
STAT #0 id=3 cnt=414 pid=2 pos=1 obj=1876 op='TABLE ACCESS FULL SOME_TABLE'
WAIT #1: nam='SQL*Net message to client' ela= 0 p1=1650815232 p2=1 p3=0
WAIT #1: nam='SQL*Net message from client' ela= 0 p1=1650815232 p2=1 p3=0
```

In this tracefile extract, there are examples of all of the attributes found in this type of trace. For this trace, timed_statistics was set true before the trace was initiated. Starting at the top of the trace, the "PARSING IN CURSOR" section shows the parsing of a new cursor and the assignment of the "#1" cursor number to it. The tokens listed in Table 3.2 describe information about the cursor and its context.

Table 3.2 "PARSING IN" Section

Token	Description
len	Length of statement in bytes
dep	Depth of execution context. Anything greater than zero indicates recursive SQL executing implicitly.
uid	User ID context in which cursor is executing

Table 3.2   continued

Token	Description
oct	Command type (see V$SESSION documentation in server reference guide)
lid	Unknown (usually the same as UID)
tim	When timed statistics set true, shows relative timestamp in hundredths of a second
hv	Hash value of the statement
ad	Address of the statement in the SQL cache

This section is immediately followed by the actual statement itself, which is terminated by the "END OF STMT" declaration. Immediately below this are the statistics for the PARSE call itself. This is the format taken for all subsequent tokens: <ACTION> <CURSOR#>: <data>. In this case, the PARSE directive reports back with the standard information used by tkprof as shown in Table 3.3.

Table 3.3   General Operation Statistics

Token	Description
c	CPU seconds used by this call
e	Elapsed time (in seconds)
p	Physical I/Os
cr	Blocks accessed through consistent read mechanism ("consistent gets" in V$SESSSTAT)
cu	Blocks not accessed through the consistent read mechanism ("db block gets" in V$SESSSTAT)
mis	Misses in library cache during parse
r	Row count
dep	Recursive depth
og	Optimizer goal (1=all_rows, 2=first_rows, 3=rule, 4=choose)
tim	Relative timestamp

The `tkprof` output for this statement would look like this:

```
********************************************************************************
select count(*)
from
 some_table where some_col=:b1

call     count       cpu    elapsed       disk      query    current       rows
-------  ------  --------  ---------- ---------- ---------- ----------  ----------
Parse        1      0.08        0.10          2         29          1           0
Execute      1      0.00        0.00          0          0          0           0
Fetch        2      0.01        0.01          7          7          3           1
-------  ------  --------  ---------- ---------- ---------- ----------  ----------
total        4      0.09        0.11          9         36          4           1

Misses in library cache during parse: 1
Optimizer goal: CHOOSE
Parsing user id: 20
```

By reading through the output in the raw tracefile, it can be seen how these standard statistics are used by `tkprof`. The count column equates to a count of the number of calls made during the lifetime of this statement. In this example, two fetch calls were made, but only one each of parse and execute. The remaining columns are totaled from all calls of that type.

The next component of the raw tracefile is the BINDS section, activated by setting bit 3 when specifying the trace level. In this section, full details of the bind variables used for this execution of the statement are provided. The initial BINDS #<cursor> token is immediately followed by an indented flow of all bind variables specified. The binds are always shown starting with "bind 0," regardless of the naming of the bind variables in the statement. The order in which the binds are listed is the order in which they appear in the SQL statement: top to bottom.

Within the BINDS section, several details are given for each bind variable, although in practice it is the `dty` and `value` fields with which we are mostly concerned. The `dty` field shows the datatype of the bind variable, where 1=VARCHAR2, 2=NUMBER, etc.: see the *OCI Programmer's Guide* for details. The `value` field shows the actual value bound to that variable. If the `value` field is absent, this means that no value was bound (`null` value) or that the variable is an output variable.

The next section in the raw tracefile is the EXEC call. It is in this execution step of a SQL statement that Oracle will build the result set for a cursor in the case of a query, or actually execute the INSERT, UPDATE, or PL/SQL that the cursor contains. The fields available here are the same as those described during the PARSE phase.

During the execution of this statement, the session passed through several wait states before the result set was built. These wait states can be serially detailed in the tracefile by initiating the trace with bit 4 set in the level (level 8 or 12). This is one of the most useful features of this type of trace, and the detail of the WAIT lines will be used later in the book. Within the WAIT line, there are some new tokens, as shown in Table 3.4.

This information is the same as that found in V$SESSION_WAIT, with the three parameter fields having different meanings depending on the actual wait state. The labels for the p1, p2, and p3 fields can be derived by querying SYS.X$KSLED, giving the name of the wait as the value for KSLEDNAM.

The next entry in the raw tracefile is the FETCH call. In this case, the call is made twice, with the second call returning no data (r=0). This is fairly common, because applications often retrieve data from a cursor until the cursor returns "no more data."

The final area of interest in the tracefile is the STAT section. There is one of these for each SQL cursor in the tracefile, and it details the actual access plan used for the statement, including the number of rows inspected in order to satisfy the request. One interesting thing to point out here is that it looks as if the version of Oracle that I used to create this tracefile has a bug, in that the STAT section is referring to cursor #0, which does not exist.

Table 3.4 WAIT Section Detail

Token	Description
nam	Name of wait state
ela	Time waited
p1	Parameter 1
p2	Parameter 2
p3	Parameter 3

The STAT section should be referring to cursor #1, as the "TABLE ACCESS FULL SOME_TABLE" operation shows.

The Oracle Call Interface (OCI) Fast Track

The impenetrable *OCI Programmer's Guide* makes OCI look like a time-intensive, difficult-to-understand environment. However, this really isn't the case, and it makes good sense, particularly when trying to build an application simulator, to develop some knowledge of OCI. The steps involved in OCI programming relate directly to the required calls from a client to the server in order to service SQL requests, and it is useful to be familiar with them.

The good news is that there is nothing at all difficult about OCI. In fact, if we ignore the fancy things such as object support, then a reasonable familiarity should only take a few pages. One of the most useful aids to learning OCI is an OCI flowchart, showing the required steps for a given statement (see Figure 3.2).

One thing to note from the flow diagram, and indeed from all the code examples in the book, is that the release 7.x OCI concepts are used. The reason for this is that OCI changed substantially in Oracle8, not least to provide object support. The effect of the changes is that the native OCI supplied with Oracle8 is nearly 100 percent different from the release 7.x OCI and adds some complexity to previously simplistic programs. The 7.x concepts lend themselves better to simplistic explanation, and all the concepts and functions are still available in the 8.x libraries for backward compatibility. Finally, retaining the old call API allows the code to be used against Oracle7 instances.

Starting at the top of the flowchart and working down, the first item is initialization of the environment. All that this means is that a structure of type Lda_Def (Login Data Area) and a corresponding HDA (Host Data Area) need to be allocated. The Lda_Def definition is found in a header file supplied by Oracle and is stored in $ORACLE_HOME/rdbms/demo; the HDA is simply an array of 256 bytes. Next, a connection needs to be made to the Oracle database, using olog(). This connects the client session to the database and populates the Lda_Def and HDA structures with context information for the connection.

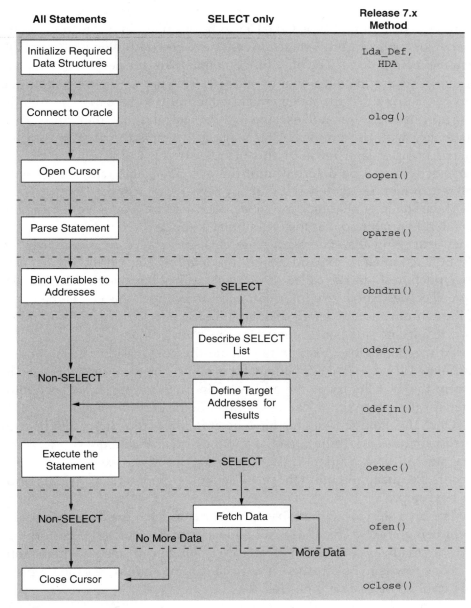

Figure 3.2 OCI call flow

The oopen() call is used to initialize a cursor for the SQL statement and requires a structure of type Cda_Def to be supplied in order to maintain the cursor context. At this stage, no calls have been supplied with any SQL statements to process. The only function that takes the actual SQL request as one of its arguments is that of oparse(). This parses the request on the server, ensuring that the statement is syntactically correct, that the submitting user has permission to execute that request, and that all required data dictionary work is complete. This stage also enters the request into the shared pool for later reuse by this or other users. The actual server-side parse activity can be deferred until the describe stage, with the oparse() call returning immediately without any server interaction.

If the statement has bind variables, a local address must be assigned to each bind variable so that the OCI library knows where to look for values when executing the statement. After this, if the request is a query, the SELECT list must be expanded into full detail by issuing the odesc() call. This function should be called repeatedly until all items in the SELECT list have been described. The information returned from this call is the name of the column and the details of datatype, size, and so on, which should be used to allocate sufficient memory for the returned data.

At this stage, it is possible to execute the cursor, although it is more logical to call the odefin() function at this point. The odefin() call is used to inform the OCI library of the addresses in memory that have been allocated for the return of the data, as defined in the describe stage.

Once the storage locations have been defined, the cursor can be executed using oexec(). If the cursor is anything other than a query, this is the final step of the execution. If the cursor is a query, the execute stage will execute the query and build the result set but will not return any data until the next step.

The final step for a query-based cursor is to fetch the data back to the client using ofen(). The ofen() call allows array fetches to be performed, and should always be used in preference to single-row fetches where more than one row is to be returned. The fetch routine should be called repeatedly until no more data is needed.

At this point, regardless of the type of cursor (SELECT, INSERT, UPDATE, or DELETE), the cursor can either be closed, freeing up the cursor on the server, or be reexecuted using the same or different bind variables. The statement does not need to be rebound to achieve this: the contents of the addresses already bound to the variables can simply be updated with the new values.

That's it. In a nutshell, that is all there is to OCI from the release 7.x perspective. There is a good deal more complexity available in OCI, but the information above covers 90 percent of all the occasions for which you would use it. The important thing is to resist being intimidated by the number of parameters required for each function call in the OCI library. At the end of the day, most of these require a 0, –1, or null pointer, because they are there for compatibility with the COBOL version of OCI. The best way to simplify your life if you expect to be doing a lot of OCI coding is to make a set of macros around the calls most used in order to fill out the redundant fields automatically.

3.5.4 Using Tracefiles to Generate a Simulation: An Introduction to dbaman

Once you have a passing familiarity with OCI, the contents of a SQL tracefile start to look very familiar. In fact, the tracefile is an accurate journal of the work performed by the server and can be mapped directly to a corresponding set of OCI calls. This allows a tracefile to be used as the source of a kind of playback utility, one that reads the tracefile and reapplies the same requests to the server in the same order and with the same parameters. One way to do this is to adopt a two-stage process involving some custom software and an awk script (see Figure 3.3).

This is the approach that will be presented over the next few pages, starting with the dbaman component of the process.

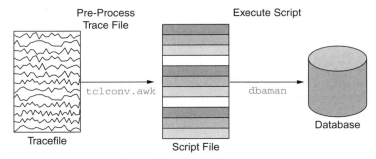

Figure 3.3   dbaman processing hierarchy

Introducing *dbaman*

dbaman is a utility that has many uses. It was originally written to enable OCI programs to be written as interpreted scripts, the idea being that it could then be used as a general-purpose development language for administration of the database, hence the name dbaman[ager]. However, it soon became clear that this tool could be used for a series of other, more specific tasks with only slight modification. The one we are primarily interested in here is tracefile replay utility.

dbaman is an extension of Tcl (Tool command language). Tcl, pronounced "tickle," was written by John Ousterhout at the University of California at Berkeley. It was designed to be an extensible scripting language—that is, a language that can be extended in functionality by the user. It is the result of Ousterhout becoming tired of developing new languages every time a new specific command set requirement came up. He therefore developed Tcl as a core scripting language that he could customize each time a new requirement appeared. This reduces the coding effort and eliminates the need to learn a new language each time.

Tcl is freely available over the Internet. The primary location for obtaining Tcl is http://www.scriptics.com, which is the commercial company set up by John Ousterhout to bring Tcl into the corporate mainstream. It offers full development environments for Tcl and professional support, although Tcl itself remains a public domain product. For simplicity, version 8.0 of Tcl is included on the accompanying CD.

When the Tcl software is built, the result is a library, libtcl.a. If a main() routine is linked in with the library, the result is the Tcl shell (tclsh). This is the Tcl equivalent of the Korn shell, on which Tcl programs (scripts) are executed. The scripting language provided by Tcl is easy to learn, flexible, and fast, making it suitable for many development tasks.

The Tcl library provides functionality that enables additional commands to be easily added to the language. It is this functionality that makes Tcl the powerful tool that it is, and is the reason that it was adopted for dbaman.

With all the extensions linked in, the result is a single Tcl shell language environment with additional capabilities, such as the ability to maintain an Oracle connection and submit requests to the database server from the shell, as can be seen in the following list of available routines within dbaman:

```
$ dbaman
% ?
ambiguous command name "?": after append array auto_execok auto_load
auto_mkindex auto_qualify auto_reset binary break case catch cd clock
close concat continue eof error eval exec exit expr fblocked fconfigure
fcopy file fileevent flush for foreach format gets glob global history
if incr info interp join lappend lindex linsert list llength load lrange
lreplace lsearch lsort namespace oci_bind_begin oci_bind_end
oci_bind_name oci_bind_pos oci_cancel oci_close oci_exec oci_fetch
oci_list oci_logon oci_open oci_parse oci_vars open package pid
pkg_mkIndex proc puts pwd read regexp regsub rename return scan seek set
socket source split string subst switch tclLog tclMacPkgSearch
tclPkgSetup tclPkgUnknown tell time trace unknown unset update uplevel
upvar variable vwait while
%
```

The example above shows all the functions that the dbaman extension externalizes to the Tcl interpreter. Used together, these additional commands allow the full playback of tracefiles against the database server. Table Table 3.5 details each of the commands and their usages.

Table 3.5   Tcl Extensions provided by *dbaman*

Tcl Call	Usage	Comments
oci_logon	oci_logon <username> [password]	Initializes structures and connects to Oracle
oci_open	oci_open ?-assign ##?	Open a cursor and return the cursor handle. A specific cursor number can be specified with the -assign switch; otherwise, the lowest available handle is assigned.
oci_parse	oci_parse <cursor#> <SQL text>	Send the supplied string to the server for parsing.
oci_bind_begin	oci_bind_begin <cursor#>	Initializes the structures used in bind process
oci_bind_pos	oci_bind_pos <cursor#> ?-date? <var offset> <value I ?-null?>	This routine is used to bind variables to their respective tags by position. Special consideration is given to date datatypes. Within SQL tracefiles, the date is always given in a specific form:

Table 3.5 continued

Tcl Call	Usage	Comments
	·	"8/1/1998 0:0:0" = 1st August 1998, 00:00 The native_date() routine is then called to turn this information into internal Oracle binary date format. All other bindings are assigned the VARCHAR2 datatype. If "-null" is used in place of the value, a null is explicitly bound to that variable.
oci_bind_name1	Set Tcl variable namesake, then call oci_bind_name <cursor#>.	Used for scripting, this method of binding allows variables to be associated with native Tcl variables.
oci_exec	oci_exec <cursor#>	Executes the statement. If this cursor is not to return data (i.e., INSERT), this is the last call required for the cursor.
oci_fetch	oci_fetch <cursor#> <array size>	Retrieves specified number of rows from cursor, putting results into local Tcl array variables
oci_close	oci_close <cursor#>	Closes cursor and frees associated memory
oci_cancel	oci_cancel <cursor#>	Cancels the execution of a query when sufficient rows have been returned.
oci_list	oci_list	For interactive use—shows cursor # and associated SQL text for all cursors.
oci_vars	oci_vars <cursor#>	Dumps SQL statements and all current bind information.

The only real complexity in this process is in the binds section. First, in order to build usable data structures containing the bind information for a given cursor, the dbaman code needs to make a half-hearted attempt at parsing the SQL text to determine which bind variables need to be bound or not bound. Second, although the VARCHAR2 datatype can be used for just about everything, the DATE datatype is the exception to that rule (as ever). Dates must be bound by position using the `oci_bind_pos -date` operation. This directive instructs dbaman to convert the date string into a native Oracle format.

Preprocessing and Executing the Tracefile

Once the dbaman executable is built, some method of generating scripts from the raw tracefile is needed. This is done using an awk script to convert the trace information into the corresponding dbaman/OCI commands. This is imaginatively named `tclconv.awk`.

This conversion script parses the tracefile and produces code that can be directly executed by dbaman:

```
oci_logon scott/tiger
oci_open -assign 256
oci_parse 256 { alter session set events '10046 trace name context forever, level 4'}
oci_exec 256
oci_close 256
oci_open -assign 1
oci_parse 1 { alter session set nls_language= 'AMERICAN' nls_territory= 'AMERICA'
nls_currency= '$' nls_iso_currency= 'AMERICA' nls_numeric_characters= '.,'
nls_date_format= 'DD-MON-YY' nls_date_language= 'AMERICAN' nls_sort= 'BINARY'
nls_calendar= 'GREGORIAN' }
# alter session set nls_language= 'AMERICAN' nls_territory= 'AMERICA' n ...
oci_exec 1
oci_open -assign 2
oci_parse 2 { SELECT EMPNO,ENAME,JOB,MGR,HIREDATE,SAL,COMM,DEPTNO,
ROWID FROM EMP WHERE (ENAME LIKE :1) }
oci_bind_begin 2
oci_bind_pos 2 0 "D%"
oci_bind_end 2
# SELECT EMPNO,ENAME,JOB,MGR,HIREDATE,SAL,COMM,DEPTNO,ROWID FROM EMP WH ...
oci_exec 2
oci_fetch 2 1
oci_cancel 2
oci_bind_begin 2
oci_bind_pos 2 0 "SMI%"
oci_bind_end 2
# SELECT EMPNO,ENAME,JOB,MGR,HIREDATE,SAL,COMM,DEPTNO,ROWID FROM EMP WH ...
oci_exec 2
oci_fetch 2 1
```

This example shows the output produced from the first 89 lines of a SQL tracefile. The trace was taken from a SQL*Forms 4.5 program that queries the EMP and BONUS tables, and is intended to serve as a simplified example of the simulation process. In this section, we connect, set our NLS preferences (generated automatically by SQL*Forms), and then run a query against EMP. A fetch of a single row is attempted, which returns no data. The cursor is then canceled, rebound, and then executed once again, this time returning data. Running this script with dbaman, we can go on to interrogate the status afterwards:

```
$ dbaman
 percent source part1.tcl
% puts $oci_error

% array names results
1,status 2,0 2,status 2,rpc 2,header
% puts $results(1,status)
OK
% puts $results(2,status)
OK
% oci_list
Cursor #1 - Text :  alter session set nls_language= 'AMERICAN'
nls_territory= 'AMERICA' nls_currency= '$' nls_iso_currency= 'AMERICA'
nls_numeric_characters= '.,' nls_date_format= 'DD-MON-YY'
nls_date_language= 'AMERICAN' nls_sort= 'BINARY' nls_calendar=
'GREGORIAN'
Cursor #2 - Text :  SELECT EMPNO,ENAME,JOB,MGR,HIREDATE,SAL,COMM,DEPTNO,
ROWID FROM EMP WHERE (ENAME LIKE :1)

% puts $results(2,header)
EMPNO ENAME JOB MGR HIREDATE SAL COMM DEPTNO ROWID
% puts $results(2,0)
7369 SMITH CLERK 7902 17-DEC-80 800 {} 20 AAABLnAACAAACoQAAA
% puts $results(2,rpc)
1
%
```

It can be seen that two cursors are open at the end of the script: the NLS cursor, and the EMP cursor. Because it was an ALTER SESSION call, the NLS cursor (cursor 1) was taken only to the EXEC stage. Therefore, it has only a $results(1,status) variable indicating its status; no data is returned from this cursor. The cursor is not closed in the script, and so the full state of the cursor is preserved within dbaman.

The EMP cursor (cursor 2) has produced many more variables in the $results array. The status of the cursor execution shows that it returned successfully from the FETCH. The oci_fetch call is the only call that will set the status variable to anything more useful than OK or NOT OK. The oci_fetch call will set the variable to "no data found," if the fetch returns no data.

The data returned from cursor 2 is put into the variable $results(2,0). One NULL, as denoted by the {} in the output list, was returned. One row was returned, as shown by $results(2,rpc), and the column names are all stored in the $results(2,header) variable. Example output from the oci_list command can also be seen, showing the SQL for each of the currently open cursors.

Using this example code fragment, we can turn this into a single user simulation using standard Tcl coding:

```
# Single user simulation demonstration using dbaman.
set sleep_time 1000
set max_iter 50

oci_logon scott/tiger
oci_open -assign 256
oci_parse 256 { alter session set events '10046 trace name context forever, level
4'}
oci_exec 256
oci_close 256
oci_open -assign 1
oci_parse 1 { alter session set nls_language= 'AMERICAN' nls_territory= 'AMERICA'
nls_currency= '$' nls_iso_currency= 'AMERICA' nls_numeric_characters= '.,'
nls_date_format= 'DD-MON-YY' nls_date_language= 'AMERICAN' nls_sort= 'BINARY'
nls_calendar= 'GREGORIAN' }
# alter session set nls_language= 'AMERICAN' nls_territory= 'AMERICA' n ...
oci_exec 1
# Main section - loop through until max_iter reached.
while {$max_iter > 0} {
        oci_open -assign 2
        oci_parse 2 { SELECT EMPNO,ENAME,JOB,MGR,HIREDATE,SAL,COMM,DEPTNO,
        ROWID FROM EMP WHERE (ENAME LIKE :1) }
        oci_bind_begin 2
        oci_bind_pos 2 0 "D%"
        oci_bind_end 2
        # SELECT EMPNO,ENAME,JOB,MGR,HIREDATE,SAL,COMM,DEPTNO,ROWID FROM EMP WH ...
        oci_exec 2
        oci_fetch 2 1
        oci_cancel 2
        oci_bind_begin 2
        oci_bind_pos 2 0 "SMI%"
        oci_bind_end 2
        # SELECT EMPNO,ENAME,JOB,MGR,HIREDATE,SAL,COMM,DEPTNO,ROWID FROM EMP WH ...
        oci_exec 2
        oci_fetch 2 1
```

```
        # Following added from original trace file to allow looping
        oci_cancel 2
        oci_close 2
        incr max_iter -1
        after $sleep_time
}
```

We now have a very simplistic single-user simulation script. In this case, it repeatedly performs the same operations, although in reality you would want to vary the actual work performed each time. This is a straightforward change to make, with this kind of a construct replacing the `oci_bind_pos 2 0 "SMI%"`:

```
switch [ expr $max_iter % 5 ] {
        0 { oci_bind_pos 2 0 "JON%" }
        1 { oci_bind_pos 2 0 "SMI%" }
        2 { oci_bind_pos 2 0 "MIG%" }
        3 { oci_bind_pos 2 0 "ALB%" }
        4 { oci_bind_pos 2 0 "WHI%" }
}
```

Again, this is still very simplistic, but demonstrates the kind of constructs that should be built into the final script. For some of the more critical data points in the simulation, you will need some kind of more generic way to supply data to the script, particularly when simulating more than one user at a time. This will be discussed in Section 6.2.

3.5.5 Validate Server-Side System Utilization

Once each single transaction is complete, run it through on your test system and compare it with a real user from the perspective of system utilization, including CPU, memory, and disk I/O. If you have done a good job, it should be possible to get the system utilization pretty close to that of a real user.

One of the checks that you should perform is to trace the simulated session in the same way that the original tracefile was produced and compare it with the original tracefile. This is the reason why the `tclconv.awk` script turns on a trace as the very first thing it executes. While there will almost certainly be differences in the number of recursive calls within the respective sessions, running the before and after tracefiles through the `tkprof` facility will quickly split these out and report back accordingly.

Tests performed on the `tclconv.awk`/`dbaman` combination have thus far yielded very good results as far as accuracy is concerned. Using a transaction from a very complex Forms application, the following tkprof summaries are created with the original Form and the simulation session, respectively:

```
Original:
OVERALL TOTALS FOR ALL NON-RECURSIVE STATEMENTS

call      count       cpu    elapsed        disk       query     current        rows
-------  ------  --------  ---------  ----------  ----------  ----------  ----------
Parse        80      0.00       0.00           0           2           0           0
Execute     147      0.00       0.00           1         157          65          83
Fetch       162      0.00       0.00           0        1436         219         324
-------  ------  --------  ---------  ----------  ----------  ----------  ----------
total       389      0.00       0.00           1        1595         284         407

Misses in library cache during parse: 0


dbaman:
OVERALL TOTALS FOR ALL NON-RECURSIVE STATEMENTS

call      count       cpu    elapsed        disk       query     current        rows
-------  ------  --------  ---------  ----------  ----------  ----------  ----------
Parse        82      0.00       0.00           0           0           0           0
Execute     149      0.00       0.00           0          15          68          35
Fetch       163      0.00       0.00           7        1913         220         326
-------  ------  --------  ---------  ----------  ----------  ----------  ----------
total       394      0.00       0.00           7        1928         288         361

Misses in library cache during parse: 0

Generated by 'TKPROF SYS=NO'
```

The `tkprof` summaries show some differences, mostly in the execute/rows cell, but otherwise all looks good. One of the reasons that this value is different is a shortcoming in `dbaman`: the inability to simulate array inserts. This results more from the shortcomings of the trace facility, because the bind variables are dumped only for one of the rows to be inserted.

More information about the accuracy can be gained by querying v$sesstat for the respective sessions and determining the differences. For a session similar to the one above, the statistics in Table 3.6 were generated.

Some of these differences could be associated with different activities going on in the database at that point in time, particularly the cluster-related

Table 3.6   Statistical Differences Between Original and Simulated Session

Name	Forms	dbaman	Accuracy[*]
SQL*Net roundtrips to/from client	306	709	132%
buffer is not pinned count	2616	1972	(25%)
buffer is pinned count	6964	3739	(46%)
bytes received via SQL*Net from client	36232	62985	74%
bytes sent via SQL*Net to client	26523	60532	128%
calls to get snapshot scn: kcmgss	149	152	2%
calls to kcmgas	2	1	(50%)
cluster key scan block gets	3	28	833%
cluster key scans	3	19	533%
consistent gets	3072	2106	(31%)
db block changes	28	76	171%
db block gets	295	319	8%
enqueue releases	6	5	(17%)
enqueue requests	6	5	(17%)
execute count	175	187	7%
free buffer requested	1	2	100%
messages sent	2	1	(50%)
no work—consistent read gets	2416	1592	(34%)
opened cursors cumulative	86	102	19%
opened cursors current	81	81	0%
parse count (total)	105	102	(3%)
recursive calls	120	146	22%
redo entries	14	40	186%
redo size	4904	10400	112%
redo small copies	13	39	200%

Table 3.6 continued

Name	Forms	dbaman	Accuracy*
redo synch writes	2	1	(50%)
session cursor cache count	18	16	(11%)
session cursor cache hits	6	4	(33%)
session logical reads	3367	2423	(28%)
session pga memory	331856	508040	53%
session pga memory max	347160	508040	46%
session uga memory	223476	325612	46%
session uga memory max	248932	325612	31%
sorts (memory)	37	21	(43%)
sorts (rows)	39	70	79%
table fetch by rowid	1749	821	(53%)
table scan blocks gotten	2673	1257	(53%)
table scan rows gotten	17103	14242	(17%)
table scans (short tables)	89	83	(7%)
user calls	287	692	141%

* Values in parentheses denote negative values.

items: these cluster statistics are attributed to recursive work performed by the session. However, there are large differences in other areas also:

- *SQL*Net.* Clearly, the dbaman tool was a good deal more verbose over SQL*Net than the original Forms session. This could be attributed mostly to the use of a different API (application programming interface) into the database server. Forms uses the proprietary UPI layer, whereas dbaman has to use OCI.

- *Memory utilization.* Again, dbaman used a good deal (30 to 53 percent) more server-side memory than the Forms session. This could also be attributed in part to the use of a different API. In addition, any variations in the other statistics could radically change this ratio.

- *Amount of data read.* The dbaman session shows that it returned more data than the Forms session. Once again, the API could come into play here, but it is most likely to be affected by differing amounts of *recursive* work performed by each session. Although the dbaman session made more recursive calls, this does not mean that it performed as much work.

- *Other.* Not all information is explicitly logged in the tracefile. Therefore, some amount of guesswork needs to be done in order to work out, for example, where cursors should be closed.

In summary, however, dbaman is capable of a reasonably good simulation of the Forms session. Some of the discrepancies may balance out over time (particularly the memory-related ones), while others are already very close on target.

3.5.6   Building a Multiuser Framework

Once we have a selection of accurate single-user simulations, we can start to think about how to convert them into a benchmark suite. In order to do this, it becomes necessary to build a simple control framework for all of the sessions. The framework should allow the following actions to be performed:

- Start specified number of sessions.
- Update active set of users.
- Update "sleep time" multiplier for each transaction type.
- Update logon/logoff rate for simulated sessions.

This kind of a framework is an important method of keeping the simulation scientific. Without this kind of control, the simulation is not controllable for long enough to gain repeatable, dependable results.

The complexity of this kind of framework varies, depending on the scale of the simulation. It can range from a simple shell script that starts up the required number of sessions, with checks that keep the number of connected sessions at the required level, all the way to a full UNIX IPC (Interprocess Communication) implementation using shared memory, semaphores, and message queues (see Section 3.6).

The extent of engineering required for the framework is dependent on the amount of control needed and the number of users that the simulator will be driving. Once several hundred sessions are trying to do the same thing on the system at the same time, some of the more simplistic techniques no longer scale adequately.

3.6 Scale the Simulator

3.6.1 Data Problems

One of the most important portions of any simulation, whether written from scratch using OCI or using a third-party tool (see Section 3.4), is the portion that provides the simulating sessions with data that

- Is usable by the application, with no greater collisions in data access than would occur in real life

- Does not provide the database server with an artificially high cache hit ratio

- Does not provide the database server with an artificially *low* cache hit ratio

- Is plentiful. (It makes no sense to run out of driving data 1 hour into an 8-hour stress test)

This is an area that is unique to each particular application and should not be overlooked: the simulation will not scale sufficiently unless the data needs of the application are satisfied.

For example, assume that we are simulating an application that allows the creation of invoices and the subsequent processing of payments against those invoices. During the invoice creation stage, the users simply type in the part number and the quantity; the details of the line items are automatically filled in by the application. When all the lines are entered, the transaction is committed and an invoice number is generated.

Later on in the life cycle of the invoice, a payment is received against it. This occurs several weeks or months after the original invoice was created. At this stage, the total on the invoice is checked, and the credit is applied.

If we are simulating this application, by whatever means, it would be tempting to have each simulated session enter an invoice using a canned set of line items and then proceed to post the credits against the invoice in order to make the simulation self-perpetuating. Unfortunately, this would result in the dreaded "optimal transaction profile," which spoils the results of many benchmarks.

The transaction becomes optimal for the following reasons:

- The same line items are used each time. This means that the database validation on the part numbers will always be resolved by a small number of cached index leaf blocks and their corresponding table data blocks. This means the blocks will always be hot in the buffer cache, ensuring that the lookups require zero disk I/O.

- The retrieval of the invoice by invoice number is also certain to be in cache, because it has just been committed by the same session a few seconds ago. In real life, the invoice is likely to be somewhat older and therefore more likely to require several disk reads to obtain the data.

It can be seen that a workload with this profile is nothing like real life. It is far more realistic to have two distinct sets of connections, each fulfilling one of the functions of data entry, or credit posting. The data that each uses should not be shared, and must be prebuilt and loaded into the database as in-flight transactions. Any lookup information should be as random as it would be in real transactions. For example, the line item lookup in the example above should be driven from a very much larger list of potential line items, making life a little more realistic for the database server.

Many of the RTE packages provide functionality to drive the sessions with different sets of data, and this kind of functionality is not difficult to build into a custom simulation suite.

3.6.2   User Control Problems

Another problem in trying to scale a simulator is control of the user sessions. In simulating many thousands of users from potentially one driver machine, the system can behave in very peculiar ways, and controlling the users may not be as straightforward as it seems.

As mentioned in Section 3.5.6, UNIX Interprocess Communication (IPC) facilities are a very good way of providing user control. Comprising shared memory, semaphores, and message queues, IPC provides a flexible way to control the sessions and to supply the simulator with the required data. Figure 3.4 shows one way in which IPC can be used to control the sessions and feed them with data.

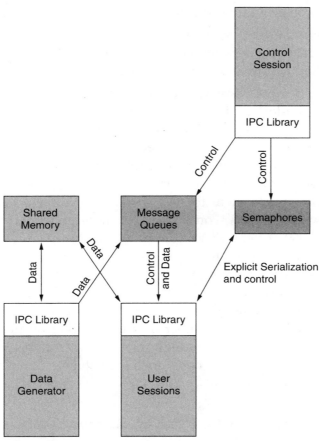

Figure 3.4 Simulation control and data supply

In Figure 3.4, all three types of IPC have been used for various reasons. Access to the IPC mechanisms is provided through a common set of libraries. The IPC in this example is used as follows:

- Shared memory is used to supply each session with the data it requires. The shared memory segment is populated by a data generator, which maintains lists of operating data in the segment. In addition, the user sessions can use the shared memory to log statistics about themselves during a run and to return data for use elsewhere.

- Message queues are used as pipes for submitting data to the sessions, in addition to providing control messages such as sleep multipliers.

- Semaphores are used by the sessions themselves for explicit serialization operations, where necessary, and as a global "active list" that ensures that the correct number of processes are active at any one time.

The use of IPC is a good way to provide a global control point for the system, although caution needs to be observed in regard to the way some systems behave when many sessions all use the same instance of the IPC mechanism. For example, I once worked on a benchmark that used UNIX message queues as the mechanism for controlling the active user set. All of the sessions would sleep, blocking on the read of the message queue, until a message was sent to them to start work. The problem here was that, although only one session would receive a message to start work at any one time, all 3,000 of the user sessions would wake up (at kernel priority) and go on the run queue each time a message went on the queue. This prevented the system from scaling to the point where we needed it to go, and so another mechanism had to be found. In this case, the easiest and quickest way to fix the problem and proceed was to define *many* messages queues and have a smaller number of users waiting on them. This certainly fixed the problem well enough for us to proceed with the testing, although we would probably have done it in some other way if the circumstances had been different.

3.6.3   Simpler Methods for Use with dbaman

Although IPC is very flexible, its use may seem a little complex or even daunting at first. If this is the case, or if time is not available to produce an

IPC solution, a more simplistic solution can yield fairly accurate results, albeit with somewhat less flexibility. In this section, we will cover a more simplistic approach that can be integrated into a dbaman simulation with only simple script and infrastructure changes.

The following section describes what is available in this infrastructure.

User Control

The user control process allows one-time setup prior to the execution of the test and a way of terminating the test cleanly, which are considered the bare essentials required during a benchmark. Highly desirable control points such as midflight timing changes, live status messages, and guaranteed active user counts are not provided in this model.

Data Supply

The simulator is provided with data on a per-process basis with pre-prepared datafiles for each process.

If these facilities are adequate, it can be relatively straightforward to build the required infrastructure. First of all, a common start-up script needs to be created, containing all the presets for the run:

```
#############################################################################
# Simulator startup script
# Usage: startup <ID> <TX script to run> <userid/password>
#############################################################################
#
###########
# Globals
#
# All timing values are in SECONDS
###########
set tx_sleep 120
set think_time 2
set max_iter 1000
set my_id [ lindex $argv 0 ]
set dfiles /sim/input
set ofiles /sim/output
set userpass [ lindex $argv 2 ]
###########
# Common functions
###########
proc get_data {} {
```

```
        global data_fd
        return [ gets $data_fd ]
}
proc logit { wstr } {

        global log_fd
        return [ puts $logfd $wstr ]
}
##########
# Open files
##########
set data_fd [ open "$dfiles/scr$my_id.txt" ]
set log_fd [ open "$ofiles/ses$my_id.log" w ]
##########
# Execute script
##########
source [ lindex $argv 1 ]

close $data_fd
close $log_fd
```

Calling this start-up script from a master program that assigns unique IDs to the start-up script, all the scripts can pick up a private datafile from which they read a line for each transaction. If we were to use this to simulate the invoice entry example, we would invoke the simulator as follows:

```
cnt=1
while [ $cnt -le 1000 ]
do
        cnt=`expr $cnt + 1`
        dbaman startup.tcl ${cnt} inv_entry.tcl user${cnt}/pass${cnt} &
done
```

This would initiate 1,000 invoice entry users, each trying to connect with a username derived from its ID number and attempting to use a datafile with the same ID number. The datafile would contain the part numbers that the session was to enter and would need to be prerandomized in order to avoid the optimal transaction profile.

The script itself can be modified to take advantage of all the facilities now available:

```
oci_logon $userpass
.... menu navigation ....
while { $max_iter > 0 } {
      set start_click [ clock ticks ]
      set tx_data [ split [get_data] { }]
      foreach part_num $tx_data {
            ..... enter line items .....
            after [ expr $think_time * 1000 ]
      }
      .... wrap up transaction ....
      logit [expr [clock ticks] - $start_click ]
      after [ expr $tx_sleep * 1000 ]
}
```

This script now logs in as the specified user and reads through its private datafile, inputting line items every $think_time and pausing for $tx_sleep between each complete invoice. Nominal logging has been provided by the total transaction time being logged after each transaction.

This is just a simple example and does not provide a great deal of control. However, it can be seen that most changes are relatively simple to implement owing to the use of a scripting engine for the simulator.

3.7 Make It Easy to Run

Once the simulation software is complete, or fully configured if third-party software has been used, it is important to finish the process by making the entire process *shrink-wrapped*.

3.7.1 Portability

It is likely that, after all the effort you have just expended, you will want to reuse this software on numerous occasions. The first step toward this is to make sure that there is nothing in the benchmark suite that is terribly non-portable. This includes all the usual C coding portability warnings, such as relying on the size of a pointer, but equally includes any reliance on the location of system files, Oracle files, and so on. This is worth thinking about at the start of the development, and all the way through whenever something potentially system-specific is used.

A good finishing touch to all of the portability work is to have one central file that contains all of the lookup information required by the simulation, such as:

```
PWDFILE=    /etc/passwd
ORATAB=     /etc/oratab
```

This file then serves as a checklist after the installation of the software as to what will need to be configured.

3.7.2   Packaging

Again, you will probably want to run this software a few times, so make it easy to install. Package the software on a single tape (or a range of tapes for maximum portability), and provide setup and running instructions with the software. Make the directory structure for the simulation intuitive, and keep the content of each directory concise for all the main directories. This would include keeping all the source code, the binaries, the driving data sources, the run statistics, and the log files separate from each other.

3.7.3   Start-Up Scripts

When you are developing the simulation, you will become an expert in all the nooks and crannies of the software. It makes sense to use this knowledge to write some start-up scripts for the simulation, because you will have become tired of typing in the same old commands, with their many parameters, over and over again. This is especially useful because during execution of subsequent benchmarks, the start-up process could be executed many times a day.

The benefit of having good, well-documented start-up scripts extends far beyond the laziness element of typing them in all the time, however. Benchmarks frequently run long and late into the night, and having good start-up scripts can make the difference between stupid mistakes and high-quality, measurable benchmark results. In addition, the next time the simulator is installed, it is likely that you will have forgotten many of the idiosyncrasies of the software.

3.7.4   Automating Information Retrieval at Closedown

When a successful benchmark execution has been performed, it is likely that there will be a lot of data in widely distributed places that you will want to keep and log for that test. Among such data are the following:

- Test start-up parameters
- Test notes, including reason for test parameters, changes since last run, and why changes were made
- Response time and throughput statistics from the simulator sessions
- System statistics from all machines involved
- Database statistics from database server
- the `init.ora`

It is very frustrating to forget to retrieve some of this information at test closedown, because it could invalidate the entire test at the analysis stage. Therefore, invest sufficient time in creating information gathering and filing systems. These routines can also be responsible for the clearing down of logging areas at the end of a test phase in order to facilitate the next test session.

3.8 Define Limitations in Advance

3.8.1 A Benchmark Is Never Perfect

As we discussed earlier, it is almost impossible to create a 100 percent accurate simulation of a system. It is possible to get it pretty close, however, and it is important that the proximity to real life be documented. Some of the specific areas that would definitely need to be documented as deficiencies were noted in Section 3.2.3, but there are many more that will come up in the development of the simulator. It is important to accept that the perfect simulation is not possible, and to make sure that all limitations are clearly defined and made available for use in any results analysis.

3.8.2 Measure the Impact of the Inaccuracies

Assuming that the benchmark is not perfect, how far off the mark are we? What is the impact of being erroneous? Which areas of the system must we get absolutely correct, and which areas allow some room for error?

These are all good questions to answer up front. If the simulation shows that it is using 5 percent less CPU per user than a real user, then this needs to be factored into the analysis, and a risk assessment needs to be produced. If the results show that an eight-processor machine is needed, and the machine will scale well up to 12 or 16 processors, then this is not a critical issue, because the option of adding more processors is available if all else fails.

3.9   Chapter Summary

Throughout this chapter, we have covered a wide variety of topics, ranging from choice of tools to development of a custom tool. This is indicative of a real benchmark, because a successful benchmark depends on diverse skill sets from the people developing and running it.

A complete solution to the benchmark problem has not been presented in this chapter. To a degree this has been intentional, because the most important attribute of all is to *understand* every minute aspect of the benchmark operation. The intent of this chapter has been to provide pointers and a starting point for what is a very complex task.

When you are actually executing the benchmark, paranoia is a fine quality. If something doesn't seem quite right, or somebody does something that magically solves a problem, please be suspicious and ask questions. It is easy to have the wool pulled over one's eyes, and there is a good deal of wool involved in most benchmarks.

Most of all, enjoy the process. At the end of the benchmark, you are likely to understand a great deal about all aspects of the system, including the application, the tuning approach required for Oracle, the quirks of the hardware platform—everything.

3.10   Further Reading

Aho, Alfred, B. W. Kernighan, and P. J. Weinberger. 1988. *The AWK Programming Language.* Reading, MA: Addison-Wesley.
Ousterhout, J. 1994. *Tcl and the Tk Toolkit.* Reading, MA: Addison-Wesley.
Various. "Oracle Call Interface Programmer's Guide." *Oracle RDBMS Documentation.*

Chapter 4

System/Database Monitoring

4.1 Why Monitor?

Monitoring is a frequently overlooked component of essential system development. Whether you purchase a third-party software product or develop your own techniques for monitoring the system, it is important not to underestimate either the effectiveness of good system monitoring or the effort required to develop this capability.

The benefits provided by monitoring fall into three categories:

- Providing proactive fault-detection capability
- Providing rapid fault diagnosis capability from available data
- Providing historical performance records for capacity planning and analysis

These are substantial benefits that even if taken alone would justify the cost of implementing a quality monitoring solution.

4.1.1 Proactive Fault Detection

In an ideal world, fault detection would occur before the actual problem arose, and the problem could therefore be fixed before it happened. This is, of course, complete nonsense. However, using proactive fault-detection techniques, it should be possible to preclude a selection of your least favorite problems. Very often, major problems are caused by the combined effect of several minor problems and can be prevented by providing early warnings of these problems.

For example, let's say that an Oracle Parallel Server system is capable of handling 100 distributed lock operations per second under normal loading and has 20 percent idle CPU during this loading. It is also known that servicing of 20 lock operations could take up to 5 percent of the system CPU. If something happened to increase the number of lock operations to 160 operations per second, this would not impose a response time problem on the user community, and under many operational environments this event would go unnoticed as a result. However, with a monitoring system, this would be detected and an alert would be triggered indicating that something had changed significantly and that the system was now very vulnerable to increases in CPU utilization. The system would now be running at 95 percent utilization, and even a small problem would cause user discomfort.

It can be seen that, using a suitable monitoring system, this problem can be avoided. This is one of the greatest strengths of a monitoring system.

4.1.2   Rapid Fault Diagnosis

Another advantage of a monitoring system comes into play when the system is not performing properly. In this instance, when the support person is called out, considerably more information can be made available to him or her than if the system were not monitored. For example, if one of the tablespaces in the database had filled up, the only thing the users might get (if using Forms) would be an "unhandled exception" error. If the system were not being proactively monitored, the DBA would have to work through systematic checks to discover that the tablespace was a problem. With a monitored system, however, the problem could be relayed to the support person as "tablespace full," and the DBA could rectify the problem immediately.

Typically, a DBA uses scripts, one at a time, to look through several "hot buttons" in order to determine the operational status of the database. With an adequately monitored system, the DBA has an enormous advantage over script-based DBAs for determining the performance of the system. If the monitored data is well presented to the DBA, such as through some kind of histogram-based Graphical User Interface (GUI), trends and correlations between many statistics can be immediately observed and interpreted.

For example, it is very simple to observe the relationship between the user commit rate (as measured by "user commits" in v$sysstat) and the use of the redo allocation and redo copy latches: when one increases in rate, it is accompanied by a jump in the reported statistics from the related areas. Viewing the rate that users enter wait states, in conjunction with the usage rates for the relevant resource, can show where the pain threshold lies for key areas of database operation. A good example of this would be monitoring the number of "latch free" wait events in conjunction with the number of latch gets for each type of latch. This shows where the system starts to have problems keeping up and provides explicit targets for application tuning exercises.

4.1.3 Historical Performance Records

Whichever method you adopt for system monitoring, it is important to make sure that historical records of all the performance data are kept for later review. By doing this, you gain the ability to track gradual problems (such as adverse row chaining in the database causing excessive I/O), determine the effects of software releases in terms of system utilization, and even perform high-level capacity planning by extrapolating resource trends as business volumes increase.

Historical records are also useful for determining the impact of system upgrades and database changes. For example, a recent upgrade of Oracle on one of our production database servers allowed the use of "hard locked SGA." This is a facility that locks the SGA into real memory, removing the possibility of it being paged out onto disk. The benefit of this is more than is immediately apparent. First, because it does not need to be considered by the virtual memory system for paging, there is no swap space allocated for the SGA. Second, the UNIX kernel can start to share *Process Table Maps (ptmaps)* for each process that attaches to the SGA (every user process and all Oracle background processes). A ptmap is the space map kept by the kernel that provides VM information about all pages of memory the process has mapped. On this particular system, this means that it needs to allocate 4 bytes (i.e., a 32-bit address) for every 4KB memory page that it maps. If each of your processes on the system is mapping a 500MB SGA, this means that the effective size of their process goes up by 500KB, just in management overhead. This can become a major issue when there are 1,000 users or more connected to your system, because this equates to a 500MB memory overhead.

Historical monitoring was a useful tool here to determine how much memory we would need in the system once this facility was implemented. We were able to plot charts of memory consumption over a period of more than 1 year and to determine the impact.

4.2   Low-Intrusion Techniques

If you decide to develop your own monitoring suite, or even if you use the framework of a third-party tool with your own collectors, you will need to make sure that the collection methods are *low-intrusion* methods. This means that the methods used for the collection should not impose too much on the system when they are running—that is, you should not be affecting the behavior of the system you are trying to monitor. This could result in response time problems for the user community and could also spoil the quality of any data that you collect from the system.

4.2.1   Go Easy on the System

When developing statistic-collection tools, taking care of the system should be of primary concern. Most of the time, this will mean simply minimizing the amount of CPU that the collector uses. However, when the system has especially severe scaling requirements, it is important to factor in all the types of resources that need to be minimized:

- Processor
- Disk I/O
- Memory
- Single-threaded resources

The first three resources may be fairly obvious, but the last one is not. It is included here as a catchall for any type of resource that is a potential bottleneck in the system. Within Oracle this typically equates to latches, but can include anything that has the same mutual exclusion effect. If it is possible to implement the collector without using any single-threaded resources, then that should be one of the primary design goals.

4.2.2 Avoiding Single-Threaded Resources

A good example of this might be the "ST" enqueue within Oracle. This is visible in V$LOCK and is the enqueue that needs to be acquired by Oracle before it can do a *space transaction*, which includes allocation, deallocation, and coalescing of space in the database. This lock is taken out by your user process (during recursive SQL) when you require an extent on disk to extend a sort into, because the free extent table (SYS.FET$) and the used extent table (SYS.UET$) need to be updated to reflect this.

The big problem with the ST enqueue is that, by design, there is only one of them. This means by implication that only one session in the database can be doing any space transactions at any one time, and has been the reason for the ST lock to be aliased "Single Threaded" and "Seriously Throttling."

So, avoiding the need to take out the ST lock is one good consideration that you should make, both to ensure that you are not impacting the system and to ensure that the monitoring is not affected by resource contention for ST. This is often not as simple as it sounds, as the following SQL demonstrates:

```
SELECT a.name,b.value
FROM v$statname a,v$sesstat b
WHERE a.statistic#=b.statistic#
AND a.name like "db file%'
```

In this query, a join operation needs to occur between v$sesstat and v$statname. Whereas this may not be a problem in most systems, imagine what happens on a 2,000-user OLTP system, where there is a very small sort area by design. A disk sort segment needs to be allocated, because you are joining tables of approximately 400,000 rows and 200 rows, respectively, and this cannot be serviced out of the small sort area (areas as small as 16KB are not unusual).[1]

---

1. This is less of an issue now that the sort_area parameters can be dynamically altered by each user session: the monitoring session can invest in a larger sort area than the online users in order to keep the impact to a minimum.

Of course, you would not be running the query above in an automated monitoring system, but you may want to run queries like it in online diagnosis sessions. There are several ways around this type of problem:

- Avoid joining tables where it is not necessary; reference `v$sesstat`, for example, directly by `statistic#` instead of joining it against `v$statname`.

- Use the "virtual" column indexes on the X$ tables found in Oracle 7.1 and above.

- Rely on the latch managed "sort segments" facility found in Oracle 7.3 and above. Note that while this helps a great deal, you should be aware that the disk sorting is still occurring (and is expensive) and you can still end up using ST if the sort segments are badly tuned.

- Use foreground (or application layer) joins. In extreme cases where you have no other option, you could implement the joins as a series of separate cursors in the monitoring application with which your application then deals. This has a resource overhead all its own, but is an option that is open to you under unusual circumstances.

Another single-threaded resource to be careful with is the library cache latch. More details on the use of the library cache latch can be found in Chapter 6, but for now we can simplify it by saying that it is taken out for each SQL *parse* made on the system. Therefore, for each SQL parse made on the system, the library cache latch needs to be taken out first, preventing any other sessions from parsing. This is largely relieved in Oracle 7.2 and above with the introduction of multiple library cache latches based on the SQL hash value of the statement. However, in heavily loaded systems, it does not make sense for an automated monitoring system to allocate these latches every n seconds when it does a sample. There is also a processing overhead in this scenario that does not need to be there.

Therefore, another good thing to do is to "parse once, execute many" for all the statements that make up the monitoring suite. Once the statement has been explicitly parsed once, it is only necessary to reexecute the cursor and suck down the results. From the OCI discussions in the preceding chapter, it should be clear how this can be easily achieved, and in fact I will be showing ways of implementing an Oracle data collector using `dbaman` later in Section 4.5.

4.3   Introduction to V$ Views

4.3.1   What Are the V$ Views ?

The V$ views are views that are based on the X$ fixed tables. Although referred to as tables, the X$ tables are not actually tables at all. An X$ table simply presents data in a format that looks like a table in order to allow standard SQL queries to be executed against it. However, the data is extracted from a variety of sources, including memory structures and file headers (see Figure 4.1).

The data available in the X$ tables is unrelated to the application data stored in the database. Instead, the data in the X$ tables describes the operational state of the database server at any point in time. The actual contents of the V$ views and X$ tables are discussed in more detail in Section 6.10. In this section we will concentrate on the *methods* of accessing them, rather than on the contents themselves.

The structure of these tables is based on the underlying data structures and subsequently has table names and column names that are unintelligible to anyone without strong source code knowledge of the RDBMS. They

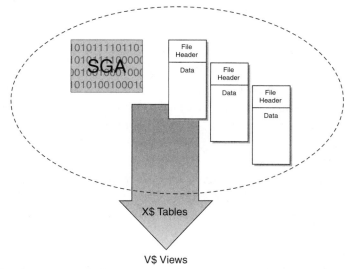

Figure 4.1   Data sources for V$ Views

are also subject to a good deal of change between releases, as the architecture of the underlying software changes.

It is for these reasons that the V$ views are supplied by Oracle and that their usage is recommended over the X$ tables. This having been said, there are specific occasions for which knowledge of the underlying X$ tables is beneficial, and advice will be given accordingly when such occasions arise.

4.3.2 Accessing the V$ Views

The V$ views are all owned by the SYS user. The catalog.sql script creates public synonyms for all of the V$ views and grants SELECT to the SELECT_CATALOG_ROLE role. Therefore, anybody with a privileged role can access these views.

The method used to allow non-SYS users to access the views is worth observing, because this is the method that is necessary for allowing non-SYS access to the X$ tables also. The necessary steps are:

- Connected as SYS, `create view x_$<name> as select * from x$<name>;`
- `create public synonym x$<name> for x_$<name>;`

When these steps are used, any of the X$ tables can be externalized for other database users to view.

4.3.3 Structure of the V$ Views

The V$ views have definitions, just as all other views in the database have. The difference is that the V$ views are not visible in the DBA_VIEWS view, because they are not real views.[2] To see how a V$ view is defined, one needs to query the V$ view V$FIXED_VIEW_DEFINITION. to find the definition.

The first thing you will notice when querying this view is that all the V$ views seem to be simple views based on the like-named GV$ view. A GV$ view is a new feature of Oracle8 that provides a global view of all the

---

2. However, the V_$<name> view exists, because it was created as a standard database object in catalog.sql.

instances that have the database open. The way to get the real definition is to query V$FIXED_VIEW_DEFINITION for the respective GV$ view, which will give the actual definition of the V$ view.

Many of the V$ views are composed of more than one X$ table, with a join condition. An example of this is V$SESSION_WAIT, which joins X$KSUSECST (the actual data) and X$KSLED (the names of the wait conditions) to provide the readable information that is presented.

In addition to the table joins, the V$ views are frequently aggregated rollup views of an underlying X$ table. An example of this is the V$SQLAREA view, which provides a view of summary information of the cursors stored in the library cache. Although a single cursor may have several child cursors as a result of different bind variable thresholds, for example, only one row will be returned from V$SQLAREA for any single identical piece of SQL, because of the GROUP BY clause in the view definition.

The performance of many of the views has been significantly improved since release 7.0. The reason for this is the inclusion of virtual indexes on selected columns within the underlying X$ tables. Another view, V$INDEXED_FIXED_COLUMN, details which columns of the X$ tables have indexes maintained on them. Although these indexes are somewhat limited in scope, their use can significantly improve the usability of some of the views, particularly when joining against other fixed views or tables.

4.3.4 Overhead of Using V$ Views

Alhough many of the V$ views access structures that are memory-resident this does not mean that they have a low overhead on a large system. In fact, the larger the system, the more resource is consumed in processing queries on V$ views. For example, a very large buffer cache may be covered by 1,000,000+ latches and the library cache by 100,000+ more. A subsequent query on V$LATCH involves a row for every one of these latches, making a very large data set.

Likewise, joining V$SESSION to V$SESSTAT on a system with a substantial user population (3,000+) results in a large join operation.

Other attributes of the V$ views that somewhat aggravate this problem include

- Table joins
- Aggregations
- Latch allocations

We have seen how table joins and aggregations are introduced, through the actual views themselves, but the problem of latch allocations is not immediately obvious. As many of the X$ tables are based on rapidly changing memory structures, Oracle needs to protect the lists that it traverses to obtain the results in order to prevent the list from being changed by another session. If this were to happen, the X$ query could easily find itself in a piece of list that is no longer valid, and could return corrupt results or crash the session. Therefore, when an X$ query is executed, latch operations take place.

To demonstrate this to yourself, try the following on an idle instance:

```
SELECT gets FROM V$LATCH WHERE name='library cache';
SELECT gets FROM V$LATCH WHERE name='library cache';
SELECT count(*) FROM V$SQLAREA;
SELECT gets FROM V$LATCH WHERE name='library cache';
```

The first query is executed twice to demonstrate the constant number of library cache latch gets that occur just from the execution of the V$LATCH query (ten on my test system). The query to V$SQLAREA allocates the library cache latch many times during its execution (more than one latch get per cursor) and therefore contends directly with the users on the system that are trying to parse SQL statements.

Table joins and aggregations can cause problems greater than just the CPU overhead of the required sort. If the sort is too large for the sort area, the sort will become a disk sort in temporary tablespace. Although the sort_area_size parameters are now dynamic parameters (they can be changed on a per-user basis as required), the number of rows involved in some of these queries often makes it impractical to extend the sort area to this size.

4.4 Minimizing Overhead

Now that we have seen the overhead of using the V$ views, it should be apparent why there are cases where the X$ tables should be accessed in preference. One such example is the use of V$LATCH in a continuous sampling environment.

The V$LATCH view can take up to 15 seconds of CPU time to execute in a large configuration, owing to the large number of rows in the underlying X$ tables. V$LATCH aggregates this data into a summary view of all the underlying child latches (V$LATCH_CHILDREN).

If this data is required, it makes sense to rewrite the view to reduce the amount of data returned from each X$ table used in the view. This is especially important if you intend to execute the query many times in succession, such as in an automated monitoring environment, because the amount of overhead imposed without good reason can really mount up.

Finally, it is common to join several V$ views in order to obtain the desired result. Many of the V$ tables have relationships between them, and it is beneficial to join them in this way. However, many of the views also use the same underlying X$ tables, and the entire query can be rewritten in order to eliminate any unnecessary extra accesses that may occur. When joining the X$ tables, you should also try to join on the indexed columns (usually the ADDR column), because this can make a huge difference on some of the larger views.

4.5 Using dbaman to Optimize Data Collection

Now that we have a general-purpose scripting interface to the OCI API, it makes sense to use that interface to automate the low-intrusion data collection process. In this section, we will look at ways to implement dbaman as a general-purpose monitoring tool.

4.5.1 Defining the Cursors

First of all, we don't want to end up with a system that needs to be reprogrammed every time we want to monitor something new. So, a standard method is required for entering SQL statements in a user-friendly manner.

One way to do this is to provide a separate file containing the SQL, formatted as a simplistic Tcl script that loads up all the SQL strings:

```
##############################################################################
# sqllist.tcl - list of statements to sample with
##############################################################################
#
##############################################################################
# Setup required procedure
#####
set next_ind 1
catch { unset sql_list }
proc add_sql { stmt } {
        global next_ind
        upvar sql_list x

        set x($next_ind) $stmt

        incr next_ind
}


##############################################################################
# Actual SQL Statements. All must be of the form "add_sql { <del|abs> { SQL } }"
#####
# Delta System Stats.
add_sql {
del {  select name,value
       from v$sysstat
       where statistic# in ( 4,40 ) }
}

# Absolute System Stats.
add_sql {
abs {  select name,value
       from v$sysstat
       where statistic# in ( 1 ) }
}
```

Each call to the defined add_sql procedure loads up the SQL along with its processing requirements to the array sql_list. The processing types adopted for this implementation are del and abs, denoting delta processing and absolute processing, respectively. In delta processing mode, the SQL is executed, and the delta (difference) is returned between its result set and the result set from the prior execution. In absolute mode, the absolute value is returned directly from the SQL execution.

The format of the SQL in the setup file should be such that the query always returns data in two columns, tag and value. In addition, all SQL submitted for delta processing must always return the same number of rows. If this is not the case, the deltas cannot be processed.

4.5.2 Parsing and Executing the SQL

Once the SQL is all loaded up into a local variable within dbaman, we can go through the array in sequence, parsing all the SQL one at a time, and storing the cursor handle each time:

```
###########################################################################
# parse_all - parses all statements in $sql_list()
###########################################################################
proc parse_all {} {

        global sql_list
        upvar cursor l_cur

        foreach stmt [ array names sql_list ] {
                set l_cur($stmt) [ oci_open ]
                oci_parse $l_cur($stmt) [ lindex $sql_list($stmt) 1 ]
        }
}
```

This step needs to be executed only *once*, in order to keep the processing overhead (and use of the library cache latches) to a minimum.

Now we need a procedure that will go through each of the statements and do the right thing accordingly:

```
###########################################################################
# exe_all - execute all the statements, and fetch all the data.
###########################################################################
proc exe_all { } {

        global sql_list oci_error cursor results

        foreach stmt [ array names sql_list ] {

                oci_exec $cursor($stmt)

                while { [ lindex $oci_error 0 ] != 1403 } {

                        oci_fetch $cursor($stmt) 30

                }
        }
}
```

This procedure executes each statement and fetches all the available data in array fetches of 30 rows at a time. As all the data from oci_fetch is stored in the global namespace, all this data will be accessible from everywhere else in the program.

4.5.3 Process the Result Sets

Finally, we need a routine that will perform the specified processing on each set of data. It should put all the results into a specific array so that the output stage can just traverse the array and output in the desired format:

```
##############################################################################
# calc - go through each statement and calculate the correct values. Put the
# results into an array when finished in order to make display easy.
##############################################################################
proc calc { } {

global sql_list display prior results

set now [ clock seconds ]

foreach stmt [ array names sql_list ] {
        switch [ lindex $sql_list($stmt) 0 ] {

"abs" {
foreach row [ array names results "$stmt,\[0-9]*" ] {
set display($row) [concat [ list \
                [clock format $now] ] $results($row) ]
            }
        }

        "del" {
                foreach row [ array names results "$stmt,\[0-9]*" ] {
                        if {[ catch { set prvval [ lindex \
                        $prior("$stmt,[lindex $results($row) 0]") 1 ] } ]==0} {
                                set prvtmsp [ lindex \
                                $prior("$stmt,[lindex $results($row) 0]") 0 ]
                                set nowval "[lindex $results($row) 1].0"
                                set difftm [ expr $now - $prvtmsp ]

                                set display($row) [ list [ clock format $now ] \
                                [ lindex $results($row) 0 ] \
                                [ expr ($nowval-$prvval)/$difftm]]
                        }

                        # Set up for next fetch
                        set prior("$stmt,[lindex $results($row) 0]") [ list \
                                $now [lindex $results($row) 1] ]
                        }
                }
            }
        }
    }
```

In this procedure, we attempt to set as many of the $display array ele-
ments as possible. In the case of the delta processing, if there has been no
previous execution, the $display array element is simply not set. If there
has been no prior corresponding row it is also ignored, apart from setting
up the prior data for the next row. If there *has been* a corresponding prior
data point but there is none on this runthrough no delta will be calcutlated
for the data point. *However,* if the data point reappears at some point in the
future, a delta will be calculated at that time, using a delta calculation
based on the stored timestamp of the prior sample (whenever that was).

4.5.4   Pulling it Together with a Main Loop

Once we have all the required procedures, we can build a main loop that
takes care of the repetitive execution of the procedures:

```
##########################################################################
# Main routine for dbaman-based sampling monitor
##########################################################################
#
###
# read in all the support procedures
###
source all_procs.tcl
###
# read in the SQL configuration file
###
source sqllist.tcl

oci_logon /

parse_all

set fd [ open [lindex $argv 0 ] a+ ]
set sample [ lindex $argv 1 ]

while { 1==1 } {

        exe_all
        calc
        foreach dpoint [ array names display ] {
                puts $fd $display($dpoint)
                unset display($dpoint)
                flush $fd
        }
        after [ expr $sample * 1000 ]
}
```

That's about all that is needed to get a fairly low-intrusion, dbaman-
based monitoring system. The actual monitoring process can be run on a

nonproduction platform, because it will use standard Oracle client/server connections to the actual database server. This ensures that the intrusion on the actual server is kept to a minimum. Combined with well-written and well-understood SQL statements, the result is a useful monitoring system.

This main routine is very simplistic—just writing out all the data to a file. More complex monitor presentations can be created by linking the TK component into the `dbaman` shell in order to gain a full GUI capability. Once this has been performed, there is practically no limit to how the data can be presented.

4.6 Processing Statistics

4.6.1 Data Transports

After going to the trouble of making a low intrusion data collector, it makes sense at least to run the database collector in client/server mode, as shown in Figure 4.2. This means that only the actual data extraction, and

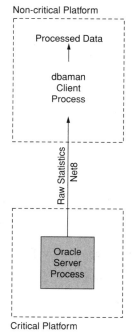

Figure 4.2 Running *dbaman* in client/server configuration

none of the pattern matching and actual delta processing, is performed on the database server.

Wherever possible, all other data processing of the statistics should take place on noncritical resources such as, for example, a development server. One project that is slightly beyond the scope of this book but worthwhile nonetheless is building a network infrastructure among all the monitoring components (dbaman, system monitors, etc.) in order to funnel all the data to a central place in real time. This allows several activities to be performed on the data, such as data analysis and data display.

The latest version of Tcl supports both client and server network sockets (socket command) and is a good starting point for building such an infrastructure. In this example program, we have most of the makings of a network data concentrator:

```
#############################################################################
# journal.tcl
#
# A TCL based concentrator for producing a serialized journal for all
# incoming streams.
#
# Usage: tclsh/dbaman journal.tcl <output file> <listen port>
#
# J.A. Morle, November 1998
#

proc main { outfile listen_port } {

        # Open the server socket, to listen for incoming requests
        set a [ socket -server { add_stream } $listen_port ]

        # Open the output journal
        set outfd [ open $outfile a+ ]

        # Loop forever accepting connections and writing out the data
        while { 1 } {
                after 300 { set vwait_ret 1 }
                vwait vwait_ret
                write_logs
        }
}

proc write_logs {} {

        upvar sock_arr l_sa
        upvar outfd l_ofd
```

```
        # Go through each socket connection, and write out every line in the
        # buffer. This is not very fair share, as it allows one stream to
        # dominate if it desires.
        foreach elem [ array names l_sa ] {

                while { [ gets $l_sa($elem) out_line ] != -1 } {
                        puts $l_ofd $out_line
                }
        }
        flush $l_ofd

}

proc add_stream { sockd addr port } {

        global vwait_ret
        upvar sock_arr l_sa

        # Setup the client socket connection
        fconfigure $sockd -blocking false -buffersize 524288
        set l_sa($addr,$port) $sockd
        set vwait_ret 1

}

main [lindex $argv 0 ] [lindex $argv 1]
```

The program works by first of all setting up a server socket. A server socket is a socket that listens for incoming requests and creates a new client socket for any such requests that come in. This action frees up the server socket and allows multiple connections by connecting to the same port. The new client socket is assigned a port that is guaranteed to be unique.

Every 300 milliseconds, or less if a new socket connection interrupts the sleep, the program wakes up, scans all the defines client socket connections, and writes all the data from each socket to the file supplied on the command line.

This is a fairly simplistic version of what is needed and will actually work well as long as no exceptional circumstances arise. One such exceptional circumstance is noted in the source code, where a single session can effectively lock the write_logs procedure by never giving it a chance to finish on that socket. However, there would need to be a great deal of data flowing in for this to happen.

In order to use this framework with the dbaman-based database data gatherer, we need to amend the main routine to use the network instead of a local file:

```
############################################################################
# Main routine for dbaman-based sampling monitor
############################################################################
#
###
# read in all the support procedures
###
source all_procs.tcl
###
# read in the SQL configuration file
###
source sqllist.tcl

oci_logon /

parse_all

set sendaddr [lindex $argv 0 ]
set sendport [lindex $argv 1 ]
set sample [ lindex $argv 2 ]

set sd [ socket $sendaddr $sendport ]

while { 1==1 } {

        exe_all
        calc
        foreach dpoint [ array names display ] {
                puts $sd $display($dpoint)
                unset display($dpoint)
        }
        after [ expr $sample * 1000 ]
}
```

The only changes in this program relate to opening a socket instead of the file, and using puts to write down the network instead of to the local file.

4.6.2   Alarm Propagation

Once a network forwarding infrastructure has been implemented, this infrastructure is also an ideal vehicle for centralizing and reporting on all subsystem alerts. Useful things to include are

- The Oracle `alertXXXX.log` files
- The UNIX hardware error log
- Any middleware or application logfiles

It does not make sense to ship the entire logfile, however, because this is not much more useful than the original logfile. Instead, a text filter can be applied to the logfile in order to extract only specific types of messages. These messages can then be distilled and rewritten prior to shipping across the network, with the end result being a much more useful set of messages, all in a central location.

This example code fragment of one such text filter searches its input for ORA-00600 errors, the dreaded internal error:

```
/^ORA-00600/{ sub("[[]"," ");
              sub("[]]"," ");
              sprintf("STATUS: Oracle Internal error: type %d.",$6);
            }
```

This `awk` pattern match and action detects the ORA-00600 error, extracts the arguments of the string, and reports only the fact that there is an internal error, of the type denoted by the arguments.

This could be run as follows:

```
$ tail -f alertDB.ora | awk -f filter.nawk | sendmesg dev_host 12345
```

This command line filters all the future output from the alertfile and pipes the output to a command called `sendmesg`. This is a fabricated program that simply takes standard input and pushes it down an open client socket to the host and port specified on the command line.

In the ORA-00600 example, we prefix the message with a string denoting the severity of the message. All that is now required to make a simplistic alert console is to tail the single journal that is now being created and `grep` for the type of message required (STATUS, ALARM, etc.).

4.7 Defining the "Flight Envelope"

4.7.1 What Is a "Flight Envelope"?

A flight envelope is the way that the operating characteristics of an aircraft are specified. For example, a plane may be able to fly at 300 knots at 20,000 feet but at only 150 knots at 3,000 feet. This is very similar to the way that large complex systems work.

In your system, you may be able *either* to cope with 3,000 pageouts per second *or* to run at 90 percent CPU utilization. If the system were to start paging at 3,000 pageouts per second while your system was at 90 percent CPU utilization, the system would be in big trouble, with end user response times being degraded accordingly. This is a simplified version of a system flight envelope.

A flight envelope is a very useful thing to define, both for your own benefit and for the benefit of people who simply cannot understand the complex interactions of the system.

4.7.2 How Do I Define a Flight Envelope for the System?

Much of the definition of the flight envelope comes down to "getting a feel" for the particular system on which you run your database. The hardware vendor may be able to provide some raw statistics about on the system's capability, but these numbers need to be used with a good pinch of caution.

In fact, one of the best ways to define a flight envelope is to break it out into several child flight envelopes. Certain operational parameters within the system will directly compete against each other, while others will work in their own discrete groups.

For example, there is a direct correlation between the number of latch acquisitions per second and the amount of idle CPU on the system, because of the impact of spinning to obtain latches. Whereas a normal latch get is not very CPU-intensive, a spin get of a latch is very CPU-intensive. Therefore, one of the system flight envelopes may be how the latch get potential relates to idle CPU on the system (see Figure 4.3).

This envelope shows that the number of potential latch gets increases linearly up to a certain point. At this point, a proportion of the latch gets must be acquired by spinning, and therefore the act of gaining the latch starts to eat into the idle CPU. As the available CPU is reduced, the latch acquisition problem is compounded, and so the number of potential latch gets per second is further reduced.

These kinds of flight envelopes can be as scientific as you like; sometimes the best metric of all is "I can do up to *n* transactions per second before the response time degrades."

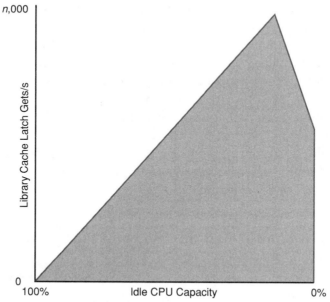

Figure 4.3 Latch gets versus idle CPU flight envelope

4.8 Using Excel Spreadsheets for Data Visualization

Microsoft Excel spreadsheets provide an excellent way of visualizing trends in otherwise meaningless streams of data. Typically, they provide an entire spectrum of different plotting options that should always provide you with enough choices to produce meaningful results.

Unfortunately, there are also several limitations that probably don't normally affect standard bean-counter users of the spreadsheet products (unless they have unusually large numbers of very complex beans to count). The first one is the row count limitation. In Excel, this is limited to 16,384 rows in version 7.0 and to 65,536 in the 97 version. It is amazing how easy it is to exceed 16,384 rows in your data; for example, if your data collector is sampling every 15 seconds, it only takes 68 hours of one statistic to exceed the limit, and proportionately less if you are showing several instances and a small number of different statistics. This comes down to only 5.67 hours if you are trying to plot four different statistics over three database instances, for example.

The other problems with using Excel for this type of function relate to the assumptions it makes about the size and complexity of the spreadsheet that you can use on it. The spreadsheet is always memory-resident, for example, which can cause havoc with the Windows virtual memory system when large sheets are used.

Related to this is the fundamental assumption from the charting tool in Excel that you are plotting "a few" data points. It clearly is not expecting 16,383 (the first row is the heading row) points to plot, because otherwise it would not redraw the chart in the "Chart Wizard" box every time you changed the settings.

Despite these problems, however, Excel is still one of the most powerful tools in the domestic tool bag for data analysis. Using Excel to best effect requires several preliminary steps in order to make the most of the charting facilities it contains.

The most fundamental requirement is that you massage the data before trying to do anything with it in Excel. This is necessary because of the variety of different sources from which the data may originate. More often than not, data from different sources will have different sample periods, different snapshot times, and widely different numbers of samples. It is often these mismatched data points that you will want to chart together on a single chart—for example, charting transaction rate against CPU utilization.

In order to achieve this with high-quality results, several steps must be taken. First, all the data must be quantized to common snapshot times and sample periods. This can be achieved using one of the powerful text-processing languages such as awk or perl.

Quantization means time-aligning the data points from the separate data sources. Individual circumstances will determine the most suitable granularity for the quantization, but using nearest whole minutes often works very well.

The input data may look like this:

```
1997/12/17 23:42:26 882430946 dbmon BMA2.user_commits 14.58
1997/12/17 23:42:59 882430979 dbmon BMA2.user_commits 14.79
1997/12/17 23:43:32 882431012 dbmon BMA2.user_commits 15.30
1997/12/17 23:44:06 882431046 dbmon BMA2.user_commits 14.79
1997/12/17 23:44:39 882431079 dbmon BMA2.user_commits 13.79
1997/12/17 23:45:12 882431112 dbmon BMA2.user_commits 14.58
1997/12/17 23:45:46 882431146 dbmon BMA2.user_commits 14.33
1997/12/17 23:46:19 882431179 dbmon BMA2.user_commits 13.00
1997/12/17 23:46:53 882431213 dbmon BMA2.user_commits 14.50
1997/12/17 23:47:27 882431247 dbmon BMA2.user_commits 14.97
1997/12/17 23:48:00 882431280 dbmon BMA2.user_commits 15.27
1997/12/17 23:48:34 882431314 dbmon BMA2.user_commits 15.18
```

All of the samples lie on almost random time boundaries as a result of rounding in system timers, scheduling glitches, and so on. This makes such data very difficult to match up with any other data.

The following awk script will take data in the form above and time-align it to whole-minute boundaries:

```
# Quant.awk -
# Quantizes to fixed minute boundaries
# J.A. Morle
# Input should be of form:
# 1997/12/17 23:43:32 882431012 dbmon BMA2.user_commits 15.30
# Output is of form:
# 23:43:00,882431012,15.06
#
{       now_min=substr($2,4,2);
        now_hr=substr($2,1,2);
        now_sec=substr($2,7,2);
        now_tstamp=$3;

        if (last_min!=0 && last_min!=now_min) {
            if (go==0) {
                now_value=(now_tstamp%60*$NF);
                nsec+=(now_tstamp%60);
                go=1;
            }
        }

        if (go==1) {
            if (now_min==last_min) {
                #Add weighting to value
                now_value+=(now_tstamp%60*$NF);
                nsec+=(now_tstamp%60)-(last_tstamp%60);
            } else {
                #check for "missing minute"
                if ( ((now_min=="00") ? 60 : now_min)-last_min != 1) {
                    l_hr=last_hr;
                    l_min=last_min;
                    l_tstamp=last_tstamp;
                    for(i=0;i<((now_min=="00") ? 60 : now_min)\
                        -last_min;i++) {
                        printf("%02d:%02d:00,%s,%0.2f\n",\
                            l_hr,l_min,\
                            l_tstamp,now_value/nsec);
                        if(++l_min>59) {
                            l_min=0;
                            if(++l_hr>23)
                                l_hr=0;
                        }
                    }
                }
            }
```

```
                #add partial piece
                if (nsec!=0 ) { # ie NOT the first sample set
                        nsec+=(now_tstamp-last_tstamp-(now_tstamp%60));
                        now_value+=((now_tstamp-last_tstamp-\
                            (now_tstamp%60))*$NF);
                        printf("%s:%s:00,%s,%0.2f\n",last_hr,last_min,\
                            last_tstamp,now_value/nsec);
                        now_value=(now_tstamp%60*$NF);
                        nsec=now_tstamp%60;
                }
        }

    } # last_tstamp!=0

    last_min=now_min;
    last_hr=now_hr;
    last_sec=now_sec;
    last_tstamp=now_tstamp;


}
```

The program takes all the samples, or portions of samples, that fall within the boundaries of the minute. A weighted average is then calculated for the minute, and the output timestamp is adjusted accordingly.

This results in data of the following form:

```
23:42:00,882430979,15.30
23:43:00,882431012,15.06
23:44:00,882431079,15.55
23:45:00,882431146,16.94
23:46:00,882431213,18.67
23:47:00,882431247,15.13
```

This data is now ready for the next step.

The next step varies depending on the amount of data analysis required. If one-off charting of a few choice statistics is all that is required, the next step is simply to load up the CSV (comma separated value) file into Excel and perform the charting.

If the requirement is in-depth analysis of hundreds of statistics, spanning multiple days and possibly multiple systems, the next step should be a little more preparation, in order to save a good deal of time later.

One of the best (and most enjoyable) ways to proceed in this case is to use Oracle and Open Data Base Connectivity (ODBC) to aid the process. I used this technique after a large benchmark and found it to be a most flexible method of rapidly comparing and cross-checking results from numerous tests from both benchmark sites.

The first step is to create a table in an Oracle database:

```
Name                                   Null?     Type
------------------------------------   --------  ----
STIME                                            DATE
SYSTIME                                          NUMBER(10)
VENDOR                                           VARCHAR2(10)
ID                                               VARCHAR2(20)
NAMESPACE                                        VARCHAR2(10)
STATNAME                                         VARCHAR2(80)
VALUE                                            NUMBER
```

This table stored the date and time, the UNIX date/time (seconds since epoch), the vendor name, the test ID, the namespace of the statistic (e.g., db, system), the statistic name (e.g., user_commits), and the actual value.

On top of this, four bitmap indexes were built—on VENDOR, ID, NAMESPACE, and STATNAME. No other indexes were required. The total number of data points in this particular analysis was just over 1 million.

Owing to the quantization effort prior to this, any statistic for a given timestamp could be directly compared with any other for that timestamp. This is a fundamental requirement for when we start using pivot tables in the Excel product, because any inconsistencies will result in "gaps" in the data, where the value suddenly crashes down to zero every few samples. This results in false spikes in the data owing to quantization errors.

Next, an ODBC/SQL*Net connection is defined between the database server and the PC running Excel. Once this is running, a pivot table can be created that drives from a query to the Oracle database. This is defined when you initially invoke the pivot table, specifying that you want to use an "external data source." You are then given the opportunity to define the query that will act as the data set for the pivot table. The screen shot in Figure 4.4 shows one of the master pivot tables used to flip quickly between different tests at the different vendor sites.

The pull-down-menu-type cells (B1:B2) change the parameters for the data selection from the database, and the query is reexecuted in order to define the new set of data to display on the pivot table.

In this particular example, the tabs on the bottom of the workbook point to predefined chart worksheets: when a test is recalled from the

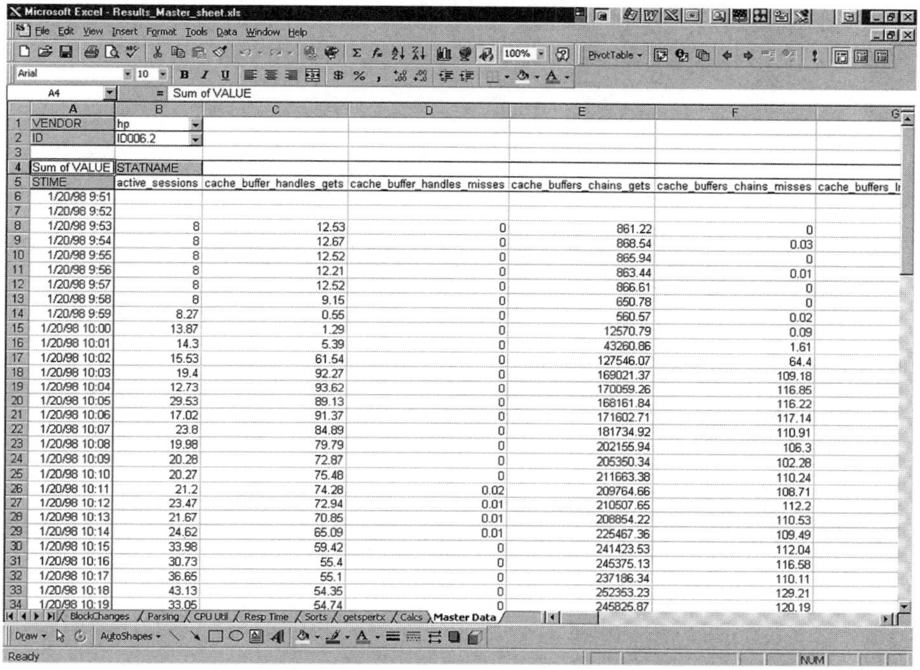

	A	B	C	D	E	F	G
1	VENDOR	hp					
2	ID	ID006.2					
3							
4	Sum of VALUE	STATNAME					
5	STIME	active_sessions	cache_buffer_handles_gets	cache_buffer_handles_misses	cache_buffers_chains_gets	cache_buffers_chains_misses	cache_buffers_l
6	1/20/98 9:51						
7	1/20/98 9:52						
8	1/20/98 9:53	8	12.53	0	861.22	0	
9	1/20/98 9:54	8	12.67	0	868.54	0.03	
10	1/20/98 9:55	8	12.52	0	865.94	0	
11	1/20/98 9:56	8	12.21	0	863.44	0.01	
12	1/20/98 9:57	8	12.52	0	866.61	0	
13	1/20/98 9:58	8	9.15	0	650.78	0	
14	1/20/98 9:59	8.27	0.55	0	560.57	0.02	
15	1/20/98 10:00	13.87	1.29	0	12570.79	0.09	
16	1/20/98 10:01	14.3	5.39	0	43260.86	1.61	
17	1/20/98 10:02	15.53	61.54	0	127546.07	64.4	
18	1/20/98 10:03	19.4	92.27	0	169021.37	109.18	
19	1/20/98 10:04	12.73	93.62	0	170059.26	116.85	
20	1/20/98 10:05	29.53	89.13	0	168161.84	116.22	
21	1/20/98 10:06	17.02	91.37	0	171602.71	117.14	
22	1/20/98 10:07	23.8	84.89	0	181734.92	110.91	
23	1/20/98 10:08	19.98	79.79	0	202155.94	106.3	
24	1/20/98 10:09	20.28	72.87	0	205350.34	102.28	
25	1/20/98 10:10	20.27	75.48	0	211663.38	110.24	
26	1/20/98 10:11	21.2	74.28	0.02	209764.66	108.71	
27	1/20/98 10:12	23.47	72.94	0.01	210507.65	112.2	
28	1/20/98 10:13	21.67	70.85	0.01	208854.22	110.53	
29	1/20/98 10:14	24.62	65.09	0.01	225467.36	109.49	
30	1/20/98 10:15	33.98	59.42	0	241423.53	112.04	
31	1/20/98 10:16	30.73	55.4	0	245375.13	116.58	
32	1/20/98 10:17	36.65	55.1	0	237186.34	110.11	
33	1/20/98 10:18	43.13	54.35	0	252353.23	129.21	
34	1/20/98 10:19	33.05	54.74	0	245825.87	120.19	

Figure 4.4 Using pivot tables with ODBC connections

database, all of the required charts are already drawn and finished on the other sheets in the workbook, by virtue of the fact that they contain static references back to the data in the pivot table.

4.9 Chapter Summary

Having the right tools is an essential part of building a large system. Without the data provided by such tools, it is very difficult to make scientific decisions and hypotheses about the system—you are quite literally in the dark.

Hopefully, some of the building blocks presented in this chapter will be of use in building some of the fundamental tools required, in addition to allowing rapid development of any subsequent tool requirements (using `dbaman`).

## PART III

How Oracle Works

Chapter 5

Physical Oracle

5.1 Introduction

Oracle can be viewed as having two different groups of aspects that work very closely together and are difficult to separate cleanly for explanation. These two groups of aspects are the physical aspects, such as files and blocks, and the operational aspects, such as the memory architecture and the Oracle kernel.

This chapter covers the physical aspects of Oracle. It is not intended to replace, or to be a subset or superset of, the *Oracle Server Concepts Guide*. Instead, it is a look at some of the more important aspects of Oracle operation—aspects that are most important in building a very large system using Oracle. None of the various Oracle cache or process architectures are covered in this chapter; these features are covered in the next chapter.

5.2 Overview

What is Oracle? This chapter details the common understanding of what Oracle is—a front end to a load of data on disk. I frequently like to think of Oracle in terms of the other aspect—a complex operating system that also stores a bunch of data—and this is the aspect presented in the next chapter. Anyway, in order to cover the physical structure, we will briefly discuss the higher level and then drill down to some finer detail throughout the chapter.

The Oracle database consists of several different types of files that support its operation (as shown in Figure 5.1):

- Control files
- Initialization files
- Datafiles
- Logfiles

5.3   Control Files

The control files within Oracle store information about the physical database. Within each control file is the following information:

- Datafile information (names, locations, status, etc.)
- Operating information (database name, number of threads, number of datafiles, etc.)

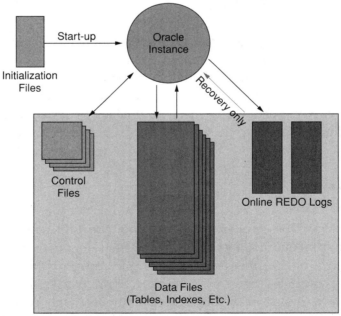

Figure 5.1   The physical Oracle

- Redo log thread information
- Redo log information
- Log history
- Backup information (if using Oracle Recovery Manager)

Although these files are usually quite small (typically less than 3MB if not using Recovery Manager), their importance should not be overlooked. Therefore, it is common practice to have two or more control files for each database, placed on different disk drives and controllers to increase availability in the event of a failure. Oracle automatically mirrors (i.e., keeps two or more copies in sync with each other) the control files once they have been configured into the system.

In previous releases of Oracle, the loss or corruption of a control file while in operation would result in a database crash. This appears to have been fixed in Oracle8, where certain failures can be sustained provided that at least one of the control files is still available. If the control file that is lost is also the primary control file (i.e., the first-named control file), certain operations requiring the control file (such as queries on v$datafile) will fail, but the instance will remain in operation.

5.3.1 Datafile Information

Within the control file, there is a directory of all datafiles in the database. The control file stores

- Full pathname
- Size of file in Oracle blocks
- Oracle block size
- File status
- "Stop" SCN (system change number)

The first three of these items are self-explanatory. The file status can be set to one of many values depending on whether the file is online, offline, needing recovery, and so on. The "stop" SCN is the change number up to which media recovery will continue for that file. This is set to infinity when the file is online but to the current change number when the tablespace it belongs to is taken offline or made READ ONLY. This allows the media recovery operation to recover the tablespace only to the point in time at which it was taken offline or made READ ONLY.

5.3.2   Operating Information

This portion of the control file includes how many redo threads are currently open, how many datafiles there are, and how many logfiles there are. In addition, the maximum numbers of datafiles, logfiles, and instances specified at database creation time, and whether or not the database is currently running in ARCHIVELOG mode, are recorded.

5.3.3   Redo Log Information

This part contains information about each of the redo groups—which thread it belongs to, whether the thread is public or private, and which log group is the currently active one. It also contains more detailed information about the individual logfiles, including the full pathname, the size, the low and high SCN numbers for that log, the log sequence number, and thread allocation information.

5.3.4   Log History

This is the source of the V$LOG_HISTORY view. It contains historical information about logs that have been archived, including low and high SCN numbers and timestamp. The maximum number of entries for historical information is controlled by the MAXLOGHISTORY section of the CREATE DATABASE command.

5.3.5   Backup Information

If the database backup is performed using Oracle Recovery Manager, the control file is also used to store information about backups and file copies that have taken place. This information is used on recovery of the datafiles if the Recovery Catalog is not available.

5.4   The init.ora File

I make no apology for this section of the book, because it is not going to be a verbatim regurgitation of the *Server Reference Guide* as found in some "tuning" books. The purpose of this section is to give real advice on putting together a safe, usable initialization file to be applied to a large-scale database system. However, explanations of some of the more important init.ora parameters are included as an appendix, because explanations are more meaningful once the concepts are understood properly.

5.4.1   Rules for init.ora Creation

On the face of it, the init.ora looks to be a fairly straightforward entity—that is, it simply contains multiple parameter=value declarations. This is almost true, and for the most part, simplistic declarations are all you need to worry about. However, there are some lesser-known facts about the way Oracle parses the init.ora that you should understand, because your life will be a good deal simpler and less confusing if you do.

Value Overrides

First of all, beware of inadvertently assigning a value to a parameter twice, and thus overriding the original value. This should not happen if you follow strict layout procedures as detailed in "Layout Recommendations" but if it does it can cost you many lost hours chasing system performance problems. A good example of this would be the setting of our old friend db_block_buffers. If you are the proud owner of a file that looks like this

```
    .
    .
db_block_buffers= 10000
#changed by JM
#db_block_buffers= 100000  ◀———————
    .
    .
```

then you are asking for trouble. Using this example, it would be very easy for the file to be changed accidentally (say, during maintenance) to

```
    .
    .
db_block_buffers= 10000
#changed by JM
db_block_buffers= 100000
    .
    .
```

Once the maintenance was completed and the database started up, every-thing would probably look good. It is likely that you wouldn't even notice the extra zero on the size of the database buffers section of the SGA on instance start-up.

The rest of this story is painfully obvious, involving "missing" mem-ory on the database server, poor performance, and a very well hidden problem in that the initial setting all looks OK. In general, you should avoid retaining multiple settings for the same parameter, except under very specific circumstances, as detailed in the next section.

Value Concatenation

There are some `init.ora` parameters that can be legitimately specified sev-eral times in the file without overrides occurring. A good example of this is the `event` specification, used to set system-wide database events (nor-mally for debugging purposes). If there is more than one event to set in the `init.ora` file, this can be achieved without overriding the previous one by keeping all the event settings bunched together in the file. This means that no other parameters can be set in between, as shown below:

```
# Correct way to specify events

event = "1547 trace name errorstack"
event = "4031 trace name errorstack level 1"



.
.


#Incorrect way to specify events

event = "1547 trace name errorstack"
processes = 3500
event = "4031 trace name errorstack level 1"
```

In the first example, both of the events are successfully set for the instance. However, in the second example we would end up with the 4031 event being the only one set, because Oracle has legitimately overridden the 1547 event.

This rule also applies to all other multiple-value parameters, such as `rollback_segments` and `control_files`.

init.ora *File Sizes/Limits*

When working on init.ora files, it is important to be wary of the limits Oracle puts on init.ora files. There are limitations on both the size of any individual file and the length of the string assigned to a parameter.

These limitations have been lifted in Oracle8 to the extent that they are unlikely to become a problem, even with enormous numbers of comments. However, caution should be observed on the remaining Oracle7 databases in your company.

The limits in Oracle7 are port-specific, but the values given in Table 5.1 are very typical for Oracle 7.3 on a UNIX platform

Layout Recommendations

When implementing a large system, it is important to maintain a highly readable init.ora file and to incorporate strict change controls. This helps to prevent costly mistakes when making changes in the database configuration parameters.

The first rule to follow when putting together an init.ora is to create and maintain the file in sections. This makes it easier to find specific components of the file when editing it and creates some structure in the file.

In the *Oracle Reference Guide*, it is recommended that all parameters be grouped together alphabetically; I don't like this idea, because it puts unrelated parameters adjacent to each other, but the choice of grouping should ultimately be something that makes sense to all the people who could edit the file.

Each of the recommended groupings will be presented individually.

Change Control Header.   The first section of an init.ora file should be a change control header. This can also be formalized by the use of a source

Table 5.1   Parsing Limits for init.ora File

Name of Limit	Size of Limit
Size of a file (init.ora, or ifile)	8,192 bytes
Size of a string assigned to a parameter	512 bytes

code management system such as rcs or sccs, but such a system should be used in *addition* to the inclusion of a header at the top of the actual file. The header should include the following information:

- Name of system
- Name of file
- Owner of file
- Purpose of file
- Change history

This is a very formal approach to file headers but makes all aspects of the file absolutely clear. Don't forget, DBAs come and go, and you don't want to have to explain every minute detail of the system to each new recruit. Here's an example of a header for an init.ora file:

```
######################################################
# $Id: initRMS1.ora,v 1.44 97/02/14 19:18:34 foobar Exp $
######################################################
# Copyright (c) 1997 xyz Limited
######################################################
# System        : Reservations Management System
# File          : initRMS1.ora
# Owner         : Production Database Administration
# Purpose       : Instance RMS1 initialisation file #
#
# Change History
# --------------
#
# Who           Date           Change
#============   =========      ============
# J.A.Morle     01-Jan-94      Initial Creation
#
# J.A.Morle     08-Jan-94      Increased
#                              shared_pool_size->200MB
#                              to alleviate ORA-04031
#
# A.Einstein    01-APR-95      Added event 1547
#
######################################################
# ...etc...
```

It is important to keep the change descriptions meaningful, because over the life of a large system, it is likely that the reasons for change will be forgotten.

Common, Database-Wide, and Parallel Server Parameters

```
#######################
# Instance/Thread Definition
#######################
thread          = 1
instance_number = 1
#######################
# Common Parameters
#######################
ifile           = /opt/oracle/RMS/initshared.ora
```

This section includes all Parallel Server settings, if used. These may appear to be strange things to include as the first settings, but there is a reason for this, which will become clear when the contents of the initshared.ora file are shown. This file is located on a shared-disk volume, in order to be accessible by all nodes in the OPS cluster. It is therefore readable by all instances, which will all specify the ifile instruction in the main init.ora for that instance.

```
#######################################################
# $Id: initshared.txt,v 1.44 97/02/14 19:18:34 foobar Exp $
#######################################################
# Copyright (c) 1997 xyz Limited
#######################################################
# System      : Reservations Management System
# File        : initshared.ora
# Owner       : Production Database Administration
# Purpose     : Instance independent (Common)
#               initialisation parameters
#
# Change History
# --------------
#
# Who          Date           Change
#===========   =========      ============
# J.A.Morle    01-Jan-94      Initial Creation
#######################################################

db_name       = PRDRMS
control_files = ( /opt/oracle/RMS/ctrl1.dbf,
                  /opt/oracle/RMS/ctrl2.dbf,
                  /opt/oracle/RMS/ctrl3.dbf )
db_files      = 256
dml_locks     = 0
ccf_io_size   = 4194304
optimizer_mode = RULE
..contd...
```

This is the first part of the ifile, used for setting parameters that are common to all instances but are not Parallel Server parameters themselves. Notice the change control header at the top of the file, describing the usage of the file.

If Parallel Server were *not* in operation on this system, this part of the file would be included (inlined) as part of the main `init.ora` file, because the logic is no longer there to maintain a separate file. This is the reason for including this section first in the breakdown—it is common practice among DBAs to include the `db_name`, `control_files`, and so on at the top of the main `init.ora` file when running a single-instance database.

The eagle-eyed will have spotted the `dml_locks` parameter and will be wondering why it declared as a common parameter between instances—surely there can be different settings on each instance, can't there? Yes, and no. There can be different settings *unless* any instance has it set to zero, which is why it must be a common setting. More information as to why one would set it to zero can be found in the Parallel Server section of this book.

```
.....contd..
########################
# Parallel Server
########################
gc_lck_procs = 6
gc_freelist_groups = 100
gc_rollback_segments= 164
gc_rollback_locks = 40
gc_save_rollback_locks = 64
gc_segments = 1800
gc_db_locks = 29000
gc_files_to_locks ="1,34=4000EACH"
gc_files_to_locks = "7-8,18-19,21,30-31=1000EACH"
```

This is the final part of the `initshared.ora` file, containing all the settings specific to Parallel Server operation for this database. The `gc_files_to_locks` parameter is another good example of using multiple lines to build up a complex parameter value, such as demonstrated with the `event` specification in the next section.

Event Specification

Returning to the main `init.ora` file, we maintain a separate section for the event specifications:

```
#######################
# Events
#######################
#
#   1547 - To create a trace file when a tablespace runs
#          out of space.
#   4031 - To dump the cause of a ORA-600 [4031]
#          " out of shared memory when trying to allocate %s bytes"
event                       = "1547 trace name errorstack"
event                       = "4031 trace name errorstack"
```

Again, note that both of the event specifications are on contiguous lines, with no other parameters between them.

Other Groupings

Rather than waste paper by listing the remainder of the example init.ora file, the list in Table 5.2 should prove useful. It suggests categories for each of an example set of parameters.

Table 5.2   Parameter Grouping Suggestions

Section Heading	Example Parameters
High water marks	processes, sessions, transactions
Platform and version specifics	compatible, use_asyncio, _lock_sga, async_write, use_listio
Rollback information	rollback_segments, transactions_per_rollback_segment
Cache parameters	db_block_buffers, sequence_cache_entries, shared_pool_size
Process specific	sort_area_size, sort_area_retained_size, session_cached_cursors
Logging	background_dump_dest, user_dump_dest, max_dump_file_size
Archive and REDO logs	log_buffer_size, log_archive_dest, log_buffer, log_simultaneous_copies, log_checkpoint_interval
Miscellaneous	spin_count, use_readv

Further Tips

Although in Section 5.4.1 it is advised that value overrides should be avoided, there is one special case in which it actually can be safer to have them than not to have them. That special case is when a special maintenance `ifile` is created and referenced at the bottom of the main `init.ora` file. The contents of the file could be

```
sort_area_size    = 10485760
dml_locks         = 1000
db_block_buffers  = 100000
```

and the tail end of the main `init.ora` file could look like this:

```
    .
    .
    .
###############
# Maintenance Parameter specification
###############
#ifile     = maint.ora
```

When maintenance parameters are set in this way, they are very easy to take in and out in order to perform maintenance—only a single comment character needs to be toggled in front of the `ifile` specification.

Setting Up a Maintenance Instance

Another excellent way to toggle in and out of maintenance mode is to set up an alternative instance. This method is very flexible and completely removes any risk of leaving parameters unsuitably set when you enter production mode once more. The method for doing this is simple.

First, create another `init.ora` file with a name totally different from that used for the production `init.ora` file—for example, `initMNT.ora` file to indicate the MaiNTenance mode of the database. Within this file, use the same `db_name` and `control_file` parameters as in the production `init.ora` file. This will allow the newly created instance definition to access the production database. Next, set up all of the required maintenance parameters in the `initMNT.ora`, such as `db_block_buffers` and `sort_area_%`. If space is available, rollback segments can permanently exist in the database. These can be included in the `initMNT.ora` in order to bring them online for use during maintenance.

The maintenance instance is now ready for use. In order to use the maintenance instance, the following procedure should be followed.

1. Shutdown the production instance cleanly.

2. Ensure that all processes related to the production instance are cleaned up. This can take a few seconds to complete even after the instance has closed cleanly. If some of the processes do not die off naturally, manually kill off the remaining processes.

3. Ensure that the shared memory segment used to accommodate the SGA has been removed. If it has not, remove it manually.

4. Reset ORACLE_SID to point to your new instance definition (i.e., ORACLE_SID=MNT).

5. Start Oracle, and perform maintenance tasks.

6. When complete, shut down the instance and switch back to the production instance. It is vital to take good care that all traces of the maintenance instance have been cleaned up, in the same way as the production instance was cleaned up in step 2.

Using this technique, a totally different environment can be safely and easily set up for database maintenance. It is also worth noting, from a safety standpoint, that the production instance cannot be started while the maintenance instance has the database mounted, and vice versa, because Oracle takes out an exclusive lock on the datafiles.

5.5   Data Storage

5.5.1   Overview: The Physical Picture

It is important to have a full understanding of tablespaces (see Figure 5.2), segments, objects, extents, and so on. If you do not have a comprehensive understanding of these concepts, it is important that you read the *Oracle Server Concepts Guide*. This section deals exclusively with the different types of Oracle blocks, where they are found, and what they are used for.

5.5.2   Blocks: An Introduction

Every datafile[1] is comprised of blocks, as illustrated in Figure 5.3. The size of the block is defined in the init.ora (db_block_size) when the database is created and cannot be changed thereafter. All I/O operations within

---

1. A "datafile" is a file containing information from a tablespace. Logfiles and controlfiles are not considered datafiles in the Oracle naming convention.

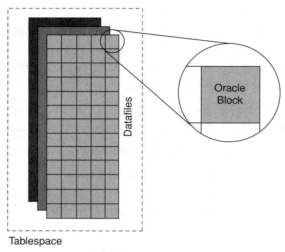

Figure 5.2 Oracle physical storage hierarchy

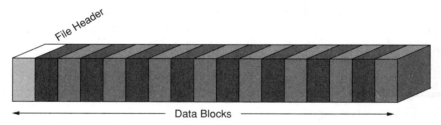

Figure 5.3 Oracle datafile

Oracle are performed in some multiple of the block size. Blocks are used in order to simplify the I/O, storage, and caching algorithms used within Oracle.

The block size chosen for any particular implementation affects the fundamental operation of the database and therefore needs to be set to an optimal value at database creation. This is actually not as daunting as it sounds, because there is generally one range of sizes that are optimal for transaction-based systems and another for read-intensive systems such as data warehousing. The setting of the block size is a matter of balancing the read and caching advantages of a large block against the caching advantages of a small block when *write* activity is high. In this way, the determination of the correct block size is very much dependent on the operation of the database and will be covered later in this book.

Several different block types are used in Oracle.

First, there is a *data block*. The term "data block" is used to describe a block containing table data, index data, clustered data, and so on. Basically, it is a block that contains data.

Next, there are blocks that are associated with internal Oracle operation, such as header blocks and freelist group blocks. These blocks do not contain any user data but contain important structures that the implementor should be aware of when building a large system.

Data Blocks

The structure of a data block (see Figure 5.4) is the same whether the block belongs to a table or to an index.

Block Header.   Each block contains a block header. This portion contains the block's identity in terms of

- Address of block
- Type of block (index, table, rollback, etc.)
- Interested Transaction List (ITL)

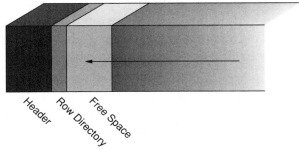

Figure 5.4   Oracle data block format

Although this piece is of variable size, it remains on the order of 100 bytes. This should be considered when assessing the efficiency of using small Oracle blocks: A 2,048-byte block would lose 5 percent in overhead, whereas a 4,096-byte block would lose only 2.5 percent.

An important part of the block header from a read consistency standpoint is the ITL portion. This is a variable list of "interested transactions" for that block, and the number of entries is determined by the settings of INITRANS and MAXTRANS. For each of these entries, the undo (rollback) block address, the transaction ID, and the system change number are recorded. This information is used by Oracle to facilitate the read consistency model, for which a small explanation is necessary.

When a query starts, the SCN is recorded in order to determine the start time of the query. This SCN is then compared against the SCN of the actual block when it is read in order to determine whether the version of the block is consistent with the query start time. If the SCN is greater than the expected SCN, a new version of the block (called a constant read [CR] block) is created in the buffer cache out of the applicable undo entries to get the prior version of the block. These undo entries are determined by reading the ITL, and so the ITL is the entry point for constructing the CR block. Note: The CR block is a cache entity only—it is *never* written to disk.

Once the relevant undo records have been applied, the SCN of the block is checked once again. If the SCN is still greater than the required SCN, the ITLs are reviewed again—because the entire block had undo applied to it, including the block header, the ITL entries in the new CR block also reflect the state of the block prior to the last change. Therefore, this process can be continued until the desired version of the block is created, or the required undo records are no longer available, due to forced reuse. At this point, the query session receives a "snapshot too old" message, because the read-consistent version of the block can not be constructed.

Row Directory. The row directory is the secret of how Oracle finds a specific row within the block. It is what its name suggests: a directory of the rows contained in the block. It contains the offset in the block for each row it contains. Therefore, the block does not need to be scanned beyond the row directory before the index to the row data required is found.

Take, for example, a single-row lookup for which Oracle has already determined the rowid of the required row from the index on the table. Part of the rowid is the *row number within the actual block*, and therefore Oracle can read the row directory out of the block header and proceed directly to the actual row data.

It is worth noting that the row directory is not subject to any shrinking when rows are deleted. The space allocated for the row directory is never returned to the block but is reused on subsequent inserts. This does not present a problem in practice, because the rows that are subsequently inserted are typically of the same size as the deleted rows, therefore yielding the same number of rows per block. Anyway, we're not talking about a large amount of space for the row directory, unless you have tables with a *very* small row size.

Free Space. Free space is the currently unoccupied portion of the block that is used when new rows are inserted or when existing rows are extended.

Row Data. At last! This is where the actual data is stored for the block. The row data (or index data) is stored in `length:value` pairs for each column. That is, if a column for a particular row contains the value "YES," this is recorded as 3:'YES'. When a NULL column is stored, it is stored as a length zero, with no data associated with it. If these NULL columns all occur at the tail end of the column list, nothing is stored at all, because the start of the next row implies that the row had trailing NULL columns.

It is worth bearing in mind that when ordering the columns in a table it makes sense to put all the NULLable columns at the tail end of the column list in order to reduce storage and the amount of data Oracle has to read to determine that there are NULL columns.

Data Block Dump. The following block dump of a table block will help to demonstrate some of these attributes:

```
buffer tsn: 1 rdba: 0x00805003 (2/20483)
scn:0x0000.00054c1c seq:0x02 flg:0x00 tail:0x4c1c0602
     frmt:0x02 chkval:0x0000 type:0x06=trans data

Block header dump:  0x00805003
 Object id on Block? Y
 seg/obj: 0xaf7  csc: 0x00.54c19  itc: 1  flg: -  typ: 1 - DATA
     fsl: 0  fnx: 0x0 ver: 0x01

 Itl        Xid                 Uba         Flag Lck        Scn/Fsc
 0x01   xid:  0x0003.02d.0000018e  uba: 0x00000000.00001.00  ----    0  fsc 0x000
 0.00000000

data_block_dump
===============
tsiz: 0xfb8
hsiz: 0x8c
pbl: 0x4010c844
bdba: 0x00805003
flag=-----------
ntab=1
nrow=61
frre=-1
fsbo=0x8c
fseo=0x233
avsp=0x1a7
tosp=0x1a7
0xe:pti[0]        nrow=61 offs=0
0x12:pri[0]       offs=0xf81
0x14:pri[1]       offs=0xf49
0x16:pri[2]       offs=0xf10
0x18:pri[3]       offs=0xed7
0x1a:pri[4]       offs=0xe9e
0x1c:pri[5]       offs=0xe66
0x1e:pri[6]       offs=0xe2d
0x20:pri[7]       offs=0xdf4
0x22:pri[8]       offs=0xdbb
0x24:pri[9]       offs=0xd82
0x26:pri[10]      offs=0xd4a
0x28:pri[11]      offs=0xd11
0x2a:pri[12]      offs=0xcd8
..... contd. ....
0x8a:pri[60]      offs=0x233
block_row_dump:
tab 0, row 0, @0xf81
tl: 55 fb: --H-FL-- lb: 0x0 cc: 7
col  0: [ 7]   77 c6 01 0f 14 10 01
col  1: [ 5]   c5 09 55 5d 06
col  2: [ 2]   68 70
col  3: [ 7]   49 44 30 30 35 2e 31
col  4: [ 4]   42 4d 41 32
col  5: [17]   43 52 5f 62 6c 6f 63 6b 73 5f 63 72 65 61 74 65 64
col  6: [ 3]   c1 04 33
tab 0, row 1, @0xf49
tl: 56 fb: --H-FL-- lb: 0x0 cc: 7
col  0: [ 7]   77 c6 01 0f 14 11 01
col  1: [ 6]   c5 09 55 5d 06 3d
col  2: [ 2]   68 70
col  3: [ 7]   49 44 30 30 35 2e 31
col  4: [ 4]   42 4d 41 32
col  5: [17]   43 52 5f 62 6c 6f 63 6b 73 5f 63 72 65 61 74 65 64
col  6: [ 3]   c1 1f 28
.... etc ....
end_of_block_dump
```

Starting at the top, we have the *rdba*, or *relative data block address*, of the block. The rdba is an internal rowid format for every block and is used by Oracle for every operation that addresses a specific block.

The SCN for the block is listed next, as described in "File Headers" below. The "tail" field is the last 2 bytes of the SCN, combined with the "type" and the "seq" for the block. This value is the mechanism used by Oracle to determine whether the entire block is consistent with itself after a recovery operation. The "tail" value is physically stored at the tail end of the block and should always match the SCN, seq, and type stored at the head of the block. If not, recovery needs to be performed on this block to bring the entire block into sync with itself.

Next, we have the block header information. The "Object id on Block?" piece is a throwback to version 6—it should always be "Y" now, indicating that the "seg/obj" value below it is the actual object number stored in SYS.OBJ$ (main constituent of the DBA_OBJECTS view).

The "csc" is the cleanout system change, or a short extract of the SCN used to show when block cleanout was last performed on this block. Block cleanout is covered in Section 5.5.3.

The "itc" value is simply a count of the ITLs on the block, which are listed farther down. The "flg" is either "-" or "O', where "-" means that the block is not on the freelist (i.e., more than PCTUSED used in the block), and "O" means that the block is on the freelist. The remaining fields denote which ITL's freelist the block appears on (if any).

Next are the actual ITLs themselves, containing the information described at the beginning of this section, required in order to construct CR blocks out of committed or uncommitted transactions that have modified the block. This represents the end of the transactional portion of the block header.

Then comes some information about the space usage in the block and the row directory, used to locate specific row offsets within the block. Included in the general information are the following:

- tsiz is the actual usable space in the block on which PCTUSED and PCTFREE are calculated.

- ntab is the number of tables (if this is a cluster).

- nrow is the number of actual rows in the block.

- fseo is the start of row data above header overhead.

The section beginning "0xe" is the start of the row directory, which shows once again that there are 61 rows in this block. This is immediately followed by the row directory entries, which are in the following format:

<directory_address>:pri[rownum-1] offs=<offset_address_into block>

One interesting thing to note here is that the rows are inserted into the block starting at the end of the block. In other words, the row data grows *toward* the row header, not away from it. This is reflected in Figure 5.4, where the free space is shown as being adjacent to the row directory.

The last thing in the block dump is the actual data, formatted as described under "Row Data" above. Above each row is a header showing the row number in the block and a summary of the content:

- t1 is the total number (in bytes) of the row plus the header.
- fb is a set of flags where, in this example, we have a "H"ead of a row, and we have the "F"irst piece and "L"ast piece of the row: this row is not chained.
- cc is the column count for this row.

The actual data follows, one line per column. In this dump, the first two columns are SYSDATE and NUMBER(10), respectively, stored in Oracle internal format. The following four columns are VARCHAR2 columns, and their contents can be viewed by turning the hexadecimal values into ASCII characters.

Header Blocks

There are several different types of header blocks.[2] Each of these types of header blocks has a very different purpose and will be covered in turn.

File Headers.   The first block of a datafile contains the file header. Stored in this block is information such as the file number, the database that it belongs to, and the last change number for that file. The overhead of this

---

2. Header blocks should not be confused with block headers (see "Block Header" above).

block is important to remember when creating datafiles within Oracle using raw disk devices.

When sizing the raw disk partitions, it is important to remember to add the overhead of the file header block. It is common to find raw disk based Oracle databases with the file size within Oracle defined as 99M, 199M, 499M, and so on. This is because the raw disk partitions have been sized to exactly 100M, 200M, 500M, and so on, and no provision has been made for the file header.

In this situation, Oracle will fail to create a datafile of size 100M, because a 100M+1 block is required. It is very good practice to slice the disk in order to allow for the additional Oracle block. This makes the space management tasks for the database far easier because more *human numbers* are used in calculating free/used space.

The change number information is used by Oracle to determine the version number of the file in order to perform recovery on the file if necessary. During a hot backup,[3] this change number is frozen, and a hot backup "fuzzy bit" is also set in the file header to indicate that the file is in the process of being backed up *hot*. The change number is frozen in order to determine where recovery should *start*.

In Figure 5.5, the file (or rather the tablespace containing the file) is put into hot backup mode using the ALTER TABLESPACE .... BEGIN BACKUP syntax. At this point in time, the system change number (SCN) is 23, and all the blocks in the file are guaranteed to be at the same version number as a result of the implied checkpoint when the file is put into backup mode.

During the backup, changes *continue to be applied* to the datafile, contrary to many beliefs. Therefore, the image that is recorded on tape will look a lot like the middle picture; many of the blocks have the original change number (i.e., have not changed), but a great deal of them have changed during the actual saving of the file to tape.

In fact, two of the blocks are denoted as having two version numbers. This is known as a "fractured block" and is the result of having an external reader operating on the file. When the UNIX kernel issues a read from the file (in 512-byte increments), the block is not guaranteed to remain the

---

3. Not using Oracle Recovery Manager.

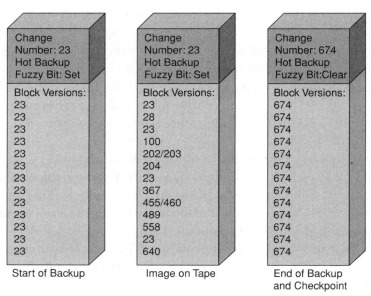

| Start of Backup | Image on Tape | End of Backup and Checkpoint |

Figure 5.5 Hot backup recovery principle

same until it has read the entire block, because this could entail many physical read operations. Oracle could be in the process of writing this particular block at the same time, resulting in the tail end of the block having a newer version than the older header portion of the block shows. The physical mechanism for this will be shown in "Segment Headers" below.

This is the key difference between this standard hot backup approach and the Oracle Recovery Manager approach. The Recovery Manager uses the Oracle buffer cache to copy the blocks out of the file onto tape, therefore guaranteeing that a consistent, nonfractured copy of each block is made on tape.

For the standard hot backup approach, Oracle has to make a change in the way it writes redo information to the redo log for the duration of the backup. The first time Oracle writes a particular block to the redo log, it records a before-image of the entire block in addition to the changes to the block. Although the full block is recorded only on the *first* change to that block during backup mode, this can result in a significant increase in the amount of redo information recorded during the backup, especially if batch processing is running at the same time.

The end of the backup shows all the blocks having the same version number, because a checkpoint is performed following the backup. This checkpoint is recorded in the redo log and marks the minimum recovery point for this backup.

When this file is recovered onto disk, it will look like the middle picture once again. However, Oracle is aware that this file was copied out in backup mode (due to the fuzzy bit being set) and starts to apply redo information to the file beginning with the SCN stored in the file header. This process ensures that all blocks in the file are updated to consistent versions and that all fractured blocks are repaired accordingly.

Segment Headers.   The segment header is an important header for us to understand when building databases for maximum scalability. Contained in the segment header are

- Segment identification information, such as object number
- Extent information, such as a map of extents allocated (start address, size), the high-water mark of used extents (used for ALTER TABLE xxxx DEALLOCATE UNUSED)
- Freelist information
- Segment-specific information (such as the transaction table in a rollback segment)

Freelist information is stored in the segment header of each segment. What is a freelist? It's exactly what its name suggests: a list of free things. In the case of a segment freelist, it is a list of the free space in the segment, as determined by the PCTUSED setting for the segment. If a segment had data stored as shown in Figure 5.6, the freelist would contain entries for the last two blocks only, because both of the blocks have greater than PCTUSED of the block free.

A segment header can contain several freelists, each of which is protected (locked) individually during use. This allows the number of concurrent inserts in the table to be increased, because multiple freelists are available.

In the case of Oracle Parallel Server, this does not mean multiple inserts from different instances, because the buffer for the segment header cannot be concurrently held in exclusive mode on multiple nodes. For Parallel Server installations, the concept of *freelist groups* is used to provide this facility, which assigns additional blocks for freelists. This gives each instance preferential access to that block, thereby allowing concurrent access by multiple nodes.

Segment Header Block Dump.   A block dump of a table segment header looks like this:

```
buffer tsn: 1 rdba: 0x00805002 (2/20482)
scn:0x0000.00054c5d seq:0x0a flg:0x00 tail:0x4c5d100a
      frmt:0x02 chkval:0x0000 type:0x10=DATA SEGMENT HEADER - UNLIMITED

  Extent Control Header
  -----------------------------------------------------------------
  Extent Header:: spare1: 0       space2: 0      #extents: 14     #blocks: 2139
                  last map  0x00000000  #maps: 0      offset: 2080
     Highwater::  0x00805684  ext#: 13     blk#: 236    ext size: 710
  #blocks in seg. hdr's freelists: 28
  #blocks below: 1665
  mapblk  0x00000000  offset: 13
                  Unlocked
    Map Header:: next  0x00000000  #extents: 14   obj#: 2807   flag: 0x40000000
  Extent Map
  -----------------------------------------------------------------
   0x00805003  length: 4
   0x00805007  length: 5
   0x0080500c  length: 10
   0x00805016  length: 15
   0x00805025  length: 20
   0x00805039  length: 30
   0x00805057  length: 45
   0x00805084  length: 65
   0x008050c5  length: 95
   0x00805124  length: 140
   0x008051b0  length: 210
   0x00805282  length: 315
   0x008053bd  length: 475
   0x00805598  length: 710

   nfl = 1, nfb = 1 typ = 1 nxf = 1
   SEG LST:: flg: UNUSED lhd: 0x00000000 ltl: 0x00000000
   XCT LST:: flg: USED   lhd: 0x00805652 ltl: 0x00805062 xid: 0x0001.028.00000193
```

The initial portion is identical to the dump of the table data block above. After that comes the extent information for the block. Here we see that this segment has 14 extents and 2,139 blocks, and the high-water

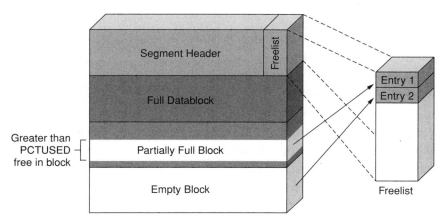

Freelist

Entry 1
Entry 2

Freelist

Segment Header

Full Datablock

Greater than
PCTUSED
free in block

Partially Full Block

Empty Block

Figure 5.6 "Free" definition in Oracle freelist management

mark (i.e., any blocks above this point have never been used to store data) is at 0x00805684. This is 236 blocks into the 13th extent, which has 710 blocks allocated to it. We can see that there are 28 blocks reported in the segment's freelist(s).

It's worth noting that the high-water mark is not the same as the freelist. When Oracle goes to allocate space for a new row, it will use one or the other of these pieces of information to find space for it according to the following algorithm:

- If space is available in the segment freelist (also called the process freelist), it will be allocated from there. Each process is restricted to one segment freelist that it can search, allocated by the algorithm illustrated in Figure 5.7.

- If not, the process will search the "master freelist" for the space. The master is simply one of the segment freelists that is nominated as the master. If space is found in this list, it is allocated to the process.

- If no space is found there, the "transaction freelists" are searched. These are freelists that are created when a process gives space back to the segment during a transaction. There can be many of these freelists per segment, and they can be searched by any process. If space is found, it is allocated to the process.

- If space is not found in any of the above freelists, the high-water mark must be increased. When it is increased, all space gained from the increase is allocated to the segment freelist. This is done to allow subsequent inserts to be satisfied by the first freelist search in this sequence.

- If the high-water mark is already at the top of the final extent, a new extent must be allocated.

The respective freelists can be seen at the tail end of this block dump, showing (nfl=1, nfb=1) that we have one freelist per freelist block (a.k.a freelist group) and one freelist block. We have a currently unused segment freelist and a used transaction freelist, which stores the 28 blocks that are in the segment header's freelists.

In the extent map for the segment, we see that all the extents are five blocks in size *except* the first one—because the first extent stores the segment header, and if additional freelist groups were assigned to the segment (at creation time), the usable size of the initial extent would be reduced accordingly.

When multiple freelists and freelist groups are created in a segment header, they are assigned to processes using a simple modulo hash. The freelist group used is determined by *<thread#>/<number of freelist groups>*, and the freelist within the freelist group is determined by *<process id>/<number of freelists>*. For example, if a segment has three freelists and two freelist groups, it is used as shown in Figure 5.7.

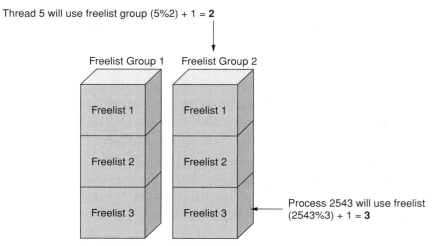

Figure 5.7 Freelist allocation algorithm

The "+1" addition in the example is to prevent the algorithm from mapping to freelist group 0, which does not exist.

5.5.3 Block Cleanout

Block cleanout is an optimization made by Oracle to speed up the commit process. When a transaction is committed, Oracle will only perform the minimum amount of work in the block required to guarantee the transaction. In addition to this work, there is an amount of housekeeping that needs to be performed in order to keep the database running smoothly. Oracle does not perform this housekeeping at the commit phase in order to keep the commits as fast as possible.

Block cleanout is the name given to these housekeeping tasks, and it is performed by the next session to read the block. The idea of this is that many sessions could be doing the housekeeping in parallel, therefore keeping the overhead for any single session to a minimum.

During block cleanout, the following duties are performed, where applicable to the prior transaction:

- The SCN in the block header is updated to reflect the contents of the ITLs.

- The ITL entry is cleaned, including free space credit given back to the block, and the SCN is updated to reflect the current state of the block.

- The freespace in the block is updated in the row directory.

- The row directory is updated to show the deleted rows (gaining a tag of `sfll` instead of `offs`).

- The row data is actually purged instead of being flagged as deleted.

Block cleanout is a frequently forgotten part of the operation of Oracle, and it can affect the performance of the system significantly.

For example, data purge is mostly performed as part of the batch cycle in the evenings. Even if the deletes are kept separate from any batch access to the affected tables, the subsequent batch jobs will still be very much slower than the evenings in which the deletes do not occur. In fact, after a mass delete, it could take many times longer for a read-only batch job that follows it to complete. One good procedure for at least keeping things predictable in this scenario is to always perform full table scans on tables that have had large numbers of deletes performed against them.

The other side effect of block cleanout is that you might notice a sudden increase in redo writes that does not relate to the execution of a batch job (i.e., it has already finished). This is the logging of the block updates necessary as part of the block cleanout operation.

5.6   Redo Logfiles

The redo logfiles are responsible for the integrity of the database. All changes in the database, both committed and uncommitted, are written to the redo log.

Unlike writes to the data files[4] in the database, the redo log does not operate through the buffer cache in the SGA. Instead, the redo log is accessed through the redo log buffer, which will be covered in the next chapter.

The redo logs are used to record all changes in the database by recording the changes made to the actual blocks. This includes changes made to rollback segments, and so the complete state of the database can be rebuilt by reapplying the redo information to a recovered database. When a commit is issued, all the session's redo records are written out to the redo log by the Log Writer (LGWR) process, in addition to a commit marker for that transaction. If several other sessions are to commit while this write activity takes place, all of the commits are serviced concurrently by the LGWR, in a process called *group commit*. In this way, the rate of writes to the redo log is not proportional to the rate of commits, and the system can scale more efficiently.

During a database recovery operation, the database is rolled forward to the specified point. During this rollforward from the redo log, all the rollback segments are rebuilt and any committed transactions are recommitted back to the database. Think of the rollforward as a more efficient replay of the work recorded in the redo logs. Once the recovery is complete, any uncommitted transactions left in the rollback segments are rolled back, in order to return the database to a consistent state.

---

4. Excluding temporary tablespaces, which neither generate any redo information nor go through the buffer cache for read or write activity.

Owing to the serial nature of the redo logs, it is important that the logs be optimized for write performance, because sessions issuing a commit will wait until the records are all synchronously (i.e., we wait for the operation to complete) written to disk. Therefore, locating the redo logs on a UNIX file system is almost always a bad thing to do unless special support is provided by the operating system for direct writes, because of the additional overhead of the file system buffer cache, where it provides no benefit to the write-only operation.

Often, the best way to optimize redo log placement is to build the logs on raw disk partitions and place the logs on their own disk, preferably with their own controller (although this gets less important when Ultra SCSI or fibre channel is used). In this way, the writing to disk is not interrupted by an external influence, such as another file operation or file system cache contention.

When the redo logs are placed on their own disks, the physical drive spindle is much more capable of sustaining a high write throughput, because very little (if any) seeking is required by the disk head. The optimal way to lay out redo logs on a large system is shown in Figure 5.8.

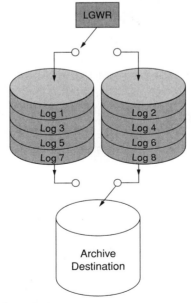

Figure 5.8 Optimal redo log placement

Figure 5.8 is more of a schematic than an I/O channel configuration. What it shows is that, at any one time, the LGWR process has a dedicated write channel through to the redo log. When Oracle switches the active redo log to the next defined log, it implicitly switches to another disk spindle, allowing the archiver process a free channel on which to archive the full log to the archive destination.

5.7   Key Database Objects

5.7.1   Rollback Segments

Rollback segments are also known as *undo segments* because of their role in database operation. During a transaction in the database, data manipulation language (DML) statements modify the actual data blocks that are affected by the operation. In order to have the ability to undo these operations, the *before-image* of the changed data is stored in the rollback segment. When the user issues a rollback command, or some kind of failure implies a rollback, this rollback information is applied back onto the data blocks, restoring them to their state before the transaction started.

In addition to undoing uncommitted transactions, the rollback segments are also used to construct a read-consistent view of the data blocks for all other users who access the blocks prior to the commit of the transaction.

The Oracle consistency model is covered in detail in the next chapter, because it uses many different attributes of the Oracle system, not the least of which is the buffer cache layer. In this chapter, we will concentrate on the physical types of rollback segments and their usage.

User Rollback Segments

User rollback segments are used to store the undo information for user transactions—that is, for nonrecursive SYS transactions. All rollback segments except the SYSTEM rollback segment are considered user rollback segments.

Full information on the physical usage of rollback segments can be determined from the *Oracle Server Concepts Guide* and won't be repeated here. However, some of the pertinent points will be restated.

If a long-running query is running against an object in the database, and other sessions are writing to that object at the same time, none of the undo information for the writing sessions can be released until the long-running query is complete. This occurs because the undo information for the writing sessions is required to reconstruct a read-consistent version of the modified blocks on behalf of the reading session. If the rollback segment needs to reuse these blocks that were retained for consistent read, it will do so and cause the reading session to fail with a "snapshot too old" error. The creation of consistent blocks will be covered in the next chapter.

A rollback segment's extents are reused in a circular fashion. If the tablespace that contains the rollback segment is full, or if maxextents is exceeded for the rollback segment, this affects how a rollback segment is deemed to be "full." As an extreme example, take the scenario where the first and last extents of the rollback segment contain active transactions. When a new transaction requires space in this rollback segment, it will attempt to reuse the first extent and will fail because active transactions reside in that block. This makes the rollback segment effectively "full" despite all the extents between the first and last remaining empty.

A common practice among DBAs is to use the OPTIMAL setting for rollback segments. This allows the segment to be automatically kept close to the specified size by Oracle. It does this by deallocating the oldest inactive extents in the segment until the segment is close to the requested size. This is a popular option, because it allows runaway jobs to operate in a common "pool" of rollback segments without leaving one or more of the segments dominating the space in the tablespace.

However, for a large-scale implementation, this is probably not an "optimal" approach, because it is working around a more fundamental problem. The problem is: What is the runaway job in the online pool of rollback segments? If it is a batch job, then it should use the SET TRANSACTION USE ROLLBACK SEGMENT call in order to assign it to some large, prebuilt rollback segments. If it is an online session, it probably shouldn't use so much rollback.

The online user session can only be using a lot of rollback for one of two reasons: either it is making a lot of changes in the database, or it is holding a cursor open for a long time, requiring a great deal of consistent read support from the rollback segment. In the first case, if the changes are

UPDATE or DELETE, the session is committing a worse sin than growing a roll-back segment, in that it is locking many, many records in the database and probably causing TX enqueue contention in the database. In the second case, it would be unusual to find a requirement that called for this kind of long-lasting, read-consistent view in an online session.

The other reason to avoid the OPTIMAL setting is that it can severely limit the capability to retain consistent reads, even for short periods, because extents that are maintained only for consistent reads are eligible for deallocation in order to shrink the segment back to its optimal size.

System Rollback Segment

The SYSTEM rollback segment resides in the SYSTEM tablespace. It is used in the same way as user rollback segments are used, but only for recursive transactions in the database, otherwise known as data definition language (DDL) statements. If no other rollback segments are created, this segment is also used for user transactions.

Deferred Rollback Segments

Deferred rollback segments are temporary rollback segments that are created in the SYSTEM tablespace automatically as needed. They are used to store undo information that cannot be applied because a tablespace is offline at the time of the rollback operation.

5.7.2 Read-Only Tablespaces

When a tablespace is defined READ ONLY, this tells Oracle that no writes can occur to the tablespace. If no writes can occur, there is no need to update the SCN for the file either, because nothing can change.

This tablespace declaration is most useful in data warehousing applications, where tablespaces can be marked READ ONLY once they are loaded. As the former restriction of a table residing in only one tablespace is now removed (when using partitioning), this becomes a very useable way of controlling the backup requirements for very large data warehouses.

Once a particular partition is loaded and is residing in its own tablespace, this entire tablespace can be made READ ONLY. After this is done, the files that make up the tablespace can be backed up to tape, possibly multiple times to protect against bad tapes, and then can be stored forever at an offsite location. As the files never change (unless they are taken out of READ ONLY mode), this backup is all that is required to effect a full restore of the tablespace.

5.7.3   Temporary Tablespaces and Temporary Segments

These two entities are closely related and overlap in function. A temporary segment can exist in any tablespace, but a tablespace of type TEMPORARY can store only temporary segments. Specifically, a TEMPORARY tablespace can contain only sort segments.

In release 7.3, Oracle introduced a tablespace of type TEMPORARY, and also introduced the principle of SORT_DIRECT_WRITES[5] for all writes to temporary segments.

All users in Oracle have a tablespace assigned to them as their temporary tablespace. This tells Oracle where it should create sort segments when it needs to sort on disk. Complex join operations, GROUP BY operations, ORDER BY operations, and so on, can all result in a disk sort. In addition to temporary segments needed for the sort, temporary segments are created in the target tablespace of a CREATE INDEX operation, used for the actual construction of the index. Both of these types of temporary segments benefit from the direct write capability.

The direct writes functionality instructs Oracle not to use the buffer cache when writing sort segments—they can be written directly to the datafile by the active session.[6] In addition to this, Oracle does not generate any redo information for the temporary blocks written. These two factors combined allow far greater performance for large queries than was possible before.

In addition to this change, the ability to create a tablespace of type TEMPORARY was introduced. This is a special type of tablespace solely for use in disk sorts and cannot be used to store permanent objects. In addition to

---

5. This parameter is now obsolete. The functionality still exists, however, and is managed automatically by Oracle.

6. Apart from some sort directory information, which is still maintained in the buffer cache.

gaining the direct write capability for all writes to this tablespace, the concept of a *sort segment* was introduced.

Sort segments were implemented to relieve the pressure exerted on the space transaction (ST) enqueue in the database. The ST enqueue is the lock that needs to be held before any space management can be done in recursive SQL. Whenever any new extents are created in or removed from the database, the ST lock must be acquired; if it is already in use, you must wait for it to become available. In a system where a great deal of this activity takes place, such as a busy system with a several disk sorts occurring at any one time, there can be fierce contention for the ST lock. This is massively compounded in a Parallel Server environment, where there is still only a single ST lock for all instances that are running.

The introduction of sort segment practically removes this type of ST contention. When a sort segment is first created, it requires the use of the ST lock, just as before. However, instead of acquiring the lock again to remove the segments once it becomes free, the segment is handed over to a pool of sort segments managed by instance-local latches instead of a database-wide enqueue. The next session that requires a sort segment can check the pool and reuse any free segments that the instance has allocated to it.

The net effect is that, once the instance has built enough sort segments using the ST lock, their management is then handled by the local sort segment management, leaving ST free for its other tasks.

5.7.4   Tables

The concept of a table is no longer as simple as it once was. In addition to the standard table and clusters that have existed since version 6, we now have partitioned tables, temporary tables, and index-organized tables. The index-organized table is covered as an index, because it resembles an index more closely than it does a table.

Standard Tables

A standard table is still the most common table in most Oracle databases. The structure of the standard table was covered under "Row Data" in Section 5.5.2.

Partitioned Tables

Partitioning is one of the big changes in Oracle8. This facility allows the administrator to break up large tables into several smaller partitions while accessing the table in the normal manner (see Figure 5.9).

The table is split into partitions based on key ranges on one or more columns, either by direct value or by hashing[7] the value to gain the partition number. The choice of how the partitioning is performed is up to the administrator. In this example, the "bookings" table is broken up into four partitions by the first letter of the booker's name. Each of the partitions is stored in its own tablespace, although they could all be stored in the same tablespace if desired.

A good way to view partitions is as "subtables" of the global table. Oracle handles all the joining of the partitions to form a single view of the data, but also takes care of *partition elimination* (or *pruning*) using the cost-based optimizer. In partition elimination, the optimizer excludes certain partitions from the execution plan of a given piece of SQL based on the predicates in the query.

Partitioning brings three important features to the table:

1. Manageability

2. Performance

3. Scalability

The manageability comes from being able to perform maintenance at a partition level without affecting the other table partitions. Using partitions, we

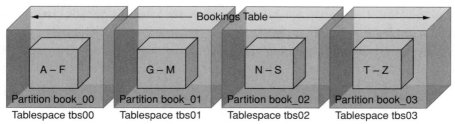

Figure 5.9 Partitioned table "bookings"

---

7. In Oracle 8.1 and upward.

can lock an entire partition (for data maintenance, or to do local index builds[8]) while users continue to execute against the remaining partitions. Likewise, if a file goes offline as a result of hardware problems, only the partition that is within the file is affected; the rest of the table is accessible and does not require recovery.

We can also remove certain partitions from the table, either by turning these partitions into tables in their own right or by dropping them. If a table is partitioned by a range that also works well for the purge rules, the delete process can be as simple as dropping the oldest partition when its data becomes older than the required retention period.

In addition to purging of data, partitions allow far greater flexibility performing data loads. Data that needs to be loaded into the large partitioned table can first be loaded into an interim table that has the same definition. When all the data is loaded, the table can be merged into the partitioned table as an additional partition, making the data load comparatively transparent to the end user.

Performance gains in partitioned tables come from the fact that the optimizer can now physically exclude data from the search path. This is true for all dimensions: We now effectively have multiple tables where we previously had only one. Therefore, all operations on the table can be performed much faster, provided that the access paths are evenly distributed across the partitions.

In the case of INSERTs, we now have several segment headers from which to retrieve freelist information, and so the contention on the segment header is reduced accordingly. In the case of DELETEs and UPDATEs, a new facility is available in partitioned tables called *parallel DML*. Using parallel DML, these two operations can be executed in parallel from a single session, as long as the operations fall in different partitions.

The scalability advantages come from two dimensions that span the manageability and performance categories. As a table gets past a certain size,[9] it simply becomes unmanageable in terms of indexing, backups—

---

8. See "Partitioned Indexes" in Section 5.7.5.

9. The meaning of "a certain size" keeps changing: as I/O and processing get faster, the "line in the sand" gets farther away. However, we are normally pushing way beyond wherever the line is drawn anyway.

everything. A system cannot scale if the objects within it become unmanageable. With partitioning, a table can be processed in pieces, doing only what is required for one partition at a time.[10]

In a data warehousing environment, it makes sense to load the data by date range if possible. In this way, the data can be loaded into different partitions when the current one gets unmanageable to backup (this could mean a day, a week, a month, or any time period). When the loads start to go into a different partition, the previous one can be made read-only and can be archived off to tape as a one-time exercise. When local indexes are used (see Figure 5.15), the index building can be restricted to the comparatively small (relative to the whole table) partition.

From the performance perspective, we will cover less obvious reasons why partitions scale well later in the book. The more obvious reasons are the use of *partition elimination* in queries, which reduces the amount of unnecessary work that the database performs. Partition elimination is the process that the cost based optimizer (CBO) uses to determine whether or not certain partitions need to be read. Based on the values submitted for predicates using partition columns, the optimizer can elect to omit irrelevant partitions from the execution plan.

Hash Clusters

Hash clusters have been in the Oracle product for quite some time. Despite this, they remain relatively unused in the field, despite their performance and scalability advantages. The reason for this is that they also come with several limitations that make them unsuitable for most purposes.

The theory behind a hash cluster is that a column, or several columns, can be passed through a hash algorithm so as to produce the approximate location of the actual data in the database.

In the example shown in Figure 5.10, a user submits a query to the database with a single set of criteria: ID = 346782, Name = Jones, Flight = ZZ437. Oracle takes these values and performs a hash operation on them, deriving a hash value of 8465874852. Neither the user nor the administrator needs to know what this value is.

---

10. Global indexes are the exception to this rule.

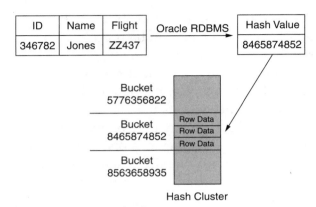

Figure 5.10   Hash cluster access method

The content of the hash cluster is physically stored on disk according to the same hashing algorithm. Therefore, if the data exists in the cluster, it must exist under the same hash bucket that has just been calculated for the user's query. In this example, there are three rows that reside in this hash bucket, and so Oracle will check each one for equality against the supplied predicate and then return the data.

It is important to remember that a hash cluster will provide good performance only when

- There are a small number of records for a given hash value

- The data is accessed mostly through direct lookup as opposed to any type of scan

Keeping the number of records low for a given hash value is achieved by setting the HASHKEYS parameter appropriately on hash cluster creation. You will need to know a good deal about the current and future row counts for this table in order to set this parameter adequately, because the correct setting is likely to be different in six months as a result of table growth. Keeping the row count per hash low allows Oracle to go straight to the correct row based on the hash value, with no subsequent scanning of peer rows in that hash bucket.

Full table scans are very inefficient in hash clusters because of the relatively sparse block population resulting from a well-configured hash cluster. Likewise, range scans across the cluster key are not very efficient because of the number of blocks required to satisfy the request.

In summary, hash clusters work well where the data is relatively static and where the cluster is configured correctly for the number of hash keys. They scale well as a result of the small number of block visits (probably only one) needed to retrieve the single row requested. This eliminates the root and branch block contention encountered on very busy B-tree indexes. Hash clusters are ideal for very large reference tables, for all of these reasons.

5.7.5 Indexes

Gone are the days when there was only one type of index. We now have as many as *five* variations on the indexing theme. Although the old B-tree index continues to suit most purposes well, the performance requirement on indexing has increased over time, and new data access methods have been implemented to improve the capability of the database.

Structure of B-Tree

A B-tree index in its purest form is a binary tree structure that maps the path to the required leaf block by making yes/no answers. Figure 5.11 illustrates the structure of an Oracle B-tree.

Unless the index is very small (only one block required for all keys), it will have at least a root block and probably many branch blocks. There is

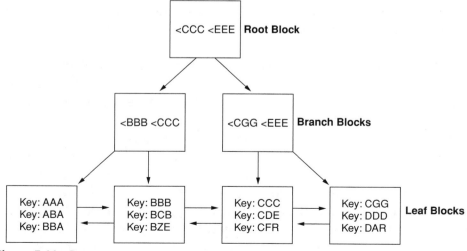

Figure 5.11 B-tree structure

no difference between a root block and a branch block except that the root block is always the entry point for the index and is therefore a kind of "super branch block."

When Oracle needs to find a row, and the query contains predicate information to allow Oracle to use an index, it will start by going to the root block of the appropriate index. The root block contains the information required to get to either the leaf block itself (in the case of small indexes) or the next branch block. The next branch block homes in further on the actual leaf block, based on the supplied data values.

The leaf block contains all the data values for the indexed columns and the rowid for the corresponding row in the table. If the query can be satisfied using only the columns in the index, the rowid is not used any further. However, if additional columns are required from the table, the rowid is used to access the row directly, without any scanning.

If the query contains a range of possible values for the key, Oracle can elect to perform a "range scan." Oracle will start at one end of the supplied range and use the links between the leaf blocks in order to go directly to the next applicable index block, without going back to the root and branch blocks.

Oracle maintains very *shallow* B-trees. This means that the number of root/branch blocks read before the actual leaf block is hit is very low—typically two (one root, one branch), with a maximum of four levels. This directly correlates to the size of the Oracle block, because this is the ultimate limit on how many pointers to the next level can be stored.

When an index block is filled, Oracle allocates another block from the freelist, as described previously. However, owing to the B-tree structure, Oracle normally cannot start to use the block immediately, because the inserted key value is likely to fall somewhere between existing keys (e.g., the inserted value is 1,000, and the leaf block contains a range from 500 to 4,000). In this case, Oracle performs an index *leaf block split*, which means that the upper half of the keys are transferred to the new block while the lower half remain in the old block. This way, the key can be applied to the correct leaf block in the B-tree. When the split is complete, the branch block above the blocks must be updated to reflect this new block's keys and location, in addition to updating the key range for the old block.

Reverse Key Indexes

Reverse key indexes are primarily an Oracle Parallel Server optimization. They are exactly what their name implies: The key is reversed before being inserted into the index. This allows a far more scalable spread of index keys when an ascending key is used for the leading edge of the index (see Figure 5.12).

This spread of keys is critical in a Parallel Server configuration where many instances can be inserting rows into a common, indexed table. One example of this would be invoice records, where each instance is creating invoices and by implication requiring insertion into the exact same leaf block. This can cause huge cross-instance contention, because the leaf blocks must be pinged between the nodes each time.

For insertion into a standard table, this is not a problem, because free-list groups allow each instance to maintain its own set of freespace for the inserts. This is particularly true when entire extents are explicitly allocated to certain freelist groups. In the case of a standard B-tree, this does not apply, because Oracle *has to* insert keys into specific blocks in order to preserve the structure of the B-tree.

When a reverse key index is used, the least significant portion of the key suddenly becomes the most significant, and the index keys "stripe" across the entire range of leaf blocks, reducing the likelihood of a hot leak block.

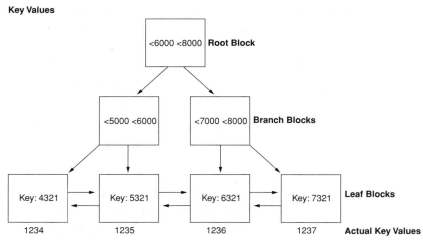

Figure 5.12   Reverse key indexes

This benefit does not come without restrictions, however. As a result of the key now being reversed, a range scan is no longer an option, because Oracle may need to scan the entire set of index leaf blocks hundreds of times, or full scan the whole index, before the complete range is satisfied. Therefore, reverse key indexes are useful only where single-row fetches are used to retrieve the inserted rows. If this is not possible because of application design, alternative methods for reducing index leaf block contention must be considered in a Parallel Server environment.

Bitmapped Indexes

Bitmapped indexes were introduced in release 7.3 and were the first variation on the trusty B-tree index. Primarily designed for decision support queries rather than transaction processing, bitmapped indexes provide both excellent performance and comparatively small size.

They are referred to as *bitmapped* indexes because they provide Oracle with simple true/false answers as to whether the keys match certain criteria. In physical terms, the equivalents of branch blocks now contain the possible combinations of key values in the indexed column, equivalent to performing a SELECT DISTINCT column_name on the table.

The leaf blocks contain bitmaps for a range of rows in the table, declaring which combinations the row matches (i.e., TRUE) and which it does not (i.e., FALSE). These bitmaps are very small, and therefore the entire bitmapped index can be scanned very quickly.

For example, if we had a table called STUFF with a column called TYPE that contained the values GOOD, BAD, and INDIFFERENT, the result would be entries in the index leaf block of the form

```
col 0: GOOD
col 1: start dba
col 2: end dba
col 3: <bitmap>
```

This example shows the key to which this bitmap relates, followed by a range of dbas to which this bitmap corresponds. The bitmap consists of an array of bits set to 1 if the row it relates to has the value "GOOD," and to 0 if it does not. Every row is reported here, including NULL columns, which never "equal" anything. This makes a bitmapped index an acceptable method for counting all the rows in a table or where something IS [NOT] NULL.

Bitmaps are particularly useful in conjunction with other bitmaps, including themselves. To continue with the example, if a query were written as

```
SELECT count(*) FROM stuff WHERE TYPE in ('GOOD','INDIFFERENT');
```

there would be a bitmap "merge" of different portions of the same bitmapped index on STUFF. The "GOOD" and "INDIFFERENT" bitmaps would be ORed together to produce another bitmap that could be used to satisfy the query by counting all the set bits in it. This technique applies equally to different bitmaps, on different columns.

Bitmapped indexes are useful only if there are a small number of *distinct* values for the indexed column. If this is not the case, the overhead of building a bitmap for every combination can quickly make the bitmapped index unwieldy, and the advantages become liabilities.

Updates to a table covered by a bitmapped index are deferred until the entire DML operation is complete. This means that if one row or one million rows are changed, the bitmap will not be updated until the end of the operation. This does not affect readers, because the bitmap will always be updated before any other session needs it, because the update always completes before the updating session issues a commit.

Locking of the bitmap index is done on a dba range basis in order to maintain the whole bitmap portions. This is logical, considering the way that Oracle stores the bitmap fragments in the leaf blocks; managing multiple updates within a single bitmap would be very difficult. Despite being logical, however, this makes bitmaps tricky to use in a transactional environment, because the concurrency of updates is directly affected.

Partitioned Indexes

Just as tables can now be partitioned, so can indexes. However, in the case of indexes, there are more considerations to be made.

Indexes now have terminology associated with them that declares the scope of table coverage for the index. An index can be either *global* or *local* under this terminology. A global index covers all partitions of the underlying table, whereas a local index covers only the table partition to which it is assigned. A global index can be partitioned or nonpartitioned, and a local index is partitioned by implication that it covers a partition of a table.

When a global index is nonpartitioned, it is exactly the same as a standard B-tree index. It does not have to be built on a partitioned table.

The index illustrated in Figure 5.13 can be partitioned only in one of the two possible ways—that of a *prefixed index* and a *nonprefixed index*. A prefixed global index is partitioned on the leading edge column within the index. That is, if the index in Figure 5.13 were built on `book_ref` and `book_time`, the prefixed index would be split into several partitions based on ranges of `book_ref` or of `book_ref` and `book_time` combined. It could not be partitioned on `book_time`, because this would be a global *nonprefixed* index, which is not provided for by Oracle. The result is shown in Figure 5.14.

Global prefixed indexes are not as preferable as local prefixed indexes. However, sometimes it is not possible (or practical) to build local prefixed indexes, because the required indexes for any given table will often lead on columns other than the table partition key (as required for local prefixed indexes). Also, there are situations in which a partitioned index may be preferable for contention management reasons and partitioning of the table is not required at all.

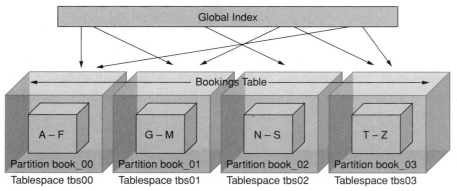

Figure 5.13   Nonpartitioned global index on a partitioned table

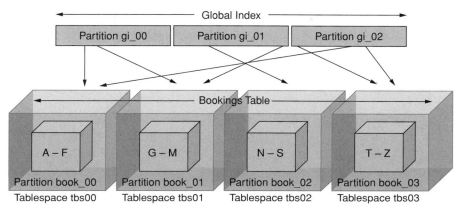

Figure 5.14 Partitioned global index on a partitioned table

The specific situation in which this may be desired is the case of heavy index *root block contention*. This kind of contention is possible for many reasons and can even occur when the index is simply being read a great deal. In this case, the object of contention is the latch protecting the piece of cache in which the root block is stored. In this situation, there is not much else to do (apart from checking for strange data pathologies) than to partition the index to form *multiple root blocks*. If the partition ranges are carefully chosen (by access rate, rather than by strict storage ranges), this kind of partitioning can result in multiple blocks in the cache, each protected by its own latch (assuming that the cache is well tuned—see Chapter 6).

Local indexes can be built only on partitioned tables, but can be either *prefixed* or *nonprefixed*. When prefixed, the index is partitioned on the same column and range as the table partition, shown in Figure 5.15.

With local prefixed indexes, each index partition directly maps to one corresponding table partition. The index can include additional columns but must *lead* on the same columns as the table partition.

With local nonprefixed indexes, the index columns *do not* have the same leading columns as the table partition. However, the index partitions contain only data related to the table partitions they cover: Leaf blocks in a local nonprefixed index point only to rows in the related table partition, not to any other partitions.

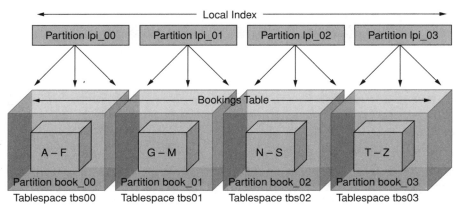

Figure 5.15 Local index partitions

For example, assume that the bookings table were partitioned on book_name range, as shown above. A prefixed index on this partitioned table would be built using the same ranges of book_name. A local nonprefixed index could be built on book_time, and each local index partition would contain a mini B-tree of book_time keys, built locally on each table partition of book_name.

When one is determining which type of index to build, the following performance consideration must be taken into account. Prefixed indexes allow Oracle to determine which index partitions will be needed at execution time. When the index is nonprefixed, Oracle cannot know which partitions can be excluded from the search. Therefore, all index partitions must be examined at runtime in order to determine the locations of all the data, unless they can be eliminated on the basis of other predicates in the query.

Index-Organized Tables (IOTs)

Index-organized tables are also known as index-only tables. The best way to visualize an IOT is to view it as a normal B-tree index in which, instead of a rowid partnering the key columns, all the columns in the table are included in the actual leaf block (see Figure 5.16).

With all the columns included in the "index," the storage of an actual table is not necessary, and so the B-tree itself becomes an IOT, accompanied by a few changes in the way the table is accessed.

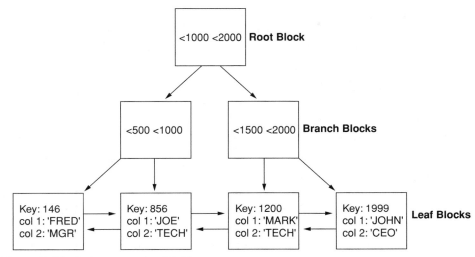

Figure 5.16 Index-organized tables

The major change is that an index does not have a rowid—only tables have rowids. The new unique row identifier is now the primary key on which the table is organized. In order to support the creation of additional indexes on the IOT, a new logical rowid is created in the new index in an attempt to allow direct access to the row without traversing the branch blocks of the actual IOT when a different index is used to access the table.

Unfortunately, the physical location of a given row in an IOT is not fixed, owing to the index block split phenomenon required to maintain the structure of the B-tree when inserting rows. For this reason, Oracle refers to the physical portion of the logical rowid as a *"physical guess."* This guess is stored in the logical rowid, along with the primary key of the row. When accessing the table through a secondary index, Oracle probes the guess point first to see if the row is still present. If it is not, Oracle must traverse the IOT, starting at the root block, in order to locate the row. In this instance, the physical guess is considered *stale*.

The only way that stale guesses can be rebuilt is by a physical rebuild of the secondary index. This includes a full scan of the IOT, because the physical locations cannot be determined in any other way.

Full table scans are still possible on IOTs, with the interesting side effect that the rows now come out in primary key order, regardless of the order in which they were inserted into the table. This occurs because the full table scan equivalent for an IOT is an index range scan.

Prior to Oracle 8.1, IOTs were not very usable, because several capabilities of a standard "heap" (normal) table were absent from IOTs. Included in this list were support for additional indexes, support for large object (LOB) columns, and the ability to partition the table. These restrictions have been removed in Oracle 8.1.

More importantly, Oracle has made a significant change in database operation that makes IOTs more attractive for widespread use.

Over time, tables become fragmented within the rows themselves, because rows are deleted from the table over time and updating of rows can result in row chaining. The only way to reorganize these tables, and to compact the data into the blocks, is to rebuild the table physically. In previous releases, these tables could not be rebuilt online, because a full table lock was the only way to ensure that the table was not updated while the rebuild was underway.

In release 8.1, this is still true. However, in this release, Oracle allows indexes to be rebuilt online, while DML continues against the underlying table. Because this also applies to IOTs, it therefore allows for full database reorganization online, including tables (IOTs *only*) and indexes.

5.7.6   Other Database Objects

Some objects do not fit under any of the prior headings, but are still worth reviewing in terms of their impact on the database.

Sequences

Sequences, or sequence number generators, are automatic number generators that are used mostly for the provision of generated primary keys for tables where this is preferred. These numbers can be cached within the SGA to improve the throughput for requests made against them. The implementation of the cache is simply the storage of a single number in the SGA, which can be incremented in memory without touching the on-disk representation.

The disk value is updated each time the cached "bundle" of numbers is depleted, and the value reflects the next value after the cache is all used

Table 5.3 Sequence Caching Process

Step	On-Disk Value	Cache: Instance 1	Cache: Instance 2
Both instances cold started	1000	N/A	N/A
First access from instance 1	2000	1000	N/A
First access from instance 2; instance 1 has used 45 numbers	3000	1045	2000
All numbers used on instance 1 and cache refreshed from disk; 645 numbers used from instance 2	4000	3000	2645

up. This is a benefit for the DBA but a potential problem for application developers. Table 5.3 shows how caching relates to disk values in a two-node Parallel Server configuration.

This table clearly shows that the two instances can maintain very distinct ranges of numbers from each other through the use of caching.

The downside of this is that if instance 1 is shut down in the third step in Table 5.3, all 955 numbers in its cache will be "lost," because Oracle cannot write back the lower number after the other instance allocates its higher cache range. This will always result in lost sequence numbers, much to the frustration of application developers who were relying on sequentiality of numbering in order to provide, for example, invoice numbers.

Other ways in which numbers can get lost (in both non-OPS and OPS configurations) are (a) abnormal instance termination (crash) and (b) flushing of the shared pool when sequences are not pinned using the DBMS_SHARED_POOL.KEEP package.

The moral of this is that developers should be clearly told that sequence generators will guarantee *only* uniqueness. They do not, and will not, guarantee sequentiality.

The final implication of the cache model is that if the ORDER flag is specified on the sequence generator, this will implicitly defeat all caching and will go to disk every time the NEXTVAL is gotten. In frequently accessed sequences, this will result in contention in the SYSTEM tablespace and a large increase in recursive SQL in order to retrieve the next value from disk.

Packages, Procedures, and Functions

Packages are bundles of stored procedures and/or functions. They are provided to enable server-side processing using PL/SQL, aimed primarily at reducing the number of round trips to the application client over SQL*Net and improving code reuse across modules. Packages can become very large in complex applications and can impose large processing burdens on the database server.

As the database server is fundamentally the least scalable point in the network, it makes sense to review carefully the use of packages in the database and to have them perform realistic duties rather than being just convenient places to store large program modules. For example, use of packages as conduits to database server-based batch processing should be avoided.

Since release 7.3, packages have been able to use noncontiguous fragments of free memory in the shared pool when loading for the first time. This change made a huge difference in the impact of loading a large package into a fragmented shared pool. It is still very advisable, however, always to pin database packages into the shared pool at start-up, using the DBMS_SHARED_POOL.KEEP package. The method required for doing this is to reference the package once (for example, call a small function in the package) and then issue the KEEP package against it. The list of packages to keep should include the SYSTEM packages as well as the application packages.

A package is always executed with the identity and authorization levels of the owner of the actual package, not those of the user who executes it. The execution of the actual SQL within the package therefore shows up as recursive SQL calls, not user calls. Likewise, all statistics logged by the integral package contents are rolled up and also logged against the call to execute the package, in addition to the actual statements.

It's worth mentioning here that functions are very often abused by application programmers. It is commonly believed that a function is a very fast method of converting data and that this can be done on the server prior to sending the data back. However, it is impossible for a user-written function to perform anywhere near as fast as the built-in functions such as TRUNC(), because of both the language that the routines are written in and the code path required to get there.

Built-in functions are written in C and compiled into native machine instructions by the machine's optimizing compiler. They are called by branching to the function's memory location when required by the SQL engine. Conversely, a user-written function is written in PL/SQL an interpreted high-level language. It requires many orders of magnitude more machine clock cycles to process a given line of PL/SQL than to process a similar line of C. To execute it, Oracle must leap up through several functions, take out several latches, call the PL/SQL interpreter, and then go through the code. There is obviously no comparison between the impacts of these executions.

Try to limit the use of functions to the areas where no other solution is possible. When they are used in the select list, limit the row count to the number of rows that are actually required. This can be done using simple business logic (does the user really need a list of 3,000 reservations in a scrollable box?), or by some kind of arbitrary rownum restriction on the tail end of the query.

Triggers

Triggers provide a way of executing PL/SQL based on certain events occurring in the database. They can be fired BEFORE, AFTER, or INSTEAD OF the actual event that fired the trigger, and can operate on DML, DDL, and database events.

For example, a trigger can be set up to fire AFTER an UPDATE to a certain table. This is an application developer's favorite way of implementing audit requirements, because it requires no special considerations to take place on the part of the application. However, this is also an expensive way to implement what is already an expensive operation.

When the trigger is fired, it goes through the same kind of code path as demonstrated above in function execution. Typically, the code that processes updates will compare all the old values with the new values to determine which columns have actually been updated. This too is a very expensive operation, when the application already has this information.

Using triggers in this way is an attempt to gain some of the advantages of a multitier application without the work. Unfortunately, the work still has to be done, and it has to be done from scratch each time by the database server, with no context to start with.

The new INSTEAD OF trigger type is useful in allowing updatable views, because the trigger is fired instead of actually attempting the update or insert. Once again, however, be aware that this convenience is not without significant performance degradation when compared with accessing the underlying tables directly.

Perhaps one of the best uses for triggers is that of the database event triggers. These can be fired whenever there is a server error, log-on, log-off, or start-up and shut-down. Using the start-up trigger, for example, a package could be executed to take care of post-start-up tasks such as pinning packages.

Security Roles

Database roles are a facility in Oracle that allows transparent, role-based privileges based on login ID. These roles are designed to group together certain privileges in the database and to be able to assign them to users as single entities.

For example, a role could be created to allow users to connect to the database, to execute the ALTER SESSION command, and to access a set of specific tables in the database. This role is then assigned to a user, and that user can then perform any of the allowed functions.

A user can have several roles assigned, and can switch between roles based on location in the application and password authentication.

Although the use of roles is very flexible, allowing simple management of privileges within the database, it currently does not scale very well. In a very large system, where several thousand users are defined, in addition to more than 100 defined roles, the overhead of queries on the %_ENABLED_ROLES views, for example, can be very unwieldy. One example of this is on a large Oracle8 system, where a single user could generate 8 million buffer gets from a single roles query.

It does not take very complex use of the roles facility for this kind of burden to become evident. For example, Form 4.5 (in Developer/2000 1.X) uses database roles in order to implement menu security. This is not a very sophisticated use of the roles, but was the reality behind the 8 million buffer get example above. In this case, the problem was removed by

- Moving all the data from the database roles configuration to user tables
- Creating correct indexes on the new user tables
- Dropping the FRM45_ENABLED_ROLES view and recreating it so that it referenced the new user tables
- Changing all code that issued CREATE ROLE, ALTER ROLE, and so on, simply to INSERT, UPDATE, and DELETE the user table.

This made all accesses to this data go from 200 to 8,000,000 buffer gets to about 4, with subsequent improvements in both response time and system utilization on the server.

There can be an additional side effect that compounds the performance problems of using database roles. If the dictionary cache is squeezed to a small size in the shared pool, owing to an unruly set of SQL statements in the library cache, many of the calls to check database roles do not get hits in the dictionary cache. The impact of this is that many of the 8 million buffer gets end up going to disk, the recursive calls rate goes through the roof, and the system performance goes down.

5.8 The Data Dictionary

The data dictionary is a widely misunderstood entity in the database. It is comprised of two components:

1. The objects in the SYS schema
2. The dictionary cache (a.k.a. the rowcache)

It's true, the dictionary cache is the same thing as the rowcache. It is known as the rowcache because the unit of management is a row out of the SYS tables, rather than a block unit in the buffer cache for user tables. The dictionary cache itself will be covered in Section 6.8. For now, we will concentrate on the physical elements of the dictionary cache.

The data dictionary is physically stored in the database as objects within the SYS schema. For all intents and purposes, these tables are just the same as normal user tables in any other tablespace. However, the consistency model is completely different for these tables, and they should therefore never be written to directly by the user, even if the user has a good understanding of their usage.

Table 5.4 shows some of the more interesting tables in the SYS schema, along with their parent clusters. Many of the tables in the SYS schema are mostly joined with each other and therefore merit the use of a cluster for their storage.

The main time to be aware of these tables is when looking at the definitions of the DBA_% views and other SYS views. These views will break out into views of these underlying tables, and it is useful to be able to interpret the view definition, potentially to write a more efficient version of the view for specific reasons.

5.9   Chapter Summary

In this chapter, we have attempted to cover Oracle from a physical standpoint, without venturing into the operating architecture of Oracle. These two areas are finely interwoven, and some of the concepts in this chapter or the next may not make much sense in isolation from each other. For this reason, Part III should be read as a single unit.

Oracle is a complex product and has many more physical attributes than those covered in this chapter. It is for this reason that it is imperative to be well versed in all areas of physical Oracle, at least from a "Server Concepts" perspective, before attempting to implement anything on a large scale.

5.10   Further Reading

Various. *"Oracle 8i Concepts,"* Oracle RDBBMS Documentation.

Table 5.4 Selected SYS Schema Tables

Cluster Name	Table Name	Comments
C_FILE#_BLOCK#	SEG$	Segments and Used Extents Table. SEG$ provides the guts of the DBA_SEGMENTS view, while UET$ provides the DBA_EXTENTS view.
	UET$	
C_OBJ#	ATTRCOL$	Fundamental information about each object in the database, including tables (TAB$), indexes (IND$), and clusters (CLU$). Includes column definitions (COL$).
	CLU$	
	COL$	
	COLTYPE$	
	ICOL$	
	ICOLDEP$	
	IND$	
	LIBRARY$	
	LOB$	
	NTAB$	
	REFCON$	
	TAB$	
	TYPE_MISC$	
C_TS#	FET$	Free extent table and tablespace definitions. FET$ forms the basis of DBA_FREE_SPACE; TS$ forms the basis of DBA_TABLESPACES.
	TS$	
C_USER#	TSQ$	User creation records and tablespace quota settings.
	USER$	
None	DUAL	Normal table, despite existing in the SYS schema; infamous table, used to dummy out queries.
	FILE$	Datafile information
	OBJ$	Object definitions
	UNDO$	Rollback definitions
	VIEW$	View definitions
	PROPS$	Database properties, mainly NLS definitions

Chapter 6

Oracle8 in Operation

6.1 Introduction

This chapter will cover the other side of the Oracle database—the process and memory architecture. These are the aspects of Oracle that make it a scalable database as opposed to a static filestore, and a good understanding of these concepts is essential for building a very scalable Oracle system.

The combination of these operational aspects of Oracle form the *Oracle kernel*.

6.1.1 The Oracle Kernel

The Oracle kernel is not a kernel in the same sense that an operating system kernel is. All execution on the host operating system occurs in user mode, with standard system calls made to access system functionality. Oracle does not have any special privileges with regard to memory visibility or system function.

Instead, the Oracle kernel is a set of processes and shared a memory segment upon which they operate. The processes and shared memory combined form an *instance* of Oracle. The physical side of Oracle on which the instance works is an Oracle *database*. Although these two entities are very much intertwined, Oracle Parallel Server provides ways to allow multiple instances to operate on the same database. This will be covered in Section 6.9.

Having declared that Oracle is not like an operating system kernel, it is time to contradict myself in some respects. The Oracle kernel is very much like an operating system kernel in that it performs the following functions on behalf of user connections:

- File I/O (through the operating system)
- Caching
- Process scheduling
- Runtime memory management (especially when using multithreaded server)

However, Oracle does not provide the following operating system kernel functions:

- Virtual memory
- Cache coherent multiprocessor support
- Timesliced process execution
- Direct hardware interfacing

These functions are all provided by the operating system and are fundamental to the operation of Oracle. They are so fundamental, in fact, that most hardware vendors provide a variety of special facilities in their operating system kernels for Oracle to use. These facilities include

- Asynchronous I/O to take the I/O scheduling burden away from Oracle
- Physically locked virtual memory that is not subject to any further virtual memory management, such as paging
- The ability to stop processes from being preempted by the operating system (OS) kernel for short periods while holding latches

In this chapter, we will look in detail at some of the services provided by the Oracle kernel.

6.2   Process Architecture

This is the most straightforward part of the Oracle system to understand. An Oracle instance consists of two different types of processes:

- Shadow (or server) processes
- Background processes

All processes in an Oracle instance are considered to be part of the Oracle kernel. In fact, all background and shadow processes are invoked from the same binary image—that of $ORACLE_HOME/bin/oracle. In this way, Oracle can rely on the fact that all the connected processes will follow the same rules about accessing objects in the SGA, and will not corrupt other sessions as a result of invalid writes to the shared areas.

6.2.1 Shadow Processes

The shadow processes constitute the server-side portion of a user TWO_TASK connection and therefore are also known as "server processes." There are two different architectures provided in Oracle8 for database connections: the dedicated server and multithreaded server (MTS). Whichever option is adopted, the shadow process is the process that performs the actual request servicing within the database.

Each process attaches to the Shared Global Area (SGA) for read and write use of the global caches. The process waits for requests to come over the network either directly (dedicated server) or through a dispatcher (MTS). When a request comes in from the client application, the server process interprets the request through the Net8 software that forms part of the process.

When the Net8 work has been completed, the process acts directly on that request on behalf of the user. Although the shadow process has Oracle kernel privileges and can do anything at all to the database or SGA, the process will not allow this unless the user connection is authorized to do so. However, when the user session has permission, the shadow process will do all the I/O, sorting, package execution, and whatever else the user session has requested.

In this way, the shadow process can be considered a proxy worker for the client application. The client application never accesses the SGA or the database itself directly, but only through the shadow process. It is the responsibility of the shadow process to enforce the security of the database and to service all work on behalf of the user.

Dedicated Server

Dedicated server processes are private to the user. That is, there is one process for each connected user, and that process is dedicated to the processing of that user's requests only.

The `oracle` executable is renamed on execution to become something like

```
oracleSID (LOCAL=NO)
```

or

```
oracleSID (DESCRIPTION=(LOCAL=YES)(ADDRESS=(PROTOCOL=beq)))
```

for remote and local connections, respectively. Note that the actual `oracle` executable on disk is not renamed; only the name of the *running* process is changed.

The dedicated server process maintains its own private working space and caches in a private piece of memory called the Process Global Area (PGA). The working memory is also known as session memory and is the portion of memory that stores the context of the session for the user session.

The dedicated server process listens on the direct network connection that was setup when the user connected to the database. The network connection is private between the dedicated server shadow process and the user application client—no other processes can use this network connection.

With one physical process for each user connection, large dedicated server-based systems can put a large burden on the host operating system in scheduling the processes, in addition to an increased overhead in memory management.

Multithreaded Server (MTS)

The multithreaded server removes dedicated shadow processes from the system by switching user connections in and out of a pool of shared servers.

In Figure 6.1, three users are connected to the database using both dedicated server and the multi-threaded server. Where the dedicated server maintains a one-to-one relationship with its corresponding client process, the MTS clients are sharing just two servers from a common pool.

The key component to consider in an MTS configuration is the dispatcher process. The dispatcher process acts as a software switch, listening for incoming requests from the client and connecting the client to a free server when required. The client is said to have a *virtual circuit* to the server process. During the time that the server is processing the request for the client, it is unavailable for any other session. Really, shared servers are not multithreaded at all, but serially reusable.

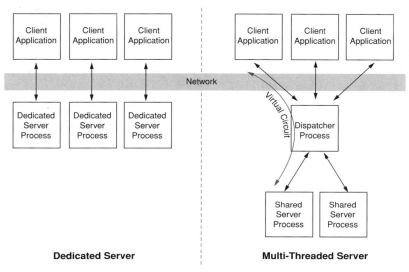

Figure 6.1 MTS operation

In order to support this server reuse by multiple client sessions, Oracle moves the session information, which was formerly stored in the PGA of the server process, into the SGA. Specifically, the memory is allocated from the large pool, or from the shared pool if no large pool is defined. This memory allocation is not insignificant and can increase the size of the SGA by many hundreds of megabytes in a large system. In reality, the memory savings offered by MTS are not great, if any.

The increase in required SGA memory can have other consequences on some systems. Many 32-bit platforms have quite low restrictions on the maximum size of the SGA, for example. On some platforms, this can mean that the maximum size of the SGA is less than 1GB, which somewhat limits the maximum number of connections possible with MTS.

In addition, the enlarged SGA can cause problems with the virtual memory management of the host operating system. If the host does not support the locking of the SGA into real memory, each server process that attaches to the SGA must maintain page table entries (PTEs) for each of the (typically) 4KB pages that make up the SGA. With a 4GB SGA, this equates to around one million additional page table entries to manage for each process. If the SGA can be locked into memory, all processes can share a common set of page table entries and so this is less of a problem.

The MTS shared servers are classified as background processes by Oracle, as are the dispatchers. However, unlike the other "real" background processes, Oracle will not crash if the processes are killed from the operating system. The impact of killing shared servers is minimal; the termination will be detected, and a replacement server will be started. All sessions will be unaffected by this operation *unless* they were active in the shared server at that time. Killing a dispatcher will terminate all sessions connected through it.

6.3   Net8

Net8, formerly known as SQL*Net, is the software used on both sides of the client/server connection in order to provide a platform-independent transport layer between client applications and the database server. It has become increasingly complex over the last few years, but the principles remain the same from a tuning perspective.

We are not going to cover any of the Net8 functionality here; this is well covered in the Oracle documentation. Instead, there are a few basics that need to be understood, particularly if your application is to be rolled out over a large geographic area.

The fundamental thing to bear in mind with Net8 is that it operates over a network. A network, like any communication medium, has two primary measures of "speed": latency and bandwidth. It is frequently the latency aspect that is overlooked, resulting in poor application response times for the user.

If an application is written in SQL*Forms, and each user runs the actual form locally on their PC, the Net8 communication is between the actual user PC and the database server. If the two are separated by a wide area network (WAN), problems frequently arise as a result of the latency of the underlying network rather than any particular Oracle problem.

As an extreme example, imagine locating a worldwide database server in North America and user PCs as far away as Asia. This wide area network could be implemented using satellite technology, providing a high-bandwidth network at relatively low cost. Unfortunately, the latency of a satellite-based network is approximately 0.5 second for each hop between the client and the server. This means that a round trip takes about 1 second and forms the *minimum* response time for any database access.

Database access includes parsing, every fetch, and so on. This means that a query on `sys.dual` will take about 3 seconds using this network. Increasing the bandwidth of the network will not improve this problem at all, because it is the latency of the network that causes the problem.

Therefore, the first rule of Net8 should be to keep network latencies between the client and the server to a minimum, preferably on the same physical local area network (LAN) in the datacenter.

The second rule of Net8 also relates to the underlying network. There is a tunable for Net8, specified in the `tnsnames.ora`, called the SDU (session data unit). This is the size of the data that Net8 will send to the native network transport for sending across the network.

There are occasions when the default setting of the SDU is not appropriate and the value must be increased. Typical reasons for increasing this value include

- Client performing large array fetches from the server
- Large number of requests not fitting in one physical network frame

The second reason is of particular importance where the network has a higher latency than desired. One symptom of a small SDU is when sessions are frequently found to be in "`SQL*Net more data to/from client`" wait states.

6.4   The SGA Components

6.4.1   High-Level View

The SGA is the area of shared memory that Oracle creates on start-up. All Oracle processes (background and shadow processes) connect to this shared memory when they are started. The various areas of the SGA are provided to meet the following needs of the database system:

- Caching
- Concurrency

- Consistency
- Control

On its own, the SGA does nothing at all—it is just a piece of shared memory. It is the use of the SGA by the Oracle kernel that provides all of the above-listed attributes of the database.

The SGA, shown in Figure 6.2, is composed of four distinct components:

1. Fixed region
2. Variable region
3. Buffer cache
4. Redo buffer

All of these areas, with the exception of the redo buffer, are comprised of many other subareas.

6.4.2   Fixed Region

The fixed region is very small, typically on the order of 40–60KB. Within this region Oracle stores singleton latches, such as the redo allocation latch, in addition to the parent latches for variable lists of latches. The contents of this region are defined by a platform-specific assembly language source file called `ksms.s`. This file used to be resident in `$ORACLE_HOME/rdbms/lib` prior to release 7.3, but is no longer shipped. It was used as the mechanism for relocating the SGA, but

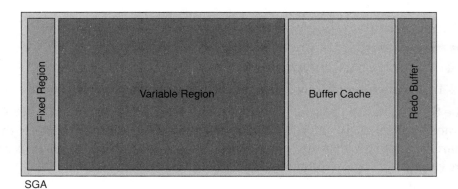

SGA

Figure 6.2   SGA components

this is now handled through init.ora parameters, and the assembly language file is no longer needed.

This is a shame, because the file was essentially a symbolic map of the fixed region of the SGA. For example, there was an entry showing

```
.set    kcrfal_,sgabeg+19072
```

This shows that the structure for kcrfal (redo allocation) is stored in the fixed region, 19,072 bytes from the beginning of the SGA. Part of this structure is the actual latch itself.

The names of structures relate to the names of the software modules that contain them and therefore are considered Oracle Proprietary (and therefore cannot be published). Anyway, it's immaterial now, because ksms.s is no longer shipped.

Essentially, the fixed region contains the structures that relate to the contents of V$LATCH: If you subtract the lowest ADDR from v$latch from the highest ADDR, you will get an approximate size of the fixed region. It is called the fixed region because this component is sized at compile time. No amount of change in the init.ora will change the size and structure of the fixed region, only its location in memory.

Now is a good time to get into some specifics of how Oracle implements latches.

Anatomy of an Oracle Latch

In the example above, we state that the kcrfal structure starts at an offset of 19,072 bytes from the beginning of the SGA. This structure might look a little like that shown in Figure 6.3.

The latch is physically stored at the head of the structure. Due to the serialization provided by the system bus, we already know (from Chapter 2) that we can perform atomic writes to memory locations of certain sizes. The limit on the size of the location that can be atomically updated is dependent on the platform (processor) architecture.

In this example, we assume that a 32-bit atomic memory write is available. Therefore, the mechanism for acquiring the latch is simply a test-and-set operation on the memory location at 19,072 bytes into the SGA memory region. If the test-and-set operation is successful, you have acquired the latch and can continue to modify any other part of the structure, copy data

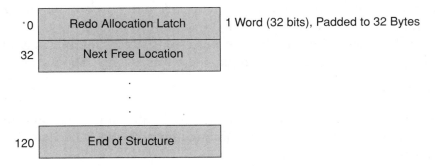

Figure 6.3   Conceptual view of a latch structure

into buffers, or modify several elements in a linked list of which this structure is the head. When the work is complete, the memory location is reset back to the "unset" value, and other sessions can allocate the latch.

You may have noticed that the latch location has been "padded" to 32 bytes in length. This, again, is just an example and assumes that the length of a single CPU cache line is 32 bytes on this platform. The reason for the padding is to guarantee that the latch itself is isolated in its own cache line and is not coexisting with another, unrelated latch. If this were not the case, it would result in false contention on the cache line, making the allocation of a little-used latch as difficult as that of a highly-contended-for latch.

6.4.3   Variable Region

The variable region contains the following elements:

- Shared pool
- Large pool
- Variable lists of latches (i.e., all the *cache buffers chains* latches)
- All lists (cache buffers chains, LRU lists, etc.)

In turn, the shared pool contents include the following elements:

- Library cache
- Dictionary cache
- NLS loadable objects
- Session and process context

- Enqueue resources
- Session memory (if running MTS and no `large_pool` is defined)

The large pool contains:

- Session memory (if running MTS)
- Parallel query buffers
- Oracle backup work areas

6.4.4   Buffer Cache

The buffer cache is an area of the SGA that is set aside for the caching of data blocks. From release Oracle8 onwards, it can contain up to three distinct "buffer pools," which are separately managed caches for different types of data usage:

- DEFAULT
- KEEP
- RECYCLE

The default buffer pool is the buffer cache that is created by default and has all objects assigned to it by default. This can be directly compared to the single buffer cache found in Oracle7. Optionally, two other buffer caches (pools) can be defined, which can be tuned to behave more suitably for specific situations. These two additional caches are the KEEP and RECYCLE caches (see Figure 6.4).

All three of the buffer pools have separate allocations of buffers and LRU lists that manage the buffers. The RECYCLE and KEEP pools are explicitly defined in the `init.ora`, whereas the DEFAULT pool allocates the remainder of the buffers and LRU lists for itself.

There are subtle differences between the three buffer pools, and some of these are highlighted next. One of the major differences, however, is that we now have the ability to individually tune the pools individually, dependent on their use.

RECYCLE Buffer Pool

The idea of the RECYCLE buffer pool is to use it more as a work area than a cache; this pool is used to store blocks that are virtually never reused after

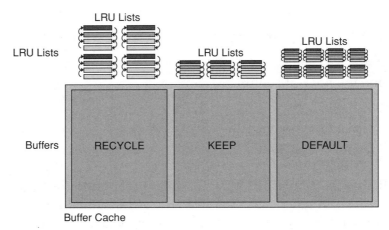

Figure 6.4   Organization of buffer pools

the initial read. Even though the blocks will rarely be reused, Oracle still needs to run all database blocks through the buffer cache in order to maintain consistent read views, and thus a buffer cache is still necessary for these blocks.

However, in a single buffer cache configuration, these single-use blocks could quickly dominate the buffer cache, implicitly flushing out other blocks that *will* be reused. Blocks that are frequently referenced are not affected by this cache pollution, because they will always be at the most recently used (MRU) end of the LRU lists. It is blocks that are reusable, but are not necessarily used very often, that are affected by this kind of cache pollution.

One operation that can pollute a cache is random single-row lookups on a table that is much larger than the cache itself. Each time one of these rows is read from disk, it must occupy an entire buffer in the cache. If these reads are part of an index-driven scan across the table, all of these buffers will need to be allocated from the cache, quickly dominating the space in the cache. Other blocks will need to be flushed from the cache to make space for these incoming blocks.

In this case, the table that is being accessed in this way can be moved to the RECYCLE pool. The idea of this pool is that we just give Oracle a work area for the blocks but don't really expect any kind of reusability. This having been said, the standard LRU mechanism still applies to this buffer pool but is managed in isolation from the other buffer pools. Therefore, if a few of the blocks in this table are reused from time to time (such as an index root block, as opposed to the leaf blocks), they will still remain in the cache if the access frequency merits the retention of the block.

When allocating a RECYCLE pool, we typically want it to be just large enough to allow contention-free allocation of the buffers. If the buffer is created too small, there will be too much demand for the number of buffers available, and potentially reusable blocks will be eliminated from the cache before they are requested again. However, this cache is typically not directly aiding system performance a great deal and so should not be wasting memory that could be used by the other caches. The sizing of the RECYCLE pool can require a little trial and error, and Oracle recommends an initial setting of one-quarter the number of buffers that the object occupies in the DEFAULT pool prior to being moved.

KEEP Pool

The KEEP pool is for the allocation of buffers for objects that are accessed with medium frequency, or those for which a consistent response time is desirable. Blocks that are accessed very often will remain in cache anyway, even in the DEFAULT or RECYCLE pools. The KEEP pool is for the blocks that are not accessed quite enough to remain in cache, or those with a mixture of hot blocks and warm blocks.

Using the KEEP pool, it is possible to assign just a few small objects to the cache and thus have the peace of mind of knowing that the buffers will never be aged out by unrelated blocks over time. This allows consistent response times for queries that access that object.

In order to support this a little more than the DEFAULT pool, some subtle changes are made in the algorithms used for the KEEP pool. First, to minimize cache pollution by excess CR versions of buffers (see Section 6.5.5), these buffers are not created in the KEEP pool. As they are assumed to be short-lived, CR versions of buffers in the KEEP pool are created in the DEFAULT pool in order to keep the content of the KEEP pool as static as possible.

In addition, the LRU algorithm used in the KEEP pool is slightly different. This will be discussed on Section 6.5.3.

6.5   Operation of the Buffer Cache

6.5.1   Introduction

The buffer cache is a portion of the SGA that is set aside for the caching of database blocks. As memory access is approximately 100,000 times faster than disk reads, it is highly desirable to service as many data requests from buffers in the cache as possible, without going to disk.

This is the ultimate goal of the buffer cache and is often the only information needed about the buffer cache in order to run a system fairly effectively. Simply keep an eye on your cache hit ratio:

Hit ratio = 1 – [physical reads / (db block gets – consistent gets)][1]

However, when the buffer cache is pushed very hard, it is useful to understand the workings of the buffer cache.

The buffer cache is a set of buffers in memory, each sized as one Oracle block. When a query needs a block of data from disk, Oracle first checks the buffer cache for the presence of that block in memory. This search is performed using *hash chains*.

6.5.2   Hash Chains

The hash chains are fixed-depth lists of pointers to the actual buffers in the cache. A conceptual view of the list elements is shown in Figure 6.5.

When Oracle has determined which block it requires, it can then hash this dba[2] to gain the ID of the hash chain that it should search. The buffer pool that the object is assigned to does *not* form part of this hashing algorithm; the entire set of hash chains is shared among all

---

1. Many people are not sure about the definition of this formula. db block gets are blocks retrieved without going through the CR mechanism, such as segment headers. consistent gets are blocks retrieved through the CR mechanism. The two combined make the total number of blocks retrieved, whether as a cached read or as a physical read.

2. Remember that dba stands for data block address and is the way that Oracle identifies disk blocks.

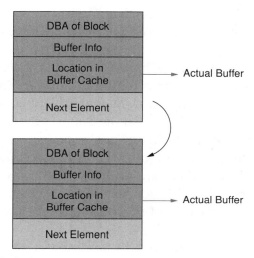

Figure 6.5 Hash chains

the buffer pools, with the chain ID determined by dba only. This means that an object that is cached in the RECYCLE pool could easily share the same hash chain as an object in the KEEP pool by virtue of dbas that hash to the same value.

Oracle maintains many hash chains, and they can be explicitly set using the _db_block_hash_buckets parameter in the init.ora. The maximum total number of elements in all of the hash chains is the same as db_block_buffers, because the hash chains are a list of the contents of the actual buffer cache.

Let's start an example that highlights this concept and the others that follow. In this example, we assume that we are using a single buffer pool, as in Oracle7.

A user submits a query to the database. It is determined that dba 15^3 is required as one of the blocks that is needed to execute this query. Oracle then hashes this dba, using the total number of hash chains as one of the hashing parameters. This yields a result of SEVEN, and so Oracle has determined that this dba will be listed in hash chain number 7 if it is present in the cache.

---

3. This dba value is nothing like a real dba, of course. It is used for simplicity only.

Oracle then starts at the top of hash chain 7 and checks the actual dbas of all the entries until it either hits the end of the chain or finds a match on the requested dba.

If the dba is matched in the hash chain, Oracle then checks to see if this buffer is OK to use. The information required to determine this is also likely to be stored within the hash chain element itself. One reason that the buffer may not be OK to use could be that the buffer is for an incompatible CR version of the block. If the buffer is not available for use, the hash chain is traversed further to determine whether more buffers store the same dba. If none of these buffers are available, or no further matching buffers are found for that dba, Oracle does not have a buffer in the cache that can satisfy the requirement and must go to the LRU list to create a new one (see Section 6.5.3).

If the buffer is found and deemed to be usable, Oracle can *heat the buffer* on the LRU list (again, see Section 6.5.3) and pin the buffer while it is in use. This pinning operation is a little like a latch but operates on a single element in the chain.

At this point, the buffer request has been serviced for the query, and Oracle can proceed to read the buffer and to read the actual contents of the buffer to act on the query. After use, the buffer is unpinned and is available for other sessions.

Twice in this section we have mentioned the LRU list, so let's go into some more detail on this.

6.5.3   LRU Chains

In order to have a cache that is based on frequency of use, a list that shows how often the blocks have been accessed needs to be maintained. In the Oracle kernel, this is implemented using an ordered LRU list, where the blocks with entries at one end of the list have been accessed most recently and the blocks entered at the other end of the list have been accessed least recently. This is the basis of a simple LRU chain.

In Chapter 1, we saw an example of an LRU chain in operation (see Section 1.5.4). This is the way Oracle managed its LRU chain right up until version 7.2. In this release, Oracle split the single LRU chain into multiple LRU chains in order to improve the scalability of the system.

We have two scenarios passed down from the section on hash chains:

1. Heating the buffer when it is located successfully in the hash chains

2. Finding a buffer to use when a block is not present in the cache, or when one is needed to create a CR version of the block

A simple view of the heating procedure is covered in Chapter 1 (see Section 1.5.4). Each time we access a block, it becomes the most recently used (MRU) buffer by implication. Therefore, the buffer is heated to the MRU of the LRU list. This heating process ensures that blocks that are not used as often as others will get implicitly aged down the LRU list by the heating process of the other blocks. When they get to the LRU end of the list, they become targets for replacement.

This is where the buffers come from in the second scenario. Oracle will go to the relevant LRU list when it needs a buffer and will take the first available buffer slot from the list. *Note:* The buffers at the LRU end of the list may not necessarily be available for use, because they could be dirty buffers (modified, but not written to disk).

The buffer is then heated to the top of the LRU list and is moved from its prior hash chain to the correct hash chain for the dba of the new block.

With the introduction of multiple LRU lists, sessions can no longer assume the location of a single LRU list. Instead, each session will round-robin between the multiple LRU lists, based on the buffer pool in which the object is cached. If an LRU is locked, the session will move onto the next LRU without waiting.

This is the basis of a simplified linear LRU mechanism, applied to the Oracle buffer cache. However, Oracle implements LRU slightly differently in order to gain better performance from the cache.

Oracle 8.1 Buffer Cache LRU

This description applies to Oracle 8.1 only. Prior (and probably future) releases of Oracle do not (will not) necessarily operate in this way.

When Oracle reads a block into the default buffer cache, it is *not* heated to the MRU end of the list immediately. The new block is generally inserted into the middle of the LRU list, because it is not known at this stage whether the block will be accessed enough to deserve a slot at the MRU end.

There then follows a short period of time during which the buffer will not be heated, even if it is accessed again. This timeout period is designed to be used in situations in which a block could be read and updated in quick succession and then never used again. One example of this would be a single row update: Oracle reads in the block in order to determine whether it meets the criteria for update and then modifies the block. This kind of activity could quickly dominate the MRU end of the cache in an OLTP system if the timeout period were not imposed. If the block continues to be accessed outside of this period, it will be heated to the MRU end of the list.

In the KEEP pool, the blocks are all assumed to be useful, especially because the kernel does not need to cater to CR buffers in its LRU algorithm. Therefore, all new blocks going into the KEEP pool are heated on first access.

Oracle 8.1 adds further optimizations for the LRU algorithm. Using the simple "read and heat" algorithm, every access to a block requires an LRU operation in order to heat the buffer, imposing a significant overhead in buffer access.[4] In order to improve on this, 8.1 implements an LRU algorithm that keeps a reference count for each buffer. No heating occurs at all, unless the buffer hits the end of the LRU list and has a high enough reference count. This way, the required LRU manipulations are very much reduced.

6.5.4 Latch Coverage

The buffer cache is covered by a large number of latches, typically more than all other parts of the Oracle kernel combined. This is vital, because the buffer cache needs to be completely free of corruption and yet retain a high degree of concurrency in access.

First, every hash chain is protected by a latch. These latches are the "cache buffers chains" latches and, like all child latches, are reported in v$latch_children. This is one of the important aspects of a system to watch, especially when the application is very heavy on the buffer cache.

Viewing v$latch_children, the number of gets and sleeps can be determined for each child latch. It is possible and likely that a small number of these child latches are requested much more often than the others. This is

---

4. Oracle has always had an algorithm that does not heat a buffer if it is close to the MRU end. This significantly cuts down on the number of LRU manipulations.

sometimes attributed to a single block being heavy, but more often than not it is the result of several blocks hashing to the same chain. When this happens, a large proportion of accesses to the buffer cache become serialized through this latch. The following query will report on the hottest hash chains:

```
SELECT  a.HLADDR,a.DBARFIL,a.DBABLK,b.GETS,b.SLEEPS
FROM    v$latch_children b,
        sys.x$bh a
WHERE   a.HLADDR=b.ADDR
AND     a.state != 0 /* ie, currently in use*/
AND     b.sleeps > ( SELECT 100*avg(SLEEPS) from v$latch_children
                     WHERE name='cache buffers chains' )
ORDER BY b.SLEEPS desc
```

The output from this query might look a little like this:

HLADDR	DBARFIL	DBABLK	GETS	SLEEPS
AA416498	158	3139	538830353	1588779
AA416498	208	374	538830353	1588779
AA416498	480	3343	538830353	1588779
AA41CED8	480	3543	1974346642	950985
AA41CED8	158	3339	1974346642	950985
AA33A8C8	157	12803	555346192	112729
AA3F5268	307	1283	148471828	93581
AA340B98	85	71701	263159467	81874
AA3C1498	480	783	554143110	78639
AA3E48C8	72	58417	358435709	46844

This shows several things about the operation of the hash chains in Oracle. First, there are multiple completely different blocks in the database on the same hash chain (HLADDR). This shows the hashing process sharing the chain among a diverse range of dbas. Second, it can be seen that there is still heavy contention for the first hash chain. There are 50 percent more sleeps occurring on the latch protecting this chain than on the next hottest chain, even though it has been acquired only one-quarter as often. This is likely to be caused by the duration of each latch operation that protects the chain, or by a series of "burst" allocation requests.

In this example, a good next step is to create more hash chains using the _db_block_hash_buckets parameter. The top two hash chains have two file/block combinations that could be the objects contended for: File 480, blocks 3343 and 3543; or File 158, blocks 3139 and 3339.

The only way we can determine which of the objects is getting requested so much is to create more hash buckets and hopefully split up the dba ranges into different hash chains: The guilty object would then be clearly visible.

The second set of latches over the buffer cache come from every LRU chain being protected by a latch, shown as "cache buffer lru chains" in v$latch_children. There are many times fewer LRU chains than there are cache buffers chains, because there is a minimum ratio of buffers to LRUs enforced at start-up time of 50 buffers per chain.

6.5.5   CR Versions

CR (consistent read) block creation was first discussed in "Block Header" in Section 5.5, in the anatomy of an Oracle block. In order to support the CR model provided by Oracle, the buffer cache must be employed to supply buffers that contain versions of a given block that differ from its on-disk representation. There may be several different versions of the same block in cache at any one time. This is a CR block.

When a CR version of a block is needed by a query, it will first of all determine if there is any version of the block in cache at that point. If so, it will choose the version that has a version number closest to, but no lower than, the desired one. If the version number were lower than the desired number, the block would need to be rolled forward from redo log; CR is supported from undo information only.

If a buffer is found that can be used to construct the CR block, it is cloned onto a free buffer in the cache and assigned to the same hash chain as the original. If no version can be found, the block is read off disk.

Once the buffer is available for constructing the CR block, the last relevant piece of undo information is applied to the block, as determined by the ITL entries in the block. This rolls back both the contents of the block and the ITL entries themselves. This process repeats until the change number of the block matches that of the start of the query. At this stage, we have a CR version of the actual block.

As previously discussed, this block is *never* written to disk. It exists only in the cache, as a reflection of a previous version of a block. Writing the block to disk would mean corrupting the database.

6.5.6   DBWR Operation

In our discussion of the LRU list, we referred to a dirty buffer that could be found at the tail end of the LRU list. The list of dirty buffers is also maintained within the LRU structures. The reason for this is simple: There is no point in writing out dirty buffers if they are about to get updated in the very near future.

However, it can be seen that without a formal way to clean (write out) these buffers, the cache would quickly become full of dirty buffers. This never happens in reality, because a given session will search only a certain percentage of the LRU list for a clean, reusable buffer. If it does not find one before hitting the threshold, the session will post[5] the database writer and wait on "free buffer waits" until buffers become available for reuse.

Every time the database writer is woken up to write out some dirty buffers, it will start at the cold end of each LRU and scan toward the hot end until a complete *write batch* full of dirty buffers is found. The size of this write batch is determined by the write batch size. This used to be a parameter in the init.ora but is now derived according to the algorithm in the *Oracle8 Tuning Guide* ("Internal Write Batch Size").

Another way in which the database writer is woken is by the checkpoint process. The checkpoint process doesn't actually do the writing associated with the checkpoint; it simply posts the database writer to write dirty blocks that are less than a given change number out to disk. This is an incremental checkpoint, because not all the dirty buffers need to be written out at each checkpoint. Each time a checkpoint occurs, this determines where rollforward recovery must start in the event of a failure prior to the next checkpoint.

Multiple database writers can operate on a given buffer cache/instance. Each database writer will work on LRUs in a round-robin fashion, ensuring that they do not contend with themselves for the latch. This implementation of *true* (i.e., independent) database writers is an improvement on Oracle7, where multiple database writers were implemented as a master/slave arrangement.

---

5. Posting is the term used by Oracle for telling a process to wake up.

6.5.7 Flowchart Summary of Buffer Cache Operation

The flowchart presented in Figure 6.6 should serve as a useful reference for the operation of the buffer cache. It is not a complete view of the operations but provides a simplified version for ease of use. In particular, the two items marked with asterisks should be viewed in conjunction with the text in the relevant preceding sections.

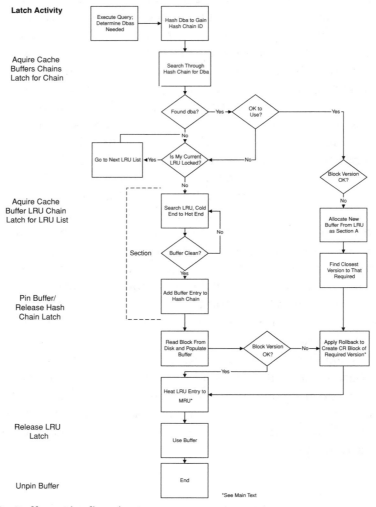

Figure 6.6   Buffer cache flowchart

6.6   Shared Pool Structure

The shared pool (see Figure 6.7) is a portion of the SGA, and itself contains several components.

These components compete for space within the space allocated to the shared pool. This means that if a poor cache hit ratio is being achieved in the library or dictionary cache, the other caches in the shared pool will be reduced in size proportionately, attempting to allow the badly controlled area to stabilize.

The "Other" portion of the shared pool is used to cache other structures needed for operation of the instance. The detail of the components in the shared pool (and the rest of the SGA) can be found by querying v$sgastat:

```
POOL           NAME                            BYTES
-----------    --------------------------    ----------
               fixed_sga                           47852
               db_block_buffers                167772160
               log_buffer                        1048576
shared pool    free memory                     294079744
shared pool    miscellaneous                     5625880
shared pool    transactions                      3424000
shared pool    db_files                           264736
shared pool    table columns                       72928
shared pool    SEQ S.O.                           336000
shared pool    KGK heap                            24408
shared pool    db_handles                        1470000
shared pool    KQLS heap                         8121648
shared pool    fixed allocation callback            3560
shared pool    branches                           960240
shared pool    Checkpoint queue                   347888
shared pool    PLS non-lib hp                       2104
shared pool    ktlbk state objects               1712000
shared pool    partitioning d                      32024
shared pool    db_block_hash_buckets             6062232
shared pool    DML locks                         1856000
shared pool    State objects                     2913312
shared pool    KGFF heap                          383656
shared pool    trigger defini                      18360
shared pool    distributed_transactions-          392168
shared pool    db_block_buffers                  8683520
shared pool    dictionary cache                 37045784
shared pool    state objects                      886728
shared pool    messages                           504000
shared pool    PL/SQL MPCODE                     1899184
shared pool    enqueue_resources                  576000
shared pool    library cache                   201110312
shared pool    table definiti                      23448
shared pool    sql area                        115850968
shared pool    processes                         2632000
shared pool    sessions                          8384000
shared pool    kxfp buffer su                   14932792
shared pool    event statistics per sess         9920000
shared pool    PL/SQL DIANA                      1616072
shared pool    transaction_branches               736000
shared pool    kxfp subheap                       240616
```

Shared Pool

Figure 6.7   Shared pool composition

6.7   Shared Pool: The Library Cache

6.7.1   Introduction

The library cache was introduced in Oracle7 as a means of cutting down on the amount of processing required just to parse an SQL statement. Prior to Oracle7, all incoming SQL requests were individually parsed each time, regardless of whether or not the statement had been parsed before. The CPU cost of performing a parse is high, and it was determined that a method of reducing parsing was needed.

In Oracle7, the library cache was introduced as the mechanism of reducing the amount of parsing in the database.

6.7.2   Cursors

All SQL statements are classed as cursors. Physically, a cursor consists of the following components:

- Client-side runtime memory (SQL runtime library)
- Server-side runtime memory (known as runtime memory)
- Server-side private SQL area (known as persistent memory)
- Server-side shared SQL area (the library cache)

When a cursor is opened and parsed, Oracle determines (as detailed next) whether or not the statement is identical to a previously submitted cursor. If it is, Oracle will reuse the parse information from the prior execution of the cursor.

6.7.3 The Parsing Mechanism

In order to convert a SQL request, which is essentially just a human readable text string, into an executable request, Oracle *parses* the statement.

Hard Parse

There are several steps involved in parsing a statement:

- Semantic and syntactic checking of the statement
- Dictionary validation that all the objects and columns exist
- Name translation of objects (i.e., synonym expansion to actual objects)
- Checking user privileges on the objects accessed in the cursor
- Production of an execution plan by means of the optimizer
- Loading of the statement into the library cache

These steps comprise the extreme of parsing—a *hard parse*. At this stage, although the cursor exists in the shared pool, it is not currently actually *shared*, other than by the session that created it. It exists as *sharable*, but the final steps have not been performed to make it usable by another session. These steps occur during the first execution of the statement by another session.

Cursor Representation in the Library Cache

When a statement is loaded into the library cache, two different entities are created:

1. Cursor head
2. Cursor body

When the statement is first parsed, it creates one head and one body for the statement. The cursor head can be thought of as the master record for that statement, containing the following information:

- The SQL text

- The optimizer goal

The head is locked when the cursor is first opened and is unlocked only when the cursor is closed by all sessions. The head cannot get aged out of the library cache while it is locked. When the head is unlocked, it is eligible for aging out of the cache, at which point all the corresponding body entries are also flushed out.

The body contains all the specifics for the cursor, such as the actual execution plan and the bind variable information. A cursor may have many bodies for its single head, even though the text is the same for each. The number of bodies is reported in the VERSION_COUNT column of v$sqlarea, and each body's statistics are reported in v$sql.

Identical executions of the same statement will reuse both the head and the body of the statement. New bodies are created under the following conditions:

- Bind thresholds differ greatly from prior executions.

- Optimizer plan changes as a result of bind variables supplied.

When a SQL statement is submitted using bind variables, Oracle builds a cursor body that can cater to bind variables of that specific length. The body will also cater to bind variables that are similar to that length, subject to different buckets of sizes. For example, if a query has a bind variable for NAME, the first time it is executed the value bound to the NAME variable is 6 bytes, and Oracle creates bind information to cope with up to 50 bytes in that bind position. The next time it is executed, NAME is 200 bytes in length (a really long name), and Oracle cannot reuse the existing body—the runtime requirements of the statement go beyond the definition in the current body. At this point, Oracle will create a new body to cater for—say, 65 to 256 byte bind variables at that point. The previous body will remain for future use, subject to being aged out.

The optimizer plan can also change between executions, owing to the existence of histograms for the values for a column. If a value is supplied that can be approached in a more efficient way as a result of cardinality, then a new plan is created and put into a new body for the statement.

Cursor bodies are eligible for aging out at any time, regardless of whether the cursor is open or not. If a cursor is open and the body is aged out, the head (which is locked) contains sufficient information to reconstruct the body for when it is next used. This is classed as a reload, and the hit rate of executions to reloads can be determined by the following query on V$LIBRARYCACHE:

```
SELECT 100*sum(reloads)/sum(pins) Reload_Ratio
FROM v$librarycache
```

Soft Parse

Prior to the steps of a hard parse, Oracle hashes the statement to produce an identifier to look for in the library cache. The range of the hashing algorithm is very broad, and most of the time there will be only one statement for a given hash value. It is not guaranteed to be unique, however, and the ADDRESS of the statement in the shared pool should always be used in conjunction with the hash value in order to gain uniqueness when querying the library cache. If this hash value corresponds with one already stored in the library cache, and further checks prove this to be the same statement as one that has already been parsed, then this statement only requires one of the three types of soft parse instead of the full hard parse.

Soft Parse Type 1.   The first time a session attempts to use a sharable cursor (i.e., one that resides in the shared pool but has never been executed by this session), two actions are taken by Oracle. First, a name translation occurs, just as in the hard parse. The reason for this is that this session is not the same user as the original, and it must be determined that this session is referring to the same objects.

Second, the user has to be authenticated on all the objects in the cursor. Once this has been completed, the user is put on the authentication list.

Soft Parse Type 2.   The second time a session attempts to use a cursor, it is now classed as shared because of the prior name translation and authentication steps. However, because grants may have changed since the last execution, the authentication step must still occur.

Soft Parse Type 3: Session Cached Cursors.   When session cached cursors (session_cached_cursor init.ora parameter) are used, it is the third parse call for a cursor that creates the entry in the session's cursor cache. Once in the session cursor cache, any CLOSE calls to the cursor are ignored, and the statement does not need to be reparsed, up to the number of cursors specified in the init.ora.

Parse Hit Ratio

Once the hash value for the statement has been determined, Oracle goes to the library cache and determines whether the statement is already cached. If so, Oracle uses that information to reduce the steps needed to execute the statement. This is known as a *soft parse*, and there are up to three different severity levels for this type of parse.

The ratio of hard parses to soft parses should as close to zero as possible. In this case, good sharing of SQL is occurring, and the system is running efficiently from the library cache. The cache hit ratio for the library cache can be determined by the following query:

```
SELECT 100*(1-(gets-gethits)/gets) Ratio
FROM v$librarycache
WHERE namespace='SQL AREA'
```

This query reports the hit ratio as a percentage, and should be as close to 100 percent as possible.

6.7.4   Latch Coverage

The library cache is protected by latches, in the same way as are the other memory structures in Oracle. Prior to Oracle 7.2, this was performed using a single latch on the entire library cache, and scalability was a big problem on systems that had heavy parse overheads.

Since 7.2, Oracle has maintained multiple library cache latches, where the latch used is based on the hash value of the statement. The default number of latches is the nearest prime number greater than the number of CPUs on the system, but can be explicitly set using the _kgl_latch_count parameter in the init.ora. The inclusion of multiple latches protecting the library cache allows for far greater work to be achieved on the system.

Work occurring in the library cache must be carried out while holding the relevant library cache latch. For most requests, the library cache latch is acquired and released several times before the request is complete. The number of times the latch is required depends on the severity of the operation. For example, a simple SELECT * FROM DUAL acquires the library cache latch 29 times to hard parse the statement, but only 19 times for the next execution, and only 10 times for executions after that. The amount of work performed in the library cache decreases each time, owing to the different levels of parsing.

A badly sized shared pool, or an application that does a poor job of sharing SQL, will quickly fill up the shared pool. In this eventuality, Oracle must start to age items out of the library cache using a "modified" LRU algorithm.

When space must be found, Oracle starts at the cold end of the LRU and flushes out cache entries until a contiguous area is available that is large enough for the minimum contiguous size required by the statement being parsed. The actual amount of memory freed up by this process could be far in excess of the actual required memory, because the entries that are aged out are unlikely to be contiguous themselves. This means that a fairly severe flush is required to gain the space needed for the new statement. Each time this aging process occurs, the demand on the library cache latch increases greatly as a result of the extra strain put on it by the aging process.

As time goes on, the shared pool becomes more and more fragmented, resulting in more and more pressure on the library cache latch. There comes a point where the miss rate on the library cache latch becomes unacceptably high, and the shared pool must be flushed explicitly to relieve the pressure on the latch. Even having to hard parse all the requests for the foreseeable future is not as bad as having a full and fragmented shared pool.

During the aging-out process, Oracle can age out only objects that are not currently being executed, pinned in memory, or locked (i.e., cursor heads). If an area of library cache needs to be found for the parsing of a large object, this can result in Oracle being unable to flush any further objects out of the cache and still not finding enough space for the object. In this case, an ORA-04031 error is returned, and the request fails. The shared pool is dangerously undersized and/or badly treated by the application if this occurs.

The latch cost of a 4031 error can be estimated by a simple test. With a large shared pool, a connection to the database using SQL*Plus requires approximately 3,357 latch gets. The same test performed on the same instance with a small shared pool (to provoke 4031 errors) takes out the latch 4,596 times. These measurements reflect only acquisition counts, but it is also likely that the period during which the latch is held will increase when the management overhead is increased in this way. These two factors combined result in high latch contention on a busy system.

6.8   Other Memory Structures

6.8.1   Dictionary Cache

The dictionary cache is a special cache designed expressly for the caching of certain objects in the SYS schema, as described in Section 5.7.6. It is also known as the *rowcache*, because it operates on a row-by-row basis rather than the block basis on which the buffer cache works. These two terms are used interchangeably in Oracle documentation.

The purpose of the dictionary cache is to speed up access to the tables that Oracle needs to operate. Included in this are all the table definitions, storage information, user information, optimizer histograms, constraints, and rollback segment information.

When an object is not found in the dictionary cache, Oracle must go to disk and retrieve the required dictionary information. The process of getting dictionary information from disk is called *recursive SQL*. Often, a single SQL statement will require many recursive calls before it can be executed, if the information is not found in the dictionary cache. The recursive calls quickly dominate the cost of executing a single statement at this point.

Due to the presence of the dictionary cache, the tables that make up the data dictionary cannot be manipulated by DML. In physical terms they can be, and Oracle will allow you to do so without complaint. However, this can cause database corruption as a result of the dictionary cache being unaware of these changes.

If SYS.FET$, for example, were to be modified by a user session, any updates would occur with a standard DML TX enqueue rather than the ST enqueue that is used when the kernel manipulates this part of the dictionary. In addition, when the update is committed, the dictionary cache would not be invalidated, therefore making the operational state of the database inconsistent with the state stored on disk.

6.8.2 Log Buffer

The log buffer is the buffer that stages database changes prior to being written to the redo log. When a change is made to database blocks, they are written to both the buffer cache and the log buffer. If a commit occurs on the system, regardless of origin, all data in the log buffer is written to the redo log. This is the way Oracle guarantees that committed transactions are on disk; the dirty buffer cache blocks can be re-created from the redo log in the event of a crash.

The log buffer is a circular buffer, as shown in Figure 6.8.

This means that the log writer "chases the tail" of the new buffers being copied in. It also means that the new buffers can chase the tail of the log writer. To prevent the buffer from filling up, the log writer will start to write out the buffers when the log becomes one-third full, or every 3 seconds.

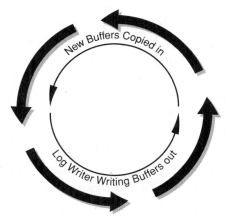

Figure 6.8 Circular redo buffer

In reality, a busy system commits a good deal more often than every 3 seconds, and so this typically is not a problem (at least in a transactional system). The important thing to ensure is that the log buffer is large enough to allow the log writer to catch up before any burst writes to the buffer threaten to fill it up.

When a commit is issued, Oracle writes a commit record to the redo buffer for that transaction and flushes all of the buffer to disk. If any commits are issued while this is happening, they will all be handled as an atomic unit by the log writer when it returns. This is known as a *group commit* and reduces the amount of time a session will wait for a commit confirmation.

Latch Coverage

The log buffer is ultimately protected by just one latch—the *redo allocation latch*. This latch is serialized by design, because it is the only point in the design of the Oracle database that is inherently serial. All records must be written to the buffer in order, and without interfering with each other.

However, a single latch would not scale very effectively, as sessions must copy potentially large amounts of redo records into the log buffer. This could take a long time and would result in high contention for the latch as many sessions waited to copy in their data. To prevent this, Oracle provides *redo copy latches*.

Redo copy latches are an abstraction of the redo allocation latch specifically geared toward reducing the amount of time that any one session holds the redo allocation latch. Using copy latches, the redo allocation latch is acquired for just long enough to reserve the amount of space needed for the copy. One of the redo copy latches is then acquired in order to perform the actual copy.

The use of redo copy latches is governed by two `init.ora` parameters: `log_simultaneous_copies` and `log_small_entry_max_size`. The `log_simultaneous_copies` parameter sets the number of copy latches to create, where `2*cpu_count` is the default. The `log_small_entry_max_size` parameter determines the threshold over which it is preferable to copy using copy latches rather than the allocation latch.

6.9   Oracle Parallel Server Concepts

6.9.1   Introduction

Oracle Parallel Server (OPS) is typically surrounded in mystery, because not many people have experience in implementing or administering such a system. However, the basic concepts of OPS are not *very* complex and should be understood by anyone involved in specifying or implementing very-large-scale systems.

Ultimately, the scalability of a single system has a limit at any given point in time. If your application looks to require three times more CPU than the largest server on the planet can provide, even after tuning, then a single-system solution is no longer an option. Without OPS, Oracle is limited to the scalability provided by the hardware vendor.

Figure 6.9 shows a high-level view of the operation of OPS. Starting at the bottom, we have a database that is accessible by all nodes that need to

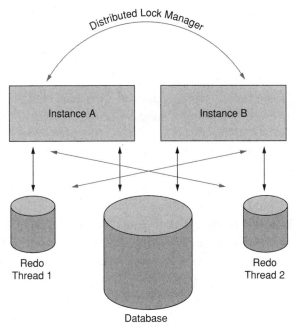

Figure 6.9   High-level view of OPS

run an Oracle instance against this database. The access can be direct, through a shared disk array found in clustered systems, or indirect, through software layers commonly found in shared-nothing MPP systems. All nodes open the database in shared mode, which allows other instances to open the same database. Each node acquires a set (or thread) of redo logs for exclusive use during normal operation. The gray arrows are intended to demonstrate that the redo logs must be available to all other instances for recovery purposes.

6.9.2   Distributed Lock Manager (DLM)

On top of the physical database, each node runs an Oracle instance exactly as normal, with the addition of the distributed lock manager (DLM) to take care of communication between the instances.

In single-instance Oracle, the state of locks is held internally as a series of structures in the SGA. When a lock needs to be acquired or released, it is simply a case of taking a latch (the enqueues latch) and updating the structures in memory. When there is more than one instance accessing the same data, a common view of lock states must be maintained for all nodes; this is the function of the DLM. In addition to standard enqueues that we are familiar with, the DLM also controls access of a variety of other resources, most notably the buffer cache by means of parallel cache management (PCM) locks. This is covered in Section 6.9.3 and is one of the fundamental differences between single-node Oracle and OPS.

In the Oracle7 days, the DLM was typically provided by the hardware vendor rather than by Oracle. This was both good and bad, depending on the implementation of the DLM.

The good thing about a vendor-supplied DLM was that it could be implemented as part of the operating system kernel and subsequently always run at kernel priority. It could also have direct access to the hardware layer in order to communicate with DLMs running on the other nodes.

The bad thing about a vendor-supplied DLM was that if problems occured (and they did, many times), the resolution of the problem lay across the boundaries of two companies. Frequently, these problems took a long time to be resolved and sometimes never got fixed because neither side believed it to be their issue. The other bad thing was that the Oracle software had to communicate with the DLM through a published API. This prevented Oracle from being able to change things from release to release and drastically reduced the speed at which improvements could be made in the DLM architecture. These problems have all gone away in Oracle8, due to the introduction of an integrated DLM in the OPS version of the RDBMS.

The DLM is implemented as a new set of background processes with special hardware support in the operating system for the best internode communication method for that platform. On SMP platforms, this is typically a private Ethernet LAN or some kind of proprietary interconnect. On MPP systems, the communication is performed over the MPP interconnect. It is the latency of the DLM communication medium that is one of the prime limiting factors in an OPS environment, because it directly affects the time taken to service each remote lock request.

The existence of the DLM allows multiple Oracle instances to synchronize their use of shared resources.

Not all Oracle resources are shared, even in an OPS environment. Examples of this would be the redo allocation latch and cache buffer LRU chains latches. These entities are private to the local instance and therefore do not need to be coordinated through the DLM.

Therefore, in an OPS configuration, Oracle has a total of five different types of resources to consider:

1. PCM locks

2. Global enqueues (non-PCM lock)

3. Global locks (non-PCM lock)

4. Local enqueues (non-PCM lock)

5. Local latches (non-PCM lock)

The first three of these resources are handled by the DLM, and the remainder are handled the same as in a single-instance configuration.

6.9.3 Parallel Cache Management

The concept of a parallel cache is fundamental to OPS. It is important to understand this concept thoroughly before attempting to recommend or implement an OPS solution.

What Is a Parallel Cache?

In a single-instance configuration of Oracle, a buffer cache is used to speed up access to frequently used pieces of data, to provide a fast commit mechanism, and to reduce the overall number of writes to disk. These attributes of the Oracle buffer cache are absolutely essential, and if OPS were to remove any of these advantages it would not be a viable option.

However, to retain these features in an OPS configuration, a cache on every instance is required. This is not an issue if the database is purely read-only, but in a deferred write environment such as Oracle, data corruption would occur as multiple instances all wrote differing data to common blocks on disk.

To eliminate this problem, and retain most of the advantages, OPS has the concept of a *parallel cache*. This is simply a fancy name for multiple Oracle buffer caches glued together with a DLM. However, the DLM cannot coordinate the access to every buffer on every instance, because its latency would cause all buffer operations to slow to a crawl, not to mention use a great deal of resource. Instead, Oracle implements *parallel cache management* (PCM) locks, over the datafiles in the database, and coordinates the use of these locks with the DLM.

Note: PCM locks are not related to transaction locks in any way. This will become clear as we go on.

Each PCM lock can cover one or more actual data blocks in the files, and they are used to group data blocks together into commonly managed resources. This dramatically reduces the number of resources managed by the DLM and also reduces the overall communication between the nodes, provided that the application and database implementation have been performed adequately.

When an instance wants to access a block covered by a PCM lock, it must ask the DLM for the PCM lock covering that block and must obtain it in a mode suitable for the intended operation. In simple terms, this means Shared Mode for read and Exclusive Mode for write, although more states than this are used by OPS.

If another instance has the PCM lock in any mode higher than Shared Mode, the DLM will not grant the lock to the requesting instance right away. The fact that another instance has a higher-level lock than Shared means that the other instance has modified the block. In this case, the DLM downgrades the Exclusive Mode lock of the other instance to a Shared Mode if the new request is for read or to NULL Mode (i.e., no lock) if the new request is for Exclusive Mode. This forces the other instance to flush the block from the buffer cache back onto disk and to report back when complete. When this synchronous operation is complete, the DLM grants the requested lock to the instance requesting it. This operation is known as a *ping* (see Figure 6.10).

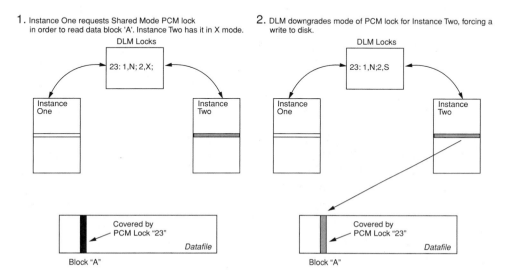

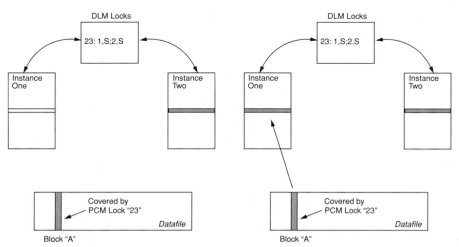

Figure 6.10 OPS ping for READ

As stated earlier, a PCM lock is not the same as a transaction lock. A PCM lock has the granularity of a single database block at best, whereas a transaction lock has the granularity of a single row within a block. Therefore, the PCM operations cannot interfere with the critical ability to perform row-level locking in Oracle.

Oracle achieves this isolation by keeping transaction and PCM locks totally independent of each other. While a transaction will typically cause a buffer to be written to in the first place, it is not linked to the PCM operation in any way, or vice versa.

In the example above, an update of block "A" by Instance Two caused the buffer to be dirty in the first place. This update has not been committed at this point. When the request comes in from Instance One, the transaction has still not been committed, but because PCM and transactions are not related, the buffer can be written to disk and used by the other node. The other node is only trying to read the block and so is not affected by the fact that there is an outstanding TX lock on one of the rows (remember, writers don't block readers). When Instance Two is ready to make more changes in the block, it will request that its lock be upgraded to an Exclusive Mode once more and will continue work.

CR Server

Of course, in this example, Instance One has just gained permission to read a block that is of no use to it. The block it read from disk has uncommitted data in it, and the query running on Instance One needs to see the version of the block before it is changed by Instance Two. Therefore, an additional ping is required of the transaction table and undo information in order to rebuild the old version of the block. This is known as reader/writer contention in the OPS world and is the reason that the CR server has been implemented for Oracle8.1. The CR server vastly improves this type of contention by constructing the correct version (that's where the CR part comes in) of the block using required undo (on Instance Two in this case), and ships the buffer directly over to the buffer cache of Instance One. No disk writes occur, because CR blocks are useless anyway once they are finished with by the requesting session; they should never be written to disk.

Types of Locks

Further complexity now arises; it is impractical to have a PCM lock for every block in the database. Doing this would cause an enormous memory burden on each instance in the configuration, because each PCM lock requires memory to be allocated for the lifetime of the instance. The exact amount of memory varies among platforms and releases, but it is reasonable to estimate this memory burden at 100 bytes per lock. This would make 11GB of memory overhead per instance for a 450GB online database.

To alleviate this problem, Oracle provides two types of locks:

1. Fixed PCM locks
2. Releasable PCM locks

Fixed PCM Locks

A fixed PCM lock is one that is created at start-up and not released until instance shutdown. Therefore, every instance has a copy of each lock, potentially in a NULL Mode if it has not been used. Fixed locks cover between one and n blocks of the database for each lock, although fixed locks are typically used to cover multiple blocks. Therefore, the rest of this subsection will concentrate on hashed PCM locks—the type used to cover multiple blocks with a single PCM lock.

Hashed locks are specified on a per-file basis in the init.ora and are evenly distributed across the file according to the blocking factor specified (used as the modulo in the hash), as shown in Figure 6.11.

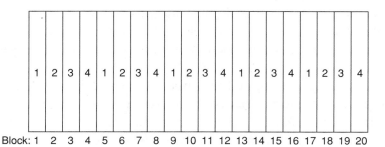

Figure 6.11   Hashed PCM locks distribution

In this example, a 20-block datafile is configured to have four locks covering it, with a blocking factor of 5. This means that every fifth block is protected by the same PCM lock.

Hashed locks have a serious problem when covering files with a comparatively small number of locks. As the number of locks covering a file decreases, the probability of lock collisions increases proportionately. A lock collision is where, say, one instance is updating block 6, and another instance wants to read block 18. Both of these blocks are covered by PCM lock "2," and so the DLM has to downgrade that lock on the other node's behalf, causing a ping. This situation is known as a *false ping*, because it did not need to be performed in order to preserve coherency between the buffer caches. In reality, one false ping can potentially cause many, many disk writes, and so should be avoided wherever possible.

As previously mentioned, it is not really practical to allocate one fixed PCM lock per block in the database. Therefore, another option is needed for situations where block level PCM is needed.

Releasable PCM Locks

A releasable lock is a PCM lock that is allocated from a pool defined in the init.ora. If a lock has not been used, it does not exist on any instance, but only as a blank entry in the common pool. Although the coverage of releasable locks can be specified as hashed, covering many blocks, this rarely makes sense because of the additional overhead of using releasable locks for each lock operation. Therefore, releasable locks tend to be most useful for covering one block or a few blocks for each lock.

As their name suggests, releasable locks are released when they are no longer in use. That is, there is no concept of a NULL Mode lock with releasable locks—they are simply released. This allows a relatively modest pool of releasable locks to be used to provide block level locking across the entire database.

Unfortunately, nothing in life is free. There is about a 30 percent overhead imposed by using releasable locks, because the lock must be created and destroyed for each NULL-to-X or anything-to-NULL conversion pair. Therefore, greater performance can be achieved using fixed locks as long as the false pinging can be tuned to acceptable levels.

6.9.4 Design Considerations for OPS

The whole point of the preceding section is to give you a feel for operations that occur in an OPS configuration. Although this topic really needs an entire book in its own right, hopefully you will have realized that careful design and planning are required when implementing an OPS system.

Application Design

The application design component of OPS is probably the single most critical component in obtaining good horizontal scalability (i.e., more nodes) from OPS. Primary in this is the concept of *partitioning the application*.

Application partitioning has nothing to do with table or index partitions, although the partitioning strategy may elect to use those features. Rather, it involves the partitioning of function within the application to allow users on different instances of the OPS database to operate without incurring too much synchronization overhead from the DLM. To achieve this, the data access for users on a given node should be as independent of the data access on other nodes as possible.

Specifically, the ideal application would be one that shared only read-only data in the database, such as reference information. This is known as a hard partitioning of the application. However, this is rarely a practical proposition, particularly when many nodes become involved.

The flipside of a hard-partitioned application is a soft-partitioned application. This is where the application designer has quantified where read/write and write/write synchronization is required between nodes and provides functionality in those areas to allow measures to be taken in the database to reduce the synchronization.

In practice, a combination approach is usually required, using hard partitioning wherever possible and soft partitioning elsewhere.

Step 1. Determine how much partitioning is required. A two- or three-node OPS system is significantly easier to design than a ten-, 50-, or 150-node system. In systems where the node count is significantly greater than the number of hard-partitionable functions in the application, most of the design attention needs to be put into the soft-partitioning effort.

As a rule of thumb, if there is a great deal of read/write and write/write sharing between functions, the hardware platform choice will become an increasingly dominant factor in the performance of the system. In this situation, considerably greater scalability will be obtained by minimizing the node count and maximizing the power in each node.

In read/read OPS applications, such as decision support, good scalability can be obtained by increasing the node count to quite high numbers. In these applications, the nodes quickly stabilize their locks into being Shared Mode, and the synchronization overhead is reduced significantly because lock operations remain local.

Step 2. The next step should be an analysis of the tables that each function in the application requires. This is the opportunity to make the high-level hard-partitioning decisions. For example, in a financial application there may be a good split between Accounts Payable and Accounts Receivable. If this split continues to look good right down to the table level, then this will already allow the application to run efficiently on two nodes of OPS owing to minimal synchronization overhead.

If there is not a clean split between functions in the initial data model, are there any changes that can be made to change this situation? For example, if one part of the application updates a table frequently, and the other function reads only nonupdated columns in the table, can the model be amended to split this table into two? This would eliminate the pinging every time the read function needed to access a row.

Clearly, changes in the data model are very much more suited to this stage in the design process, and this is why the more successful OPS applications take care of this overhead at the right time.

Step 3. Once the hard partitioning has been defined, how much further do we need to go (defined in Step 1)? In our example, we allowed the application to scale from one node to two nodes, just by finding a good hard partition in the application. Let's assume that we need twice as many nodes to support Accounts Receivable as to support Accounts Payable. In this case, we need to find a way to split Accounts Receivable. This is going to involve some support from the application to allow certain database operations to work most efficiently.

For example, in order to minimize contention on index leaf blocks for a table that is written to by both AR nodes, we may want to take either of two approaches:

1. Sequence number caching
2. Reverse key indexes

Both of these approaches have implications for the application and therefore will need application support prior to implementation in the database.

Sequence number caching was one of the first techniques to be used in gaining index leaf block separation (and therefore minimizing concurrent updating of the same block by multiple OPS nodes). The theory is that if the primary key for an index is system-generated by a sequence number generator, then the sequentiality of the numbers will force the additional row inserts to update the same block in the primary key index. This is a result of the primary key being in exactly the same part of the index B-tree due to close values being used by all nodes.

The solution is to use a large sequence cache for this sequence number on each node. This would typically be on the order of 2,000, depending on insert frequency. This means that when the first node needs a sequence number, it will read the next value from disk and update the on-disk value to be 2,000 greater. It will then have exclusive use of a set of 2,000 numbers. The next node to use the sequence will start 2,000 higher and update the on-disk version of the sequence to be 2,000 higher still. In this way, each node gets a discrete set of numbers to use as primary key values.

The impact of this is that, if the cache is sized correctly with respect to the number of keys in a leaf block, each node will typically be updating a different leaf block to the other nodes.

Here's the downside: you should never assume that sequence numbers are sequential; they are guaranteed only to be unique. If there is an instance crash, or even a normal shutdown in OPS environments, Oracle will "lose" numbers from the defined range due to the cache. In the case of a normal shutdown, the value used at next start-up will be one greater than the highest number last used. This is the only value that Oracle can use.

In the extreme case of AR, we might be using this technique to provide index separation in the INVOICES table, on the INVOICE_NUMBER column. Two situations can arise here that financial people are rarely very pleased about.

First, if an invoice is created by an AR user on one node and then cancelled and replaced by a user on another AR node, it is very feasible that the replacement invoice will have an invoice number *less than* the original.

Second, whenever there is a crash, or even a normal maintenance shutdown of the instances, numbers will get lost. Again, financial people get upset about this, because they have to account for all invoice numbers.

Both of these issues can be catered for with application reporting, user signoff, and so on, but they need to be taken care of up front.

Reverse key indexes are another database-level change that affects the application. Using reverse key indexes, a noncached sequence number can be used to generate the keys (although this requires greatly increased synchronization on the sequence generator itself), and the key will be inverted by Oracle before determining which leaf block it belongs to. For example, key 123456789 would become 987654321.

This ensures that the most significant digits of the index are the ones that change every time there is a sequential insert. When the key is read by Oracle, it is simply flipped back to the way the application expects it. However, all is not as transparent as it seems.

Now that the keys are inverted in the actual index, range scans can no longer be performed on the index. The only way this could occur would be for Oracle to perform either a Full Fast Scan of the index and check each key to see whether it was in the required range, or to perform potentially thousands of physical index range scans. Neither of these options bodes well for performance, and so the application designer needs to ensure that no range scans are required on this index.

Step 4. Don't forget the batch cycle. Is there a defined batch window for the system? If batch needs to run concurrently with the users, is the user count a great deal smaller at that point? Can the batch processes be hard partitioned?

The reason these questions need to be answered is that batch typically runs while some users are still operational and traverses many areas of the database schema in order to produce the desired result. In this case, massive amounts of pinging can occur as a result of the large synchronization overhead.

In order to minimize this, the ideal solution would be to hard partition all the batch processes. Unfortunately, this is very rarely possible, simply because of the nature of batch processing. Instead, it often becomes an operational solution that is required.

During the batch cycle, the system can normally be operated with a single node because of reduced user load at night. This involves some kind of change in the login process during the batch window to ensure that users connect to the same system. Once all the users are on one node, batch can also be executed on that node.

This is a strange one to sell to management sometimes. They see that batch is running slow and that there are loads of unused CPUs on the idle instances. However, the real issue is the cost of synchronization. Even if the single batch node is at 100 percent CPU, it is unlikely that moving jobs to the other nodes will speed things up—usually the contrary.

Database Design

Once the application design is OPS-friendly, all the attention has to be turned to the database. While the application design phase is likely to have included database changes to reduce data sharing, the physical database implementation requires a great deal of attention in order to scale the system effectively.

Removing Contention for Blocks

Contention for blocks is the single most gating factor in scaling OPS systems because of the required DLM synchronization between the nodes, which is many orders of magnitude slower than within a single instance. Therefore, contention for blocks and the resultant pinging must be minimized wherever possible. There are several options open to the DBA at this point, and some of them should be used by default in an OPS implementation.

The first of these "must haves" are *freelist groups* and *process freelists*. These were covered in some detail in Section 5.5.2, where the usage of these entities was discussed. In summary, freelist groups remove segment header contention from the Parallel Server synchronization list, because each node now has its own freelist block to update. As the overhead of freelist groups is so minimal, it is almost not worth thinking about where they are required; they can be added to every table in the database. For example, in a five-node clustered OPS system with 1,500 tables (i.e., a complex application), the total overhead would be 7,500 database blocks, or approximately 30MB. This is a very small price to pay for the advantages it gives with little complexity.

With Oracle8, another "must have" became available. Partitioned objects allow physical separation of data, including freelists, high-water marks, and in many cases the indexes for the table. To use partitioned objects for OPS, some kind of node identifier needs to be used as the partition key, and this clearly has an impact on the application. Partitioned tables should be used wherever practical, not necessarily just on large objects.

If there are any tablespaces that are truly read-only, consider changing their status in Oracle to read-only. Not only does this reduce the amount of data that needs to be backed up regularly, but also removes the tablespace from the DLM's consideration.

Once all the physical measures have been taken, including the methods mentioned in the application design section, all that remains is the tuning of the PCM lock allocations with the init.ora parameters, especially with a view toward reducing false pinging.

This is where a more in-depth analysis of the application is required, including knowledge of SELECT, UPDATE, INSERT, and DELETE frequencies and distribution to all of the tables in the application. This will allow the type and distribution of the PCM locks to be set accordingly. Consider Table 6.1. when planning for PCM lock distribution.

There are many shades of gray in the way a table is accessed, and other approaches are required accordingly. It is important to go through the kind of thought process presented in Table 6.1 for each of the situations, in order to come up with the correct allocation and type of PCM locks.

Removing Contention for Non-PCM Locks

In addition to the PCM lock synchronization that occurs in OPS, there are several non-PCM locks that must be coordinated. The most straightforward of these is the TX or row-level lock and its associated TM table lock.

The careful use of TX locks is not really an OPS design issue, but rather an issue for any application. It is not good design to allow users to hold row-level locks for any extended period. The TM locks are created implicitly when a TX lock is created and are a preventative measure.

Table 6.1 PCM Lock Approaches

Table Access Method	PCM Lock Tuning	Why
Read-only, all nodes	If the table is in its own tablespace, set the tablespace to read-only.	Take it out of the DLM equation.
Mostly read-only, all nodes	Cover the file with comparatively few fixed hash locks. False pinging will not be a problem if the table is rarely written to.	Save memory by using few locks. The table access will still be fast owing to fixed locks. Rare writes will not present large synchronization problems.
One node updates, other nodes read	CR server should be considered, in addition to covering the file with fairly fine-grained fixed hash locks.	Updates can occur all over a table. The use of CR server minimizes the pinging required by the readers, because no undo needs pinging.
Heavy insert from all nodes	Partitioned table, partitioned by presence of instance number in partition key. Sparse PCM lock coverage, potentially using releasable locks.	Physical separation removes synchronization problems.
Heavy update from all nodes	Fine-grained fixed locks, CR server on all nodes.	Updates cause reads and writes, and high CR requirement.

A TM lock is held in a non-NULL mode when a TX lock is created in the table, because this prevents the table from being dropped, or locked in exclusive mode (such as for building an index), while the transaction is active.

In OPS mode, it is preferable to remove this synchronization overhead by either setting `DML_LOCKS=0` in the `init.ora` or using the `ALTER TABLE ...` `DISABLE TABLE LOCK` directive. The implications of using either of these approaches are as follows:

- No TM locks are created.
- All attempts to lock the table are rejected.

When Oracle knows that nobody can lock the table, it does not need to synchronize the lock states between the instances, therefore cutting down on the DLM overhead.

One lock that needs very careful attention in an OPS environment is the ST (space transaction) lock. In the event of a great deal of work to be performed while holding ST, such as a large amount of free extents to coalesce, the additional overhead of passing the ST lock around the many nodes can quickly bring a system to its knees. This is especially true when anybody needs to create a new extent while the ST lock is already in demand from SIMON doing cleanup work.

One situation in which new extents are frequently created and discarded is that of temporary disk sort areas. For this reason, tablespaces of type TEMPORARY and *sort segments* should always be used in OPS environments, as discussed in Section 5.7.3.

6.9.5   Summary

The goal of this section has not been to provide exhaustive OPS information. Rather, it has been to provide enough information for you to be aware of when OPS is a viable scaling option for a large application. Further reading is strongly encouraged before any attempt is made to implement OPS, as detailed below.

6.9.6   Further Reading for OPS

The best place to learn the details of OPS is the *Oracle8 Parallel Server Concepts and Administration Guide*. This is a very comprehensive guide to OPS and is surprisingly readable. Included in this manual are comprehensive worksheets to aid the application design and analysis required for successful OPS deployment, in addition to background information and configuration syntax.

6.10   V$ Views Exposed

In this section we visit several of the more interesting V$ views and present some examples of how they should be interrogated to extract information that can be used for operational, tuning, and capacity planning purposes.

The information in the V$ views can be put into three high-level categories:

- Session-level information
- System-level information
- Miscellaneous information

In this section we will cover the first two of these categories in varying detail. Full details of all the V$ views can be found in the *Oracle Server Reference Guide.*

6.10.1 Session-Level Information

A great deal of information is available about individual sessions connected to the database. Connected sessions include everything that attaches to the SGA, including all the Oracle background processes. This information is centered around the V$SESSION view, and we will use this view as the driving table as we go through the session information, as shown in Figure 6.12.

V$SESSION

V$SESSION contains one row for every connection to the database. Connections to the database include any shadow processes (the server side of the two-task architecture) and all of the background processes, such as DBWR and any parallel query slaves. Table 6.2 is the master record of every session in the database and contains foreign key information for gaining greater detail in a variety of areas.

The primary key for this table is the SADDR column, but this is not the most useful column for using this table. It is far more useful to use the SID,SERIAL# combination as the primary key, because this provides many more join options against other tables. The reason that the serial number is present is to define this session uniquely: If this session were to log off and somebody else logged on, they could very well pick up the same SID. Therefore, a different SERIAL# is assigned in order to distinguish among the session information for the respective sessions.

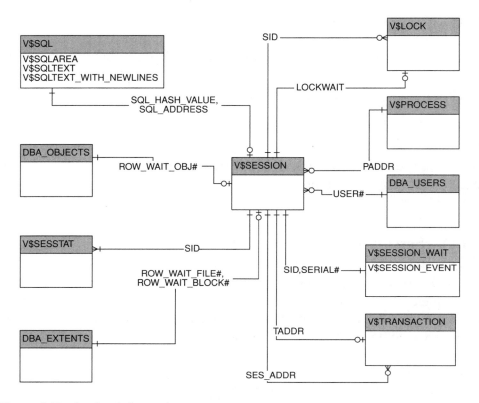

Figure 6.12   Session information

Continuing on through the view, skipping AUDSID, the next column is PADDR. This is a very useful column, because it is the foreign key used to join against the V$PROCESS table on the ADDR column (see Table 6.3).

An important distinction needs to be made between the SPID column of V$PROCESS and the PROCESS column of V$SESSION; the SPID is the Unix PID of the server-side shadow process, whereas the PROCESS is the PID of the client process (sqlplus, f45runx, etc.). Before returning to V$SESSION, we can go through the V$PROCESS information.

Highlights of V$PROCESS (apart from the server side SPID) are the LATCHWAIT and LATCHSPIN columns. These columns show the address of the latch on which the process is waiting or spinning, respectively, and can be a good source of information when aggregated as a count.

Table 6.2 V$SESSION Detail

Column	Type	Useful Joins/Notes
SADDR	RAW(4)	Session address (V$TRANSACTION.SES_ADDR)
SID	NUMBER	V$SESSION_WAIT.SID, V$SESSTAT.SID, V$SESS_IO.SID, V$LOCK.SID
SERIAL#	NUMBER	Increments each time SID is reused. Used to identify this session uniquely.
AUDSID	NUMBER	
PADDR	RAW(4)	V$PROCESS.ADDR
USER#	NUMBER	DBA_USERS.USER_ID SEG$.USER#
USERNAME	VARCHAR2(30)	DBA_USERS.USERNAME
COMMAND	NUMBER	Command type. See *Server Reference Guide.*
OWNERID	NUMBER	
TADDR	VARCHAR2(8)	V$TRANSACTION.ADDR
LOCKWAIT	VARCHAR2(8)	V$LOCK.KADDR
STATUS	VARCHAR2(8)	ACTIVE, INACTIVE, KILLED. Killed status exists until PMON cleans up the session.
SERVER	VARCHAR2(9)	DEDICATED. SHARED, NONE (an inactive MTS session has no server associated with it)
SCHEMA#	NUMBER	
SCHEMANAME	VARCHAR2(30)	
OSUSER	VARCHAR2(15)	Operating system user ID for the client process.
PROCESS	VARCHAR2(9)	Client process ID
MACHINE	VARCHAR2(64)	Client machine name

Table 6.2 continued

Column	Type	Useful Joins/Notes
TERMINAL	VARCHAR2(10)	Client terminal ID
PROGRAM	VARCHAR2(48)	Program name for client
TYPE	VARCHAR2(10)	USER or BACKGROUND
SQL_ADDRESS	RAW(4)	V$SQLAREA.ADDRESS, V$SQLTEXT.ADDRESS, V$SQL.ADDRESS, V$SQLTEXT_WITH_NEWLINES.ADDRESS
SQL_HASH_VALUE	NUMBER	V$SQLAREA.HASH_VALUE, V$SQLTEXT.HASH_VALUE, V$SQL.HASH_VALUE, V$SQLTEXT_WITH_NEWLINES.HASH_VALUE
PREV_SQL_ADDR	RAW(4)	As above. This reflects the last statement for the session.
PREV_HASH_VALUE	NUMBER	
MODULE	VARCHAR2(48)	The application can set these columns using DBMS_APPLICATION_INFO package. This is highly recommended for any complex application, but should not be used for very small components of the application.
MODULE_HASH	NUMBER	
ACTION	VARCHAR2(32)	
ACTION_HASH	NUMBER	
CLIENT_INFO	VARCHAR2(64)	
FIXED_TABLE_SEQUENCE	NUMBER	This increments each time a session does any work. Can be used to determine which sessions are active at any one time, within the granularity provided by LAST_CALL_ET.
ROW_WAIT_OBJ#	NUMBER	These four columns identify which row a session is waiting on. The row in question will be locked by another session if these are populated.
ROW_WAIT_FILE#	NUMBER	
ROW_WAIT_BLOCK#	NUMBER	
ROW_WAIT_ROW#	NUMBER	
LOGON_TIME	DATE	Hmm...
LAST_CALL_ET	NUMBER	Number of seconds since last activity

Table 6.2 continued

Column	Type	Useful Joins/Notes
PDML_ENABLED	VARCHAR2(3)	Yes/No
FAILOVER_TYPE	VARCHAR2(13)	OPS failover type
FAILOVER_METHOD	VARCHAR2(10)	NONE/BASIC/PRECONNECT
FAILED_OVER	VARCHAR2(3)	Yes/No
RESOURCE_CONSUMER_GROUP	VARCHAR2(32)	Name of resource consumer group

Table 6.3 V$PROCESS Detail

Column	Type	Useful Joins/ Notes
ADDR	RAW(4)	V$SESSION.PADDR
PID	NUMBER	Oracle PID. Used by the Oracle kernel and not related to any UNIX PID.
SPID	VARCHAR2(9)	Unix PID for shadow process
USERNAME	VARCHAR2(15)	UNIX username for owner of server process
SERIAL#	NUMBER	
TERMINAL	VARCHAR2(10)	
PROGRAM	VARCHAR2(48)	Always "oracle," unless using single-task executable.
BACKGROUND	VARCHAR2(1)	Yes/No
LATCHWAIT	VARCHAR2(8)	Address of the latch this process is currently waiting on
LATCHSPIN	VARCHAR2(8)	Address of the latch this process is spinning on

The other columns in the view are not especially useful in a client/server architecture, because the program is always "oracle," and the username is also "oracle." In a multithreaded server (MTS) environment, there will be multiple session records that can map to a single entry in V$PROCESS, because there are multiple sessions sharing the same physical server process. Latch waits always operate on a process level, and so this is the correct location for this information.

Back in the V$SESSION view, we find the username information in both text form and numeric ID format. The next column is the COMMAND column, which shows the command type of the last statement parsed. A full reference to all the command types is included in the *Server Reference Guide* but typically will be 2 (INSERT), 3 (SELECT), 6 (UPDATE), 7 (DELETE), or 45 (ROLLBACK).

The OWNERID column is used to identify the owner of a parallel query operation. All the parallel query slave processes started on this instance have an entry in V$SESSION, showing the username to be that of the calling session. However, this is not sufficient to identify the session uniquely—particularly if the initiating session is actually connected to another instance of a parallel server database. In this case, the value of this column is a 4-byte value, with the low-order bytes identifying the session ID and the high-order bytes identifying the instance number.

The TADDR column is a good one to remember. It is the foreign key reference through to the V$TRANSACTION view (see Table 6.4) and uniquely identifies the transaction that the session holds active.

Many of the columns in V$TRANSACTION are of use only in very specific debugging situations. However, there are other columns that are invaluable in tracking down common problems and determining how long rollback operations are going to take. These columns are

- XIDUSN
- START_TIME
- USED_UREC/USED_UBLK
- LOG_IO
- PHY_IO
- CR_GET
- CR_CHANGE

The XIDUSN column shows the (U)ndo (S)egment (N)umber for the transaction—that is, the rollback segment number. This is useful when tracking back users of a particular rollback segment, going back to the session information by means of the SES_ADDR column. The START_TIME column is a character representation of the time at which the transaction started and can be used to locate long-running updates.

Table 6.4 V$TRANSACTION Detail

Column	Type	Useful Joins/ Notes
ADDR	RAW(4)	Joins against V$SESSION.TADDR
XIDUSN	NUMBER	Undo segment number (SYS.UNDO$.US#)
XIDSLOT	NUMBER	Undo slot number
XIDSQN	NUMBER	Undo sequence
UBAFIL	NUMBER	File number of *current* undo block
UBABLK	NUMBER	Block number of *current* undo block
UBASQN	NUMBER	Sequence number of *current* undo block
UBAREC	NUMBER	Record number of *current* undo block
STATUS	VARCHAR2(16)	Mostly ACTIVE in nondistributed, nonparallel-DML environments
START_TIME	VARCHAR2(20)	Character representation of actual start time
START_SCNB	NUMBER	SCN when transaction started
START_SCNW	NUMBER	Wrap number when transaction started
START_UEXT	NUMBER	Extent number of *initial* undo block
START_UBAFIL	NUMBER	File number of *initial* undo block
START_UBABLK	NUMBER	Block number of *initial* undo block
START_UBASQN	NUMBER	Sequence number of *initial* undo block
START_UBAREC	NUMBER	Record number of *initial* undo block
SES_ADDR	RAW(4)	V$SESSION.SADDR
FLAG	NUMBER	<Unknown>
SPACE	VARCHAR2(3)	These four columns contain Yes/No answers to denote whether the transaction is a space transaction (i.e., implicit operations on the extent tables of the data dictionary), a recursive transaction, a "noundo" transaction (i.e., DISCRETE_TRANSACTION), or a parallel DML transaction, respectively.
RECURSIVE	VARCHAR2(3)	
NOUNDO	VARCHAR2(3)	
PTX	VARCHAR2(3)	

Table 6.4 continued

Column	Type	Useful Joins/ Notes
PRV_XIDUSN	NUMBER	Transaction information for previous transaction
PRV_XIDSLT	NUMBER	
PRV_XIDSQN	NUMBER	
PTX_XIDUSN	NUMBER	Parent transaction information for parallel DML
PTX_XIDSLT	NUMBER	
PTX_XIDSQN	NUMBER	
DSCN-B	NUMBER	SCN on which this transaction is dependent. In an environment where multiple redo threads are associated with recovery, the dependent SCN determines the sequence of recovery.
DSCN-W	NUMBER	
USED_UBLK	NUMBER	Number of used undo blocks
USED_UREC	NUMBER	Number of used undo records
LOG_IO	NUMBER	Logical I/Os used by this transaction
PHY_IO	NUMBER	Physical I/Os used by this transaction
CR_GET	NUMBER	Number of consistent read gets for transaction
CR_CHANGE	NUMBER	Number of blocks constructed for CR prior to update

The USED_% columns show how much real undo space is being used by the transaction. Probably the most useful of this pair is the UREC column, which shows the number of data records in the undo segment. This is an effective way to determine how long a rollback operation will take on the transaction, because it decreases in real-time during rollback operations.

The remaining four columns provide a nice summary of the block operations that have occurred during the transaction.

V$SESSION_WAIT

V$SESSION_WAIT (see Table 6.5) is one of the primary views for determining the cause of poor response time. It provides a snapshot view of every connection to the database and what the session is currently waiting on. If the session is not currently waiting, it provides the last wait event for that session.

Table 6.5   V$SESSION_WAIT Detail

Column	Type	Useful Joins/ Notes
SID	NUMBER	V$SESSION.SID
SEQ#	NUMBER	Increases each time the session starts a wait. Used to differentiate between consecutive waits of the same event type.
EVENT	VARCHAR2(64)	The name of the wait event
P1TEXT	VARCHAR2(64)	All the P% columns are different for each event type. They represent three different parameters that relate to the specific wait event. The PxTEXT columns contain the name of the parameter, and the Px and PxRAW columns contain the value in decimal and RAW formats, respectively.
P1	NUMBER	
P1RAW	RAW(4)	
P2TEXT	VARCHAR2(64)	
P2	NUMBER	
P2RAW	RAW(4)	
P3TEXT	VARCHAR2(64)	
WAIT_TIME	NUMBER	A value of ZERO means the session is still waiting. Negative numbers show time last waited, unless it is –1 (WAITED SHORT TIME) or –2 (unknown wait time).
SECONDS_IN_WAIT	NUMBER	If TIMED_STATISTICS is enabled, shows the number of wall clock seconds the session has been waiting on this event
STATE	VARCHAR2(19)	WAITING, WAITED SHORT TIME, WAITED UNKNOWN TIME, WAITED KNOWN TIME

Initial queries to this table should aggregate the data to provide a readable view of the wait states in the system:

```
    SELECT event,
           count(event)
      FROM v$session_wait
     WHERE wait_time = 0  /* i.e. still waiting */
  GROUP BY event;
```

This query provides a rolled-up view of all the sessions in the system that are currently in a wait state. While this is useful information, it is often more useful to include all sessions in this query, not just sessions that are currently waiting. The reason for this is that it gives a more accurate feel for the trend of the system and often exaggerates problems enough for them to be easily identified. For example, the query above may return the following results:

```
EVENT                                                            COUNT(EVENT)
----------------------------------------------------------------  ------------
SQL*Net message from client                                              988
pmon timer                                                                 1
rdbms ipc message                                                          4
smon timer                                                                 1
db file sequential read                                                    9
db file scattered read                                                     1
```

At first glance, this looks like a reasonably healthy system: Most users are not in a wait state other than waiting for a new request from the application. However, the "db file sequential read" may not be as normal as it looks. If the query is executed without the WHERE clause, the following is produced:

```
EVENT                                                            COUNT(EVENT)
----------------------------------------------------------------  ------------
SQL*Net message from client                                              988
SQL*Net message to client                                                 20
pmon timer                                                                 1
rdbms ipc message                                                          4
smon timer                                                                 1
db file sequential read                                                  198
db file scattered read                                                     4
```

Now a potential problem is evident. This clearly shows that several sessions have been waiting for single-block physical I/O from disk.[6] It is now time to drill down, using some of the other columns in the view.

We need to get more detail on the sequential read wait event, so we need to incorporate the general-purpose columns p1, p2, and p3 into our query, and exclude the wait states that we are not interested in. The parameter columns (p1, p2, p3) have a different meaning for nearly every different wait event, and so the p?text columns should be used to find out what the values relate to. This can be done in two ways, either by

```
SELECT * FROM V$SESSION_WAIT
WHERE event='db file sequential read" AND ROWNUM=1;
```

6. The two statistics "db file sequential read" and "db file scattered read" are a little confusing in naming convention. A "sequential" read is a single block read, usually indicating the use of an index. A "scattered read" indicates a full table scan or index fast scan, and is so named (presumably) because of the use of multiblock reads.

or by

```
SELECT * FROM V$EVENT_NAME
WHERE event='db file sequential read';
```

V$EVENT_NAME is a simple view of X$KSLED, which is one of the tables used by the V$SESSION_WAIT view. From either of these two techniques, we find that the parameter columns for "db file sequential read" are as shown in Table 6.6.

In this case, we do not really care about P3, because it is likely to always be 1 anyway (single-block read). When we run the following query:

```
SELECT p1,FLOOR(p2/100),count(*)
  FROM V$SESSION_WAIT
 WHERE event='db file sequential read'
GROUP BY p1,FLOOR(p2/100);
```

the following discovery is made:

```
    P1 FLOOR(P2/100)   COUNT(*)
---------- ------------- ----------
    15            10         ·2
    42           139        103
    42           140         93
```

This shows that 196 of the 198 sessions that have waited for physical I/O have been reading from the same file and the same block ranges. This is likely to be a rogue query, and so the next step for this particular problem is to join V$SESSION_WAIT and V$SESSION in order to find common hash values for running SQL:

```
SELECT se.sql_hash_value,count(se.sql_hash_value)
  FROM V$SESSION se,
       V$SESSION_WAIT sw
 WHERE se.SID=sw.SID
   AND sw.event='db file sequential read'
GROUP BY se.sql_hash_value;
```

Table 6.6 Parameter Descriptions for "db file sequential read"

Column Name	Column Value	Description
P1	FILE#	File number of file being read
P2	BLOCK#	Block number of file being read
P3	BLOCKS	Number of blocks being read

This query joins the two tables by their common primary key, the SID of the session. This query produces output like this:

```
SQL_HASH_VALUE COUNT(SE.SQL_HASH_VALUE)
-------------- ------------------------
     828483197                      186
             0                       10
    1356206681                        2
```

The guilty hash value is clearly 828483197, and this can now be extracted from the library cache using the V$SQLTEXT view.

This is one example of how to interrogate the V$SESSION_WAIT view in order to find the causes of problems in the system. Frequently, this type of approach is the only one necessary when reacting to performance problems in the system, because it provides an instant view of sessions that are spending time waiting rather than working.

6.10.2 V$SESSION_EVENT

One of the drawbacks of V$SESSION_WAIT is that it provides only a transient view of the current wait state. V$SESSION_EVENT (see Table 6.7) is the cumulative view of wait states for all the sessions in the database. It reports the same wait events as V$SESSION_WAIT and provides a history of wait states and durations for that session.

Table 6.7   V$SESSION_EVENT Detail

Column	Type	Useful Joins/ Notes
SID	NUMBER	V$SESSION.SID
EVENT	VARCHAR2(64)	Name of event, as seen in V$SESSION_WAIT
TOTAL_WAITS	NUMBER	Number of times this session entered the wait routine for this event
TOTAL_TIMEOUTS	NUMBER	Number of times the wait timed out and had to be restarted for this event
TIME_WAITED	NUMBER	Total time this session waited for this event
AVERAGE_WAIT	NUMBER	TIME_WAITED/TOTAL_WAITS
MAX_WAIT	NUMBER	Maximum time waited on this event

This view is useful for getting an idea of the severity of waits in the database. Take a look at the following example:

```
EVENT                              TOTAL_WAITS  TOTAL_TIMEOUTS
---------------------------------- -----------  --------------
SQL*Net message to client             16465777               0
SQL*Net message from client           16465776               0
db file sequential read                4938379               0
buffer busy waits                       829199             125
SQL*Net more data to client             637883               0
SQL*Net more data from client           328281               0
latch free                              153494          118651
free buffer waits                        11314            1656
db file scattered read                     811               0
file open                                   81               0
library cache pin                           15               0

11 rows selected.
```

In this example, the session has waited a large number of times on SQL*Net messages to and from the client. This is an indication of the number of requests this session has made of the server—in this case, the session has executed many short queries against the database.

The worrysome thing in this example is that a high number of timeouts have occurred waiting on the "latch-free" event. This event is a catchall for every latch in the system, but in this kind of situation it is typically one latch that is causing the majority of the timeouts. Multiple latch wait timeouts are normally an indicator that latch contention is occurring and should be investigated further.

V$SESSTAT

The V$SESSTAT (see Table 6.8) view provides approximately 200 different statistics related to the operation of each session in the database. The names of these statistics are recorded in the V$STATNAME view (see Table 6.9), where they are also grouped according to the type of statistic reported.

These statistics are identical to the ones reported for the system level, and accordingly some will be more useful as a global total.

Table 6.8 V$SESSTAT Detail

Column	Type	Useful Joins/ Notes
SID	NUMBER	V$SESSION.SID
STATISTIC#	NUMBER	V$STATNAME.STATISTIC#
VALUE	NUMBER	Actual value for this statistic

Table 6.9 V$STATNAME Class Types

Class	Type of Statistic
1	Session activity, such as CPU used, SQL*Net activity, calls made, private memory usage
2	Redo activity on behalf of this session (sesstat), or globally (sysstat)
4	Enqueue activity
8	Buffer cache centric statistics
16	O/S statistics (port-specific)
32	Parallel server instance coordination (SCN management, non-PCM locks) and parallel query
40	Global (parallel) cache management
64	Data access (sorts, table access statistics) and SQL layer statistics (parse calls, execute calls, session cursor cache statistics)
72	Buffer pin statistics
128	Rollback statistics/SCN

6.10.3 System-Level Information

Most of the remaining v$ views refer to system-level information. It does not make much sense to go through all of the remaining views, because many of the views are very rarely used. Instead, we will take a look at some of the most useful views in common use.

V$SYSSTAT, V$SYSTEM_EVENT

These two views show the same statistics as their session-based counterparts. v$system_event can give a fast overview of the system wait states, while V$SYSSTAT can give detailed information on all of the actual activity in the database.

V$FILESTAT

Joining this table to V$DATAFILE yields statistics about physical I/O occurring against the datafile that comprise the database. Several conclusions can be made about the usage of certain datafiles based on the relationships of columns in this table. For example, if PHYBLKRD/PHYRDS is greater than 1, full table scans or index fast scans are occurring on this file.

V$SGASTAT

This view shows the component parts of the SGA and their respective sizes. The most common use of this information is to determine whether or not there is free space in the shared pool. Monitoring the free space in the shared pool is a vital step in maintaining a smoothly running system.

V$LIBRARYCACHE

Following up on maintaining sufficient space in the shared pool using V$SGASTAT, V$LIBRARYCACHE will report on the efficiency of the cached objects in the library cache. For example, if the shared pool is correctly sized, and the application reuses SQL efficiently, the GETHITRATIO for the SQL AREA namespace will be close to 1 (100 percent hits).

V$ROWCACHE

An incorrectly sized shared pool will also result in an undersized dictionary cache (a.k.a. rowcache) as a result of the SQL area squeezing out other namespaces. If this is occurring, misses will start to occur on dictionary cache objects. The cache hit ratio is reported in this view as GETHITS/(GETHITS+GETMISSES).

V$DB_OBJECT_CACHE

This view shows statistics about tables, views, indexes, sequences, packages, and even cursors. Historically, this table was once used for objects that had owners, not anonymous SQL statements. It was used to show whether an object was currently cached and whether or not it was "kept" in memory using the DBMS_SHARED_POOL package. Now that this package supports the "keeping" of cursors in the shared pool, the cursors are also listed.

V$BH

This view is reported in the Oracle documentation as a parallel server view. However, it is now created as part of the catalog.sql script and therefore present in every Oracle instance. The BH in this view name stands for buffer hash and refers to the actual buffers in the buffer cache; there is one row in V$BH for each buffer in the cache. Simple queries can be run against this view to determine such things as population of the buffer cache by a given object, and it is thus very useful for maximizing the potential of the cache by ensuring that it is fairly used.

V$LATCH_CHILDREN

Many of the latches in an Oracle instance consist of a parent latch and many child latches. One good example of this is the "cache buffers chains" latch. This view reports on all the child latches for those parent latches.

The columns in the V$LATCH% views are worth discussing some more. When a latch acquisition fails, this is deemed to be a miss. A success is deemed a hit. When a miss occurs, Oracle then attempts to acquire the latch by spinning on it spin_count times. If this is not successful, Oracle puts the process to sleep (sleeps) and then reattempts the get. If this is unsuccessful, the process is put to sleep for an exponentially longer period each time until the acquisition is successful.

The columns from SLEEP5 upward are no longer used by Oracle.

V$LATCH

This view is an aggregate view of statistics for all the latches in the system. Statistics for any latches that are composed of many child latches are rolled up into a single row in V$LATCH. This view also contains statistics for all the singleton latches, which are not reported in the V$LATCH_CHILDREN view.

V$LOCK

All locks are reported in this view, whether they are enqueue locks or otherwise. When sessions are found to be waiting on a lock, this view can be queried to find the holder of the lock. The columns LMODE and REQUEST are used for this; LMODE shows the lock mode that the session currently has on the lock, and REQUEST shows the mode in which the session is trying to obtain the lock.

Incidentally, there is an easy way to determine for which lock type a session is waiting on "enqueue" in V$SESSION_WAIT. The P1 value in this instance is named "name|mode," which means that the name of the enqueue is OR'd together with the mode in the value for P1. The net effect of this is that if you take the P1RAW value (hex version of the value), and use the first two bytes (first pair of two characters) this is an ASCII representation of the enqueue name. The character values for these bytes are easily determined using the "man ascii" command at the UNIX prompt.

V$WAITSTAT

When an Oracle session waits for a block to become available for use for some reason (such as another session having it pinned for exclusive use), Oracle increments a counter in V$WAITSTAT for that type of block. In normal use, one would expect the "data block" class to be the block type most frequently waited on. Problems are evident when other types of blocks are waited on frequently. For example, many waits on "segment header" demonstrates segment header contention, probably due to heavy inserts into a table resulting in freelist contention.

V$BACKUP

When the old hot backup method (i.e., not Recovery Manager) is used, each file that is in backup mode will have a status of ACTIVE in this view.

V$SORT_SEGMENT, V$SORT_USAGE

When a tablespace of type TEMPORARY is created, it is used solely as storage for sort segments. These are segments that are used for on-disk sorting of data and are not automatically freed after use. Instead, they become eligible for reuse by other sessions under the control of the `sort extent pool` latch instead of going through all the overhead of using the single ST lock.

6.11   Chapter Summary

The operation of Oracle is tightly linked to its physical side. As it all operates in memory structures, however, so this is not immediately apparent. Documentation of these aspects has historically been poor, and word of mouth was the only way to determine answers to some questions. Hopefully, this chapter has been enlightening and interesting in this respect.

Use of the `v$` and `x$` tables are the window to Oracle's soul, and it's important to stay on top of the new views/tables that appear in each release. Oracle is fairly unique in the amount of information it divulges, and this should be used to your advantage.

6.12   Further Reading

Various. *Oracle 8i Concepts,* Oracle RDBMS Documentation.
Various. *Oracle8i Parallel Server Concepts and Administration,* Oracle RDBMS Documentation.
Various. *Oracle 8i Tuning,* Oracle RDBMS Documentation.

PART IV

How UNIX Works

Chapter 7

Introduction to UNIX

7.1 What Is a Kernel?

The most fundamental level of UNIX is the kernel. User programs execute under the protection of the kernel and use its services. The kernel provides a standard interface to the system hardware and provides standard services over and above that to ease the process of developing and executing software on the hardware platform.

7.1.1 "That Picture"

I must apologize for Figure 7.1. This kind of representation never helped me when I went through the familiarization process myself. That having been said, it does provide a concise view of the structure of a UNIX system, and hopefully a little verbiage will make it clear.

This diagram is supposed to represent the various layers in a UNIX system. Going from bottom to top, the software engineering effort becomes less complex and less shared. For example, every program in the system uses the virtual memory subsystem, although this is a very complex part of the system. It is a sharable part of the system, but each of its users is protected from the inherent complexity by the layers below it. This is the overriding mission of the kernel: to protect users from each other, and from the complexity of the system.

Starting at the lowest level, we have the platform itself, or the hardware domain. Included in this domain are all the physical attributes that

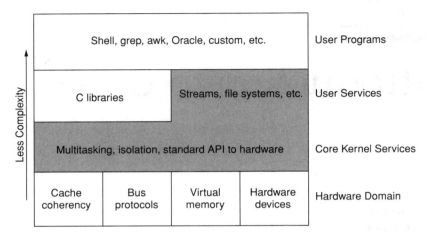

Figure 7.1 UNIX hierarchy

need to be taken care of in order to execute software on the system. Some of these things are partially taken care of by the hardware but still require explicit action from the software on the system to instruct the hardware how it should, for example, ensure that the CPU cache reflects valid data for the next process to use.

Moving up the stack, we get to the core kernel services. This layer ensures that all layers above it are taken care of, in addition to providing standard interfaces to the hardware domain. For example, one of the overriding concepts of the UNIX model is that everything is a file. The core kernel services take care of this interface, providing the upper layers with a way of viewing (nearly) all hardware objects as a linear file.

This layer also provides the *process abstraction*. This is essentially how executing programs are handled by the system, providing each process with the illusion that it is operating independently on private hardware. It also takes care of isolation between these processes, ensuring that one process cannot corrupt the execution environment of another in any way.

In addition, the kernel also provides value-added services that can be used by the user programs. These are software modules that are not essential for the operation of the system but provide a more usable interface for the user. A prime example of this is the availability of many filesystems. A filesystem does not contribute directly to the running of the system but is more than just a simple service. It must have access to kernel memory for the sharing of the filesystem buffer cache and must have fast access to the hardware itself.

Everything else on the stack is user code. That is, it is not directly associated with the kernel. The C libraries are reusable software modules that are used to aid the rapid construction of user software. Note that Oracle is associated with the user processes at the very top of the model.

This is probably the highest-level view of what the kernel *does*; now it is time to take a look at how this is achieved from an implementation perspective.

7.1.2 Execution Modes

The UNIX operating system operates in two distinct modes: kernel and user. The kernel does not do anything mysterious; it is just software like the rest of the system:

```
$ file unix
unix: ELF 32-bit LSB executable 80386 Version 1
$ file /bin/grep
/bin/grep: ELF 32-bit LSB executable 80386 Version 1
```

or

```
$ file vmunix
vmunix:        ELF-64 executable object file - PA-RISC 2.0 (LP64)
$ file iotest
iotest:        ELF-64 executable object file - PA-RISC 2.0 (LP64)
```

It is executed on the same processors as the user software. However, the kernel has special duties and normally operates with a privileged status from a *hardware* perspective, able to access and modify addresses and registers that user mode cannot. This mode of execution is called *kernel mode*.

There are two distinct situations in which kernel mode is entered, excluding the boot process:

- A user process executes a system call or raises an exception (explicit kernel processing).

- System housekeeping occurs, such as time-slicing and servicing interrupts (implicit kernel processing).

7.1.3 Explicit Kernel Processing (Process Context Kernel Mode)

Starting with the user process, let's have a look at UNIX from a user perspective in order to see where the kernel fits in.

A user connects to the UNIX system by some mechanism, such as a login process for a shell user or an SQL*Net connection for a database user. Whichever way the user connects, the net result is a *process* on the system. This process is the executing context of a user program, and it is supported by the kernel with an operating environment. The environment for a process consists of

- A private memory map, including private stack and program counter

- A share of available processor capacity, up to 100 percent of one CPU if required and available

- The system call interface

The private memory map is a set of memory pages over which the user has exclusive rights. This memory map is actually a virtual memory map, which will be discussed in Section 7.3.2. For now, it is enough to think of this memory as a contiguous block of memory that is private to the user process. The block of memory is composed as shown in Figure 7.2.

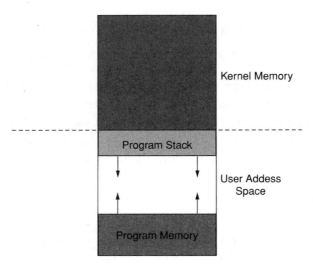

Figure 7.2 Process memory map

The lower portion of the memory map is accessible to the process, and the upper half of the map is a shared mapping of the kernel memory. All user processes have the kernel memory in their address spaces but cannot access it. In 32-bit UNIX implementations, it is common for the lower 2GB of the 32-bit address range to be used for user memory and the upper 2GB for kernel memory.

The "program memory" in the Figure 7.2 refers to all memory used to execute the user program, excluding the stack. This memory is further divided into as many as five types:

1. Text (the program itself)

2. Data (initialized variables)

3. BSS (uninitialized variables), including heap memory allocated by the malloc() family

4. Shared libraries (can include all items above for each library)

5. Shared locations (shared memory, memory mapped files)

The program stack is typically started at the top of the user address space, growing downward, while the program memory starts at the base and grows upward.

If this process is executing a program that operates only within that private memory map—that is, never requests more memory (program memory or stack), never causes an exception, and never needs to do any I/O—this process will never explicitly switch into kernel mode.

Considering that any kind of output, including screen output, is I/O, this hypothetical program would not be very useful to anybody. In order to perform I/O, however, the process needs to access the hardware of the system, which it cannot do in user mode. In this case, the process will execute a system call, which invokes a few actions on the system and results in the process running in kernel mode. This mode of execution is considered as *process context kernel mode*.

In modern systems, kernel mode is a hardware state invoked by a hardware trap on the processor. This puts the processor into kernel mode and allows the executing process to perform the required privileged operations. In order to continue, the kernel must first save the processing context of the user process—that is, program counter, general-purpose registers, memory management information, and stack pointer. It's worth noting that a switch to kernel mode usually does *not* need to perform any processor cache management, because the memory map does not change. Kernel mode and user mode both exist within the same process context, so no cache lines need to be invalidated on a switch into kernel mode. In fact, it is likely that the kernel processing will require some of the user pages, particularly the *u-area* (see Section 7.2.1), and any buffers required to process system calls. Once the transition to kernel mode is complete, the kernel can start to process the system call request.

While a process is in kernel mode, it has access to both kernel memory and user memory. However, no user code is executed while the process is in kernel mode. Instead, the user request is validated and, if permitted, performed on *behalf* of the user mode side (user context) of the process. Kernel execution occurs in the same process context as the user program, so all processor cycles consumed during this process are logged against the process under SYS mode (as viewed with sar -u).

It was mentioned earlier that a process could cause an *exception*. An exception is caused by a process attempting to do something that is either impossible or prohibited. Examples of this include segmentation violations (a process attempting to access memory that has not been allocated to it) and divide-by-zero exceptions. In this case, the kernel processes the relevant exception handler for that event, such as initiating a core dump, within the context of the process.

7.1.4   Implicit Kernel Processing (System Context Kernel Mode)

The second way that kernel code executes is when certain events occur in the system. These events basically consist of software and hardware *interrupts* and occur for various reasons. By processing these interrupts with *interrupt handlers*, the kernel ensures that

- All runnable processes receive a "fair share" of the CPU.
- All hardware interfacing is performed.

When a processor receives interrupts, it stops executing the current process and executes the *interrupt handler* for that interrupt. This happens regardless of whether the process was operating in user mode or in kernel mode, although the kernel has the ability to block interrupts selectively.

Interrupts are asynchronous with respect to the currently executing process and are caused by events that are not directly initiated by the process itself. Therefore, the handler must execute outside the context of the current process and neither logs its execution cycles against that process[1] nor accesses its address space.[2] This type of execution is considered as *system context kernel mode*.

The kinds of things that generate interrupts are I/O devices returning a completion status (including network traffic) and the hardware clock.

There are situations in the execution of the kernel code in which an interrupt handler cannot be serviced. One prime example of this would be if the kernel were already executing kernel code for a prior interrupt of that type. In this case, the kernel could corrupt its own address space by having incomplete memory updates from the first interrupt when the second is received. This situation is prevented through the use of *interrupt priority levels (IPLs)*.

Using IPLs, the kernel can instruct the processor to ignore interrupts that it receives that have a lower priority than the specified level. Therefore, the kernel can set the interrupt level at a suitable level prior to processing a critical (i.e., protected) section of code. Any interrupts that have a lower priority than the one set are ignored by the processor, and the critical section can complete safely.

Interrupt levels are hardware-dependent entities and thus vary among processor architectures. Typically, there are several hardware interrupts, and a smaller number of software interrupts that can be programmed. The highest interrupt level is always reserved for machine exceptions: If there is a fatal problem in the hardware or the operating system, all processing must cease immediately to protect against widespread data corruption resulting from unknown states in the system. When a fault of this nature is

---

1. Some implementations log these CPU cycles on the process that was executing on the processor before the interrupt was received.

2. Unless the interrupt is directly related to the process—for example, a context switch or the return from an outstanding I/O.

detected, the highest-level interrupt is generated in order to generate a "panic" of the system.

The next level down is usually reserved for the hardware clock, followed by various peripheral interrupts (disk, network, etc.), and software interrupts have the lowest priority level. Below all of this comes level zero, which is the level at which user mode processing occurs. This allows *anything* to interrupt user mode processing.

The Hardware Clock

The hardware clock is a critical component of a UNIX system. It not only determines the rate at which the processor is driven (this is why it is known as *clock speed*) but also generates interrupts that the kernel uses to implement *timeslicing*.

When the system boots, the kernel programs the hardware clock to interrupt the processor at defined intervals. Each time this interval arrives, a high-priority interrupt is received that is processed by the kernel's *clock interrupt handler*. This handler runs in system context, because it has nothing to do with any user process.

The period that the clock interrupts is determined by the value for one *tick*, frequently set at *100 Hz*, or *10 milliseconds*. Every 10 milliseconds, the interrupt handler is fired and must perform several critical functions, such as incrementing the system time, updating the system and user time statistics for running processes, and posting alarm() signals to processes that have requested them. The clock handler also ensures that the illusion of concurrent execution is maintained on the system by providing the mechanism for implementing *time sharing*.

Time Sharing

Every process in the system is assigned a *quantum*, which is the maximum amount of time the process can execute on the processor, before other processes must be considered for execution. This period varies between platforms and between scheduler classes, but is typically 100 milliseconds, or ten ticks of the hardware clock.

When the quantum is used up, the kernel checks the run queue, and determines whether the process must be suspended from execution and put back onto the run queue. If there are no processes on the run queue of sufficient priority, the process is allowed to execute for another quantum. If the process is taken off the processor, it remains dormant until it is scheduled back onto the processor when it reaches the head of the queue. This period is typically very short and is weighted by the priority of processes on the run queue.

In this way, the kernel can provide the illusion to all the processes in the system that they are concurrently running on the processor. This, combined with the private memory map, provides a private environment for each process. More detail is provided on process scheduling in the next section.

7.2   Processes

In the preceding section, a level of detail was reached with regard to what a process *is* from an execution standpoint. From a high-level perspective, a process is simply the kernel's abstraction of all the attributes of a running program, in order to control its execution.

All user processes in the system have an entry in the *process table*, with the following attributes:

- A private, virtual[3] memory map
- A runtime context (program counter, registers, stack pointer, etc.)
- System resources

7.2.1   The Process "Table"

The process table is the master reference for the process. Although the detail of the process table is not directly useful in implementing large Oracle systems, an understanding of the concepts is useful and helps when developing monitoring hooks into the system.

In physical terms, the process table exists as two structures for each process: a proc structure and a u structure (or u-area). Historically, the proc structure was a table of fixed size that was set at kernel link time and was

---

3. The "virtual" part will be covered in Section 7.3.

not changeable at runtime. This is the reason for the quotation marks around the word "table" in the head—it really isn't a "table" any more.

The proc structure contains all the information that the kernel could require when the process is not running, and so exists in kernel memory that is always mapped. By contrast, the u-area contains information that usually is needed only while the process is actually running; the u-area is stored in the private memory map of the process.[4]

The reason for using two structures to maintain the process control information is that some of the information does not need to be accessible by the kernel when the process is not running. It does not make sense to tie up global kernel memory for information that is typically not required when the process is not running.

Depending on the specific implementation, the u-area can contain the following information for each process:

- File descriptor table
- Process control block (execution context of the process, including general-purpose registers, stack pointer, MMU registers, etc.)
- Per-process kernel stack
- Pointer to corresponding proc structure

Though the list above covers the major items, many other pieces of information can be stored in the u-area.

The proc structure focuses on the more globally accessed attributes of a process:

- User credentials
- Signal masks
- PID
- Active process list pointer (see Section 7.2.2)
- Queue list pointers for run queue
- Priority information
- Indirect pointer to u-area

---

4. Some modern implementations have migrated much of the u-area to the proc structure in order to increase flexibility.

All of the items listed above, with the exception of the PID, can be written to by other processes in the system or the kernel, and therefore need to be globally accessible. The list pointers will be covered in more detail in Section 7.2.2.

When the process information is divided among such structures, it can complicate the retrieval of this information. UNIX commands, such as `ps` and `fuser`, use information from both of these structures and therefore require access to all of this information, even when the process in question is not active and could even be swapped out to disk. When the process is swapped out to disk, this includes the `u-area`, and so special access methods need to be available for gaining access to this information from the swap area. This can be achieved using special system calls or through the use of a custom API. The actual method used is implementation-dependent.

7.2.2 Process Scheduling

The subject of process scheduling is one that can have a direct bearing on the performance of your Oracle database. Although this has been touched on already in this chapter, it merits some more detail.

As previously mentioned, UNIX is a time-sharing system at heart. This means that the kernel will provide the illusion to all the processes on the system that they all have their own CPU to run on. On a large database server with 4,000 processes, it is not practical (or scalable) to provide a processor for each process, and so it is the time sharing that allows a far smaller number of processors to provide this illusion.

The key to providing this illusion is the hardware clock, as previously discussed, and *context switches*. Context switching is best covered in Section 7.3, and so for now it is safe to view context switching from the high level of just switching processes on and off processors. Also, to make this discussion simple, assume that we are referring to a uniprocessor UNIX platform.

Process Scheduling Primer: Uniprocessor Platforms

When a process has used its time quantum (i.e., when the hardware clock interrupt handler has fired) and another process is waiting to execute (the other process is termed *runnable*), it is switched off the processor and the new process is switched onto the processor. The switching of processes, and the entire clock interrupt handler, must be very efficient in order to minimize the overhead of processing small time slices. If this operation is a noticeable percentage of the quantum itself, then this is the percentage of system that is "wasted" on the task of time sharing.

This simplistic view of time sharing is useful in gaining an initial understanding of the concepts. However, the actual implementation of time sharing is a good deal more complex, having to deal with such things as different priority processes, balancing throughput against response time, managing CPU cache warmth on multiprocessor machines, and so on. The handling of this complex time-sharing requirement is called *process scheduling*.

There are several variables that affect which process will be placed on an available processor:

- Priority of process
- Recent CPU usage for process
- "Nice" value
- Machine load average
- Position in run queue

When a process becomes runnable, it is placed on a run queue—that is, a queue for the processor in order to be run. This is achieved by adding the `proc` structure of the process onto a linked list that makes up the run queue.

The architecture of the run queues is very platform-specific, especially when the platform supports complex hardware arrangements such as NUMA. In order to keep this discussion simple, we will refer to the Berkeley software distribution (BSD) run queue architecture.

BSD maintains several run queues, each of which queues processes of a specific priority. When a process has used its quantum on the processor, the scheduler scans the run queues in order, from highest priority to lowest priority. If a process is found on a run queue with a priority greater than or equal to that of the currently executing process, the old process is switched off the processor and the queued process is switched on. If there are no processes on queues with priority greater than or equal to that of the currently executing process, the process is permitted to continue running for up to another quantum before the queues are checked once again.

If a process of higher priority becomes runnable, the current process is preempted off the processor even if it has not used its entire quantum.

The priority of a process is governed by two factors and will be constantly adjusted by the kernel during the lifetime of the process based on the system load average. These factors are the estimated recent CPU usage by this process and the "nice" value of the process.

The nice value of a process is specified by the user at process start-up using the `nice` command. This value ranges from –20 to +19, with the default being 0. Superuser privileges are required to decrease the nice value, because this increases the priority of the process above the normal priority for user processes. A user can elect to put a larger nice value on the process in order to run at a lower priority and therefore be "nice" to the other users of the system.

The recent CPU usage of the process is calculated using several algorithms. It is not necessary to go into the specifics of these algorithms, because they are covered comprehensively in various other books (see Section 7.9 at the end of this chapter). It worthwhile discussing the basics, however.

If a process is using a good deal of CPU, this will be reflected in the recent CPU counter, which in turn is used as a negative weighting factor in the algorithm that determines the priority of the process. Therefore, CPU-intensive processes cannot dominate a system unless there are only lower-priority processes in the run queue or the system is idle. Likewise, if there are two processes trying to use as much CPU as possible, they will end up on the same low-priority run queue and will compete against each other.

The recent CPU counter is incremented for every tick the process executes. This value is then weighted once a second, using the system load average[5] and the process nice value in order to give the counter a decay over time. The load average is used as the amnesia factor in keeping track of the used CPU; if the system is very heavily loaded, the CPU counter will take a long time to forget previous CPU usage, and the priority of the process will be

---

5. The system "load average" is a set of numbers, calculated over 1-minute, 5-minute, and 15-minute intervals, using several types of scheduling statistics such as run queue length, priority waitlist length, and so on. The actual algorithm varies among implementations.

proportionately lower. If the load average is small, the used CPU will be forgotten relatively quickly, and the process will gain a higher priority.

If a process needs to block while it is running, such as waiting for an I/O operation to complete, it is taken off the processor and placed on a different type of queue—one of the *sleep queues*. The process stores a *wait channel* in its proc structure and puts itself onto the correct sleep queue for that resource. The wait channel is typically the address of the structure on which the process is waiting, which is hashed to obtain the correct sleep queue. When a resource becomes available, its address is hashed by the kernel to find the correct queue, and all processes waiting on it are woken and put back on a run queue.

If the process was blocked waiting for the completion of a system call, such as a read(), the process is put on a high-priority run queue until the process completes the switch back into user mode. At this point, the process priority is reduced, typically resulting in the process being switched off the processor in order to service processes of higher priority.

When processes are executing on a processor, they are neither on a run queue nor on a sleep queue. At this point, the process is active and exists on another list. In SVR4, this list is known as practive and is a linked list of all the processes currently on the processor, linked against the "active processor link" item in each proc structure.

Advanced Scheduling: Multiprocessor Process Scheduling

When multiple processors are present in a system, the scheduling algorithms become more complex. In the case of NUMA systems, this is an attempt to keep active processes close to their resident memory. In SMP machines, it is implementation-dependent: Some platforms do no extra scheduling work, whereas others do.

SMP. With multiple processors (sometimes referred to as *engines* by kernel engineers) and a relatively low number of runnable processes at any one time, some major optimizations can be made by maintaining cache warmth in the CPU caches. This is known as *cache affinity*.

An algorithm can be implemented, using the number of clock ticks since the process last ran, which determines whether the process is likely to have cache warmth on the processor on which it last ran. Waiting for the correct engine to become available may incur a delay in the execution of the process, and so this algorithm needs to be well tested with real applications.

In testing with and without affinity, OLTP Oracle workloads have been shown to exhibit as much as 15 percent more throughput when affinity is enabled.

NUMA. In NUMA configurations, it becomes more critical that the scheduler place processes on the correct engine. Although some NUMA configurations support dynamic page relocation between NUMA nodes, this is expensive at best, and the majority of memory for a given process will always reside on one node or another anyway. Therefore, it is a fair assumption that the scheduler should always attempt to schedule processes on engines on the same node as the resident set of the process.

This results in several per-node run queues, in order to ensure the locality bias in selecting processes to run. It's worth noting that the scheduler cannot factor in the location of any mapped shared memory, because this is not part of the process's private memory. In the case of all the processes in the system all running the same binary (such as `oracle`), the operating system may elect to store a single shared text segment local to each NUMA node in order to maximize the locality of reference.

7.2.3 Signals

Signals are the mechanism used to notify processes of asynchronous events. Even novice users are familiar with the `kill` command, which is used to send these signals to processes.

Most users are aware of the signal mechanism only from the user perspective—that of killing a process in order to terminate its execution. In fact, signals are very much more flexible than a simple termination mechanism, and most can be trapped and controlled in a programmable manner by the process.

Signals are passed to the process by the kernel. They can be initiated by other processes in the system or by the target process itself. The kernel

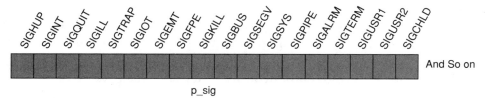

p_sig

Figure 7.3   Signal bitmask in `proc` structure

passes the signal to the process by setting a bit that corresponds to the signal in the `proc` structure for the process, as shown in Figure 7.3.

This bitmask is called `p_sig` in SVR4 and `p_siglist` in BSD-based implementations. The bitfield is used to store *pending signals* for the process.

Before the pending signal bitmask is updated, however, the kernel checks that the signal has not been explicitly ignored by the process. If the signal has been ignored, the kernel will not even set the bit in the bitmask. Once the bit is set in the `proc` structure, the kernel will attempt to wake up the process in order to receive the signal (if it is not already running). After this, the processing of the signal is entirely the responsibility of the process itself.

The signal bitmask is checked

- Every time the process returns to user mode from kernel mode
- Before going to sleep in kernel mode
- On waking from an interruptible sleep

The trend here is for the bitmask to be checked prior to returning to user mode from kernel mode. The reason for this is that some signals (namely `SIGKILL` and `SIGSTOP`) cannot be processed in user mode, because their handlers are not programmable. Once the bitmask is checked, the signals that have been received are processed by the process *in kernel mode*. The first action the kernel takes is to check if the signal is `SIGKILL` or `SIGSTOP`. If so, the actions are taken in kernel mode without returning to user mode. These actions terminate the process, or suspend the process and put it to sleep, respectively.

If the signal is not one of these two, the kernel checks the `u-area` for the process to find out if it has a handler declared for this signal. If there is no handler, the default action is taken, as shown in Table 7.1.

Table 7.1 Signal Names

Name	Description	Default Action
SIGHUP	hangup	exit
SIGINT	interrupt	exit
SIGQUIT	quit	core dump
SIGILL	illegal instruction	core dump
SIGTRAP	trace trap	core dump
SIGIOT	illegal operation trap	core dump
SIGABRT	abort and dump core	core dump
SIGEMT	EMT instruction	core dump
SIGFPE	floating point exception	core dump
SIGKILL	kill (cannot be caught or ignored)	exit
SIGBUS	bus error	core dump
SIGSEGV	segmentation violation	core dump
SIGSYS	nonexistent system call	core dump
SIGPIPE	write on a pipe with no one to read it	exit
SIGALRM	alarm clock	exit
SIGTERM	software termination signal	exit
SIGUSR1	user-defined signal 1	exit
SIGUSR2	user-defined signal 2	exit
SIGCHLD	death of a child	ignore
SIGPWR	power fail	ignore
SIGWINCH	screen size change	ignore
SIGURG	urgent condition on socket	ignore
SIGPOLL	selectable event pending	exit
SIGIO	socket I/O possible (SIGPOLL alias)	exit

Table 7.1 continued

Name	Description	Default Action
SIGIO	socket I/O possible (SIGPOLL alias)	exit
SIGSTOP	stop process (cannot be caught or ignored)	stop
SIGTSTP	interactive stop signal	stop
SIGCONT	continue process	ignore
SIGTTIN	input from background	stop
SIGTTOU	output from background	stop
SIGVTAL	virtual timer expired	exit
SIGPROF	profiling timer expired	exit
SIGXCPU	CPU limit exceeded	core dump
SIGXFSZ	file size limit exceeded	core dump

Any signal without a default action of "ignore" will not switch back into user mode. Instead, the process will exit, core dump, or be suspended, all without leaving kernel mode. If there is a handler defined for the signal, the kernel will switch into user mode and execute the signal handler.

It's worth noting that a process may not act on a signal for a comparatively long time. If the process is blocking on a noninterruptible kernel resource or is swapped out to disk, the process may remain unchanged in the system for a while before the signal is acted on.

7.2.4   Process Lifecycle

To finish up with processes, several the concepts in this section are summarized in Figure 7.4, which shows an example mini-application in which a network listener process listens for connections and creates a slave process in order to process requests as they come in.

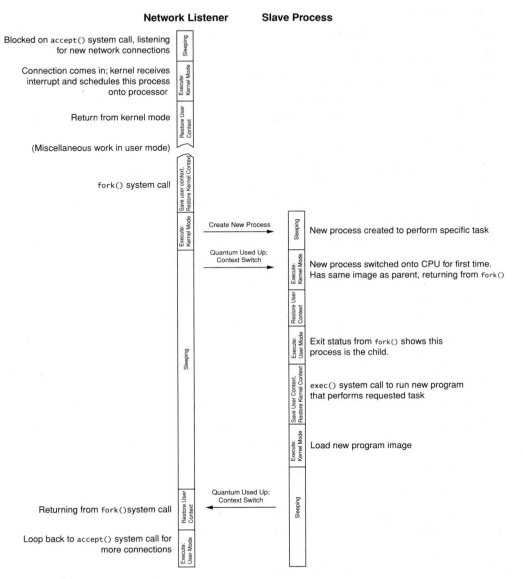

Figure 7.4   Listener application

7.3   Memory Management: The Virtual Memory System
7.3.1   Introduction

In simplistic, single-tasking computer systems, programs can be compiled to
locate themselves, and run, at specific memory addresses within the available
physical memory. The flow of control is passed from task to task on completion, with potentially only one program in memory at any one time.

A very simple operating system, for example, has an operating system
"kernel" compiled to run at a specific address and all user programs compiled to run at another specific address. The control of the system starts with
the operating system, from which other programs can be executed. The other
programs all locate themselves at addresses separate from that of the O/S; the
O/S can remain in memory while this happens. Once the program is complete, the operating system gains control of the system once more.

There are several problems with this arrangement:

- Little or no memory protection between programs: All programs can
  read or write all memory locations.

- Programs are limited to an unknown, finite amount of physical memory on the system.

- Programs must execute serially and, unless compiled for physically separate memory ranges, must overlay the previously executing program.

The last problem has two serious implications:

1. The system cannot support multitasking.
2. Software development is complex and machine-dependent.

These implications go directly against two of the design goals of UNIX, and
so this arrangement is a nonstarter. Another scheme must therefore be
adopted—*virtual memory* and its associated *memory management*.

7.3.2   Virtual Memory Introduction

UNIX systems implement virtual memory. Virtual memory separates the
address space seen by a process from real physical memory addresses.
This is achieved using memory address translation as an operating system
function.

Address Translation

Address translation allows all processes in the system to address the same locations as if they were private, with the system ensuring that the physical address used is distinct from other processes.

In Figure 7.5, there are two processes, each using half of the physical memory in the machine (for simplicity of example). Each of the two processes has an identical address space, or memory map, that is the same size as the physical address space. Although these processes are using physically different memory locations, both are under the illusion that they start at address zero[6] and have contiguous memory allocated beyond that (plus stack).

Each of the cells in Figure 7.5 represents the smallest unit of granularity that the UNIX system considers from a memory management perspective—a *page*. The concept of a page is used in order to reduce the space

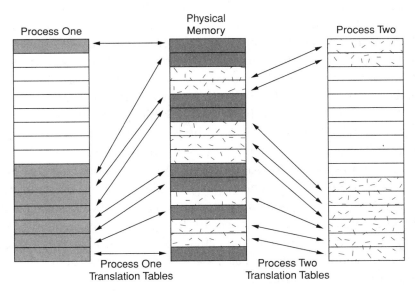

Figure 7.5 Address translation

---

6. Most implementations reserve address zero in order to catch program errors. When a program dereferences a null pointer, a segmentation violation error occurs because this page is not part of the process address space.

and resource overhead of managing a large amount of memory on the system. It is common in modern systems for the page size to be set at 4KB,[7] although some systems now support variable page sizes in order to increase the efficiency of very large memory (VLM) applications.

The glue that holds this process together is the *address translation tables*. These tables hold the mapping of virtual addresses (those that the process uses) to physical addresses (actual memory locations). In UNIX systems, these tables normally come in the form of *page tables* and, optionally, *translation lookaside buffers (TLBs)* in the processor *memory management unit (MMU)*.

The page table consists of several *page table entries (PTEs)* for each process, arranged as an array, as shown in Figure 7.6.

For a given *virtual* page frame (00 to 07 in Figure 7.6) of a process, there is a corresponding PTE, located at the same offset in the array that makes up the page table. So, the first page that makes up the address space of the process in this example is mapped to the page starting at *physical* address 0x000E1000. The actual offset within the page remains the same as the offset within the virtual page.

It was mentioned earlier that some systems now support variable-size pages. This is a result of the overhead now imposed in managing the huge quantities of memory found in very large systems. For example, if an Oracle database server has a 4GB SGA, this typically means that each connection to the database needs to have a page table large enough to cater for every page in the SGA in addition to the process memory itself. Each PTE is typically 32 bits, and so a 4KB page size would yield a 4MB (1 million times 4 bytes) page table for each process. Not only does this size of page table mean the kernel is spending a good deal of time managing page tables, but this memory is also located in kernel memory, not user memory. If 5,000 users are due to connect to this system, this means the kernel memory needs to be greater than 20GB. When variable page sizes are used, the SGA can be assigned, say, 4MB pages, thus reducing the size of the page table for the mapping.

The actual structure of each entry in the page table is defined by the hardware architecture—specifically the MMU of the processor. Each proc-

---

7. SPARC architectures use an 8KB page size.

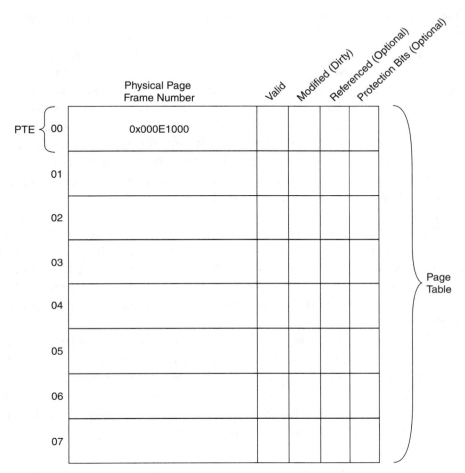

Figure 7.6 Process page table

essor family has its own structure for defining virtual to physical mappings in the MMU, and some support more functionality in the hardware than others, specifically in the area of *memory protection* and the presence of a *referenced bit*.

Although the hardware dictates the structure of the page table entries, it is the UNIX kernel that is responsible for all the manipulation of the entries in the table and for ensuring that the MMU is using the correct PTEs for the running process. At this stage, it is worth mentioning the effects of the two major variants of CPU cache architecture: *physically mapped* and *virtually mapped*.

A physically mapped architecture is laid out as shown in Figure 7.7. This is the traditional approach to caching, because the operating system does not need to be aware of the operation of the cache. Whenever a request for data is made by the CPU, the address (which remains as a virtual address) is passed through to the MMU, which does a conversion of the virtual address to a physical address. It does this using the TLB, which is a *fully associative cache*. This means that it has the ability to search all the lines (fully associative access) in the TLB concurrently, to determine the physical address to search for in the cache.

The TLB contains PTEs specified by the kernel, and this is the reason why the structure of the PTE is dictated by the CPU architecture. The kernel is responsible for loading the registers of the TLB with the correct PTE information for the active process. For any given process, the kernel mappings will not change, because all processes have the kernel mapped in their address space. On the right of the MMU in Figure 7.7, all addresses are physical.

It is clear that having to precede even the cache access with a lookup on the TLB can impose a significant overhead. In the case that the TLB does not contain the PTE required for the operation, a reference to main memory needs to be made in order to prime the TLB. Luckily, this normally means that the page has not been accessed for a comparatively long time, and so the impact is not felt very frequently.

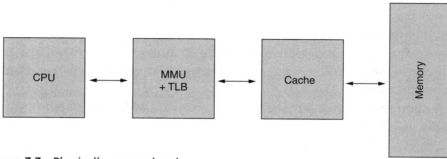

Figure 7.7   Physically mapped cache

In some modern systems, a different approach has been taken with the cache. Instead of using the physical address to determine the correct line and tag within the cache, the virtual address is used (see Figure 7.8).

The effect of this is that the CPU can request data from the cache directly by virtual address. The MMU needs to be used only when a cache miss occurs and a physical memory access is required. The requirement for a TLB is less in this arrangement, because the MMU is now positioned in a slower part of the system than it is in a physically mapped architecture. This having been said, many architectures implement virtual caches with TLBs for enhanced performance.

The downside of a virtual cache is that the kernel is now required to manage much of the cache coherency, because the hardware is unaware of the differences among the many identical virtual addresses that refer to different physical memory locations. Address 0x1000 for process A is *not* the same memory location as address 0x1000 for process B.

To alleviate the ambiguity in the cache, the system typically uses the process ID of the relevant process as part of the tagging infrastructure in the cache. The hardware has no concept of process IDs,[8] and so the coherency of the cache must involve the operating system: At a minimum, the kernel must inform the processor of the identity of the current process in order for the correct tags to be checked in the cache.

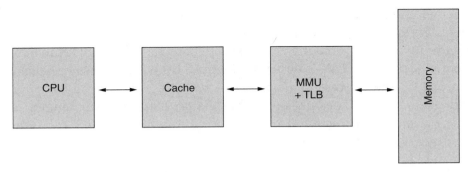

Figure 7.8 Virtual mapped cache

---

8. With the exception of a hardware register populated by the operating system to reflect the current context/process.

Cache coherency across DMA operations is also more complex, because the majority of I/O devices have no concept of virtual addresses; they transfer to and from physical memory addresses.

Context Switch

When the operating system switches one process off the processor and puts a different one on, several actions must be taken to

- Preserve the context of the prior process.
- Restore the context of the activated process.

These actions constitute the formal definition of a *context switch*. The context of a process typically includes the following:

- Stack pointer
- Program counter
- Other general-use registers in CPU
- Virtual address mapping

The first three attributes are referred to as the *process control block*, or PCB, and relate directly to saving the execution context of the process. The last attribute is that of the PTEs, and their presence in the TLB.

When a new process is switched onto a processor, the MMU must be informed of the new address mappings for that process. This applies whether the cache is virtual or physical. If a TLB is present, the kernel must also ensure that any mappings that are not relevant for the new process are invalidated, making the MMU reload the correct mapping from memory on access. This is necessary because the MMU does not have any concept of the process executing on the CPU, and merely changing address mappings does not mean that the process has just changed. The classic example of this would be a process issuing an exec() call, which results in all prior mappings changing to support the new program.

The kernel will load up the MMU's registers with the location of the new page table for the process, followed by a flush of the irrelevant TLB entries for the new process. The new process will keep all of the kernel TLB entries, because these addresses will continue to have the same mapping for the new process.

Once this process has been completed, the new process is allowed to run.

Further MMU Considerations

The operation of the MMU and associated TLB are somewhat complicated by the following aspects of modern UNIX systems:

- Memory protection
- Presence of swap area
- Multiprocessor (MP) architectures

The MMU determines whether or not a page can be read from or written to. This includes mapped pages with memory protection bits set in the PTE and unmapped pages that the process cannot use. In either case, the MMU raises a trap for the kernel to deal with.

The presence of the swap area is discussed in Section 7.4, where we complicate the virtual memory system further by using more memory than we physically have.

In multiprocessor systems, the presence of the TLB introduces further cache coherency considerations that are unrelated to the CPU cache coherency. For example, if the virtual-to-physical mapping or memory protection for a *kernel* page changes, TLBs in *all* MMUs must be updated to reflect this change. Another example would be shared memory accessed by several processes. This includes explicit shared memory segments and also *copy-on-write* data segments for a program that has executed fork() with no exec(). Copy on write will be discussed in Section 7.4.3.

In this case, the kernel must initiate a "TLB shootdown" in order to ensure that all other TLBs are current with the new information. This is an explicit operation, for which the kernel typically maintains a set of data structures that map which PTEs are located in the various TLBs on the MP system. Using this map, the kernel can explicitly invalidate the changed PTEs in all the TLBs.

Any changes in the PTEs are typically *not* loaded into the various TLBs, because doing so would be a very expensive default operation. Instead, the entries are simply invalidated, forcing the MMU to reload the entry on the next reference. In many cases, the reload will not be required before the process is switched off the CPU, and so the work is prevented altogether.

7.4 Virtual Memory Hierarchy

The preceding section concentrated on the generic attributes of virtual memory (VM), where a finite amount of memory is available on the system and is the maximum amount of memory that can be used among all the processes.

In reality, many of the pages of a given process do not need to be resident in memory all the time, and making them so would be wasteful of the valuable memory resource. A good example of this is Oracle Forms, where the size of the physical process may be 16MB or more. In a running system, experience has shown that only around 8MB of these pages need to be in memory at any one time in order to execute the Forms application with performance quite comparable to that of a fully resident image.

In order to support this optimization of real memory, the memory hierarchy needs to be extended to physical disk, the next step down in the memory hierarchy (see Figure 7.9).

7.4.1 The Memory/Disk Hierarchy

The use of physical disk spindles is a natural extension of the familiar memory hierarchy between CPU cache memory and main system memory. The next step after main system memory is physical disk, which is much cheaper and slower than system memory.

Using disk to extend memory capacity was once a larger issue than it is today. In the past, memory chips were scarce and expensive, and the system architectures were not able to address large amounts of real memory. Therefore, disk-based memory hierarchies were essential to providing the capability for many concurrent users on a UNIX system.

In modern systems, memory is a far less important issue than it used to be, in terms of both cost and addressability. In fact, in building a high-

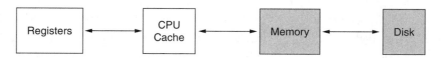

Figure 7.9 Memory/disk hierarchy

performance Oracle database server, it is preferable always to work within the confines of the physical memory on the system, and not to rely on physical disk to provide additional memory capacity.

Unlike the case of Oracle Forms cited above, Oracle Server processes share critical resources between them, meaning that one process can directly slow down all other processes in the system by holding one of the resources for an extended period. If the process needs memory that has been paged out to disk in order to complete the processing under a latch, all other processes will wait for this page-in operation before the latch is released.

The use of disk in the memory hierarchy is not limited to the sharing of physical memory, however. It also allows the rapid execution of program executables, by breaking the reliance on the entire image being in memory prior to execution. This allows the program to execute as soon as the first page is resident in memory.

7.4.2 Implementing the Hierarchy

Demand Paging

Although the full detail of the hierarchy varies across implementations, all modern virtual memory systems implement a form of *demand paging*. Demand paging extends the concepts presented in the preceding section by specifying that any given page in the system can be resident or nonresident (on disk) at any one time. This does not affect the operation on that piece of memory, because the kernel intervenes if the page is nonresident and loads the page back into memory before the operation is carried out.

The implementation of demand paging is based on the operation of the MMU and PTEs. When a page is requested, the request is serviced by the MMU. If the MMU cannot resolve the request, because the page is either not resident or not yet allocated, a page fault is generated. This is serviced by the kernel, and the appropriate action is taken, based on why the page reference could not be resolved by the MMU. If the page has never been allocated, the kernel will generate an exception for the process and send the appropriate signal.

If the page has been allocated but is located on disk, the kernel will load the page back into memory and create a new map for that virtual address, pointing it to the new physical address. The operation will then be allowed to continue.

Virtual Memory Cache Analogy

Virtual memory can be considered a cache of disk storage. This does not mean that it is the same as the buffer cache, but rather a more complex affair. However, it is safe to view the primary execution object as the on-disk copy of the memory itself. In the same way that a CPU cache mirrors the contents of physical memory in order to speed access, so the physical memory of the system is mirroring the contents of the disk in order to speed access to it.

In the case of program executables, this is a very straightforward concept to grasp: The program is on disk and, on each access to the pages that make up the file, the page is loaded into some available physical memory location in order to speed the access to the instructions in that page. The analogy to CPU caches here is the loading of cache lines (analogous to pages) from physical memory (analogous to disk blocks) before execution.

In the case of other memory objects—namely, anonymous objects such as data segments, user stacks, and so on—there is initially *no* on-disk representation. In order to deal with this, an area of disk is allocated from the swap area, a special partition or series of partitions set up for this task. This then becomes the on-disk representation of the pages allocated for this process.

When a page is first allocated to an anonymous piece of memory, nothing happens; the kernel simply ensures that the disk area is available. On first access, the page is allocated a physical memory page, which would be zero-filled by the kernel on first use. The process can now use this page as required, operating as a write-back cache (see Section 2.1.4). The disk version of this block becomes stale at this point.

This allocation is just the same as a CPU writing to a cache line for the first time; as soon as the CPU has written to it, the line in physical memory is stale, and the line in cache represents the current version.

Pager Objects

The implementation of the actual paging interface varies among different VM systems, so the method presented here represents one of the more common approaches—that of an object-based implementation.

The first concept of an object-based pager interface was introduced above; there are two different types of memory consumer, both of which are used by a process:

- File-based memory objects, such as program executables and mmap() files.

- Anonymous memory, such as program data segments, heap, and stack.

When segments of these types are created by the kernel, the kernel instantiates an object specific for that type of memory allocation. Both of the classes that define this object implement a standard interface that the kernel expects to be present (see Figure 7.10).

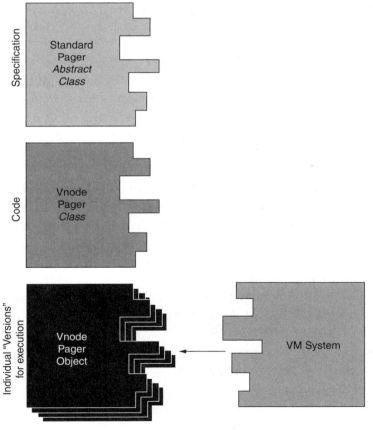

Figure 7.10 Memory objects

For those not familiar with object-oriented concepts, don't worry—it is not important that you fully understand these concepts at this stage. Basically, an *abstract class* is one that simply defines what is required from a class that *subclasses* it (it adopts the abstract class as its parent specification). A *class* is code that is fully inclusive from data and function perspectives. It contains all the data declarations and all the functions that operate on that data.[9] When a class is invoked, an *object* is created, which is basically a physical "version" of the class—one that exists in executable form in memory.

In the case of memory objects, the VM system is no longer concerned about the implementation or special requirements of a particular type of pager. As long as the pager subclasses the abstract class (i.e., specification) that the VM system expects, the VM system does not need to be cognizant of any of the detail.

The example in Figure 7.10 uses a *vnode* pager object. A vnode is an important part of the operation of modern UNIX kernels. It is the kernel's view of an active file. The "v" in vnode stands for *virtual*—that is, the vnode is an abstraction of any particular filesystem's unique file identifier. It exists in order to break the prior hard link between the kernel and a filesystem, and allows any filesystem with a vnode interface to be mounted in the same way as any other filesystem.

At the end of the vnode pointer is an actual node pointer to the physical file. Therefore, a vnode uniquely identifies a file on the system, and this is the reason that the pager object that deals with files is based on the vnode of the file.

One pager object is instantiated for every mapped file. If more than one user has the file mapped, they will share the same pager object. Whenever an operation must be performed on a page owned by this object, the VM system will call one of the standard functions on the object in order for the object to perform the operation accordingly. This includes freeing the page for another process, or reallocating physical memory for a page that has already been paged out to disk.

---

9. At least in concept. The detail is more complex, but is not required for this discussion.

The problem of handling memory mapped files is different from that of anonymous memory allocations, and so this is why there are different pager routines for each.

The pager routine for anonymous objects does not have a source file in a filesystem to pass pages to and from. Instead, these objects are transient objects that exist only for the lifetime of the process that is using them. There is no on-disk representation of these objects before they exist in physical memory. When memory pages used by these objects need to be freed, the pager writes the page out to the *swap area*, which is a dedicated set of disk partitions for this task that is shared by all processes. For this reason, this pager routine is frequently termed the *swap pager*.

Although this pager is not the vnode pager, both classes present the same interface to the kernel, using vnode and offset pairs to identify the actual page. The vnode in the case of anonymous objects is that of the swap area.

A process on the system uses both types of objects and looks a little like the arrangement shown in Figure 7.11.

Figure 7.11 illustrates the pager interfaces used by a simple executable program, such as the Korn Shell (/bin/ksh). When the program starts, a

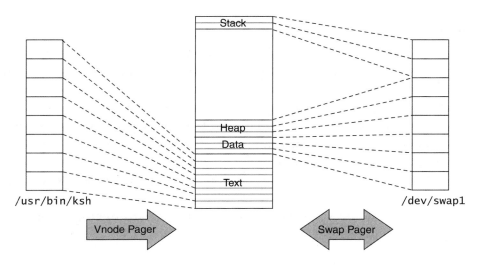

Figure 7.11 Paging interfaces

vnode pager object is created to map the executable file. The program starts to execute but cannot do so until the first page of the executable[10] is in memory. The vnode pager is called on at this point to allocate a page in memory and bring in the first page of the executable.

Almost immediately after this, the first page of the data segment needs to be available, and so a pager object needs to be made. The object would be the swap pager, because the contents of this memory will be modified during use, and this should not be reflected back into any file in the filesystem. The first page of the data segment is created by the swap pager, and execution continues.

As soon as anything needs to be placed on the stack, the kernel creates the first page of the stack segment and assigns the swap pager to it. Likewise, as soon as the program needs to use any memory on the heap, another object is created to store the heap segment, which also is a swap pager object.

In Figure 7.11, the vnode pager is a unidirectional arrow, because the mapped file is an executable (executables never get written to by the VM system). If the process were to map another file using mmap(), the vnode pager would also be responsible for ensuring that all dirty pages were first written back to the file before freeing the page.

Paging Mechanics

Now that the actual page handlers are known, we can forget about them once again and concentrate on the VM system itself and the mechanics of its operation.

The VM system varies to a large degree across implementations, but they all have the same fundamental goal: to keep as many active (i.e., currently used) pages in physical memory at any one time. They also typically all have the same basic theory for achieving this goal.

Figure 7.12 shows the four parameters used by the SVR4 UNIX memory management algorithms. Essentially, these four parameters define how aggressively the VM system should work toward freeing memory in

---

10. Or the first page of the dynamic link loader, in the case of dynamically linked executables.

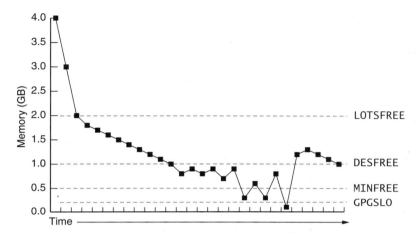

Figure 7.12 Paging thresholds

the system. The first parameter, *lotsfree,* declares that if the free memory is above this point, no action needs to be taken by the VM system to free memory—there is *lots free.* When free memory falls below this threshold, the VM system starts to find pages that can be written out to disk and subsequently free the physical memory page. This *pageout* routine is run four times per second at this point. In Figure 7.12, the rate of memory decline is reduced because the VM system starts to free infrequently used pages.

The next threshold is *desfree.* If memory falls below this point, the VM system starts *desperation paging,* because memory is getting very low. The pageout process is executed on every clock() cycle at this point, and the VM system works hard to free up memory. In the chart, the free memory level starts to become more erratic, because the requests for memory continue and the VM system is almost managing to keep the number of free pages constant. Desfree defines the amount of memory the O/S must attempt to keep free at all times.

The next threshold is *minfree.* Serious memory starvation occurs at this point, and the system becomes far more aggressive over the selection of pages to pageout. If memory still cannot be freed, and the free memory count falls below *gpgslo,* the system has to admit defeat in using the paging algorithms.

At gpgslo, the VM system changes gear and goes into swapping mode. It is deemed that memory is so scarce at this point that VM operations will dominate the CPU on the system and start *thrashing*. Thrashing is where the system spends all of its time paging in and out in an attempt to keep active pages in memory. Swapping involves paging out entire processes to the swap area, rather than trying to work out which pages should go out.

The swapping starts with the processes that are oldest. In fact, very old, inactive processes may have been swapped out much earlier in the process, just as a housekeeping action. Then sleeping processes get swapped out, followed by processes that are at the back of the run queue. At this stage, the system is essentially unusable.

In order to implement this memory management, the VM system adopts several algorithms for identifying pages to page out. One of the common ones is the not recently used algorithm, also known as the two-handed clock (see Figure 7.13).

This algorithm approximates an LRU algorithm but requires significantly less management overhead. The pages of memory are arranged as a

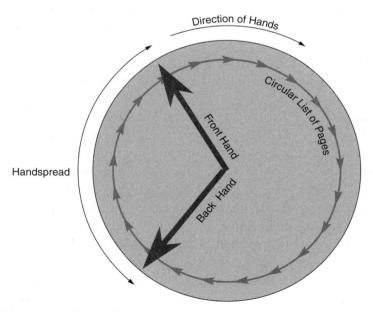

Figure 7.13 Two-handed clock algorithm

circular linked list, where the "last" element points to the first element in order to make a full loop. There are then two "hands" that are applied to searching of this list. The front hand goes through the list and turns off the referenced bit of the PTE. If the page is accessed after this, the bit is turned back on by the reference. If the bit remains off when the back hand inspects the buffer, then it is not recently used and is eligible to be freed.

The handspread is the number of buffers that separate the scans of the two hands. A small gap implies that only very frequently referenced pages will be ineligible for freeing. A large gap allows less frequently accessed pages to remain in memory. Alternatively, the speed at which the hands go around has the same effect, and this is the variable that the kernel changes depending on the amount of free memory.

When a page is to be freed, the VM system can pull the vnode and offset for the page out of the kernel structure and use this to call the correct object pager in order to carry out the procedure. The routine in the pager is called pageout(). If the page is dirty (written to but not flushed to disk), it must be written out before being freed. It is the responsibility of the relevant pager object to ensure that this occurs.

Likewise, when a page fault results in a trap, the vnode and offset for the required page are passed to the relevant pagein() routine in the pager object. This could happen for any of the following reasons:

- The page is part of an executable or mapped file and has not yet been accessed.

- The page has been paged out to swap.

- The page is a new anonymous page and needs an initial allocation.

There is a separate routine for each of these cases. In the first case, the pager simply needs to allocate a free page and fill it with the contents of the corresponding vnode and offset on disk. In the second case, the pager performs a similar operation using the swap area. The final case requires allocation of a new page, and filling of the new page with zeros by the kernel. This is defined behavior for new pages, and some programs expect such behavior.

This kind of single-page demand paging is good in theory but not very efficient in practice. In practice, just getting the required page does not make the best use of statistical facts in the way that memory is accessed.

The statistic in question, of course, is the locality of reference: If a certain page is requested, it is likely that the adjacent pages will also be required in the short term. The cost of a single page fetch from disk is so huge in comparison with the time the CPU can process that page that it makes sense to get a few adjacent pages at the same time. The additional disk overhead is tiny if the next pages are also adjacent on the physical disk, and so greater efficiency can be achieved in this way.

In addition to the standard threshold-based memory management method, some implementations adopt further optimizations. Regardless of the amount of memory left free in the system, it is also desirable to prevent proactively any processes from growing beyond a reasonable[11] size. This reduces the VM work required when the thresholds are crossed. While most VM systems keep track of the *resident set size* (*RSS*) of each process, not all allow specific action to be carried out on the basis of that number. Others, such as Sequent DYNIX/ptx, compare the current RSS of the process against a tunable parameter called *maxrs*. If the process grows beyond the defined value for maxrs, the VM system starts to pageout older pages of the process's resident set until its size comes back down to the defined limit.

7.4.3   Implications of fork() and exec()

The fork() system call is used to create new processes. The kernel creates an exact copy of the process that calls fork() and gives it a new execution thread for that process. The new process has an individual PID and retains the calling process as the parent of the process. At this point, both the parent and the child continue to execute the same application code, from exactly the same point: the return of the fork() system call.

The complexity of fork() and the reason it is present in the section on memory management have to do with the way that it is typically used. It may already be evident that the kernel will do anything to avoid work that is not necessary; this is the secret of keeping operating system overhead to a minimum. In the case of fork(), it is actually unusual for the

---

11. "Reasonable" is defined on an application-specific basis.

child process to continue executing the same code as the parent. Instead, the child typically calls the exec()[12] system call.

The exec() call invokes another program within the process that calls it. In order to do this, the address space for the process has to be redefined, making the previous set of memory mappings irrelevant for the child process. If the kernel has just gone to all the trouble of copying all the pages that comprise the parent to make this new process, that work would be wasted.

Therefore, when the kernel receives a fork() call, it typically makes an optimized copy of the parent process. This copy involves only copying of the PTEs for the parent process, thereby making the child an exact copy of the parent, including the physical memory that it uses. Of course, if the parent or the child were to write to one of the pages, it could corrupt the other process, and so another procedure is required to support this optimized copy.

This procedure is called *copy on write*. The kernel makes a copy of the parent's address space and sets up protection bits on the PTEs. If the parent or the child attempts to write to one of these pages, a protection exception is raised, which the kernel processes. Only at this stage does the kernel make a copy of the page and set the master and the copy to read/write. Therefore, if the child writes to only a few pages before issuing an exec() call, only the required amount of memory copying occurs.

BSD offers an alternative to copy on write in the form of a vfork() system call. Using this call, the child "borrows" the entire address space of the parent, and the parent blocks until the child issues an exec(). This is specifically designed for use in programs that know that an exec() always follows the fork().

7.4.4 Summary

The VM system is a fundamental part of the UNIX kernel. For large Oracle database servers, the VM system can be required to perform a good deal of work, even though the system should be configured to keep all the processes and SGA in real memory at all times.

The reason for this is that there are still a huge number of distinct processes on the system, and Oracle relies heavily on the operating system to

---

12. There are many members of the exec() family of calls, but the same concepts apply to all of them.

manage the address spaces for these processes. Each of these processes can be very large, and certainly a great deal of PTE manipulation is required.

In the case of very large SGAs, the operating system must implement changes above and beyond the provision of the standard 4KB page size. One of these optimizations—variable page sizes—was discussed in this section. Another good optimization for the reduction of PTEs in Oracle-like systems is *shared PTEs*. Just as the operating system already shares the PTEs for text segments, it is also possible to create just one set of PTEs for the shared memory segment to which all processes refer. This reduces the memory consumption of the page tables enormously.

Although the details of the virtual memory system are not essential for building a high-performance Oracle database system, a good understanding of VM can be helpful in comprehending system operation under load and in correlating system statistics.

7.5   I/O System

7.5.1   Everything Is a File

One of the fundamental design concepts of the UNIX system was to abstract all I/O operations as linear file operations. This allows the kernel to take the complexity of physical hardware devices away from programmers, and to deal with it internally instead. A good example of this would be a tape drive, which has the concept of records. A linear file has no concept of records but only of a continuous stream of bytes. Therefore, the kernel takes care of the record-based communication with the tape drive, allowing the programmer to read from and write to the tape device using standard read() and write() system calls.

This concept has mostly held true to this day, although the number of ioctl()[13] and other custom call types available has sometimes made it appear not to be so.

The rule, however, is that pretty much everything can be treated as a file. This makes I/O programming on UNIX systems very portable and

---

13. ioctl() is used to perform device-dependent actions.

straightforward as a result of the kernel (specifically the device drivers) taking the complexity away from the programmer.

Something to bear in mind when looking at system statistics is that the number of read() and write() system calls being executed does not correlate with disk I/O. Rather, these calls include logical I/O in and out of the filesystem buffer cache as well as all network and terminal I/O.

7.5.2   Filesystems

The filesystem is a user-friendly interface to the raw disk. It presents a hierarchical tree of directories and files (see Figure 7.14) and allows concurrent access to files and directories by all users with permission to do so.

All UNIX filesystems share this common interface to the user, regardless of the implementation details of the filesystem or of whether it is local or remote.

Although the interface to the filesystem is very different from the SQL interface used by Oracle, the requirement for the filesystem is virtually identical to the Oracle database. Both are tasked with optimizing the reading and writing of data, in an organized fashion, to and from physical disk.

Just like Oracle, it would be very inefficient to make all of the I/O requests physical, requiring disk I/O for every request. Therefore, filesystems perform all I/O through a cache layer known as the *buffer cache*[14] (see Figure 7.15).

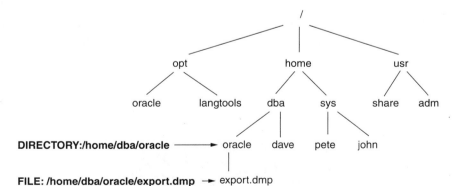

Figure 7.14 Filesystem hierarchy

---

14. Not to be confused with the Oracle buffer cache, although the two are similar in nature.

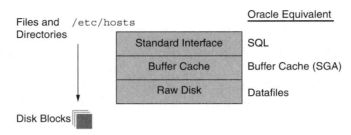

Figure 7.15   Filesystem layers

Using the layers shown in Figure 7.15, the filesystem presents a familiar interface to the user, the hierarchical view, with two types of available objects: files and directories. The access to the objects is all done by means of the buffer cache, apart from special "trusted" operations. Although the logical perspective of the file is that of a contiguous file, this is not physically true. All mappings to the blocks that make up a file are maintained by the filesystem itself.

The filesystem implementation has changed a good deal over the life of the UNIX operating system. The simplest filesystem is the System V filesystem, known as the s5fs, and we will use this as an introduction to filesystem implementations.

The s5 Filesystem maintains three different areas on disk, as shown in Figure 7.16. The *superblock* is the equivalent of a segment header in Oracle, in that it stores the freelist for inodes and data blocks and general information about the file. It is always stored as the first block on disk and is of fixed length. After the superblock comes the *inodes*.

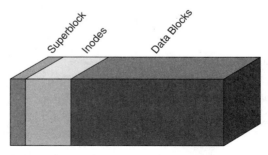

Figure 7.16   s5 Filesystem organization

Inodes are the entry points for all files. There is one inode for each file in the filesystem. Contained in the inode are pointers to actual data blocks, access information, permissions, and file owner information. The inode is read when `ls -l` is executed in a directory, in order to read the information above.

The inode is of fixed length so that each inode in the table can be addressed by a `number*size` formula. Included in this size is sufficient information to store up to ten block addresses for the actual file. For very small files (up to 10KB with 1,024 block size), this is sufficient. For larger files, the inode stores three levels of *indirect block addresses*. The first level is a pointer to a single data block that contains only further lists of block addresses. This allows for an additional 256 blocks (256KB) to be addressed. The second level of indirect block is a pointer to a block that contains only indirect block pointers. Again, 256 pointers can be stored in a single 1KB block, and so the maximum file size catered to by going to the double indirect block is 64MB (256*256*1024 bytes). Finally, there is a third level of indirection, a pointer to a block of pointers to blocks of pointers. This yields a maximum file size of 16GB (256*256*256*1024 bytes), although a 32-bit address limitation allows for only a 2GB maximum in practice, because we have to be able to `lseek()` forward and backward the full size of the file. Still, this is not too bad for an old, retired filesystem.

The first inode in a filesystem is reserved for the root directory of that filesystem. This is not the same as *the* root directory; it assumes the name of the directory at which it is mounted—that is, if a filesystem were mounted as `/opt/oracle`, the first inode would be a pointer to the "`oracle`" directory when the filesystem was mounted there. More precisely, the first inode is for the root directory of the filesystem.

A directory is simply another type of file. It is a file that has a format known to the filesystem, containing a list of names and inode numbers for the files within it. When `ls` is called without any options, only the directory is read. When a file is referred to by name, the directory is checked first to get the inode for the file. With the inode, it is just a case of going to corresponding offset in the inode table and retrieving the access information for the file.

If a directory gets too large (too many entries), its performance can be degraded. This is the equivalent of doing full table scans in Oracle; the filesystem code must go all the way through the directory "file" in order to satisfy certain requests, such as a vanilla `ls`. Likewise, `ls -l` requires a lookup of the actual inode for each entry; this is something to bear in mind when building filesystems.

Modern Filesystems

The s5fs did a reasonable job for its life span but suffered from several drawbacks, including performance. The Berkeley fast filesystem (FFS) improved on some of these drawbacks by optimizing the organization of the filesystem on disk and allowing long filenames (s5 allowed only 14 characters). However, even FFS is not suitable for commercial application, particularly if a database is to be built on the filesystem.

The drawbacks of these filesystems are

- Poor crash recovery
- Poor performance
- File size limitations

Traditional filesystems do not cope well with system crashes. Any dirty (unwritten) blocks in the filesystem buffer cache at the time of the crash will be lost, and there is no formal approach to recovering the filesystem. Instead, the filesystem must be laboriously scanned with the `fsck` utility in order to validate its integrity. Often the utility is not able to rationalize what it finds, and intervention is required by an operator, possibly resulting in file loss or corruption. This is bad enough in itself, but it also takes a good deal of time to get to this stage—possibly many, many minutes. It is essential for a large production system to recover more quickly than this, regardless of whether or not there is a hot standby system.

In order to get around the problem of unwritten dirty blocks, traditional filesystems have to support *synchronous writes*. This is the only way the database writer, for example, can guarantee that a block is actually going onto disk. This means that the database writer must wait for the completion of this write, potentially taking place at several locations on the physical disk, involving several lengthy seek operations. This results in poor performance for the filesystem.

The traditional filesystems are block-based in their addressing. This is not acceptable for large database systems, because there is an enormous administration and performance overhead from this scheme when very large files are used.

Modern filesystems have been engineered to overcome these problems and to support database systems more effectively. One of the most successful of these is the *journaling filesystem*, notably the *Veritas VxFS*. These filesystems operate even more like database servers than do the traditional ones.

Essentially, these filesystems rely on redo logs within the filesystem in order to increase its performance and recovery. When a write occurs, it can be written directly to the buffer cache and also to the redo log. The redo log is on a sequential portion of disk, and so this write is fast. The write to the actual redo log on disk only occurs at the commit point for the write, which is the end of the write. Until this point, the writes go into a redo log buffer, in much the same way as in Oracle. The redo log buffer scheme also supports group commits of multiple transactions.

The write to the data area of the filesystem is not required, because the redo log is capable of rebuilding the data area in the event of a crash. The crash recovery is based on the presence of a redo log, the filesystem check at start up needs only to roll forward the changes that have occurred since the last checkpoint of the data area. This makes recovery very reliable and fast.

The filesystem is designed for very large files, and so both the filesystem and the files within it can be very large. Instead of using single block references to the data area of the filesystem, the journaling filesystem uses extents (contiguous groups of blocks), in the same way as Oracle does. A new extent is allocated for the file, and the extent is referenced instead of a single block. This allows large files to be supported with less overhead than in the traditional block-based approach and to provide considerably greater performance as a result of the contiguous grouping of data blocks.

7.5.3 Raw Disk

UNIX allows direct access to raw disk. The interface to the disk is through a UNIX special file, which is opened using standard system calls and accessed using normal read, write, and seek calls. To an application using the raw disk, it just looks like one large file.

Raw disk partitions have several drawbacks:

- The unit of allocation to the database is the entire file.
- Cannot use standard file manipulation commands on datafiles.
- Cannot use bundled backup tools (cpio, tar, pax) to backup the files.
- Cannot easily determine how much space is free within a group of raw device files, or how large the files actually are.

They also have positive attributes:

- Not subject to any operating system locking
- Not subject to any operating system caching
- Can be shared between multiple systems

These advantages are very important. Essentially, using raw disk removes the operating system from the operation of the Oracle I/O process, with the exception of the device drivers that perform the actual I/O. Any number of processes can read from and write to the partition concurrently, if the partition resides on multiple physical disks (see Section 7.5.5). Also, raw disk is currently the only way of mounting the same Oracle database on multiple UNIX hosts for Oracle Parallel Server.[15]

In order to gain these advantages, however, it is important to work through the list of disadvantages and to produce procedures and techniques that make them operationally acceptable.

Entire File Allocations

When raw disk is used, raw partitions are supplied to Oracle as a datafile. This means that the entire file, and not just a part of it, must be allocated to Oracle at any one time. In reality, this does not present much of a problem. The physical disk can be sliced into several raw partitions of different sizes.

---

15. There now exists a clustered filesystem, based on the journaling filesystem, that works a little like a parallel server. The filesystem can be mounted on more than one node concurrently, with the coherency managed through the system cluster software (lock manager). This filesystem will support the creation and use of OPS database files.

The size and number of these partitions will vary with database requirements, but the concept maps to all databases. It makes sense to keep the range of partition sizes fairly small in order to make the management simplistic. For example, use allocation sizes of 4GB, 2GB, 1GB, 500MB, and 100MB. This allows quite large tablespaces to be built from a relatively small number of files, and the small ones to be built from small files.

Use of Standard File Manipulation Commands

Often the hardest attributes of raw disk to get used to is the inability to use the standard UNIX file utilities such as cp and mv. In reality, a well-configured database system does not require a great deal of file manipulation once it is laid out. If a disk is found to be "hot," a file can still be physically moved by using the dd command to suck the contents out of one partition and put it into a new partition.

When raw devices are used, it also makes sense to work around the naming of typical raw devices. In fact, the naming of the files is one of the major objections most people have to using them. What does /dev/rdsk/c10t5d3s4 mean to anyone, as far as the size and location of the raw device are concerned? Logical volume managers help a little here by providing more user-definable naming conventions, but there are even better ways around this.

The first thing to do after creating all the devices is to make a directory of symbolic links (ln -s). These links should be placed in a common location *away* from the /dev directory, somewhere near the Oracle codeset. A good convention is to have a root from which all these things happen, such as /opt/oracle. Under this root you can locate the codeset (say, /opt/oracle/oracle815) and the directory containing the symbolic links to the actual raw devices.

Each symbolic link should have a descriptive name, such as "db00_1000M_10_000," which means database set 00, 1000MB slice, RAID 1+0, slice number 000. With a directory called /opt/oracle/SPARE containing all these files, it is very easy to determine the types and numbers of available datafile slices and their RAID characteristics.

At database creation time, make another directory under /opt/oracle to put the used symbolic links in, such as /opt/oracle/PRD1. Creating the database would then go a little like this (assuming that the init.ora has been created and resides in /tmp for now):

```
$ cd /opt/oracle/PRD1
$ mv /tmp/initPRD1.ora .
$ ln -s $PWD/initPRD1.ora $ORACLE_HOME/dbs/.
$ mv ../SPARE/db00_500M_10_000 system_01.dbf
$ svrmgrl

Oracle Server Manager Release 3.1.5.0.0

(c) Copyright 1997, Oracle Corporation.  All Rights Reserved.

Oracle8 Enterprise Edition Release 8.1.5.0.0
With the Partitioning option
PL/SQL Release 8.1.5.0.0

SVRMGR> connect internal
Connected.
SVRMGR> create database PRD1 CONTROLFILE REUSE
     2> datafile "/opt/oracle/PRD1/system_01.dbf" size 500M REUSE
etc
```

For control files, they are ideally located in small pieces of "leftover" disk allocation. These are pieces of disk that represent the 0.1GB of a 9.1GB drive, for example, or remainder disk after rounding the allocations down. It is required that these pieces be on raw disk if OPS is used. Otherwise, it is possible to put the control files in the UNIX filesystem, although it is best to keep all the datafiles in one form or the other (raw or FS).

Backup

Backup does not present a great problem in building very large database systems. The reason for this is that you can no longer adequately manage the backup of the database using cpio or tar anyway. For a large database, it is necessary to use a fully featured backup product in order to get software indexed backups, allowing more control over tape identification and faster recovery times. In addition, the bundled archivers do not support features such as parallel tape streaming, which allows much greater backup throughput. This becomes important as the database size becomes very large.

All of the third-party backup products provide the facility to backup raw disk partitions as easily as filesystems. However, you must ensure that the symbolic link directory also gets backed up on a regular basis, because this is the tie between the location of the files that Oracle expects, and the actual location in /dev.

Space Management

When the procedures laid out above are used, space management does not present any more problems than a filesystem presents. It is very clear how much space is left for allocation to the database from looking in the SPARE directory. The only thing that is not possible with raw devices is the automatic extension of datafiles, using Oracle.

7.5.4 Filesystems Versus Raw Disk

The debate over the use of filesystems versus the use of raw disk has been raging for years. There are good points and bad points on each side, and it is not clear where the balance lies. Despite this, each has several clear advantages that factor into the decision process.

Filesystems

There are two fundamental problems associated with the use of filesystems. First, the filesystem buffer cache causes slow writes. As this is all that occurs on redo logs during normal operation, this is bad. Second, the single-writer lock imposed on a per-file basis can limit write performance to datafiles.

On the plus side, the files in a filesystem are very visible and easy to interpret and administrate. Nevertheless, when you are dealing with very large datafiles, it is undesirable to be moving 4GB or 8GB files around, so the significance of this advantage is debatable.

The other advantage of using a filesystem is application-specific—the advantage of gaining additional benefit from the filesystem buffer cache. In cache theory terms, the filesystem buffer cache can be viewed as the L2 cache, with the Oracle cache being the L1. It can also be viewed from the perspective of double buffering; there is no difference in speed between the two caches, and so there is no benefit for the frequently used blocks and a fairly significant overhead in managing the same blocks in two caches. With 64-bit Oracle, this advantage is difficult to justify any more; all the memory that would have been in the filesystem cache can now be given to Oracle across all three buffer pools.

Raw Disk

Raw disk essentially puts Oracle in the driver's seat as far as I/O is concerned. With the operating system responsible only for communication with the hardware, there is no additional CPU overhead incurred from managing filesystem caches. Raw disk is not subject to any kind of operating system locking and can be used in parallel server configurations.

From a logical perspective, there is no reason why a raw disk database system should ever be slower than a file-system-based system. The only condition under which this could occur would be a deficiency in the Oracle caching algorithms. With a file-system-based database, every miss in the Oracle buffer cache results in a read() system call. This bears a finite cost, as does the subsequent searching and cache management in the filesystem buffer cache. If there still is a miss, the physical read must occur anyway, making the true overhead for the miss twice as bad as it would be in a raw disk system (ignoring the constant cost of the disk read).

If the memory used for the buffer cache were used in the Oracle buffer cache, it is likely that there would be a hit in the Oracle cache layer, eliminating the additional system call for the filesystem logical read.

Advanced filesystem implementations provide more hooks to allow Oracle to circumvent the filesystem layer itself and go straight to raw disk. This leaves the filesystem performing only an offline administration function and not participating in the actual operation of the database. This may be the best of both worlds, providing all the advantages of the filesystem (visibility, file extension capability) without the disadvantages.

7.5.5   Logical Volume Managers

In Section 2.8, we introduced I/O and RAID levels. In Chapter 2, these levels were mostly hardware concepts focused on the disks and their performance. In addition to hardware RAID, most vendors offer some kind of *logical volume manager (LVM)*.

An LVM is an addition to the kernel that provides RAID functionality from the host. No special hardware is required to do this, only standard disk drives.

There are several reasons why this is a good thing. First, if multiple controllers are used, a stripe can be set up across all the controllers. This maximizes the performance of the controllers to gain best performance. If this approach is taken, however, care must be taken that controller redundancy is preserved, because if one of the many controllers that make up the stripe were to fail, the entire stripe array would be unavailable. In the case of EMC disk arrays, the EMC does not provide a striping function. Therefore, some kind of software stripe is required in order to perform striping on this device. Although it provides the *disk* redundancy within, controller redundancy is still required.

Second, using a software volume manager allows disk devices to be given more user-friendly names than standard disk slicing offers. This will become apparent in this rapid introduction to the operation of volume managers.

There are several fairly basic concepts used in all software volume managers. The first of these concepts is the *volume group* (see Figure 7.17). A volume group is the largest grouping used within the volume manager and is composed of several disk objects.

When the disks (or disk slices) have been added to the volume group, this volume group has a capacity equal to the combined capacities of the disk devices within it.

The next stage is to create logical volumes from the volume group. These logical volumes can be called anything at all, therefore allowing meaningful naming conventions to be implemented. From the volume group in Figure 7.17, we could create a single volume four times larger

Volume Group

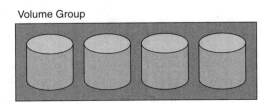

Figure 7.17   Volume group

than a physical disk. This would create a very large logical volume, but it would be practically useless because it is likely that the I/O would be concentrated within a small portion of the volume's total size.

In order to create a more useful volume, we would instruct the volume manager to create it (or, more likely, a smaller one) but to use a stripe (or chunk) width somewhat smaller than that of a physical disk. If we use a 128KB stripe width, the volume manager will go off and distribute the volume across the disks 128KB at a time, round-robin fashion. This means that a read of 512KB in the example above would include all drives in the volume group.

In Figure 7.18, six logical volumes have been created from the "bucket" of space in the volume group. All of these volumes are striped across all the disks within the volume group.

At this point, the operation of software RAID is the same as that of hardware RAID but is calculated and initiated from the host. This has two implications on the host processing. First, the administration of the RAID subsystem is now a task that the operating system must be concerned with, increasing the cost of any given I/O operation initiated on those devices. While this is a fairly small increase, it is something that should not be overlooked.

The second implication is, for the most part, valid only when LVM-based mirroring is used. When mirroring from the host, the host must make write requests to two controllers for every write request. This increases the bus utilization on write-intensive applications. In addition, when the system crashes, the host comes up trusting only one side of the mirrored pair. The other side of the mirror is marked STALE and is in need

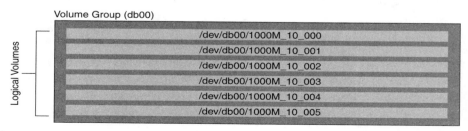

Figure 7.18   Logical volumes

of resilvering. Although this is a process that Oracle is now involved in,[16] the traditional approach to it was to perform a full disk-to-disk copy from the active side of the mirror to the stale side of the mirror. While this copy is in progress, all new writes must also be written to both sides, whereas all reads come only from the active side. This can have an enormous impact on the I/O throughput of the system, and an even bigger impact on the available CPU capacity on the system, because this operation is very CPU-intensive.

7.6 Interprocess Communication (IPC)

As UNIX systems became more powerful and complex, it became apparent that there was a need for some way to allow processes to communicate in order to coordinate processing of common workloads. All types of such communication are known as *interprocess communication (IPC)*. The first and most basic form of IPC comes in the form of the *pipe*.

7.6.1 Pipe Communication

A pipe is initiated by a process prior to forking a child process. The pipe() system call opens two file descriptors. One of these descriptors is open for reading, and the other is open for writing. In this preliminary state, anything written to the write descriptor will be available for reading from the other file descriptor. This is not very useful until a fork() call is made.

After the fork() call has been made, both processes retain all the open files that the parent had before the call. The parent closes the read file descriptor, and the child closes the write descriptor, and now there is a useful way to communicate between the processes. At this stage the communication is unidirectional only; if two pipe() calls had been made, bidirectional communication could be set up.

---

16. Recently, Oracle has gotten involved in this process. The logic is simple: If we just had a crash, why don't we assume that both sides of the mirror are out of date and reapply the redo information since the last checkpoint?

This is the mechanism used by the shell in order to enable operations such as

```
$ who -u | grep jeff
```

The shell forks once in order to continue processing with processes other than itself. This parent shell process then simply blocks (suspends) with a wait() call, waiting for the child processes to terminate execution.

The first child then initiates the pipe() sequence as above, but then takes it one step further. After the fork() of the second process, the shell (it is still just two clones of the shell; no exec() has been called yet) uses the dup() system call to reallocate the file descriptors. For the process destined to become who, the stdout descriptor is closed, and the writeable end of the pipe is associated with the usual stout descriptor using dup(). This means that this process will now send all normal output to the pipe instead of to the screen.

The process destined to become grep does the opposite—it closes the stdin file descriptor and uses dup() to make the read end of the pipe become the standard input for the process. At this stage, the two processes issue the exec() system call to become the requested processes, and the output of who is passed to grep.

This is the mechanism used by the Oracle PIPE driver for client/server communication within a common host.

7.6.2   System V IPC

System V introduced three new forms of IPC: shared memory, semaphores, and message queues.

Shared Memory

Shared memory is a simple concept: Create a piece of memory that many processes can map into their address spaces. Changes made by one user are immediately visible to the other processes, without the need for any kind of system call. Owing to the lack of required system calls once the shared memory segment has been created, this is a very fast form of IPC.

The Oracle SGA is created within a shared memory segment for providing IPC among all the processes that are connected to the Oracle database. The system call to create a shared memory segment is shmget(), which creates the segment and returns a *key* for the segment. Any number of processes can now attach the segment to their address space using the shmat() system call.

A shared memory segment, once created, is an entity in its own right. Even if no processes are attached to it, it still remains in memory. It could be created one day and only initially attached to a year later. The only thing that will clear a shared memory segment, apart from a reboot, is an explicit call to shmctl() with the remove flag set. This can be done from the command line using the ipcrm -m <key> command.

As mentioned previously, it is preferable for the operating system to provide some way of sharing page tables for shared memory regions. Otherwise, a large Oracle SGA can use a very large amount of memory in page table allocations.

Although shared memory provides no formal locking techniques, synchronization of updates can be achieved either by using the atomic operations supported in the hardware or by using semaphores. Semaphores are too slow to be used as latch mechanisms because of the required system calls, and so Oracle uses atomic memory updates with test and set to manage the synchronization of the SGA.

Semaphores

Semaphores are used for coordinating processes. They are kernel-controlled counters that support only two operations: increment and decrement. Rather confusing, for English speakers at least, is the fact that these operations are called V ops and P ops, respectively. They are referred to in this way because they were named by a Dutchman called Dijkstra, who is credited with the invention of the semaphore.

A semaphore can have any positive value, or a value of zero. Negative values are not permitted. The idea is that waiting processes attempt to decrement the semaphore, and processes that have finished running increment the semaphore. If decrementing the semaphore by the requested amount would result in a negative value, the process is blocked in the kernel until the semaphore has been incremented (by other processes) such that the operation would not result in a negative value.

Oracle uses semaphores (in non-OPS configurations) to implement slow waits such as latch *sleeps* (not latch *gets*) and enqueues. OPS configurations have to hand this task off to the DLM in order to manage enqueues between instances. In most configurations, Oracle uses semaphores to provide a communication mechanism between Oracle processes. For example, when a commit is issued, the message is sent to the log writer by way of a semaphore on which the log writer sleeps. Whenever required to perform work, the log writer is posted by incrementing the semaphore on which the log writer waits (seen in V$SESSION_WAIT as "rdbms ipc message"). The alternative mechanism for waking up processes to perform work is the *post/wait driver*. This is typically a UNIX kernel addition that allows more specific communication between the processes, through a direct posting mechanism.

Message Queues

Message queues are essentially multireader, multiwriter pipes that are implemented in the kernel. Processes can place messages on a message queue, and other processes can read these messages off the queue in a first-in, first-out order.

The reading of messages is subject to the messages meeting the criterion specified in the msgrcv() call. This criterion is a *message type*, specified as an integer. If no message meeting the criterion is found, the receiver will block (suspend) until such a message is sent to the message queue.

Message queues are not a very efficient means of communication, because a write and a subsequent read require two system calls and two copies to and from kernel memory. If the messages are large, this copying becomes prohibitively expensive in processing terms.

Message queues are sometimes useful in implementing instructions to running processes, where the message is small. Oracle does not utilize message queues.

7.7   More on System Calls

It is worthwhile to become familiar with several of the system calls available on a modern UNIX system, particularly the ones that are frequently used by Oracle. These calls can be viewed on a running process by using the O/S system call trace utility, or on a global basis using system monitoring tools.

The system calls used by a process can be analyzed in real time using a vendor-supplied utility. This utility is frequently called `truss` on machines based on System V, but other names are used on other platforms. The output looks like this:

```
execve(path, argv, envp)
 argc = 2
mmap(0x00000000, 4096, PROT_READ|PROT_WRITE, MAP_PRIVATE|MAP_ANONYMOUS, 0, 0) = 0xBFF9A000
mprotect(0x08048000, 21548, PROT_READ|PROT_WRITE|PROT_EXEC) = 0
getuid()                                 = 7688   [ 7688 ]
getuid()                                 = 7688   [ 7688 ]
getgid()                                 = 901    [ 901 ]
getgid()                                 = 901    [ 901 ]
open("/lib/libseq.so", O_RDONLY, 027777746234)  = 3
read(3, "7F E L F010101\0\0\0\0\0".., 308)    = 308
mmap(0x00000000, 188384, PROT_READ, MAP_PRIVATE|MAP_ANONYMOUS, 0, 0) = 0xBFF6B000
mmap(0xBFF6B000, 126436, PROT_READ|PROT_EXEC, MAP_PRIVATE|MAP_FIXED, 3, 0) = 0xBFF6B000
mmap(0xBFF8A000, 47144, PROT_READ|PROT_WRITE|PROT_EXEC, MAP_PRIVATE|MAP_FIXED, 3, 122880) = 0xBFF8A000
mprotect(0xBFF96000, 12288, PROT_READ|PROT_WRITE|PROT_EXEC) = 0
close(3)                                 = 0
mprotect(0x08048000, 21548, PROT_READ|PROT_EXEC) = 0
time()                                   = 922664565
ioctl(1, TCGETA, 0x08047B8E)             Err#19 ENODEV
brk(0x0805D0C8)                          = 0
brk(0x080660C8)                          = 0
lstat64("smpool.c", 0x08047AF4)          = 0
a_lstat("smpool.c", 0x08047A44)          = 0
ioctl(1, TCGETA, 0x08047142)             Err#19 ENODEV
fstatfs(1, 0x0804716C, 44, 0)            = 0
brk(0x0806E0C8)                          = 0
ioctl(1, TCGETA, 0x08047142)             Err#19 ENODEV
close(0)                                 = 0
write(1, " s m p o o l . c\n", 9)        = 9
close(1)                                 = 0
close(2)                                 = 0
_exit(0)
```

This output is from the command "`ls smpool.c`" on a Sequent platform. The format is common among all utilities of this type: system call, parameters, return code.

At the head of the trace is the `exec()` call to execute the `ls` command, followed by an `mmap()` of /dev/zero to create a zero-filled anonymous 4,096-byte page of memory in the address space. Moving on a few lines, the first `open()` represents the first stage of loading of a shared library (`libseq.so`), continuing through to the `mprotect()`. The `brk()` calls show the process allocating memory on the heap, probably using one of the function calls from the `malloc()` family. The actual requested task is carried out using the `lstat64()` system call, to get information about the file. Interestingly, if no file is passed to `ls`, it opens the directory "`.`" and uses `getdents()` to retrieve the directory entries, because no clues are given. Issuing "ls *" performs an lstat64() call for every file, because all the names are supplied implicitly by the shell wildcard expansion.

After the lstat64() returns, the process writes the output to the terminal using the write() system call, and then exits.

These utilities can be invaluable in determining strange behavior in running processes and can identify a runaway process very quickly.

It is not necessary to be familiar with all of the available system calls; that's what the man pages are for. After all, HP-UX has 324 system calls, and Sequent has 202, so the list is fairly large.

Table 7.2 identifies some of the common system calls used by Oracle. Where not specified, the return code is zero for success or –1 for failure.

Table 7.2 Common System Calls

System Call	Description	Returns
open()	Opens specified file in the specified mode	File descriptor (fd)
close()	Closes specified file descriptor	
read()	Reads *n* bytes from fd into supplied buffer	Number of bytes read or -1
write()	Writes *n* bytes to fd from supplied buffer	Number of bytes written or –1
readv()	Vectored read. Return data from many locations in specified file with one system call	Number of bytes read or –1
writev()	Vectored write. Write data to many locations in specified file with one system call	Number of bytes written or –1
lseek()	Moves position in fd to specified position	New offset or –1
select() poll()	File descriptor multiplexer—checks a series of fds for reading or writing	Sets bitmask to show which fds are ready
accept()	Accepts incoming connections from socket	File descriptor for new socket

Table 7.2 continued

System Call	Description	Returns
accept()	Accepts incoming connections from socket	File descriptor for new socket
alarm()	Sends caller a SIGALRM in n seconds	Remaining time of any previous alarm() calls
brk()	Expands heap to specified address	
chdir()	Changes working directory	
creat()	Creates file with specified mode	fd of new file, or −1
dup()	Duplicates file descriptor to first free descriptor	File descriptor of duplicate
exec()	Destroys current address space and executes this program	−1 on failure
exit()	Terminates program and sends SIGCHLD and status information to parent	N/A
fork()	Creates new child process	Child PID if parent, or zero
getuid()	Returns my UID	UID
getgid()	Returns my GID	GID
getitimer()	Gets current value of interval timer	
setitimer()	Sets up the interval timer	
getpid()	Retrieves current PID	PID
ioctl()	Device-dependent control for fd	
kill()	Sends signal to specified process	
mmap()	Maps file into process address space	Address at which mapping placed
mprotect()	Protects this range of memory, subject to supplied flags	
pipe()	Opens pipe	2 fds
semXXX()	Semaphore administration	
shmXXX()	Shared memory administration	

Table 7.2   continued

System Call	Description	Returns
msgXXX()	Message queue administration	
signal()	Changes signal handling for process	Address of prior handler
socket()	Creates network socket (endpoint)	fd for socket
stat()	Returns file information	
time()	Current time in seconds since epoch	Current time
times()	Gets time accounting information for current process and children	Elapsed time
unlink()	Decrements hard link count for file. If zero, remove file.	
wait()	Wait for child process to return and gather status information	PID of child
pstat()	<Example> system call interface to gather kernel statistics.	Varies between implementations

7.8   Chapter Summary

This chapter may have been very tough going. It has been very deep on occasion, and you may have found yourself wondering what this has to do with Oracle. The simple answer is that Oracle relies heavily on nearly all aspects of the UNIX operating system, and understanding how these functions work is an important part of total system comprehension.

When problems occur on the system, such as memory exhaustion, it is sometimes not immediately apparent what is causing the problem. An understanding of how the operating system handles its resources can dramatically speed up determination of the root cause (pun intended).

7.9 Further Reading

Vahalia, U. *UNIX Internals: The New Frontiers.* Upper Saddle River, NJ: Prentice Hall, 1996.

McKusick, M. K., K. Bostic, and M. Karels. *The Design and Implementation of the 4.4BSD Operating System.* Reading, MA: Addison-Wesley, 1996.

Stevens, W. R. *Advanced Programming in the UNIX Environment.* Reading, MA: Addison-Wesley, 1993.

Goodheart, B., and J. Cox. *The Magic Garden Explained: The Internals of UNIX System V Release 4: An Open Systems Design.* Upper Saddle River, NJ: Prentice Hall, 1994.

Chapter 8

Oracle User's Guide to UNIX

8.1   Coengineering the Oracle Kernel

The Oracle RDBMS is engineered as a platform-independent product. This means that there are many rules and procedures involved in the development cycle at Oracle, in order to ensure that the source can be built on a huge array of totally different platforms. The array of platforms that Oracle runs on includes IBM VM mainframes, Microsoft NT, VMS, and Netware, not to mention the huge array of UNIX variants. The differences among these platforms are more complex than those among different UNIX platforms; the fundamental operation of the system is totally different, including data representation formats, scheduling algorithms, interprocess communication, and "file" architectures.

In order to allow the Oracle product to run on such an array of different architectures, several steps are taken, including:

- Strict coding and naming standards in the base code
- Complete separation between host "natives" and base product

The first step involves the adherence to rules that allow the source to be built on different platforms. Examples of this would be naming conventions to cater to the lowest common denominator in linker capability, and restrictions in the use of globally scoped variables.

The second step is where Oracle adopts the *virtual operating system (VOS)* in order to provide separation of function.

8.1.1   VOS Responsibilities

In order to implement separation between the base code and the operating system specifics, Oracle divides the product source code into two distinct regions: generic (base) and operating system dependent (OSD). The base code portion contains the common base code for the product, whereas the OSD portion provides the OS-specific code.

This segregation has been a part of the Oracle product from the very beginning and is how Oracle has been able to provide the product on so many platforms.

However, until release 8.0, the interface was not 100 percent pure. This meant that OSD changes often required engineering changes further up in the base code (see Figure 8.1).

For Oracle8, an effort was undertaken to clean this up, and the VOS layer was the result (see Figure 8.2).

The VOS layer is a formalized interface to the OSD code. It allows complete separation of the generic code from the OSD code, thus making the platform-specific engineering effort *and* the base development more defined.

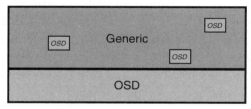

Figure 8.1   Software layers prior to Oracle8

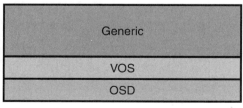

Figure 8.2   Oracle8+ software layers

The base/generic code itself is divided further into named layers, but all of these layers reside within core development from an organizational standpoint and interface with the hardware through the generic VOS interface.

The platform-specific developers build VOS-compliant OSD code for their platforms. This is sometimes a group within Oracle, a group within the platform vendor, or a combination of both. Regardless of where the work is done, it is *not* done by the same people who do the base coding of the Oracle kernel.

When an OSD developer feels that some change in the generic code would benefit the platform, this no longer results in OSD implants in the base code. Instead, the change (assuming it is a good one) is adopted in the base kernel, with a VOS interface to the OSD code. In this way, the base code stays clean, and other platforms can benefit from the change by writing their own OSD code. An example of this is covered in Section 8.1.2.

The VOS/OSD software is responsible for a variety of interfaces to the operating system, including

- Datatype specification and manipulation
- I/O interfaces (including asynchronous I/O where applicable)
- Process management and threads
- IPC
- Memory management
- Stack management facilities/other utilities

Datatype Specification

With each operating system and architecture, there may be a different specification for, say, a `long`. On one platform it may be 32 bits wide, whereas on another it may be 64 bits wide. This kind of ambiguity of data specification is avoided by Oracle by leaving it to the VOS to define the datatypes for the base code. The base code avoids the use of `int`, `long`, `double`, and so on, adopting instead an internal naming convention for data typing. Anybody who has used OCI will be familiar with the types `ub4`, `sb2`, `text *`, and so on. These names explicitly define the width and usage of the datatype; in this example, the types would be Unsigned-Byte-4, Signed-Byte-2, and a pointer to text.

In addition to the typing of data, the VOS is responsible for the handling of these datatypes in operations that are sensitive to byte ordering. The base code is not concerned with the endian (byte-ordering) orientation of the system.

I/O Interfaces

As the I/O interface can also vary a great deal among platforms, it is ultimately the responsibility of the VOS/OSD to perform the actual manipulation of files on the system. The base code calls VOS functions with common parameters in order to perform the I/O on the system. This includes the opening, closing, seeking, reading, writing, and creation of files. In addition, the VOS code is responsible for the implementation of asynchronous I/O on the platform, with the system calls and semantics of using the async I/O varying from platform to platform.

Process Management and Threads

On a UNIX system, new processes are created with the fork() system call. In other operating systems, this is almost certainly not the method for creating processes, if processes are indeed the method used in order to have multiple execution streams on that platform. Therefore, the VOS is responsible for all process creation and management from an Oracle perspective.

On the WindowsNT platform, the database architecture is implemented using threads instead of processes: All background and foreground sessions exist as threads within a single process on the system. The base code is simply calling the same VOS functions that create multiple processes on the UNIX platform, but the NT OSD implementation manipulates threads instead of processes.

IPC

Different platforms have different methods for IPC. In fact, it may be that the operating system in question does not support a process model but rather a threaded model. Once again, the base code is not concerned with this—it is only aware of requesting common services from the VOS.

Memory Management

Memory management in this case includes two unrelated items: the SGA and the process space. Both of these items are platform-specific. On UNIX platforms, the semantics are at least the same—shared memory and some kind of `malloc()` library. In other operating systems, the method for getting the required result may be very different. Likewise, this area is of increasing importance on NUMA-based UNIX servers, where the allocation memory needs to be sensitive to location.

Stack Management Facilities/Other Utilities

Oracle relies on a variety of other miscellaneous services from the VOS, including the provision of a full feature stack unwind library for the creation of trace files when failures occur. Without this facility, Oracle would be unable to support the product and therefore unable to ship it.

In addition to the stack tools, the VOS is called on for other OS interfacing, such as extraction of operating statistics, interfacing with the process scheduler, and other important aspects of operation on the UNIX platform.

8.1.2 Vendor Coengineering

Although the VOS provides the Oracle base developer with the required separation from the OS, there are also situations in which the product requires changes in both the OSD and the base code to support enhanced operation on certain platforms. This is especially true when the platform has physical attributes that directly impact the operation of Oracle, such as a NUMA system.

Case Study: Sequent NUMA-Q 2000

A good case study of Oracle coengineering is the work done by Sequent and Oracle to enhance Oracle operation on the NUMA-Q platform.[1] Although the NUMA-Q platform will *run* a standard Oracle port, the nature of the NUMA architecture allows greater scalability if certain changes are made in the way Oracle uses the platform. Several of these changes have been incorporated by Sequent and Oracle, with each release

---

1. Thanks to Kevin Closson (Sequent Advanced Oracle Engineering) for his cooperation on this subject.

adding more sophistication. In Oracle8i, the NUMA-Q port of Oracle adds the following features:

- Extended buffer cache
- SGA memory placement
- Rapid SGA creation
- Quad-local buffer preference (QLBP)

Extended Buffer Cache. The provision of an extended buffer cache capability is not a NUMA optimization but rather a 32-bit operating system optimization. Normally, a 32-bit OS can address a maximum of only 4GB per process, including the kernel memory. In order to provide very large memory (VLM) support for the Oracle buffer cache, an extended cache facility has been engineered.

The extended cache code builds logic into the Oracle processes that allows the processes selectively to map and unmap pieces of the SGA into their 32-bit address space. When the process requires a portion of the buffer cache that is not in its address space, it can make calls to the operating system to map the required buffers to a region within the 32-bit address range. Oracle can then access the buffer as usual.

SGA Memory Placement.   Owing to the distributed nature of the physical memory in a NUMA system, the location of the SGA can make a big difference in the performance of the system. By default, the operating system distributes the shared memory segment across all the quads in equal portions. Unfortunately, this typically leaves a large proportion of the fixed and variable portions of the SGA on the first quad in the system. Therefore, the first quad is the only one that gets local memory access to this portion of the SGA.

In the first of three optimizations, the portions of the SGA are treated differently when creating the shared memory segment. The fixed and variable portions of the SGA are *striped* across all the quads in the system, at a 4KB page granularity. This yields a probability of 1 divided by the number of quads that the reference will be local, with the remainder of the access distributed evenly across all of the remote cache components. The log buffer is also treated this way by default. The buffer cache is divided equally across the quads and distributed in contiguous pieces. It is not striped, because the block size could be greater than the 4KB stripe size, which would result in two or more memory references being required to retrieve a single block.

The memory striping is a good example of the coengineering between Oracle and, in this case, Sequent. Sequent provides the support in the OS for explicit placement of shared memory on the physical quads. Oracle then uses this facility when creating the shared memory in order to place the memory segments on the correct quads.

The second optimization is a restriction of the number of quads across which the SGA is spread. This allows quads that are not involved in Oracle work to be kept out of the picture, or allows separate databases to be created within their own set of quads. If a quad is not hosting active Oracle processes for a database instance, it does not make sense for any of the SGA to be on that quad—this only increases the number of remote memory references.

In the final optimization of SGA placement, the log buffer is allowed to be created on one specific quad. The idea here is that the most critical latency in the system is that of the writing of the log buffer to disk. All commits wait for this event to complete, thus ultimately gating the throughput of the system. By forcing the entire log buffer to be located on the same quad that hosts the log writer, all memory references by the log writer are kept local. When this is done, it is important that Oracle be configured so that it always copies into the redo buffer using redo copy latches, not the redo allocation latch. This is important because there is a high likelihood that any given process will have to perform the entire copy operation into remote memory; using the allocation latch will mean that the redo allocation is out of action for a longer period while the copy occurs.

Rapid SGA Creation. With all this talk of extended cache sizes and spreading the SGA across multiple quads, there comes a side effect. The initial behavior of the `shmgetq()`[2] system call was simply to allocate the

---

2. This is the Sequent-specific NUMA-aware version of `shmget()` call used by the VOS code to create the segments on specific quads, implementing the SGA placement optimizations.

memory on the correct quads as a NUMA-aware version of the standard `shmget()` call. The processor that executes the system call is then responsible for the creation of the page tables and validation of the pages for the entire segment across all the quads. This is not a big problem for small SGAs but rapidly becomes unscalable as the SGA size increases, because *most* of the memory references required to create the segment are remote.

In order to improve this situation, Sequent created a "kernel daemon" within the operating system. One of these daemons is started by the OS on every quad, and the `shmgetq()` call just makes calls to all the daemons to do the work locally. This means that the work is all performed locally, resulting in a speedup of approximately nine times compared with remote allocation.

This optimization has not required any changes in the Oracle code, including the VOS portion. However, it does demonstrate why it is very important for the operating system engineers to be clued in on the operation of Oracle.

In Oracle8i, the VOS is changed so that it can use a new `shmgetv()` system call, which also allows all the allocations to be performed in parallel, resulting in linear scalability of SGA creation time as quads are added.

Quad-Local Buffer Preference (QLBP).   This enhancement is another coengineering product. It allows the assignment of LRUs across the quads, with each LRU list comprising buffers that are local to that quad. When a buffer is required by Oracle, the requesting process determines the quad that it runs on and tries to find a free buffer on one of the local LRUs for that quad. Only if these LRUs contain no free buffers will the process try a remote LRU.

This optimization affects the following operations:

- Reading of new blocks into the buffer cache
- Creation of CR blocks
- Disk sorts
- Multiple database writers

In the case of reading in a new block, the LRU read is local, the target buffer is local, and the disk read is local. This does not provide a huge performance benefit in itself, because the latency of this operation is dominated by the disk access. However, it does reduce the overall work required to load the block into the buffer and reduces the load on the remote cache component.

In a heavy OLTP system, the creation of CR blocks in the buffer cache can represent a reasonable proportion of the system workload because of many queries and updates occurring on the same data. One of the overriding properties of a CR buffer is that it is rarely useful for any session other than the session that creates it. Therefore, when a CR block is created, it will be the local LRU that is scanned and a local buffer that it is created in, and it will probably be used only for the query executing on that quad. This provides a tremendous performance boost in CR block creation.

Large sorts—those that end up using disk storage as a secondary storage during the sort—require buffers from the buffer cache. All of these buffers would be allocated from the local LRU also.

One of the big benefits of QLBP is in its interaction with the true multiple database writers found in Oracle8. Rather than the slave writer processes of Oracle7, which performed only synchronous I/O, the database writers of Oracle8 can all perform the work associated with the old master database writer. This means they scan the LRU chains, build write batches, and issue I/O requests to write out the dirty buffers. Typically, the overhead of finding and building the write batches accounts for up to 50 percent of the database writer CPU time.

By allowing the multiple writers to be aware of QLBP, one or more database writer processes can be made resident on each of the quads that participate in the operation of the database. Each of these processes then has a preferred set of LRUs on which it will operate—the set of local LRU lists for that quad. This allows all the I/O and buffer scanning to be performed on quad-local memory and fully in parallel with the other database writers that operate on different quads and different LRUs. This enhancement allows significantly more throughput to be gained from the database writer component, and has demonstrated up to six times more throughput than the maximum amount achieved using the old writer slaves.

Further benefits are gained from QLBP and Oracle8i, because the heating of buffers in the LRU chain no longer occurs on each access and so the number of remote references is significantly lower than in prior Oracle releases.

8.2   UNIX Tools

In addition to the services provided by the kernel, several of the UNIX tools are invaluable in configuring and administering the database. A selection of these tools is presented here, with some pointers on their use in a large configuration. Some of these tools require root privileges to execute them, and this is sometimes a sticking point with the system administrator. The truth of the matter is that Oracle is the only thing that executes on the database server, and the database engineer is therefore effectively administering the system. It's important to assert some kind of easy access to root, even if it is done by means of a logged mechanism such as the sudo facility.

8.2.1   top

The top command is a shareware utility, sometimes shipped with the actual operating system as "contributed software." Written by William LeFebvre at Northwestern University, top shows real-time snapshots of the "top" processes in the system. The following screen shows the output of top on an HP platform.

```
System: vulcan                                      Fri Apr  9 18:54:21 1999
Load averages: 2.81, 2.43, 2.10
3011 processes: 2987 sleeping, 24 running
Cpu states: (avg)
 LOAD   USER   NICE    SYS   IDLE  BLOCK  SWAIT   INTR   SSYS
 2.81  67.5%   0.0%  11.8%  20.7%   0.0%   0.0%   0.0%   0.0%

Memory: 4477088K (1510640K) real, 4712176K (1584728K) virtual, 9543984K free  Page# 1/216

CPU TTY    PID USERNAME PRI NI   SIZE    RES STATE    TIME %WCPU   %CPU COMMAND
  3 rroot  5283 oracle   154 20 19036K  1036K sleep  31:59 29.17  29.12 oraclePRD
 10 rroot  4905 oracle   241 20 19276K  1284K run   221:40 23.31  23.27 oraclePRD
  4 rroot  5763 oracle   154 20 19276K  1284K sleep 234:02 23.10  23.06 oraclePRD
  8 rroot  5128 oracle   241 20 19644K  1644K run   228:06 22.74  22.71 oraclePRD
 12 rroot 22202 oracle   154 20 19260K  1268K sleep 187:33 22.10  22.06 oraclePRD
  2 rroot  5282 oracle   154 20 19276K  1284K sleep 225:26 21.70  21.66 oraclePRD
  3 rroot  4523 oracle   241 20 19276K  1284K run   224:57 21.41  21.37 oraclePRD
 10 rroot 22048 oracle   154 20 19276K  1284K sleep 188:32 21.07  21.03 oraclePRD
  9 rroot  5965 root      50 20  9968K  9564K sleep 575:27 20.81  20.77 midaemon
  0 rroot  5523 oracle   241 20 19276K  1284K run   224:54 20.55  20.52 oraclePRD
  3 rroot  5382 oracle   241 20 19388K  1400K run   226:29 20.19  20.16 oraclePRD
 11 rroot  4676 oracle   241 20 19276K  1284K run   227:39 19.95  19.91 oraclePRD
 11 rroot 22153 oracle   154 20 19372K  1384K sleep 183:21 19.95  19.91 oraclePRD
```

The main part of the screen is an ordered list of active processes on the system, including the percentage of a CPU that the process is currently using. It can also be seen that all the processes are Oracle foreground processes (oraclePRD)—this part of the display is not very useful on Oracle systems. In order to use top effectively, the PID should be used as the basis for an Oracle query to determine what that session is actually doing to be the most active in the system. This ordered list is the real value of top, in that it is immediately apparent where the CPU is being used most on the system.

This HP-enhanced version includes better support for multiple processors, including per-processor loading statistics, but most uses of top do not call on this kind of granularity. The rest of the display is virtually identical to the standard public domain version, showing load average and memory statistics for the system.

The latest version of top can be found at

```
ftp://ftp.groupsys.com/pub/top
```

8.2.2   Tcl and expect

Tcl has already been extensively introduced in this book. Its power as a general scripting language makes it an essential tool in building a large system. In addition to custom extensions such as dbaman, the popular expect extensions by Don Libes are a very powerful way to reduce the amount of time spent performing laborious tasks. Using expect, the Tcl interpreter can be used to automate previously manual tasks that require human input with a keyboard.

For example, the database start-up process often gets a good deal more complex than simply starting the database with Server Manager. It might include subsequent procedures to be run after the database start-up, such as "pinning" packages and sequences, starting daemons that connect to the database, restarting system monitoring software, and so on. Using expect, all of these things can be performed in a single operation, with exception handling all built in.

expect is an extension of Tcl that allows the script to spawn processes that have their input and output connected to the Tcl interpreter. This allows the output to be captured by the interpreter, processed, and acted on by sending the relevant action back out to the process. This sounds very complex until you consider using `telnet` as the process that is spawned:

```
spawn telnet prodbox
expect ogin:
send "tigger\n"
expect word:
send "pooh\n"
expect "\\$"
send "export ORACLE_SID=PRD\n"
expect "\\$"
send "svrmgrl\n"
expect "SVRMGR>"
send "connect internal\n"
expect "SVRMGR>"
send "startup\n"
expect "Database opened."
...
```

In this example script, a `telnet` session is connected to the production machine, and the database is started. The extensions provide a good deal of control over the response handling, beyond what is shown in this small example. In fact, there is an entire book about the `expect` extensions, called *Exploring Expect* by Don Libes, published by O'Reilly & Associates, Inc.

To download the extension, go to Don's home page at

```
http://expect.nist.gov
```

For all other available Tcl extensions, visit the Tcl consortium at

```
http://www.Tclconsortium.com
```

8.2.3   Korn Shell

One of the most important tools to be familiar with is the Korn shell (`/bin/ksh`). The Korn shell is available on all modern UNIX variants and so provides a powerful common factor among all the operating systems. Wherever it is easily possible, scripts should be written using the Korn shell, to increase portability.

The Korn shell is based on the Bourne shell but is significantly enhanced. It is beyond the scope of this book to cover all the points of the Bourne and Korn shells, so some "select highlights" will be covered.

When Oracle is used on a UNIX system, it rapidly becomes important to be able to perform tasks that cross the boundaries of both UNIX and Oracle—for example, extracting lists of used datafiles from the database to pass to a backup utility. This kind of activity is best performed using a "here-document" in the shell:

```
#!/bin/ksh -

# Get list of file from database and put into specified file ($1)

outfile=$1

sqlplus -s / <<-ENDSQL >${outfile}
        set echo off head off feed off pages 0
        select name from v\$datafile;
ENDSQL
```

In this script, sqlplus is invoked in silent mode (-s), which prevents it from displaying the usual banners. The <<-ENDSQL construct is what makes up the here-document. This construct tells the shell to take all the input for this command (sqlplus) from the following lines in the script, instead of from standard input. This will continue until the word "ENDSQL" is encountered, at which point the command is terminated and inputs return to normal. The dash (-) in front of ENDSQL specifies that the word could be anywhere on the line, not just at column 0. The word ENDSQL is for demonstration purposes only; any word can be used here. The final oddity in this example is the use of a backslash in front of the $ sign in v$datafile, which is necessary to prevent the shell from expanding $datafile as a shell variable.

Taking this concept further, the shell can be used to drive command-line utilities programmatically, by remote control. This provides a primitive version of the expect functionality shown earlier:

```
#!/bin/ksh -

sqlplus -s / |&

print -p "set pages 0 head off feed off"
print -p "select VALUE
                from v\$nls_parameters
                where PARAMETER='NLS_CHARACTERSET';"

read -p charset
```

```
if [ "$charset" = "US7ASCII" ]
then
        print -p "select name from v\$database;"
        read -p dbname
        echo "Database $dbname is US7ASCII."
fi
```

In this example, the script will return the string "Database <name> is US7ASCII." if this is the case, or nothing if this is not the case. The second query is executed only if the database is found to be US7ASCII. The start of this process is where the sqlplus command is appended with "|&", instructing the shell to create a coprocess for this command. A coprocess is a process that is started in the background, with a two-way pipe between it and the shell. This process can then be read from and written to using the -p argument to the read and print commands, respectively.

This type of process provides a very powerful way to interface with the Oracle tools from the shell level. The output from the SQL sessions can then be processed very effectively with the UNIX text processing tools, the most powerful of which is awk.

8.2.4   awk

The awk command is actually another language. It comes in several flavors, from old awk, to nawk (new awk), to the Free Software Foundation's gawk. Of all of these, I would have to recommend gawk as the most powerful, because it removes some of the restrictions imposed by the standard awk facilities, such as the 3,000-bytes-per-line maximum. From this point on, the term "awk" will refer to any of the variants and will be discussed generically.

The awk language is designed to process flat text files based on patterns within the file. It has all the constructs normally associated with a procedural language, such as for loops, while loops, if tests, functions, and array variables. In fact, the syntax is very similar to the C language, and so C programmers find they can pick it up very quickly.

The format of an awk program is a series of "test { action }" pairs, where the action is performed only if the defined test returns a positive result. The most common form of test performed is a pattern match against the current line of the input file. If the pattern matches the current line, the action is performed.

Each of the tests is performed once for every line in the file, with the exception of two special "tests" called BEGIN and END. The actions associated with these tags are executed only at the beginning and the end of the file, respectively.

The awk language is a very powerful way to process text files, whether large or small. With sufficient logic in the awk script, it is possible to write parsers with awk, which is how awk was used to create the dbaman scripts from Oracle tracefiles in Chapter 2. That script is a good example of many of awk's features.

In addition to processing files, awk can be run with only a BEGIN tag specified. In this case, no input file needs to be given—the action for the BEGIN tag is just executed and then awk exits. This often provides a faster way to generate data than, say, using the shell:

```
awk 'BEGIN { for(i=0;i<100;i++) print i}'
```

This example prints a stream of numbers from 0 to 99 without requiring an input file to drive from. More complex uses of BEGIN-only awk scripts can be written, including entire scripts, using procedures if required.

Further reading on awk is highly recommended in order to gain a working competence with the language. Having a good understanding of its capability will allow you to determine where and when the tool should be used. A good alternative to awk, although not typically part of a standard operating system installation, is perl. In terms of capability, perl is a tremendous language, allowing many more interactions with the outside world than awk was designed to do.

8.3   Further Reading

Aho, A. V., B. W. Kernighan, and P. J. Weinberger. *The AWK Programming Language*. Reading, MA: Addison-Wesley, 1988.

PART V

Implementing Oracle

Chapter 9

Scalable Transaction
Processing

9.1 Scalable Applications

This chapter demonstrates techniques for gaining maximum scalability
from a single system image. This should be considered an essential prerequisite before considering Parallel Server. If the system does not perform and scale adequately as a single entity, attempting to accept Parallel
Server will provide even worse scalability.

9.1.1 Application Design

The application design is the single most efficient area to optimize. Unfortunately, database engineers are often left to tune the database into efficient operation without input into the application. This is like trying to
tune a lawn mower into a racing car. If the fundamental design of the
application is flawed, little can be done on the server side to make the
application scale and perform adequately. This is why the first portion of
this chapter is dedicated to things that the database server engineer can do
to point the application developers in the right direction.

Maintaining Concurrency

When an application is being designed for a large user population, it is
important that the system be built to provide maximum concurrency. In
order to satisfy this requirement, the application developer needs to
develop the application using many of the same rules employed by the

developer of an operating system. One of the most vital things that the application developer needs to do is to eliminate data-based contention in the application.

Data-based contention occurs when many users of the application are competing to write to the same physical records. Oracle must maintain the data integrity of the database, and so locking is utilized to prevent concurrent writes to the same piece of data.

Oracle employs row-level locking as the default locking mechanism for maintaining data integrity. This means essentially that when a write is to occur to a particular row in the database, the database automatically locks only that row. The rest of the rows in the table, and indeed in the data block, will be accessible to other sessions for read and write. This is a major plus for the database engineer, because it means that false lock conflicts do not occur in Oracle. However, the system is still not immune to problems if locks are allowed to persist, and this should be carefully explained to the application developer. In an order-processing system, for example, the application might be designed to work as follows.

To ensure that an order is taken in its entirety, without encountering out-of-stock problems at commit time, the designer of the application decides that the inventory required for the order should be decremented as the order is taken. The entire order can then be committed as a unit at the end of the order, in the safe knowledge that all the inventory is available.

This design would work fine as a single-user system, but this really defeats the object. The problem with this design is that the first user to take an order for a particular item will hold a lock on the inventory for that item, and until the order is complete, this lock will be held and no other users will be able to use this item in their orders.

There are at least two more scalable ways to implement this system. The first way involves not doing anything until the very end of the transaction, leaving all locking operations until right before the commit. This way, locks are held only for short periods, and so lock collisions are prevented. Unfortunately, this design is also defective, because this design can easily result in *deadlocks* (more on this later in this section).

The second option is to update and commit each line item as it is entered. This also holds locks for very short periods but is not subject to deadlock because only one row is locked at any given time. However, if the session is terminated halfway through the order entry process, the inventory is corrupted because the stock is decremented without the order being completed. With a small change, this design can be made to work.

If the application creates a new order record at the start of the order, immediately followed by a commit, then there is a master record for all work that follows. When the line item is updated to reflect the decrement, a record can be inserted into an ORDER_HISTORY table at the same time, referencing the order number. As an INSERT cannot be blocked by other locks, this cannot result in a deadlock, and the order is committed as it goes along. If the session is terminated, the entry process can be continued at a later stage by querying the order record on screen and continuing the order.

With this design, all locks are held very briefly (before being committed) and yet the atomicity of the transaction is maintained. In addition, the transaction is completely *restartable*.

Restartability is very important in building any large system, for both online processing and batch processing. In the case of online processing, things must be restartable, or at least recoverable from a *business transaction* perspective, in order to lessen the impact of the inevitable system or network failures. In the case of the order entry application, it would not be acceptable for the stock to be unaccounted for in the event of a failure, nor is it practical to have developers manually *patch* the data after every such incident.

In the case of batch processing, all batch jobs need to be written under the assumption that they will be killed off part way through. This sounds severe, but batch processing has a nasty habit of interfering with the response time of online sessions, and it is likely that there will be occasions of batch overrun that necessitate the killing of such jobs. If the job is not restartable, it will need to be started from the beginning the next evening, and will be even less likely to clear the backlog *plus* the new transactions.

In the first design presented, the design was deemed to be prone to deadlocks. Deadlocks present a real problem in database systems, and thus systems should be designed around them as much as possible. In the example, we could have two order-processing users entering the following order:

User 1	User 2
1 x Foamy Soap	6 x Green Sponges
3 x Green Sponges	3 x Foamy Soap

If both of these sessions were to attempt their commits simultaneously, each would manage to update and lock the first line item in its order. When each session got to its next line item, the other user would already have this record locked, and a deadlock would be evident. There would be no way out of this situation, other than for one of the sessions to rollback and reattempt the operation after a backoff period. Oracle would intervene at this point and carry this out against one of the users, at which point an error would be reported to the session: `ORA-00060: deadlock detected while waiting for resource`.

The creation of a nonblocking application is the responsibility of the application designer, not the database engineer, and *especially* not the user. After all, if a user is *able* to provoke deadlocks and general lock contention, then the user will do so all day long.

9.1.2 Scalable SQL

Many texts refer to efficient SQL, but the real goal in building very large systems is to produce *scalable SQL*. The term "scalable" can be interpreted in many different ways when referring to SQL statements, and we will cover each in turn.

Poor Efficiency

Inefficient SQL is bad for everyone. It not only causes poor response times for the user that submits the call, but also affects all other users as a result of one or more of the following:

- Overuse of processor resources
- Overuse of disk resources
- Abuse of the buffer cache

SQL statements can be classified as inefficient for a variety of different reasons, the impact of which is dependent on the particular blend of inefficiency that the statements provoke. For example, a full table scan requires a great deal of CPU in addition to the disk bandwidth it consumes; a long index range scan pollutes the buffer cache and causes a great deal of scattered I/O.

Most new applications should now be using the cost-based optimizer (CBO), which is required in order to use the new execution plans and new features such as partitioned tables effectively. All discussions in this book assume the use of the CBO, not the rule-based optimizer.

The ultimate goal for data retrieval in a TP system is to go straight to the location of the single required row and read it in; for now, we are not concerned about whether the record is cached or not. In most cases, this kind of lookup is not possible, because some kind of overhead is required to locate the row initially. If we assumed that B-tree indexes were this lookup mechanism, the number of Oracle blocks we would expect to need in order to read the data would be from two to five, depending on the depth of the B-tree.

If all queries in the system could be written this way, life would be good. Unfortunately, it is a rare day that queries can be written this efficiently. In practice, the act of normalizing the data model implies that several fetches could be necessary in order to retrieve the single item of data required, probably in the form of a multitable join. In addition, user-friendly applications require that the user be able to search using wildcards to some degree and that certain data applies only to specific ranges of dates. All of these requirements push up the cost of data retrieval significantly.

Oracle 8.1 makes a significant improvement in the usability of the CBO in a development environment by providing static plans and user-definable plans for the CBO to use. This allows a small development database to be set up to provide the same execution plans from the CBO as from the production database. Before this innovation, developing SQL for a CBO environment was difficult to do in a reliable way.

One thing that should be considered essential when writing SQL for the CBO, whether tested against a stable plan environment or not, is the use of optimizer hints. It is almost always true that the developer knows a great deal more about the data than the CBO is able to, and the use of hints takes some of the gamble out of the CBO. The specific gamble in question is that of the CBO electing to use a different execution plan than expected, owing to a change in one or more of the statistics. The CBO is more than capable of sabotaging a query that was previously not a problem, particularly in very dynamic environments, such as a system that has recently gone into production. New systems are especially prone to erratically changing plans as a result of the rapid proportional growth of some of the tables in the system, compared with the tables it joins against.

Using a simple query against V$SQLAREA, offending SQL can easily be identified:

```
col gets_per_exe form 9999999

SELECT hash_value,buffer_gets/executions gets_per_exe
FROM    V$SQLAREA
WHERE   executions>0
AND     buffer_gets/executions>10
ORDER BY 2 desc
/

HASH_VALUE GETS_PER_EXE
---------- ------------
3359911567         2865
4279157786         1188
 607327990          121
  32929334          102
3013728279           56
2303392424           51
3565234031           37
1425443843           34
3382451116           34
 731738013           32
2407357363           26
1592329314           24
3441224864           20
1714733582           19
1428100621           15
2918884618           14
4261939565           14
3127019320           13
1737259834           12
 365454555           11

20 rows selected.

SQL>
```

Included in the V$SQLAREA view is the MODULE column. This column should be populated using the DBMS_UTILITY.SET_APPLICATION_INFO procedure by every module in the application. This is often the only way to determine the source of an SQL statement. Once this column is populated, the query can be confined to online modules, because batch jobs will always dominate the list if this is not the case.

When the priority for fixing these statements is being determined, consideration should be given to the execution rate. If the query that uses 102 buffer gets per call is executed 10,000 times more than the query that uses 2,865 gets, it is clearly a higher priority.

One of the best ways to tune a statement is to put a trace on a session that calls it, using the method detailed under "Tracing Sessions by Setting Events" in Section 3.5.3. Once a tracefile that contains the query has been obtained, a simple test case can be put together:

```
PARSING IN CURSOR #1 len=38 dep=0 uid=22 oct=3 lid=22 tim=0 hv=3024638592 ad='83842e20'
select * from sys.dual where 1234=:b0
END OF STMT
PARSE #1:c=0,e=0,p=0,cr=0,cu=0,mis=1,r=0,dep=0,og=0,tim=0
BINDS #1:
 bind 0: dty=2 mxl=22(22) mal=00 scl=00 pre=00 oacflg=03 oacfl2=0 size=24 offset=0
   bfp=4014b328 bln=22 avl=03 flg=05
   value=1234
EXEC #1:c=0,e=0,p=0,cr=0,cu=0,mis=0,r=0,dep=0,og=4,tim=0
WAIT #1: nam='SQL*Net message to client' ela= 0 p1=1650815232 p2=1 p3=0
FETCH #1:c=0,e=0,p=0,cr=1,cu=4,mis=0,r=1,dep=0,og=4,tim=0
```

The query can be pulled out of the tracefile and put into a script, using bind variables as in the original query.[1] The tracefile can also be checked for the number of buffer gets it is expected to need for those particular bind combinations. This is determined by checking the cr= token in the FETCH line. A reproducible test case can now be constructed for this query:

```
variable b0 number

begin
:b0:=1234;
end;
/

alter session set timed_statistics=true;
alter session set events '10046 trace name context forever, level 12';
select * from sys.dual where 1234=:b0;
exit
```

---

1. The reason that bind variables must be used is that the optimizer does not consider the values when servicing queries. This enhancement is proposed for a future release of Oracle8.

This test case should produce exactly the same result as the original query in the application.

When looking at high buffer gets, consider the following potential causes:

- Data skew in the underlying table/index
- Index column ordering
- Cost of joins

The first two items are related, in that they both concern cardinality problems in the table. It is important to keep indexes as selective as possible when using B-tree indexes.

The cost of the join can make or break a query, and it is occasionally worthwhile to denormalize the model a little for specific performance cases. For example, if an intermediate table is used, would the addition of another column make driving off this table more efficient?

One common misconception among SQL programmers is that it is good to try to do everything in one statement. There are some cases in which this is correct, but more often it is a very bad thing for performance. If the data is known, it is often better to break complex correlated subquery statements into two cursors and glue them together with procedural logic. Unfortunately for the programmer, this often means more typing in order to set up the variables required for coding.

Another thing to look out for is the number of records being returned by a query. For most kinds of online usage, it is not useful to return a large number of rows for the user to look through. If anything, this normally points to poor user-friendliness on the part of the application. Lists of values are best kept to a small number of rows, where "small" means a maximum of about 30 records. Obviously, there are cases in which this is inappropriate or impossible, but these situations should be exceptions to the general rule.

Large data sets can be spotted by once again using the V$SQLAREA view. With the same type of query that was used to obtain the number of buffer gets, we can obtain the average number of rows returned by a query:

```
col rows_per_exe form 9999999
SELECT hash_value,rows_processed/executions rows_per_exe
FROM    V$SQLAREA
WHERE   executions>0
AND     rows_processed/executions>1500
ORDER BY 2 desc
/
HASH_VALUE ROWS_PER_EXE
---------- ------------
  603042213        30651
 3490405195        12721
 3189300438         9600
  647382473         6840
 3399070700         4962
  893287616         3807
  327344171         3529
 3137157321         2668
 2437259511         2666
 2056336900         2513
 1767743086         2415
 1623323819         2317
 3691742970         1853
 3575556459         1749
   88760771         1692
 1074455672         1520
  980033159         1520

17 rows selected.

SQL>
```

In this example, the average number of rows per execution was restricted to 1,500 in order to reduce the list returned. It can be seen that some of these queries are returning well over a reasonable number of rows. Once the MODULE filter has been applied, this list can be worked on in order to ensure that reasonable requests are being made to the database.

Avoiding High-Contention SQL

In addition to making SQL "reasonable" and efficient, other factors need to be considered in order to ensure that the SQL does not create excessive contention in the database. These factors fall into two main areas:

1. Write-read contention: reading sessions affected by writers
2. Read-read contention: sessions competing to pin the same physical block

When a heavily read table is updated, the blocks are subject to cleanout at the next read, as discussed in Section 5.5.3. This can cause big slowdowns for the next reader of the block. The following `tkprof` output shows the cost of a given query for which no block cleanout is required:

```
select sum(MONEY)
from
  MY_CASH where CASH_ID between 10000200 and 90004611
```

call	count	cpu	elapsed	disk	query	current	rows
Parse	1	0.01	0.01	0	0	0	0
Execute	1	0.00	0.00	0	0	0	0
Fetch	2	0.78	1.17	417	420	0	1
total	4	0.79	1.18	417	420	0	1

The important fields to look at are the `cpu` and `elapsed` on `Fetch`. Compare them with the same query that needs to perform block cleanout on each block as it passes through:

```
select sum(MONEY)
from
  MY_CASH where CASH_ID between 10000200 and 90004611
```

call	count	cpu	elapsed	disk	query	current	rows
Parse	1	0.00	0.00	0	0	0	0
Execute	1	0.00	0.01	0	0	0	0
Fetch	2	1.18	3.02	417	838	0	1
total	4	1.18	3.03	417	838	0	1

The block cleanout is clearly expensive, even in this small example. The implication of this is that a relatively fast update performed during online operation of the database can affect the response times of queries for a long time afterwards. In addition, if many other sessions are also trying to read the data, they will queue up waiting on the event "buffer busy waits"—that is, waiting for the cleanout to be performed by the first session that accesses the block.

In addition to contention between writers and readers, contention between two readers can also occur. Although this occurs only at significantly higher read rates than write-read contention, it can still present response time problems if not managed adequately. Consider the following query:

```
SELECT /*+ INDEX (test_tab,ti1) */ b from test_tab where a in ('AA','AB'
,'AC','AD','AE','AF','AG','AH','AI','AJ','AK','AL','AM','AN','AO','AP','AQ','AR'
,'AS','AT','AU','AV','AW','AX','AY','AZ','A[','A\','A]','A^','A_','A`','Aa','Ab'
,'Ac')
```

call	count	cpu	elapsed	disk	query	current	rows
Parse	1	0.02	0.03	0	0	0	0
Execute	1	0.00	0.00	0	0	0	0
Fetch	2	0.02	0.01	0	71	0	35
total	4	0.04	0.04	0	71	0	35

In this query, the B-tree is traversed for each of the values specified in the IN clause. For this particular example, the BLEVEL[2] of the index is 0, meaning that it is so small that there are no root or branch blocks— only a single leaf block. Therefore, there is one consistent read for each of the rows, and one for the table reference (plus an extra get as a result of a second fetch attempt by SQL*Plus). The conclusion, therefore, is that the B-tree must be traversed from root to leaf for every fetch from it.

While this does not present a large problem for this particular (small) query, it *can* present a problem in larger tables/indexes. For example, if an index has a BLEVEL of 2, this means that there is a root and a branch block above every leaf. Therefore, three blocks must be traversed to find any given leaf. The key problem is that every access has to go through the root block—a classic bottleneck.

Although we are reading only the root block, we need to take out a latch on the hash chain that the dba belongs to in order to pin the buffer. If several queries with long IN lists all hit this index at the same time, latch contention will result on the hash chain. This shows up as

---

2. The B-tree level, as reported in dba_indexes.

an increased number of misses and sleeps in v$latch and results in response time problems as Oracle serializes on one latch:

```
select hladdr    "LATCH ADDRESS",
       dbarfil   "FILE#",
       dbablk    "BLOCK#",
       gets,
       lc.sleeps
from   x$bh            bh,
       v$latch_children lc
where  lc.addr=bh.hladdr
and    state!=0 /* ie not FREE */
and    sleeps>10000
order by sleeps desc
/


LATCH_AD     RFILE#     BLOCK# STAT        GETS     SLEEPS
--------  ---------- ---------- ---- ---------- ----------
A2F07930     311      26123 XCUR  90757897     103036
9C0A1080     157       7683 XCUR 373660716      95946
9C18A048     305     133251 XCUR  97899571      62771
9C18A048     304     476892 XCUR  97899571      62771
9C18A048     322     206671 XCUR  97899571      62771
```

This script pulls out all hash chain latches that have been slept on more than 10,000 times since start-up, identifying "hot" chains. Depending on the number of hash chains configured for the instance, one or more blocks will be reported in the output. Although it is likely that only one buffer is being contended for, all other dbas that hash to that chain will also be affected by the slow down. It can be seen from the output that the hash chain latch at address A2F07930 has been slept on about twice as many times as the latch at address 9C18A048, for the same number of gets. This indicates some kind of burst access for this buffer, such as large IN lists in a query.

If it is a root block that is contended for, the block number will correspond to the first block of the index segment after the segment header. Once a problem of this type has been identified, action can be taken to improve it. Such problems are discussed in Section 9.2.

Sharing SQL

One of the major changes in Oracle for release 7 was the addition of the shared pool and shared SQL areas. Prior to this, all SQL was parsed privately for each user who executed it. Shared SQL allows far greater throughput to be achieved on the database server, as a result of the reduction in work required to interpret the request. Full implementation of shared SQL should be considered essential for a large-scale application, because the cost of *not* doing so is very high—higher than it was prior to the introduction of the shared SQL facility.

Contrary to this need is the misuse of the dynamic SQL feature of Oracle. This feature is now present in all of the Oracle tools, including PL/SQL and Pro*C, and allows dynamic construction of SQL statements based on the flow of the code and the variables passed to it. Unfortunately, this very powerful facility is mostly abused as an easy way of constructing queries, resulting in unique pieces of SQL for every request. The proper use of dynamic SQL is to allow more structured program flow and to implement complex requests, not to embed literals in statements and to break the SQL sharing.

Dynamic SQL can still be employed in large-scale systems as long as its use is carefully managed. The important thing to remember when using dynamic SQL in a piece of code is to keep the number of potential permutations as low as possible. For example, consider a module to which are passed a variable number of parameters that are eventually needed as predicates in the WHERE clause. Anywhere from one to 400 parameters could be passed to this module, all of which must be supplied to the query in the module. The temptation is to construct the WHERE clause of the statement dynamically for every parameter supplied:

```
inputs : 1, 2, 3, 4, 5, 6, 7, 8, 9, 10, ...  399, 400

sprintf(preds,"WHERE xyz in (");

for (i=0;i<nparams;i++) {
        sprintf( tmps, "%d,",inp[i]);
        strcat(preds,tmps);
}
sprintf(preds+strlen(preds)-1,")");
```

Although easy to do, this is about the worst thing that can be done here, because it creates a totally unique statement for every execution. There are basically two levels of optimization that can be performed on this statement. The first simply uses the same code base as the original, but constructs the IN clause out of bind variables and assigns variables to those variables at the same time. While not ideal, this cuts down on the number of possibilities enormously, because any call with the same number of parameters will reuse the same cached version of the SQL statement.

A better way to do this is to define a finite number of cursors. The first cursor may allow for as many as ten parameters, the second up to 20, and so on. If a standard increment of ten parameters were maintained, this would result in a maximum of 40 cursors in this example, which would be very much more manageable.

In order to do this, the number of input parameters determines which query should be used according to the following formula:

$$queryid \ = \ (int)\frac{inputs}{increment} + 1$$

Pro*C code for constructing a finite number of "buckets" of bind variables would look a little like this:

```
/* This example uses Pro*C dynamic SQL method 4 to dynamically build
   the WHERE clause of the SELECT statement using bind variables,
   keeping the permutation count low by always rounding the number of bind
   variables submitted up to the nearest gran_size.
   i.e. if 44 parameters were passed, and gran_size equals 10, a statement will
   be constructed using 50 bind variables (the 50 variable "BUCKET"). The unused
   variables are bound to the NULL value. No rows can match a NULL in an equality check.
*/

/* Size of each bucket */
gran_size=10;

sprintf(preds,"SELECT * FROM SCOTT.EMP WHERE EMPNO  in (");

/* Calculate which 'bucket' this statement lives in */
bucket=(int) (nparams/gran_size)+1;

/* Insert unique placeholder names into statement */
for (i=0;i<bucket*gran_size;i++) {
        sprintf( tmps, ":b%d,",i);
        strcat(preds,tmps);
}

/* Terminate SQL statement string */
sprintf(preds+strlen(preds)-1,")");
```

```
/* Setup cursor from string */
EXEC SQL PREPARE new_stmt from :preds;
EXEC SQL DECLARE c1 cursor for new_stmt;

/* Setup the bind descriptor */
EXEC SQL DESCRIBE BIND VARIABLES FOR wib INTO bind_des;
bind_des->N = bind_des->F;

/* Go through the list of binds found and assign values */
for (i=0;i<bind_des->N;i++) {

        bind_des->T[i]=3; /* all int */

        if (i<nparams) {
                /* Have real value, so set indicator to 0 (not null) */
                bind_des->V[i]=(char *) malloc(sizeof(int));
                *(int *)bind_des->V[i]=inp[i];
                bind_des->L[i] = sizeof(int);
                bind_des->I[i]=(short *) malloc(sizeof(short));
                *bind_des->I[i] = 0;
        } else {
                /* Don't have real value, so set indicator to -1 (null) */
                bind_des->V[i]=(char *) malloc(sizeof(int));
                *bind_des->V[i]=0;
                bind_des->L[i] = sizeof(int);
                bind_des->I[i]=(short *) malloc(sizeof(short));
                *bind_des->I[i] = -1;
        }
}
/* Open the fully bound cursor */
EXEC SQL OPEN c1 USING DESCRIPTOR bind_des;
```

All the detail of setting up for dynamic SQL method 4 has been omitted, concentrating instead on the actual construction and binding of the statement. The trick in this particular example is to bind the unused placeholders as NULL. No value can *equal* NULL, even NULL (IS NULL is the only test that will identify a NULL value). Therefore, binding the unused variables to be NULL ensures that no data is returned for them.

The "bucket" that would be created for an input parameter count of 1 to 10 would look like this:

```
WHERE EMPNO IN (:b0,:b1,:b2,:b3,:b4,:b5,:b6,:b7,:b8,:b9)
```

The Cost of Binding. Limiting the number of permutations of a given statement is the only way that dynamic SQL can be adopted. In the very dynamic case of any number of inputs discussed above, this could also have been achieved by creating a single cursor with hundreds of bind variables. The unused variables could then be bound as NULL as in the bucket example above. However, this brings about another problem and should also be avoided.

There is a measurable cost associated with each bind operation. Each one results in work being performed on both the client side and the server side, and if the number of redundant (NULL bound) variables is high, an enormous amount of CPU can be wasted doing redundant work. To demonstrate this, I wrote a Pro*C program that executes a simple SELECT statement 500 times. The query looks like this:

```
SELECT one_column FROM my_table WHERE one_column IN ( :b0, :b1 );
```

Both of the bind variables were set to be NULL, and so no data was returned by this query. I also wrote another program that behaved exactly the same way, but bound 400 NULL variables instead of two. Table 9.1 shows the results when this program was run against a PA-8200-based database server.

The 400-bind version of the code took 333 times as much CPU to perform the same net work (returning no data). Some of this CPU will be used parsing the much larger SQL statement, and some will be spent performing the actual binding operations. At the end of the day, it doesn't matter where it is being spent—excessive binding should be avoided wherever possible.

Poorly Bound SQL

When writing SQL for an application, it is easy to fall into the trap of poorly bound SQL. This is not another reference to the use of bind varia-

Table 9.1 Cost of Binding Variables

Test	Total Executions	Total Number of Binds	Server CPU Seconds Used
2 binds	500	1,000	0.18
400 binds	500	200,000	59.96

bles, but to the careful definition of data sets within an SQL statement. A single query may have a minor footprint one day and a huge footprint the next day, all based on the data supplied to the statement. This falls into two main categories:

- Poor date definition
- Poor input enforcement

Poor Date Definition.   Most transactional systems have an abundance of date-related rules. The dates affected by these rules can range from dates on which transactions are made to dates that determine the eligibility of certain records in the database. The implication of this is that there are also an abundance of queries in the system that are constructed as follows:

```
SELECT xyz FROM abc WHERE SYSDATE between START_DATE and END_DATE;
```

As soon as such a query is written, it is guaranteed to perform a range scan of some description on the index in the date columns. If the date ranges are understood by the developer, and the data is protected from skew through the application, this still does not present a huge problem. However, it is more common for date ranges to grow quickly out of control, particularly on a new, growing system. This results in increased I/O on the system, a polluted buffer cache, and wasted CPU.

In one such scenario, certain information is considered active only if the supplied date lies between the start and end dates for that information, such as seasonal types of products in a supermarket. A certain type of chocolate Easter egg, for example, is available for order by the store manager only between January and April of the current year. The query that retrieves available products excludes items that do not have a start_date in the past and an end_date in the future.

The problem with this type of data is that it rapidly becomes very non-selective because of the way in which it is administrated by the users of the system. In this example, it is likely that 99 percent of all the available products would be made active *forever*, making any index that leads on the start and end dates completely useless. The server has no choice but to range scan most of the index, going back to the table for more information when necessary.

It is important to prevent this kind of data skew if the application is to scale well: The more data that goes into a table, the more work it takes to retrieve data from that table. If there is another attribute of the query that is more selective, that attribute should be made the leading edge of the index. Otherwise, it is likely that a full table scan is a better alternative than the huge index range scan. However, this is typically not a good solution either, and a design change needs to be investigated.

In the case of this example, it may be more practical to have a B-tree index on an "inactive flag," which is updated periodically by a batch routine. The flag would have a value only if the product was inactive for the current period, therefore keeping the number of keys in the index low. More typically, however, it is not just SYSDATE that is compared against the start and end dates, but rather some arbitrary supplied date. In this case, the adoption of an inactivity flag would not provide the required result.

Poor Input Enforcement.   The most common problem in many large systems is the lack of enforcement of controls on user input. If user input is not carefully controlled, the users have the power to wreak havoc on the system with very large, unbounded queries.

The classic unbounded query is a name search. Names are typically indexed columns and are normally quite selective apart from well-known exceptions. In a search for a customer profile, for example, the provision of a few last name characters and the first initial dramatically reduces the number of keys that need to be scanned in the index. If users are allowed to be unreasonable here, they *will* be unreasonable here—they simply don't know any better. Good practice in the name example is to require three characters of the last name before a wildcard can be added. Names of fewer than three characters don't really need the wildcard functionality to speed the user along.

I encountered an interesting case study in a furniture store one day. A price ticket was not visible for a certain table, and so I asked an employee to look it up on the computer. Unfortunately, the name of the table began with an accented character, and the employee was supplied with a U.S. keyboard that had no accented characters. I noticed that the application was Oracle, with the familiar face of SQL*Forms showing itself on the terminal.

The employee proceeded to input the only string he could in order to find the item: "%bo". Of course, while the server was grinding its way through the entire B-tree index on the product name, the employee was whining and complaining to me that the computer system was broken and that he wished they would get a new one. This is a classic problem—in this instance complicated by the need for a special European keyboard on the terminal, combined with some application field enforcement.

9.1.3   Transaction Processing Monitors

Traditional client/server applications are known as two-tier applications. Of the two tiers, the lower tier is the database, and the top tier is the application program (see Figure 9.1).

In this example, Oracle8i and SQL*Forms 4.5 have been used, in a classic two-tier pairing. In the upper tier, SQL*Forms has all of the logic to display the forms to the users, to implement the business logic, and to access the database. In the lower tier, Oracle8i consists of the database itself and a *transaction manager*.

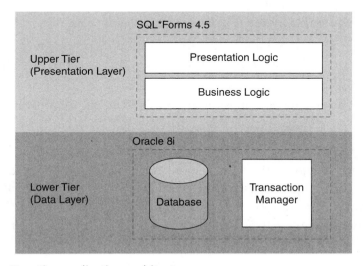

Figure 9.1   Two-tier application architecture

The term "transaction manager" is defined by The Open Group[3] as a piece of software that coordinates a transaction and enforces its atomicity. In formal terms, a transaction manager coordinates the transaction across all the involved *resource managers*, which is The Open Group's name for any shared, consistent resource. The resource manager in this case is the actual Oracle database.

In a single-database environment, the transaction manager used is the Oracle Server transaction manager, and the resource manager is the physical database. All the atomicity required for a two-tier transaction is managed within the Oracle Server, with the application logic issuing commit calls directly to the database.

The upper tier in this example contains the Forms application, which in itself consists of two logically different components: business logic and presentation logic. The same physical executable is responsible for displaying the forms to the user, following the business logic, and performing data access to the database.

This type of architecture has several problems:

- Every user of the system needs a direct database connection, wasting valuable resources on the database server.

- The same developers are responsible for both the presentation logic and the business logic.

- There is operational anarchy: No operational control over transaction flow is possible, meaning that any user can execute any part of the application at any time.

- Reuse of common business logic is difficult because of the lack of a defined interface.

- Interfacing to any other software is difficult.

These disadvantages offset the benefits of this solution: rapid development times, relatively uncoordinated development, and use of 4GL development tools. These problems are also difficult to avoid within a two-tier architecture. The way to solve them is to adopt a *transaction processing monitor*, creating a *multitier architecture*.

---

3. The Open Group is the standards body that defined the XA specification, formerly known as XOpen.

What Is a Transaction Processing Monitor?

A transaction processing monitor, or *TP monitor*, is often described as *middleware*. This means that it is software that resides between other software components. In the case of a TP monitor, this middle position lies between the presentation logic and the business logic, as shown in Figure 9.2.

In its simplest form, a TP monitor provides the following services:

- Standard, shared interfaces between software modules
- Communication and queuing facilities

The TP monitor provides a platform on which the presentation layer of an application can be created in complete isolation from the underlying business logic by providing these facilities. The TP monitor effectively provides the "glue" that holds the presentation layer and the business logic together.

In a TP monitor environment, things get renamed a little. The presentation software is called the *client*. The business logic exists in discrete programs called *servers*. These servers are advertised to the client as *services*.

The model provided by the TP monitor is that of a service provider and a client. The TP monitor provides all the communications and

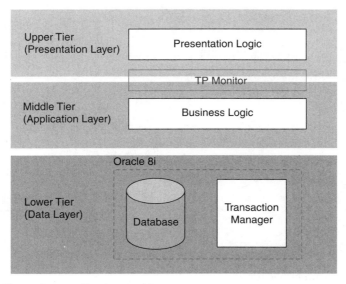

Figure 9.2 Three-tier application architecture

interfacing between the client and the servers, and takes care of advertising services to the clients.

For example, assume that the three-tier application in Figure 9.2 is the model used for a banking application. A Pro*C or OCI server could be created within the middle tier that provides the account balance for a given account number. This server is advertised by the TP monitor as an available service, and client connections can call on this service when required. This is achieved using a standard call from the TP monitor's libraries, passing the account number as a parameter for the server. The actual language, physical location, presentation style, and other features of the client requesting the information are totally irrelevant. The banking application architecture may look a little like the arrangement shown in Figure 9.3.

There are two completely different types of clients in this architecture. The first is the automated teller network, which may consist of a variety of different presentation types and operating environments across the country. The second is the cashier within the bank, running the full suite of banking services. There are three servers available in this example: a debit

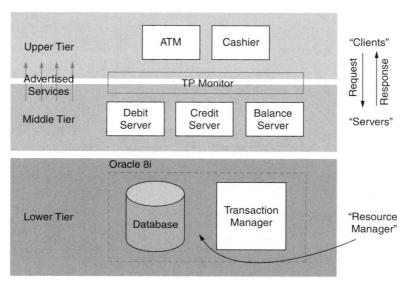

Figure 9.3 Banking application

server that debits an account, a credit server that credits an account, and a balance server that returns the current balance of the account.

The clients connect to the TP monitor *only*; there is no direct connection to the database. When the clients connect to the TP monitor, the advertised services are made available to them. The clients then send requests to the servers, in order for the server to perform the work on their behalf.

A request may be synchronous or asynchronous, depending on the requirement. If the client does not need to wait for completion of the requested task, an asynchronous call is appropriate. The server may send a response back to the client or may just complete the task. Again, this depends on the function of the server; the debit server may not send back any information, whereas the account balance server must do so.

The TP monitor also provides queuing services for the application. If the debit function is not required to take immediate effect, for example, the requests to that server may pass through a queue before being processed by the actual server. This queue can be opened or closed by the application administrator, thus controlling the throughput of the system within the application tier.

The use of request queuing is an important attribute of the TP monitor from the database server perspective. If the server system is capable of only a known number of transactions per second, the flow of requests to the database can be restricted to this number of transactions by restricting the number of available servers, keeping outstanding requests in a serial queue on the application server. This means that the waits are passive in the application tier, rather than spinning in an active wait on the database server, trying to get resource that is not available.

Further gains are made on the database server as a result of the reduced connection count on the database server. The reason the number of connections is reduced is that there are no longer any user connections into the database. Only the application servers connect to the database, thus reducing the number of required connections. The number of the application server processes required to perform the work requested by all the clients may be as few as one-tenth the number of clients, owing to the amount of "think time" that occurs in OLTP applications. The reduction of connections to the database means reductions in memory usage, scheduling overhead, context switching, and file descriptors on the server.

When an application is distributed over a wide area, a TP monitor becomes important for another reason: its communication model. When a user is a long distance from the database server, latencies are induced by the sheer distance the network covers. If the application were two-tier, and the user were 10,000 miles from the database server, these latencies would be very serious and certainly noticeable to the end user.

If the application were character-based, this would result in a delay between the keystrokes typed on the user's dumb terminal and the echo sent back by the UNIX client in the datacenter. If the application were running nearer to the user, such as on a local PC, the delays would be incurred through the use of Net8 over a wide area. Owing to the highly conversational nature of SQL*Net, several round trips can be required for each and every SQL statement sent to the database, multiplying the network latencies accordingly.

A TP monitor gets around these problems somewhat by shifting the communication model into a request/response mode. This means that the client needs only to send a single request and receive a single response for a given function. This imposes only one set of latencies over the wide area, as opposed to a large number if the communication were like Net8 or terminal character echo.

In addition to providing these benefits, TP monitors allow seamless integration of homogeneous and heterogeneous systems. An application can access a UNIX/Oracle system and a mainframe system within the same transaction, transparently to the user. This capability is provided by the TP monitor abstraction from the actual resource manager; the presentation layer is not concerned with where the data resides. The TP monitor can also facilitate intersystem data bridges and interfaces to third-party services such as computer-telephone integration (CTI) through the same abstraction.

Optionally, a TP monitor can take on the role of transaction manager, communicating with Oracle over the standard XA interface. This becomes particularly important when multiple middleware servers are associated with a single transaction, or when multiple resource managers (database) are involved in the transaction. This moves the responsibility for ensuring the atomicity of the transaction to the TP monitor, which must communicate with all of the systems involved using a two-phase commit protocol. This kind of integration comes at a price, however, and should be used only where necessary, such as in our banking application (see Figure 9.4).

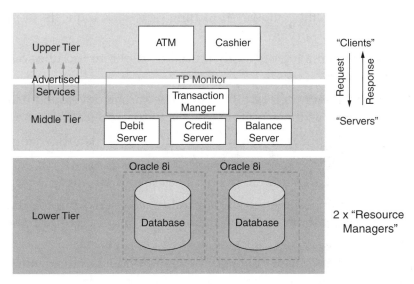

Figure 9.4 Banking application with middleware transaction management

This more closely resembles the way in which a real banking application would need to be architected. Moving the transaction manager into the middle tier is the only way that interaccount funds transfers, for example, could be implemented. The two servers involved in such a transaction, the debit and credit servers, are performing components of an atomic transaction, and therefore must either both succeed or both fail.

Alternatively, a "transfer server" could be created, performing both the debit and credit operations within a standard Oracle transaction. This would work well also, except when multiple databases were thrown into the mix. If, for example, there were a savings account on one database and a checking account on another, the transfer transaction would have to be coodinated between two servers. In this instance, there would be no alternative except locating the transaction management in the middle tier.

In summary, a TP monitor provides the following benefits for a large-scale application:

- There is lower server resource usage owing to reduced database server connections.

- The application developer can be focused on business logic *or* presentation logic, depending on skillset and assignment.

- The queuing facility allows "throttling" of work requests to prevent thrashing on the server.

- Common business logic is easily reused by different modules owing to the standard interfaces.

- Bridges and integration of other products can be developed using the same interfaces as those used in the rest of the application.

- Distributed applications can be built across heterogeneous and homogenous systems.

The deployment of a TP monitor also carries several disadvantages:

- An all-or-nothing approach of decoupling *all* users from the database (and connecting them into the TP monitor) is required to gain the most benefit.

- Application servers are generally developed in a language such as C, rather than using one of the rapid development tools.

- Skills in the development of multitier applications are not as prevalent as those used in two-tier applications.

- Software licences are required for the TP monitor software.

These negatives are easily overshadowed by the positives of using multitier technology for very large applications. For UNIX systems, there are few choices in TP monitor selection, with BEA Tuxedo being far and away the most popular. Tuxedo offers all the functionality associated with a TP monitor and runs on a variety of UNIX platforms.

Object Request Brokers

The latest development in multitier applications is the *object request broker*, or *ORB*. One of the common standards for an ORB is the *Common Object Request Broker Architecture* (CORBA) specification set out by The Object Management Group (OMG). The ORB presents a combination of the concepts of the TP monitor and object-oriented programming, providing a framework for *distributed objects*.

Distributed objects allow fully encapsulated software modules to be written, with the ORB acting as the glue that holds all the objects together. If the ORB conforms to CORBA 2.0 standard or greater, it can also provide transaction management services and security, thus providing an enhanced TP monitor environment. This new environment can be built on heterogeneous systems and in virtually any language that the ORB can interface with through the Interface Definition Language (IDL).

IDL is a language-neutral interface language, used to interface the software components to the ORB. Using IDL, stub code can be produced to allow for compile-time dependency checks and to allow software components to be produced in isolation from the complexities of the ORB and the remote procedure call (RPC) mechanisms associated with it.

Much of the actual technology supporting ORB operation is still in its infancy, though many of the industry's largest independent software vendor (ISVs) are adopting this strategy for the future. Most notably, Oracle8i provides significant ORB support. Of course, care should be taken when adopting an ORB as the middleware architecture for transactionally intensive systems, because the supporting software is relatively new. When software is as new as this, it takes time before it is ready for heavy loading.

9.1.4   Purge

A database should never be confused with a data *dump*. In OLTP-based systems, this means that the database must reach a level of equilibrium in its size; data must be deleted at the same rate at which it is inserted.

In a typical transactional database, there are two main types of data:

1. Reference data

2. Transactional data

The reference data is not normally subject to purging, because it reaches a static size early in the life of the application. The transactional data, on the other hand, grows every day the system is used and can become unmanageable very quickly. A banking application, for example, inserts many rows into each account, which are mostly read only once—when the monthly statement is produced. In this way, transactional tables can be viewed as insert-*mostly* tables.

After a period of time, this data no longer needs to reside in the production database and should be removed in order to maintain a static database size. The period of time and the rules for deletion have to be defined by the business, because there are likely to be operational and legal reasons driving the rules. The actual deletion of the data should be performed as a scheduled batch process, using deletion code that has been carefully developed.

The reasons for performing a thorough and regular purge are numerous. First, there are the date-range driven queries, as described in Section 9.1.2. As the database grows larger, these queries will become more resource-intensive as a result of the increased date range in the database transactional tables. Often this data is scanned by badly written queries even though the business is no longer concerned with it.

Second, there is the clear problem of available disk space on the database server. Things cannot be allowed to grow unconstrained, because this would result in an ever-increasing amount of disk connected to the system. In addition to this, the database must be backed up on a regular basis, and this becomes more difficult to achieve when the database is larger than the backup subsystem can deal with in the backup window. At this point, the backup needs to be spread out over several nights, complicating the recovery process in the event of a failure.

Lastly, the batch window will grow in direct proportion to the database size. This occurs because batch jobs that operate on transactional data are likely to perform a full table scan of the table in question, which would be the optimal access path for a batch job that processes a large proportion of the table. If the table were to grow without purge, the proportion of records that the batch job should consider would become slight in relation to the number of old records, thus slowing down the batch routine.

Rapid Deletion Techniques

Deletion of data often comes in tandem with insertion of data elsewhere; it is rare that data can simply be removed without storing it elsewhere first. New features in Oracle8 and Oracle8.1 have helped in both of these areas, making purge a good deal easier to implement today than in prior releases.

The first of these features is the use of partitioned objects. Partitioning a table *sometimes* allows the easiest method of deletion of all—the ability to *drop* a whole range of data from the database. This is not always available, because it depends on whether your partition key is also your purge key (i.e., date stamp) and also on whether all the indexes built on the table are partition-local (that is, no index covers more than one partition).

The ability to remove a partition can be combined with the new capability of Oracle8.1 to detach a tablespace and reattach it to another database. This allows very rapid relocation of purged data into another database for further processing. The procedure for doing this is as follows:

1. "Exchange" the designated partition with a standard table.

2. Set the tablespace to be READ ONLY.

3. Export the metadata from the catalog using

```
exp userid=<user/pass> transport_tablespace=y tablespaces=<tablespace>
```

4. Copy the tablespace datafile(s) to the target database.

5. Import the tablespace into the target using

```
imp userid=<user/pass> transport_tablespace=y datafiles='<tablespace datafiles>'
```

6. Check that all is OK.

7. Drop tablespace in production, including contents.

8. Manipulate imported tablespace in target database.

The impact on production response times for this method is close to zero, because no deletes or inserts occur. Of course, this method requires the purge criteria to be based on the same key as the partition key, because nonpartitioned columns could be spread across many partitions.

While it is often impractical to purge by partition key, an alternative is possible when the purge criteria are strictly timestamp-based and the partition key is a system-generated one, such as a sequence number. Transactional tables often meet these criteria, because the data is inserted at one end and is used less and less as it gets older. In this case, a correlation can be made between the age of the row and the partition key, assuming that the partitioning is based on the primary key. For example, although an ORDERS table may be partitioned on its primary key of ORDER_NUM, the value of ORDER_NUM will only ever increase over time. Therefore, a preliminary query can be executed to determine the corresponding key value for a given timestamp, and the purge can be executed against that derived value. This allows the partition relocation method of purging to be used.

If a partition-based purge is not possible, the only alternative is to execute deletes against the table, having previously extracted that data for insertion into the reporting environment. This is never an easy operation, because the delete process requires several resources:

- CPU
- Locks
- Undo allocation and CR blocks
- Block cleanout

Of these, CPU is the least problematic. The other three resources directly affect the operation of online sessions and batch processing, and so must be carefully managed. The first of these is the required allocation of locks to perform the delete. Normally, this should not be a huge problem either, because the data to be purged should not be getting actively updated anyway. The only legitimate activity on these rows would be reads from full table scans. However, if there are badly written batch routines out there that lock irrelevant data, they will interfere with the purge routines, and vice versa.

There are two attributes to be concerned with for the undo allocation. First, there is the requirement to have sufficient rollback segment space to allow a rollback of the entire operation. In the case of a delete, the rollback segment must include sufficient information to rebuild the entire row, should a rollback be necessary. This means that large delete operations require a large amount of rollback space with which to work.

The second attribute of undo allocation is the provision of consistent read views to other sessions. Though the rows are deleted using row-level locks, the block itself is managed by Oracle at a full block granularity. This means that any access to that block must go through the CR mechanism, regardless of whether or not the row being read is deleted. In addition, until the commit of the delete session, all other sessions connected to the database are able to read the data, thus requiring block reconstruction from the rollback segment.

If other long-running queries take place on the table being purged, all the undo information for the delete must remain for the duration of that query, even across commits by the delete session. If there is insufficient space for this, the long-running query will eventually get a "snapshot too old" error and terminate. Likewise, any updates or deletes of data in the table by online sessions must be retained in the rollback segment of the online session until the delete has completed its transaction.

Finally, there is the unavoidable issue of block cleanout. This will need to be done at the end of the purge session, whether explicitly by the purge routine or implicitly by unsuspecting users. Clearly the best solution is to perform a scan of the data explicitly after the purge, in order to perform the block cleanout operation. If CPU is available, this can be performed in parallel, speeding up the operation.

The actual delete process itself can be approached in three ways:

1. Serial delete session

2. Many delete sessions on the same data

3. Oracle parallel DML

If speed of delete is not an issue, the first option is best. This is the simplest option to develop and maintain, and so should be adopted where volumes permit. Where the volumes are too high for a serial delete, one of the parallel options can be used. The first parallel option is to use multiple delete sessions, each working on different portions of the same data set. This is fairly easy to develop but requires careful planning in order to keep the sessions in physically separate blocks. Even if the physical rows are kept distinct between sessions, multiple sessions that delete from the same block will result in unnecessary CR block creation, slowing down the process.

Probably the best option is to use Oracle's parallel DML functionality, which allows the purge code to be mostly written as the serial delete scenario while Oracle takes care of parallelizing the deletes in an efficient manner. In MPP architectures, this includes disk affinity—sending the delete streams to the node that is physically connected to the disk. In addition, the parallel delete slaves use a modified two-phase commit protocol to ensure that they effectively operate in the same atomic transaction. Block cleanout is still necessary after parallel DML and should be performed explicitly by the purge routines (i.e., perform a scan of the data).

9.2 Tuning Transaction Processing Systems

9.2.1 Goals for Tuning

When tuning a system, it is important to have clear goals set before you start. Without such goals, tuning effort will be misdirected, difficult to learn from, and hard to quantify. Perhaps most important is the learning factor; there are lessons to be learned in every tuning exercise, and it's important to be able to understand the impact of individual changes and come to a conclusion about how effective a specific tuning exercise can be.

The thing to do when planning a tuning exercise is to identify the "low-hanging fruit." Picking off the easy wins at the start allows more time for the more complex tuning along the line. The kinds of candidates for initial tuning are

- Code with high execution rate
- Resource-intensive code

The first of these is simple to determine, by querying the V$SQLAREA view for statements with a high execution count. The second is more difficult, as it is not practical to enable the timed_statistics parameter in a busy production database. Therefore, this kind of statement must be found by indirect means:

- High number of buffer gets per execution
- High number of disk reads per execution
- Very large statements
- Latch contention
- Lock collisions

You are looking for things that prevent the system from delivering good response times, either directly from the query execution time or indirectly by starving other sessions of system resources.

Once the targets have been identified, a careful evaluation of options needs to be made—that is, where the best fix for each problem lies.

9.2.2   Where to Tune

The effectiveness of tuning varies depending on what is being tuned. There is a hierarchy of impact (see Figure 9.5), where the item at the top of the hierarchy makes the largest difference and the item at the bottom makes the smallest difference (unless it is grossly wrong).

This is an important concept to grasp and to sell to others. It is a common misconception of the uninformed that application and requirement

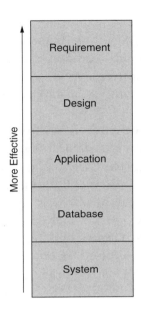

Figure 9.5 Tuning hierarchy

problems can be fixed by tuning the system. This is not true, and it is important that this be understood by all. If the system is performing badly, all areas of the hierarchy must be checked in parallel. A good rule of thumb, however, is that the impact of tuning increases by an order of magnitude (a factor of 10) as you move up each stage of the hierarchy.

Requirement

This is the high-level definition of the system. The customer typically submits a wish list, and this list is then refined into a deliverable set of requirements. Most of the time, some requirements slip through that are not essential to the customer and are extremely detrimental to the performance of the database.

One common example is the infamous default query-by-example screen. In such a screen, the user is presented with several attributes that can be either filled in or left blank. If they are left blank, all combinations of that field will be returned. If the management of a hotel had a centralized front of house system, they might have a screen containing the fields

ROOM_NO, DATE, and HOTEL_NAME, for example. The customer might have specified that any of these fields be left blank in order to return all the combinations, thinking that they might come in useful one day. This is a simple request but is completely unnecessary in reality. Why would a receptionist in one hotel need to query who was staying in every room 301 for 1-APR-1998 in *every* hotel?

These screens need to be carefully evaluated and to be revisited after the selectivity is assessed on real data. It is unusual for a user to prefer to keep such functionality in preference to good response time.

Another example of requirement tuning might be where asynchronous processing occurs automatically for user convenience, preempting the next request. In an order entry system, for instance, there may be functionality that goes out and retrieves line-item descriptions and pricing for products associated with the one last entered. The user enters "Electric Drill," and the system also gets the pricing and descriptions for various types of drill bits. As there are likely to be many types of drill bits, the majority of this preemptive processing is redundant—the customer will not be ordering all of them. Careful analysis needs to be performed in order to ensure that the automatic calls are commonly used by the user rather than passed over.

Design

When the requirement is defined, an application enters the design phase. This is the molding of all the pieces of the requirement into a cohesive application plan. Included in this phase is the database design, covering the logical model right through to the first draft of the physical implementation. Errors at this stage can have enormous knock on effects.

One frequent mistake is the "space-biased" normalization approach. Database purists typically lean hard on the side of full normalization of the data model. They have the honorable intention of reducing the data duplication, thereby reducing the risk of logical (application level) corruption and keeping the size of the database down.

A better approach is often the "time-biased" approach to normalization, in which normalization is pursued vigorously where it remains efficient to retrieve the data but relaxed somewhat where excessive table joins are likely to result in poor response times. Changes in the data model are almost impossible to implement after the application has been written, because the scope of the changes becomes too large. Therefore, it's vital to get this part of the design correct up front.

Application

Once the requirement has been defined, the application is written. Typically, a large application is written by many people of various programming beliefs, styles, and talents. With that mixture, it is inevitable that a proportion of poor quality SQL and logic makes its way through. Nonscalable SQL (as described in Section 9.1.2), unnecessary calls, and poor logical flow can result in the database server being asked to do far more work than is necessary for the required result.

This is the easiest part of the system to identify from the database view of the world; all the SQL statements are recorded nicely in the shared pool, along with a selection of their execution statistics. Ordered lists produced from the shared pool are a good way to begin this process, because this will quickly identify the worst of the bunch. Working through this list is a very effective way of prioritizing the work required for improving the system response time.

Tuning of the application can typically yield 25 percent to 50 percent of the system CPU, depending on the severity of the initial problem. This even includes applications that are fundamentally well written: If a single statement that accounts for 20 percent of the CPU on the server is improved by 50 percent in a tuning exercise, then 10 percent of the system CPU will be returned as a result (20% × 50% = 10%).

Database

The database is a service provider—it receives requests and processes them as quickly as it is able to. If the request is unreasonable, it will take a long time to service, and other requests will suffer as a result. This is a simplistic definition of what a database does, but serves well for putting things into perspective. The tuning that can be done at the database level can be viewed as improving only what is already there. Unless the database was very badly set up at the outset, it is unlikely that very large gains can be made simply by tuning it.

This declaration does not cover database work that should occur at the design stage—such work is undeniably effective. Nor is it saying that magic cannot be worked from the database angle; it certainly can, in most cases. However, it cannot make a square wheel round, and the higher-level aspects of the system should be considered with a higher priority than the database tuning.

System

The system is one level further removed from the database. It is so far removed from being able to make a big tuning impact that it is often a binary answer: Is the system configured correctly or not? If the system is not configured correctly—for example, if it allows heavy paging or swapping to occur—this will result in poor performance. If it is configured adequately, probably only very small percentage improvements can be made overall.

9.2.3 Tuning Modes

Tuning can be approached in several ways. These ways, or *modes*, are associated with different goals but often enjoy a great deal of synergy. Reducing system utilization, for example, frequently results in improved system response time. There are, however, different approaches to reaching this goal.

For a transaction processing system, there are three main modes of tuning:

- Reducing the utilization of the system
- Improving response times for specific areas of the application
- Increasing the throughput of batch processing

Reducing System Utilization

Reducing the overall system utilization is a very broad goal. Depending on the particular resource that needs to be reduced, different strategies can be followed. For a large database system, now that memory is less of an issue,[4] the resources in question are CPU and I/O.

---

4. Memory used to be an issue in large systems owing to both the price of the memory and the 32-bit address limitations of the operating system. The typical memory size of a large UNIX system in 1994 was 2GB, compared with 32 to 64GB today.

For CPU resources, it should first be established whether the system is also experiencing high I/O loads. Even if the I/O system is keeping up with the load without straying into high service times, the system could well be struggling to service all the requests and associated interrupts. Therefore, a CPU issue may in fact be a side effect of an I/O issue.

Assuming that there is not a high I/O loading, what is the cache hit ratio in the buffer cache? If the hit ratio is very high (>98 percent), the system could be doing a great deal of work without the I/O system making this evident. In this case, a more detailed analysis of the application's use of the system needs to be performed. This analysis should include a discovery of which modules perform the highest number of buffer gets (assuming that the application uses SET_APPLICATION_INFO in order to identify itself to the database) as an indicator of where to look. If the application is using a TP monitor, which server connections use the most CPU on a minute-by-minute basis?

When the system is not overloaded by one particular module of the application, this can mean one of many things:

- The system is undersized (requirements problem).

- The application is in need of tuning across the board (design problem).

- There is resource contention (database or design problem).

- Processing is occurring in the wrong tier (design problem).

An undersized system will almost certainly *not* benefit sufficiently from any tuning of the system, database, application, or design. If the system is simply too small for the required workload, changes need to be made in the requirements definition, or else additional compute resource needs to be purchased.

If all the modules of an application appear to be loading the system heavily, this is often attributed to a design problem with the application. For example, if many queries in the system need to incorporate a subquery or multitable joins, it is likely that the data model will need to be looked at. If the model looks sound, it could be that the coding standards laid down for the application were insufficient or not followed correctly. This will result in much of the application doing "naughty" things to the database server. In addition, the cardinality of indexes needs to be carefully monitored as tables grow. This is covered under "Improving Response Times."

The management of resource contention can become a very CPU-intensive task on a system that experiences heavy contention. Statements that run very fast in quiet periods will run slowly while contention occurs. Specifically, active waits on locks (i.e., latches) will use CPU just to try to acquire the latch with the minimum of wait time. In these situations, the contended latch must be quickly identified and action must be taken to reduce the contention. Such action varies from latch to latch, but typically involves the following:

- *Library cache latch contention.* Reduce parse rate by keeping cursors open, sharing SQL more effectively.

- *Cache buffer chains.* Determine why particular chains are being accessed more than others, and remedy.

Both of these forms of contention also directly impact the response time of the query; they will be covered in "Improving Response Times."

Finally, multitier application architectures allow processing to occur in several places. Often, the database is used to perform processing that is not data-dependent, thereby consuming precious resource from the least scalable part of the system (the single database). Examples include

- Packages with large amounts of non-data-related logic

- Use of SYS.DUAL to submit various ad-hoc requests to the database, such as getting the date, splitting strings using SUBSTR, and so on

This kind of practice should be discouraged whenever possible. The database server is often viewed by application programmers as a mysterious powerhouse that will run their code at lightning speed. Apart from this rarely being true, they also need to understand that they have only a very small piece of the total capacity of the server. Therefore, as much processing as possible should be performed in the application tier, saving the database server for real, data-related requests.

Improving Response Times

This approach targets improvement in specific pieces of code in the application. The improvement can come from changes in the SQL or some kind of physical intervention from the database end. As this is not an SQL tuning book, we will concentrate on database-centric modifications that improve statement response time.

Indexing. The most fundamental aspect to consider when trying to improve response time is the indexing strategy for the associated tables. Indexes are often defined inappropriately or have *become* inappropriate over time as a result of changes in the cardinality of the indexed columns. It is vital that a B-tree index be very selective (i.e., large number of distinct keys), because an index range scan very quickly becomes much more expensive to process than even a full table scan. If a particular query is found to have gone bad over time, it is almost certainly because of a change in the selectivity of the index. At this point, aggregate count() queries should be run on the underlying data in order to determine where the skew lies. The factor of performance speedup that can be expected from index improvements ranges from 1.5 to 1,000.

Queries can also create, or be exposed to, database contention, slowing down query response time as Oracle resolves the contention. The most common contention points for very large-scale Oracle systems are the library cache latches, the cache buffer latches, and the redo latches.

Library Cache. Library cache latch contention is normally caused by badly written SQL in the application. Starting with version 7.2, Oracle provides multiple child library cache latches to protect the library cache. The latch used by a given statement is determined by the hash value of the statement. The hashing algorithm used by Oracle for SQL statements is very effective, and so the child latch acquisitions are very well distributed among the available latches.

With at least as many latches as CPUs, the system is now capable of parsing SQL at full system bandwidth. However, if a large proportion of the statements in the application are not shared, the contention on the latches will increase for the following reasons:

- Hard parsing requires more time under the latch to complete in comparison with soft parsing.
- Memory management in a fragmented shared pool increases the work performed under the library cache latch.

The contention is not caused by any inherent serialization in Oracle, but as a result of the application consuming much of the system CPU cycles processing parse requests. The symptoms in this case include

- Increased miss and sleep counts for library cache latches
- Rapid consumption of free memory in the shared pool

In addition, overallocation of shared pool memory for the library cache results in contention for free memory by the other components of the shared pool. Most notably, the dictionary cache becomes squeezed down by the aggressive requirements of the library cache. The impact of this is that the system performs a great deal more recursive SQL than if the dictionary cache were allowed to grow to its optimum size.

Buffer Cache. The buffer cache is similar to the library cache in its latch coverage (*cache buffer chain latches*) and is subject to similar contention on a small handful of the many latches that cover it. The most common causes of contention for cache buffers chain latches all relate to index reads:

- B-tree indexes built on very small tables
- Multiple blocks covered by a common latch
- Root and branch block contention resulting from common search paths through the index

When an index is built on a very small table, it consists of a small number of blocks (possibly only one block). In this case, it is more efficient to do a fast full table scan because of the simpler management of such blocks in the cache. Dropping the index is the most effective solution of this problem.

The number of child latches used by Oracle is determined by the setting of _db_block_hash_buckets, which defaults to be a quarter of the configured db_block_buffers. This means that blocks share the same chain every db_block_buffers/4 in the default case. Access of any block in any given datafile is preceded by a hash of its dba (data block address), which resolves which buffer chain this block belongs to (see Figure 9.6).

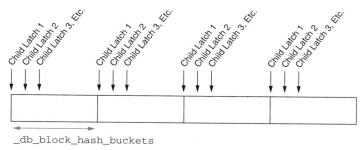

Figure 9.6 Hash bucket file coverage

On page 412, we looked at a query that will pull out any particular hot latch. If one of the child latches is being slept on a great deal more frequently, this can mean that one of the following is true:

- The latch covers more than one "hot" block.
- The latch covers one extremely "hot" block.

Whether or not the latch covers more than one hot block can be determined by running the query several times in succession and determining whether the same file and block numbers persist in the output. If so, the system will likely benefit from a finer granularity of cache buffer chains. In order to do this, the value of _db_block_hash_buckets simply needs to be increased accordingly, and the instance restarted.

If a single block is causing the problem, the solution will depend on the type of block that is contended for. The most common type of block that undergoes this contention is an index root or branch block, as previously discussed, and has typically been the most difficult problem to address prior to Oracle8.

In Oracle8, partitioned objects were introduced to increase the manageability of very large data objects, in addition to providing several performance improvements resulting from partition elimination. A less common use of partitioned objects is to directly address a problem that was not solvable prior to version 8—index root block contention. The theory is that if the root block is heavily contended for, but blocks further down the tree are not as highly contended for, then the index would benefit from having multiple root blocks in order to distribute the load over more blocks.

The multiple root blocks are created using standard partitioning of an index, where the partition key must be the leading edge of the index key. Although the index itself may well be very small (10MB, for example), it may be reasonable to partition the index into as many as 20 partitions. Although this somewhat increases the complexity of the database layout, it makes the index very much more scalable that it was before.

In addition to contention for buffers because of high read activity, contention can also result from contention for free buffers. A free buffer is required to write any new block into the cache, including any changes in an existing one. The only buffers that are classed as "free" are those that are not currently pinned and contain no unwritten data (i.e., must not be dirty). If there are no free buffers in the cache, Oracle must write dirty buffers to disk in order to allow those buffers to be made available for use by other sessions.

All these data block writes are performed by the database writer(s), and so this operation involves an expensive posting of the database writer in order to clean the dirty buffers. At this stage, the session that requires the free buffers is waiting for the operation to complete (free buffer waits), thus increasing the user response time.

If sessions are frequently left waiting for the database writer(s) to perform work, this directly impacts the response time for all users. Therefore, it makes sense to try to keep the cache reasonably clean at all times in order to preempt the requests for free buffers. This is achieved through the use of the db_block_max_dirty_target parameter in the init.ora.

Setting this parameter tells Oracle to try to limit the maximum number of dirty buffers to the specified number. Therefore, whenever the actual number of dirty buffers rises above this number, the database writer(s) will start to clean the cache (starting at the cold ends of their respective LRU chains), until the number falls below the threshold again.

The number of database writers and the number of LRUs relate directly to Oracle's ability to keep the number below the threshold. If there are insufficient writer processes to keep the cache clean, it will not be possible to keep it clean. In this case, the threshold should be raised or the number of writer processes increased.

This tuning of the cache also helps to reduce the impact of a checkpoint operation. If there are fewer dirty buffers in the cache at the time of the checkpoint, there is less work to do under the checkpoint.

Redo Allocation.   Oracle maintains only one significant point of serialization,—the redo allocation latch. Recall from Section 6.8.2 that the redo allocation latch is the only latch that covers the redo buffer. Therefore, the commit rate of the system is ultimately governed by this latch. Because a commit is really the only operation that must wait for acknowledgment of completion, it is very important that the redo management process is as fast as possible.

There are several mechanisms for mitigating the impact of this serialization. First, there is the batching of multiple commits into a single "group commit." This is provided by default and is not associated with any tuning. Second, there is the existence of the redo copy latches. During tuning for a good response time, it is vital that virtually every copy into the redo buffer occurs under one of the redo copy latches instead of under the redo allocation latch. Therefore, the setting of `log_small_entry_max_size` should be kept very low in transactional systems to force copying under the redo copy latches.

Increasing Batch Throughput

Nearly all transactional systems have a Jeckyl and Hyde existence. During the day they run many thousands of comparatively tiny transactions, whereas at night they run a substantially fewer number of very heavy transactions during the batch cycle. Both of these modes of operation are suited to different types of tuning, and yet no system outage can be taken in between in order to change things.

The only approach that can be taken in this situation is to tune the system for the OLTP users and to accommodate the conflicting batch requirements in ways that do not affect the online user. In recent Oracle releases, the number of parameters that can be dynamically altered on the fly has increased dramatically. The situation in Oracle8i is that the profile of a session can be dramatically altered while retaining the tuning of the remainder of the system.

Of note in the list of parameters that can be changed on the session level are

- `db_file_multiblock_read_count`
- `sort_area_size`
- `sort_area_retained_size`
- `sort_multiblock_read_count`
- `hash_join_enabled`
- `hash_area_size`
- `hash_multiblock_io_count`

All of these parameters can be "opened up" to allow far greater resource consumption by the batch processes. As there are many fewer batch processes, the additional impact on the system is not as large as that of changing these parameters for all database connections.

In addition to tuning the batch sessions for more optimal execution, operational factors must be considered. Perhaps one of the largest impacts on the throughput of a given batch process is the interaction on it by other batch processes. The actual form of interference from the other batch jobs varies from maintaining consistent views of the data to block cleanout and transaction locks to CPU and disk resource contention.

Keeping batch processes from disrupting each other is quite a challenge in itself, but certain measures can be taken from the programmatic and tuning perspectives to make this job easier. The first thing to do is to carefully analyze the use of transaction locks within the batch programs. Batch routines should not assume exclusive access to a table unless this is actually 100 percent true—it only takes one outstanding lock to put the brakes on any access to a given table. Performing long `select...for updates` on a table in batch can be as bad as doing so during full online use.

Related to this is the commit frequency of the program. A commit certainly has an overhead for the system, but it is very lightweight in comparison with the restriction of having large amounts of uncommitted data in the database. This results in a great deal of consistent read activity for other programs and several outstanding data locks. Reasonable commit frequency for batch jobs varies among cases, but committing every 10,000 rows or so is reasonable for mass updates, and less for more in-depth processing.

Extending regular commits further, the job should also be designed to be fully restartable. It is almost inevitable that a job will occasionally run past the normal batch window and into the online processing peaks, at which times there is no alternative but to kill the job. If the job is not restartable, this can cause problems that range from manual cleanup to long rollback operations, and almost always means rerunning the job from the beginning the next evening.

Batch processing benefits greatly from the use of Oracle Parallel Query. This extends beyond simply speeding up the individual jobs themselves, allowing a different perspective to be taken on the organization of the batch cycle. Without parallel query, a typical batch cycle will employ "operator parallelism," which means that the batch operator fires off many batch jobs in parallel in order to get the most out of the multiple processors in the system.

The effect of this disorganized use of the system and database resources is that a great deal of overhead must be incurred to manage read consistency. Parallel query allows a different approach to the batch cycle wherein all the large jobs employ extensive parallel processing to use all the available processors on the machine. While any one of these jobs is executing, no other batch is run—the jobs are run *sequentially in parallel*.

Now that the jobs are running a great deal faster within themselves, there is no need to have many other jobs running at the same time—they will complete faster in series without the overhead of consistent read.

9.3 Chapter Summary

Scalable transaction processing is all about careful design, understanding, and balance. The application needs to be designed to take into account the number of users and the concurrency required as a result. The application developer, database engineer, and system administrators need to understand what is required to build a very large, concurrent system. Above all, the overriding principle is one of balance: Many thousands of database operations occur every second, and it is only through carefully balancing the requests and tuning that these operations can coexist.

This chapter has presented several aspects of transaction processing that need attention. There are plenty of others, however, most of which are application-specific. Therefore, the important factor in making a scalable system is to understand the concepts presented in the previous sections of this book. Once these concepts have been established, and their application has become more practiced, most of the problems that arise can be resolved using logical thought processes.

9.4 Further Reading

Andrade, J. M., et al. *The TUXEDO System*. Reading, MA: Addison-Wesley, 1996.
Slama, D., et al. *Enterprise CORBA*. Upper Saddle River, NJ: Prentice Hall, 1999.
Various. *Oracle8i Tuning*. Oracle RDBMS Documentation.

Chapter 10

Pulling It All Together: A Case Study

10.1 Introduction

A great deal of detail has been presented in this book about how a large system is scaled and what knowledge is required in order to build and operate such a system. In order to demonstrate some of these concepts, this chapter comprises a case study of a large Oracle/UNIX system that I have recently been involved in building.

First of all, let's pose a question: how large is "large"? The answer is "It depends on when you ask." The system presented here is considered to be pretty large at the time of this writing, but it is likely that in two to three years, this system will not seem very large or very challenging to implement. The reason for this, of course, is that things move on, and advances in hardware and software constantly "raise the bar."

Luckily for the builders of large systems, customers' requirements have an amazing ability to track these advances in system capability almost precisely. This is often a result of compressed timescales for the development and implementation of a new system, rather than an actual increase in processing requirements. The net effect is that there will always be a requirement for very large systems.

The system in this case study is considered to be large by today's standards for the following reasons:

- It runs on the largest UNIX platform currently available, which is fully populated.

- Benchmark tests demonstrated a latch acquisition pathology that certain systems could not process, regardless of CPU capacity.

- It supports a large number of concurrent online users (2,400).

- It requires a large online database (450GB) and uses a total of 3.2TB of physical disk.

In addition to providing good response time, this system must also be highly available. This required further considerations to be made when determining the system's configuration.

10.2   Engagement Overview

10.2.1   The Business

The client has a combination of smaller offices and larger centers, situated in various locations around the world. The majority of these are in North America and the United Kingdom, with a lower number at other locations across Europe. The system described in this chapter refers only to the North American region of the business, because at the time of this writing, the UK region is not yet using the new system.

There are essentially three different types of users of the system.

1. Point-of-sale agents, thinly distributed over a large geographical area (all 50 states, plus Canada)

2. Sales agents, collected into a small number of large "sales centers"

3. Corporate users, mostly based at corporate headquarters

In total, there are more than 3,000 potential users of the system, with up to 2,400 connected at any one time. Of these connected users, most are active at any one time, normal think times excluded. The smallest collection of users in any one physical location is one, ranging up to several hundred in the sales centers.

The previous system used by our client was based on several IBM mainframes and 3270-type terminals, and was deemed to be too inflexible for business needs. The major reasons for this were the age of the application and the complexity of making changes in it. The maintenance costs of multiple mainframes and the impending Year 2000 problems in the application were also factors. Therefore, our client sought a partner for the development of a new application to support its business.

Perot Systems Corporation was successful in gaining the business, and was contracted to develop and implement a fully customized application for the client.

10.2.2 Perot Systems Corporation: The IT Partner

Perot Systems Corporation is a leading information technology services and business solutions company, serving clients in various industries, including financial services, health care, energy, and travel and transportation.

10.2.3 The Application

The client needed a fully customized application to support their business function. The application was not developed completely from scratch, however, and a little history is required to understand its current incarnation. For clarity, I will refer to the new application as "Silverstone" and to the previous application as "Monaco."

History of the Application

The application began as a project for a previous client of Perot Systems. This previous project was very large and was of vital importance to the business of the client. The client's company was formed as the result of many mergers and acquisitions, resulting in as many as 30 disparate systems in nine separate countries all loosely connected using software bridges. The tracking of data and product in this "system" was nearly impossible, and financial management was incredibly complex and inflexible. The company contracted Perot Systems in 1992 to resolve these problems, resulting in the development of Monaco.

The goal of the Monaco project was to consolidate all the systems and business processes into a single image of the company. The development and implementation of the system had to be complete in two years, and this was the driving force behind the development tools and project planning.

The development process involved the production of a single application, consisting of 5,300 modules, from scratch. The total development time was more than 300 person-years, with 330 developers working during the peak.

Because of the tight schedule, the analysis and development were attempted using CASE Designer and CASE Generator to automate much of the programming effort in the generation phase. This approach not only saved in programming effort, it drastically improved the consistency of the code that was produced. If something was wrong, it was wrong everywhere, and if it was correct, it was correct everywhere. This led to an online application that existed purely as an SQL*Forms 3.0 application, with handwritten batch programs to complement it. The entire application was centralized and two-tier in nature, with the Forms binaries running on fat UNIX "clients" and the database running on separate hardware.

One of the overriding design goals of the Monaco application was to make it compatible with Oracle Parallel Server. To be precise, it was designed to be a two-node OPS application, with sales and back office functions executed on one node, and the point-of-sale agent functions executed on the other. This was a conscious decision from day one, because we knew that even the largest available Oracle database server platform was not large enough as a single machine.

As the complete application approached reality and the sales agents were using their part of the application in production, it was clear that even two nodes of the chosen platform were not going to suffice. In fact, because this was prior to any application tuning effort, the best estimates were showing a requirement for *ten* nodes. Even if the application tuning effort *halved* the resource requirement of the application, it would still require more than twice the estimated hardware.

The hardware sizing estimates had been made on the basis of an extensive benchmark of the platform against a mock-up of the actual application, in parallel with the development of the real application. While a great deal of effort was expended in making this as accurate as possible, this example shows the difficulty of attempting to size a system accurately before the application is written.

The hardware requirements of the application meant that a new hardware platform was required in order to proceed with the rollout. At this stage, a benchmark suite was constructed using the application, in order to simulate the workload as it actually appeared. The new platform was proven and was implemented during a six-hour maintenance window.

The application was running on a two-node cluster at this stage, using Oracle7 release 7.0.15. As the rollout progressed, other problems became apparent. These problems were not gradual, but sudden, brick-wall problems, and there was rarely any warning. Many of them were bugs in the parallel server code and the vendor lock manager, whereas others were fundamental scaling difficulties in the base Oracle product at that time.

Most notable among these difficulties was the poor scalability of the library cache in this release. The certification process for the replacement platform had omitted a crucial workload attribute in its testing—parse calls. Because the simulation was implicitly "too efficient" by virtue of the fact that it did not close cursors but simply *reexecuted* the same cursors, it did not stress this portion of the Oracle product adequately.

This omission was, of course, understandable, because it is not within the scope of customer benchmarks to stress test the entire vendor product set. Or is it? Lessons learned from this exercise led to the desire to test the system in a configuration that mirrored real life. Doing this was the only safeguard against unexpected problems.

The net effect of this testing was a great deal more benchmarking, with a subsequent upgrade of the hardware to a *three*-node cluster. This marked a departure from the application design, but it was a necessary move in order to provide more bandwidth for the processing of the workload. This kind of change, however, requires extensive application rewrites. These changes were made in conjunction with extensive database reconfiguration in order to reduce the ping rate between the database servers.

The database was still running on release 7.0.15, but now it was known as 7.0.15.*Perot* owing to the existence of a special branch of the Oracle source tree to support this system. This branch had to be maintained by Oracle until all the patches on the system had been rolled up into a production release. It was only when release 7.3 went into production that all 49 of the major patches, and countless other "minor" patches, were present in a commercial release. This was the first upgrade of the Oracle codeset for this application.

During all this hardware testing and implementation, parallel efforts were proceeding to produce an application with a reduced footprint, and one that cooperated with Oracle7 a little more. Notable in this effort was the ability of Forms 3.0 to generate dynamic SQL by default—filling up the shared pool—and its overzealous closing of cursors that would prove useful later. Extensive application rework was done to work around these problems, resulting in most of the application being at least "retouched by hand" after the generation process. All the major forms were rewritten from scratch, using a significant amount of user exit code to solve the more difficult problems. In addition, the introduction of the third parallel server node meant that a good deal of the code had to be revisited once again to make the appropriate access changes to reduce the ping rate on the database servers.

The Monaco project was a technical triumph, but not without a great deal of pain and hard lessons. Hopefully this book will allow you to skip some of those lessons. As a final word on Monaco, it is worth mentioning that the system recently underwent a further upgrade. Hardware has become more powerful since the system was fully implemented, and now the Monaco system can be housed on a single node, along with a single failover node for availability. This upgrade was performed, but not without significant testing first—a benchmark was run for several months prior to the rollout of the new platform. The result of the upgrade is that Monaco now *easily* fits onto a single database server, confirming that idea of the constant redefinition of "large."

Required Changes

The new client viewed the Monaco application as an ideal starting point for the functionality and flexibility they required. The two clients were in the same business (in separate markets), so some of the core functionality was already in place. However, the business model followed by the two companies was quite different, and several changes needed to be made to Monaco before it was suitable for the new client. The changes were extensive in some functional areas, although the fundamental design of the application remained sound and provided a solid base to build on.

In addition to the business requirements, Silverstone had technical requirements that were necessary in order to deliver enhanced functionality at higher transaction rates. As a rough estimate, the new system would require approximately *four times* the throughput of the previous system.

The first of these changes was to start the migration from two-tier to three-tier. This was necessary in order to control the volatile "spikes" in activity observed during the operation of Monaco; these spikes were not controllable in a two-tier configuration. All new major functional areas were written as Tuxedo services, called by Forms using user exits. All major commit blocks were pulled out of the forms and implemented as Tuxedo services. However, all users still connect directly to the database and perform the majority of their queries directly, and the transaction management all occurs in the Oracle server.

The total effort of migrating to Silverstone was huge and far-reaching. For example, Monaco had just over one million lines of Pro*C code in addition to the Forms code. Silverstone also has one million lines of code, but only 276,077 of these are original code, and more than half of these are comments. For the Forms code, line counts are less meaningful owing to the fact that many lines of the text source are simply defaults from Forms. However, the old application had 438 forms, compared with 567 in Silverstone. Of these forms, 30% of the code is brand new—some 3,500,000 lines—performed by a large development team that peaked at 150 people during the main coding effort.

10.2.4 The Technical Solution

Supporting Silverstone requires a special technical implementation. Bearing in mind that the workload is so much greater than that of the Monaco system, there is clearly some room for things to go wrong if precautions are not taken. Those precautions were taken for the implementation of the new application, including careful sizing, platform selection, availability design, and a well-planned Oracle implementation.

Hardware

Given the size of the processing requirement, the planning and implementation of the hardware solution had to be flawless. The lessons from Monaco were not to be revisited, and so everything associated with the new implementation was approached with a healthy dose of paranoia.

The hardware was a prime example of where a formal process was followed, consisting of

1. Initial design
2. Sizing
3. Benchmarking
4. Final design
5. Implementation

Initial Design. The initial design of the Silverstone hardware solution took the best parts of the implementation for the previous client and created deliberate solutions for the undesirable parts. High priorities included

- Rapid platform failover
- Robust backup capability
- Low latency
- Simplicity

These elements were all incorporated into the initial design, leaving the finer details of availability until a later date. Initial sizing was performed prior to this stage in order to do a sanity check on the proposed architecture.

Sizing. Detailed sizing followed the initial design, where only a granular sizing effort was undertaken. During this stage, very detailed sizing information was derived from all the available data points, including

- Business metrics to determine transaction rates
- Known footprint of some portions of the application
- Estimated footprint of new portions of the application

The many metrics were taken together in a large spreadsheet, and a conceptual machine size was produced, using the Monaco system as a baseline. This included

- Database size
- Required disk spindles for I/O

- Required I/O controllers
- CPU capacity for database servers and clients
- Memory capacity for database servers and clients

All derived results were weighted according to an error tolerance, and the results were used in the next step.

Benchmarking. Benchmarking (or platform selection, in this case) involved two distinct processes:

1. Paper evaluation
2. A competitive benchmark

The paper evaluation took the data from the sizing exercise and applied it against a short list of ten potential hardware platforms. For completeness, this list did not include only UNIX servers. Each platform was then given a rating against each of several categories, including capacity and other attributes such as reliability and the support capability of the vendor. The end result of this evaluation was the selection of two platforms for a competitive benchmark. A benchmark was then developed that would represent the future operation of the application.

In order to best represent the image of the client's business, the benchmark required an accurate portrayal of the data in the database, in addition to a simulation of the application. In fact, the buildout of the database took a great deal more effort than the actual simulation of the user sessions.

The simulation of the user sessions was implemented using the Performix/TTY product, heavily customized to provide the level of control desired for the benchmark. Once the customization effort had been completed, the definition of the user simulation was fairly straightforward.

The final piece of preparation for the benchmark was the porting exercise. In addition to porting the application to the target systems, the database also had to be built on each native platform. In order to ensure that all was equal in the database, it was built using the same file layout, the same block size, and the same scripts. The net result was an identical database on each platform, apart from the operating system dependent differences in the files.

During the building of the benchmark suite, a decision had to be made as to which version of Oracle should be used. The testing was to begin in earnest at the beginning of December 1997, just five months after the launch of the initial version of release 8.0. In order to protect the progress of the benchmark from unknown bugs in a very new release, version 7.3 of Oracle was adopted for both platforms.

The benchmark was executed against both successful platforms from the paper evaluation, over a period of 12 weeks. Each vendor was allowed six weeks to complete the series of tests, strictly controlled and subject to a previously documented tuning fairness policy. This policy sets out exactly which changes must or must not be carried out at both sites. This policy ensured that an apples-to-apples comparison could be made without any unfair advantages.

The unsuccessful platform was the first to be tested.[1] The testing went very well, particularly from a reliability standpoint. Several application scaling problems arose during this phase, as the user count approached 3,000. These problems were solved, and the tests were reexecuted.

Once the problems had been resolved, certain limitations of the hardware platform became apparent at high load. Although it is possible that the limit lay just beyond that anticipated workload, this was a definite risk associated with choosing this platform. The problem was in the memory latency of the system and its subsequent ability to maintain cache coherency under heavy latch duress. The limit was near the 200,000 gets/s rate on the cache buffers chains latches, where the system simply could not process any faster. In fact, the processors were not taxed at full loading, and some were taken out to prove this observation. If anything, the latch processing capability improved at this stage. From reading Chapter 2, it is likely that you will be able to determine which hardware architecture this system is built from, given that it has memory latency challenges.

The second system to be tested was very different from the beginning. In fact, it was so different that a full transactional audit was carried out, comparing every operation on both systems, in order to sanity check the performance difference. This audit *did* in fact show a difference, but not the

---

1. The identity of the unsuccessful vendor is not disclosed: I do not want any derived conclusions of superiority of one over the other. All conclusions from this testing apply only to the versions of the hardware and of Oracle (7.3) used in the testing. This requirement is likely to be different from any other, and other cases could suit this platform very well.

expected one: The second system had an index built on a ten-block table. Even towing this boat anchor (it *doubled* the `cache buffers chains` latch acquisition rate to 500,000 gets/s), the second system processed the workload with a much more even response time and greater transactional throughput. The second system was clearly a good deal faster than the first. On exit from satisfactory fault insertion testing, and with the right commercial deal secured, this vendor was successful in securing the business.

The successful platform was the Hewlett-Packard V2250, a point-to-point SMP system. The system demonstrated itself to be well balanced from a memory latency perspective and capable of very rapid cache coherency operations. Despite having 16 processors, often all trying to spin on a single latch, the system did not exhibit negative scaling tendencies under high load. This made it eminently suitable for the latch-intensive workloads we were presenting to it. Large OLTP systems often exhibit this kind of latch-intensive workload profile as a result of the concurrency requirements of many online users.

From a procedural perspective, the entire process was documented from start to finish. Prior to the benchmark, an approach document was developed and agreed on by all parties. This was a 91-page description of everything associated with the benchmark, including rules, application descriptions, hardware architectures, project planning, operational manuals, and so on. On termination of the benchmark, an additional 61-page document was produced, including all pertinent results and observations from the testing. This was made possible by keeping a daily diary of all events at both sites, in order to recall all events correctly. In addition, the second document included a weighting table that could be applied to all the results (see Table 10.1).

For this particular exercise, this weighting table was appropriate. The only strange thing (for some) was that price was considered the least important weighting factor; in this case, where choosing the wrong platform could result in crippling downtime for the business, price appeared some way down the list.

Final Design. After the selection process had been completed, the final design phase was started. This stage determined the actual configuration of the production systems, including all availability options and ancillary

Table 10.1   Silverstone Benchmark Weighting Factors

Factor	Weighting Factor
Performance	5
Software stability	5
Reliability	5
Recovery time	4
Vendor responsiveness	4
Growth/scalability	4
Vendor experience in high-end clusters	3
Operating system environment	2
Systems management	2
Price	1
Platform longevity	1

systems. In the case of the Silverstone systems, this stage dramatically increased the inventory from the clustered database server and three application servers. The final production inventory includes some 15 servers and more than 3TB of physical disk. A good deal of the additional disk (the actual size of the database is 450GB) is used to implement several levels of fault tolerance:

- Loss of single disk
- Loss of mirrored pair
- Loss of disk cabinet
- Loss of entire cluster
- Logical loss of data (table level)
- I/O failure causing corruption

In fact, the only situation in which the production system would need tape backups to be restored would be a full disaster that took out all the production hardware. The logical view of the storage architecture is shown in Figure 10.1.

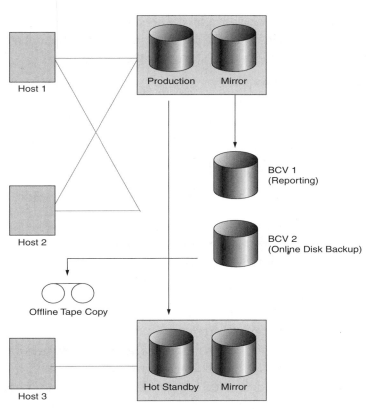

Figure 10.1 Silverstone storage architecture

Each of the disk objects represents a 450GB database "copy," thus totaling 2.7TB of physical disk. Only one of these—the mirror copy—is exactly current with the production database. The rest of the disk regions are at various levels of physical and logical distinction from the online database. First of these are the two BCV (EMC Timefinder snapshot technology, see Chapter 2) copies of the database. These snapshots are taken twice every 24 hours in order to implement the reporting requirement, the backup requirement, and the recovery requirement.

In the early hours of the morning, a snapshot of the database is taken. The procedure is to put the tablespaces into backup mode, copy the physical disk to one set of the BCV volumes, and then take the database out of backup mode. The copy on the BCV volumes now just look like a restored hot backup. These volumes are mounted on the secondary machine of the cluster and rolled forward using the archive logs from the production database. The database is then opened and several reconfiguration steps are taken, including:

- Setting a new database name
- Building rollup tables
- Building decision support indexes
- Rebuilding rollback segments
- Redefining temporary tablespaces
- Tuning initialization parameters for query-intensive work
- Making most tablespaces READ ONLY

This database is now more focused on heavy query work, although the block size cannot be enlarged during this process. When the reconfiguration is complete, the reporting database that exists on the other set of BCV volumes is shut down, and the new one is started up in its place. Therefore, the reporting facility is refreshed every 24 hours, with only a handful of minutes of downtime on each refresh.

The former reporting volumes are then used as the targets for another BCV operation from production. These volumes are copied off to tape during the day from a small, dedicated system. The disk volumes remain for as long as possible during the business day in order to allow rapid recovery from a complete failure of the primary production volumes.

In addition to the backup and reporting volumes, another set of mirrored volumes are used for further protection against lengthy failures. This set is refreshed from the production volumes every few weeks and is kept current with the production database through the use of the Oracle hot standby database functionality. As archived redo logs are produced in production, they are automatically sent over to the standby system for application to the standby database.

In the case of a failure of many disks in production—even an entire disk cabinet—the hot standby system can be brought up in a matter of minutes. This would compare with many hours if a tape restore were required. The protection provided by each portion of the storage architecture can be matched up against the claims made at the beginning of this section, as shown in Table 10.2.

Table 10.2 Storage Protection

Protection	Provided by
Loss of single disk	Online mirror
Loss of mirrored pair	On-disk BCV copy
Loss of disk cabinet	Hot standby instance
Loss of entire cluster	Hot standby instance
Logical loss of data (table level)	Reporting database (with up to 24 hours logical record loss)
I/O failure causing corruption	Hot standby instance

In fact, the design of the storage system remains the only point of potential problems in the event of failure, and this exists in any database system. If the redo logs become corrupted, the contents of the logs will be propagated to all regions of disk, thus spreading the corruption. This does not present a great deal of risk, because

- The hot standby instance is likely to detect the log corruption and complain before it becomes a problem.
- The reporting database is available regardless and is a maximum of 24 hours old.
- The backup volumes provide a clean image prior to the corrupt logs.

Once the detailed design had been completed, the orders were placed for the actual production system.

Hardware Implementation. On delivery of the production system, the implementation phase could begin. In many respects, this phase was a good deal like an extended benchmark: The systems were installed and then extensively tested during the configuration phase. This testing was a deliberate and planned event, classified as "extended benchmarking," and is highly recommended for systems that require high availability. Many lessons were learned every day of this process, which provided a great deal of additional confidence as the go-live date drew near; through these lessons, a well-trained group of technicians emerged.

Many problems were also encountered during this time. The difficulty of installing a new, complex system should never be underestimated. Even the configuration tasks that should have been simple were difficult because of the scale of the operation.

During the configuration of the system, time was spent laying down the infrastructure to control change on the system. This involved the installation of the Concurrent Versions System[2] (CVS), a public-domain source code management system. Source control systems such as CVS are not limited to program source management and can be used for version control of *all* the configuration files on a system.

Several different areas of the system were put under CVS control:

- Oracle configuration file (`init.ora`)
- Operating system configuration files
- All scripts

Owing to the client/server nature of CVS, the change repository for these files was stored on a development machine on the other side of the country. This also allowed a kind of disaster recovery capability in that all the changed files were available at short notice from a remote site.

Oracle Implementation

The Oracle implementation was tightly coupled with the hardware implementation and was not considered a separate task. A good example of this is the implementation of the backup and reporting function, as detailed above. These processes were so tightly integrated into the hardware configuration that skills in both areas were essential in implementing these parts of the system.

The implementation consisted of taking the lessons learned during the benchmarking process and merging them with operational requirements and current sizing demands. The result was an initial plan for the physical configuration and tuning of the production database instance.

Partitioning.   The immediate problem with this system was the sheer size of the database. At 450GB, the OLTP database would have been considered quite a large data warehouse just a few years ago, and managing such a

---

2. See www.cyclic.com.

large database in a 24\7 environment presents several challenges. All these challenges revolve around the time taken to scan the data in order to

- Update statistics for the cost-based optimizer (ANALYZE)
- Build/rebuild indexes
- Purge old data
- Maintain efficient batch access (full table scans)

The answer to all these problems is to use the Oracle8 partitioning option to effectively reduce the data set that is worked on at any one time.

One table in particular was estimated to reach a size of 80GB after one year in production, so this was clearly a target for partitioning. The table was divided into ten partitions, making the average size of each partition 8GB. Although still large, this made the management of this table much more straightforward.

The table partitioning keys varied, depending on the reason for partitioning. In general, it was not possible for partitioning to be based on date range for this application. It was more practical to partition by other means, such as the station ID for a given user. While this limited the ability to roll old partitions out of the database as a purge mechanism, it allowed maintenance to be carried out on a subset of the data at one time.

As detailed earlier, index partitioning can also be used to alleviate contention for a given block in the buffer cache. This was found to be the case for one of the most heaviliy used tables in the database, and so a partitioned global index was created over the nonpartitioned table in order to spread out the access pattern. This is described later in this chapter, in the description of rates engines.

Tuning. The tuning exercise retained many of the philosophies of the benchmark tuning exercise. The benchmark was the ideal system for tuning, and much of the derived wisdom was applied directly to the production tuning, specifically

- Large number of hash buckets for the buffer cache in order to minimize hot chains in the cache. Approximately one chain for every buffer in the cache means that it is less likely to have more than one hot block on a single hash chain.
- Buffer cache LRU latches set to nearest prime number greater than the number of CPUs.

- `db_block_max_dirty_target` kept at 5% of available buffers. Combined with sufficient database writer processes and deep checkpoint batches, the checkpoints are kept short and sweet.

- Plenty of parallel recovery capability to keep system failover times low.

- Very low `log_small_entry_max_size` (8) so that copying is always done under redo copy latches rather than under the redo allocation latch. Number of redo copy latches (`log_simultaneous_copies`) set to one per CPU.

- One event set: "`4031 trace name errorstack.`" Set to enable logging of shared pool problems in the alert log file.

- `spin_count` set to maximize latch concurrency, while keeping CPU usage to a minimum.

Overall, the tuning is kept as simple as possible. Once in production, a database is very difficult to tune. Tuning presents risks to the operation of the production database, potentially causing unscheduled downtime because of emergency reversal of changes. The database is tuned only when there is a specific problem, which is a very rare event after the initial implementation.

SQL*Net. The exclusion of the `listener.ora` and `tnsnames.ora` files from the CVS repository may appear strange at first. In fact, they are not required to be version controlled, because they are never edited by a person. Instead, these files are generated by a script (that is checked into CVS), which creates the desired `listener.ora` and `tnsnames.ora` configuration files on demand. This eliminates the tedious configuration of these files, which can quickly become a lengthy and error-prone process when many networks are used to carry client/server traffic.

In addition to the generation script, an `rdist`[3] configuration was developed that allows automatic distribution of the generated files to the correct hosts.

---

3. `rdist` is a utility included on most UNIX variants. It can be configured to distribute multiple files to many different hosts, with custom locations and treatments on each. Once set up, `rdist` is a single command that takes care of all software distribution.

The Rollout

Prior to actually connecting any real users to the system, the application was driven against the production system using a modified version of the benchmark simulator. This immediately uncovered a large number of unintentional full table scans and other problems. With these problems rectified, the user connections could be started.

The user rollout was deliberately staged over several weeks. In this way, bad code and scalability challenges could be determined before they became a problem and could be fixed before the next set of users came online. It is estimated that the footprint of the application was reduced by 50% during this time, and it is certain that a "big bang" approach would have resulted in a system driven way beyond its capacity.

Challenges

Any large implementation brings with it a variety of challenges. However careful the preparation, a certain amount of tension remains during the first stages of the rollout. Prime among these concerns are

- How accurate is the sizing?
- How many bugs have slipped through testing?
- How reliable are the hardware and software?
- Are the initial tuning figures in the right ballpark?

In the case of Silverstone, we came out pretty clean. This does not mean that everything was perfect, but fortunately all the technical problems could be classified as teething problems and understandable parts of a new implementation.

Application Tuning.   The vast majority of the teething issues can be categorized as "application tuning." When so much code changes during heavy production use, it is inevitable that some of it will not perform as well as it should. In fact, a tuning team was initiated even before the application was put into production, and this was simply stepped up in priority when the application became live.

One part of the system that was to benefit from the tuning exercise was the Tuxedo service known as the "rates engine," which returned pricing information for specific product combinations. This service is called on four times for every sales inquiry and once when the product is actually sold. Therefore, this service is called a great deal during the operation of the system.

The initial code for the rates engine used dynamic SQL to generate specific queries for each request. The effect of this was to deplete the 600MB of memory in the shared pool in 15 minutes flat, along with the enormous amounts of hard parsing that were necessary for all these requests.

The dynamic SQL was the first thing to change in this service, adopting a fixed string of bind variables that were filled in at runtime. This helped the global system a great deal, with the shared pool never filling up during the production day. The hard parsing was well down, and the dictionary cache was allowed to grow about ten times larger than it previously had been. Therefore, the whole system ran a great deal more efficiently than before.

Unfortunately, the performance of the rates engine itself was still not perfect, and it was still using about 40% of the database server CPU. In order to rectify this, the following steps were taken:

- Caching of some frequently used data on the client side
- Standard SQL tuning
- "Bucket"-based bind variable allocation as described earlier in this book
- Partitioning of an index to create multiple root blocks and alleviate contention on the buffer chain covering that buffer

The net result of this effort was to bring down the server-side CPU utilization to around 10 to 15 percent, and to halve the response time of the engine itself. In addition, the response times of the queries were now more predictable because of the removal of several contention points.

Oracle Challenges.   In addition to the application tuning process, the management of Oracle itself presented a variety of challenges. Foremost among them were the cost based optimizer (CBO) and the difficulties of maintaining stable response times when data volumes and ratios were exploding every day.

When a system first goes live, it is likely that it will be fully populated in *reference* data but will have very little *transactional* history. Therefore, as this transactional data grows, the following implications affect the CBO and how it approaches query plans:

- Index B-tree depths
- Table sizes
- Ratios of table sizes (reference:transactional)
- Data value skew

As a result, each day will herald new surprises in terms of queries "going bad," even if you stay on top of analyzing all the objects in the database. In fact, a few weeks into the rollout, it was deemed less risky to terminate the regular analysis procedure, and simply analyze when things were known to change. This downside of the CBO is one that will go away starting with release 8.1, in which optimizer plans can be frozen once they are satisfactory. Regardless of this, it is still very good practice for the developer to code all SQL statements with hints, because it is likely that the developer has a good understanding of how the data will look in production.

From a reliability standpoint, Oracle has been solid. Compared with the experiences of 7.0.15.Perot, the implementation and operation of Silverstone have been like a breath of fresh air. Minor problems have been encountered, but none of them could be considered serious and none merited an upgrade. Although this could be attributed to Oracle8 being less of a quantum leap than Oracle7, it is more likely that Oracle learned some hard lessons from the Oracle7 days. Oracle7 could be considered Oracle's transition into the very large-scale database market, and adjustments in process were sure to be required for this kind of step forward.

10.3 Chapter Summary

The implementation of Silverstone has been a huge success. Well-placed paranoia up front ensured that the majority of risk was removed from the project, and good planning ensured that delivery was complete and on time. The side effect of having a complete delivery is that time and attention could be applied to observing the production rollout, thus allowing any problems to be rectified very quickly.

The road from sales proposal to implemented product was long and hard, and was made possible by the very best people. At the end of the day, nothing this large can succeed without the skills of many good people. Rather like this book, the skillsets required to complete such a project range from the workings of the hardware right up to higher-level knowledge of software products and business processes. For that kind of spread, a good team is essential.

Further Considerations

Chapter 11

Building a Successful Team

11.1   Introduction

In the summary of Chapter 10, mention was made of how important a good team is to a successful system implementation. This aspect is so important that I have devoted this chapter to a discussion of my experience regarding what makes a strong team and how to go about finding the right kind of people to make up such a team.

The term "team" is used loosely here. Many people contribute to the building of these systems, from hardware engineers to end users. All of these people are vital to the construction of a world-class system. My own experience has been mostly in the teamwork required for the technical portions of the system—hardware through to application development.

Before getting into the guts of the team, let's spend a few moments talking about management.

First, let's dispel a myth. Good management does not necessarily make a good project. The opposite, however, is true: bad management *will* make a bad project. It doesn't matter how good a manager is if the people managed are not capable of thinking for themselves and acting on their own initiative. The best managers do not spend their days micro-managing their people—they spend it protecting their people and guiding them through the higher-level processes.

The best managers have the following common attributes.

- They do not believe that managers are superior to team members.
- They will *listen to* and respect the opinions of team members.
- They do not engage in a delivery role in addition to their management responsibilities.
- They have backgrounds in technical delivery.
- They have an "open door" policy.
- They lead by example, especially when the going gets tough.
- They are aware that managers don't necessarily "know best."
- They protect team members from bureaucracy, allowing them to do their work.

In short, the best managers often appear to be members of the team, whose responsibilities within the team are to administrate events that are external to the team and to suggest direction. Clearly this is not always possible, and managers rely on the quality of the team as much as they rely on themselves. However, it is clear that poor managers are those who are

- Adversarial
- Arrogant
- Stupid

We've all worked for such managers at one time or another.

11.2   Immediate Team Attributes

The traditional view of a team is the immediate team—the people with whom you work directly and who you are involved in recruiting. This section describes my personal opinions on building a successful immediate team.

Members of successful teams, like successful managers, often have similar attributes, including

- Self-motivation
- Lateral thinking
- Responsibility

- Steep learning curve
- Good communication skills
- Good work ethic

Often, this type of person is difficult to find. In fact, with the explosion of the information technology market, the average individual on the market is of a generally low quality. The reasons for this are numerous but can be fairly well attributed to short periods of service at each of a succession of employers.

The net result of this low quality, combined with massive demand, is that you typically get to choose from a selection of overpaid, underskilled individuals. This can lead to an enormous amount of frustration and wasted time when trying to find the right people for a new team, because huge numbers of interviews are necessary to get the right people on board. For this reason, it is often worth taking a different tack: Don't look for skills, look for attributes.

By making attributes your first priority, it is likely that there will be a skills deficit in the successful candidate. Don't worry about this, because a person of the right caliber will soon be running with things that the so-called skilled person would never be able to handle.

Let's run through the desirable attributes in more detail.

Self-Motivation

The motivation of the individual is critical to the success of the individual, the team, and the manager. The impact of poor motivation spreads far beyond the individual, potentially afflicting the whole team. Poor motivation on the part of any individual increases the workload of all the other team members for a number of reasons. First, the manager must spend an unacceptable amount of time trying to inject some motivation into the individual, leaving less time to perform tasks that benefit the entire team. Second, a lack of motivation is infectious. At the very least it will lead to resentment from the more motivated members and potentially can eat into their own motivation.

Self-motivated individuals allow a team to run almost on auto-pilot. If they also have the right skills, the motivated will never be idle; the manager will not need to be involved in allocating the trivial tasks. Taken one step further, the highly motivated individual will latch onto larger projects that need work, even though they are not immediately obvious to others. This kind of preventive medicine for the system will lead automatically to a more stable system.

Lateral Thinking

Many problems persist because there is no way to solve them using standard techniques. These problems can be solved only by "thinking out of the box"—flanking the problem from some other direction. If an individual is not able to think this way, much of the problem solving will be left to other individuals on the team. This can cause problems when trying to run an on-call rota, because the nonlateral thinker will nearly always end up calling another individual to solve the problem.

Lateral thinking, however, is something that can be taught to some degree. Much of the method of lateral thinking is having an expanded repertoire of approaches that can be used in place of the norm. Some investment in mentoring with a true lateral thinker can improve the nonlateralist a great deal.

An experienced lateral thinker will appear to have a "sixth sense" in finding the root cause and solution to a problem.

Responsibility

Responsibility for both one's own actions and the system in one's care are essential attributes. Nobody wants an individual on their team who will walk out on a problem at five o'clock. Likewise, being available to help one's peers in times of trouble is good for team spirit. However, being responsible does not mean being staid—it's also important to have some fun while being responsible.

Steep Learning Curve

Building and operating a large system is complicated. Therefore, even very experienced individuals must maintain a steep learning curve if they are to continue being useful; the day will never come that you can stop learning. In the case of the lesser experienced individual, the learning curve is essential. There is a magic period of about 3 months where an individual should at least be able to get around all the systems in the network and understand the whole configuration to the point of asking intelligent questions.

Good Communication Skills

Perhaps one of the most difficult attributes to acquire, communication is a tricky skill. This skill is especially important when dealing with people who are exterior to the project—support personnel, for example. Communicating all the pertinent information in a concise way is very important when there is so much information to pass on. Compounding this is the fact that with so much activity going on, it is easy to forget some of the required communication. Luckily, e-mail saves the day in many cases, because it provides the perfect method for short, FYI exchanges.

Good Work Ethic

First, what is hard work? I would assert that hard work does not necessarily equate to spending a lot of hours in the office, but rather to how efficiently those hours are spent. Often, of course, hard workers will spend many hours in the office *and* apply themselves efficiently during that time.

Closely linked to motivation, hard work is the thing that turns ideas into reality. When the hard work is all mental and not physical, it becomes even more important to keep the level of effort high. I'm sure a neurologist would laugh, but I believe the human brain to have a memory hierarchy similar to that of a computer system. If the activity level is diluted, the cache warmth will be poor, and the throughput will be an order of magnitude slower. This is evident when one is trying to write a complex program with constant interruption. An individual who is not scared of hard work will produce far greater results than one who is.

11.3 Virtual Team Attributes

The virtual team includes all the external personnel required to put a large system together, such as

- Software support personnel
- Hardware support personnel

- Consultants
- Application developers
- Kernel engineers

When building and operating the system, all of these people could be required to perform some tasks at your request, and vice versa. Therefore, they form a virtual team around your immediate team.

Often there is no choice as to who is assigned from external companies. However, if you are not happy with the attitude or skillset of an assigned individual, it is important to say so and find somebody else. One rule of thumb to use when assessing the skillsets of external people is to see if you know more than they do about their areas of expertise. It is not a good sign if you know more, although sometimes it is necessary just to get "all hands on deck," regardless of whether they deliver 10 percent or 100 percent of their advertised abilities.

When good individuals are found, it is important to treat them as members of the team. Many times, external companies will try to reassign people for no apparent reason, and this must be resisted at all costs. Finding good people at external companies is even harder than recruiting them for the immediate team.

11.4 Chapter Summary

Forming and retaining a strong team is vital to the construction of a world-class system. If you cannot recruit skilled people with the right attributes, consider waiving some of the skillset requirements. Sometimes this means doing some recruiting at colleges and just taking the smartest people, regardless of their industry experience. It is important, however, that the corporate salary structure be able to expand their compensation at the same rate at which their market value grows. If this cannot be accommodated, poor retention will be the result, a frequent downfall of university recruitment efforts.

Chapter 12

Pitfalls

12.1 Introduction

Oracle and the underlying operating system are extremely complex. Management of high load and high concurrency expose the software to many race conditions and other problems. When this situation is combined with the constant drive to implement new functionality into the products, it is inevitable that pitfalls—bugs—will arise from time to time.

The purpose of this chapter is to provide advice on how to avoid bugs, how to identify and fix them when they occur, and how to communicate with the respective vendors.

12.2 Avoiding Bugs

The best way to deal with bugs is to avoid them. This simple fact is often overlooked, and a few precautions can go a long way.

12.2.1 Initial Releases

Some people say "never go with dot-0 releases." Other people go one step further and try to associate patterns with the minor release numbers. This is clearly bogus, but the dot-0 philosophy is basically sound to varying degrees.

With large software engineering projects, code has to be frozen from change in order to produce the release. In order to do this, various techniques are used by the code management teams, ranging from conceptual freeze dates to complete shutdown of the code management system. Whatever the technique, a freeze is achieved.

When a hard freeze is set like this, it is almost inevitable that some of the changes will be checked in only partially complete, or rushed through with inadequate testing. It should not be this way, but human nature demands it. The net result of this is that bugs creep into the product.

The more experienced the development team, the less likely that nasty bugs will make it through. The reality for massive projects such as an RDBMS or an operating system is that even a small turnover of people results in a large number of fresh faces for each release.

One way around these problems is to avoid new feature code, because this code is the most likely to contain the bugs. Unfortunately, it is difficult to tell which pieces of the code have been changed the most, because some "old features" may well have been overhauled for this release in order to improve scalability, for example. If one wants to avoid the new features of a dot-0 release altogether, then one should look instead at the most recent release of the prior version.

12.2.2   Known Problems

Shortly after any release, be it a dot-0 or otherwise, problems will start to be reported to support. Therefore, it is always worth waiting at least a few weeks after a release before using it. Before upgrading, check with support and get the list of known bugs in that release. If the bugs are in areas of the product that you use heavily, this is probably not a good release to move to for the present.

12.3   Bug Diagnosis and Resolution

The ultimate treatment of a bug involves both a diagnosis and a resolution of the problem. The ultimate resolution may involve a software patch, but an interim solution can sometimes be used to work around the problem.

This is something that Oracle often tries to offer as a band-aid solution to the real problem.

Within Oracle development exists a team dedicated to repairing any problems that arise in the product. This team is known as the Defect Diagnosis and Resolution (DDR) group and in many ways offers more capability than a core developer of the product can provide. These people have a much broader knowledge of the software than a typical kernel developer has and are very experienced in sniffing out the root cause of a problem. When a problem is determined to be in a certain portion of the software, the DDR individual will either fix the problem personally or involve the kernel developer who developed that portion of code.

The DDR gorup is the kernel group interface to support, which itself is divided into several levels of escalation. The final line of support is known as Bug Diagnostics and Escalation (BDE), which is the equivalent of DDR on the support side. Once again, BDE personnel are typically versed in the source code of the product and have enormous experience in diagnosing problems. Much of the information below is derived from discussions with BDE. In front of BDE are the usual levels of support, depending on the support tier adopted in your contract.

12.3.1 Finding and Fixing Bugs

Finding bugs is often not as straightforward as it may appear. Sometimes a genuine user error can appear to be a bug, or a bug can appear to be a user or code problem. Finding a genuine bug can often require a good deal of research and testing on the part of the database administrator before it is accepted as such by support.

There are several possible bug scenarios in Oracle:

- ORA-0600 errors
- ORA-7445 errors
- Functionality-related problems
- Performance-related problems
- Memory leaks
- Oracle Parallel Server problems

For all of these scenarios, support personnel will need the following information:

- Full Oracle version (e.g., 8.0.4.2.1)
- Any ad hoc patches installed
- Operating system version (possibly including patch information, but support will ask if this is required)
- Hardware platform
- Background of the problem

The first scenario—the ORA-0600 error—is an Oracle internal error. This means that Oracle has encountered an unexpected condition within the kernel and that the developer has included a check for this in the code. An ORA-0600 error can be considered a "process panic" and normally arises as the result of a race condition. These errors are reported to the session that encounters the error and within the alert file, and so they are quite easy to spot.

Despite a popular misconception, not all internal errors are desperate cases. Unless the internal error is encountered in one of the *background* processes, it will not cause an instance failure. However, there is little diagnosis that can be done by the administrator for this type of problem, because it is by nature a wildcard. The good news is that an ORA-0600 is definitely a bug rather than a problem attributed to user error, and the following procedure should be followed when an internal error occurs.

1. Call it in to support. There is a good chance that there is already a fix for the problem. Support will need the arguments (the values in square brackets on the error line) in order to locate the source of the problem.

2. While support personnel are looking up the bug, get a good trace dump of the error, ready to send off.

3. If the problem has not already been fixed, try to produce a test case, if possible.

When sending off tracefiles to Oracle, whether for an internal error or otherwise, check that the tracefiles are not all of the same size. If they are, it is likely that they have all been truncated as a result of exceeding `max_dump_file_size` and will not be of much use to support. If a process is still writing out a tracefile, you can get to it quickly with the `svrmgrl` oradebug facility and `unlimit` the trace in order to ensure a full dump. Otherwise, you will need to set the global limit higher in order to produce good tracefiles.

The second type of problem you may encounter is an ORA-7445 error. This type of error results in a core dump of the process that encountered the error and normally a tracefile that contains a stack trace of the problem. These errors are essentially the same as ORA-0600 errors but do not have traps encoded by the developer. The net result is that this error is somewhat less expected than an ORA-0600. In the case of an ORA-7445, the procedure should be the same as for an ORA-0600, but it might be less likely that you will get an immediate fix. However, ORA-7445 errors are still bugs and will be accepted by support without question.

Functionality-related problems are frequently subject to debate and can be harder to log as bugs than other problems. Before calling support, you should be sure that you have read the relevant documentation thoroughly and really understand what is going on. Sometimes, a perceived functionality bug is little more than an incorrect assumption on the part of a user who has not read the manual. If you are sure that it is a bug, it is normally fairly straightforward to create a test case for the problem and to supply this test case at the time of opening the call. This will allow support to work on the problem without repeatedly coming back for further information.

Performance-related problems are more difficult. There can be so many factors that affect performance that you need to have a good case in hand to clearly demonstrate your problem to support. There are several specific types of problems that fall into the area of performance:

- SQL-related problems (e.g., CBO errors)
- Scalability problems
- General performance problems
- Complete hangs

For SQL-related problems, the minimum information that support will need is the output of `tkprof`, preferably with the `explain` option enabled. If this is not sufficient to demonstrate the bug, further information will be required. If the query has gone bad because of an event such as an upgrade, a "before" tracefile will be most useful.

Scalability problems are very difficult to demonstrate and often require extensive investigation before making a determination. As scalability has been covered in some detail in this book, it should be clear that poor scalability can arise for many reasons. Proving it to be an Oracle problem is often difficult. However, if you are observing a problem such as severe latch contention and cannot determine why this should be the case, it is worth talking to support.

General performance problems always require a `utlbstat/utlestat`[1] this report to be sent to support. Even if you have checked this yourself, support personnel will not be happy to look any further unless you send the request in first. They will also need to know how you have determined that performance has deteriorated. Does this problem seem to be related to workload, to an upgrade, to a new machine, etc. The more evidence you can gather that an Oracle problem is causing the performance problem, the faster you will receive answers back from Oracle.

If you experience a total freeze of the instance, do not shut down the instance until you have gathered some diagnostic information for support. Specifically, before looking at a total hang, support will need a systemstate dump:

```
$ svrmgrl

Oracle Server Manager Release 3.0.4.0.0 - Production

(c) Copyright 1997, Oracle Corporation.  All Rights Reserved.

Oracle8 Enterprise Edition Release 8.0.4.2.1 - Production
With the Partitioning option
PL/SQL Release 8.0.4.2.1 - Production

SVRMGR> connect internal
Connected.
SVRMGR> oradebug setmypid
Statement processed.
SVRMGR> oradebug unlimit
Statement processed.
SVRMGR> oradebug dump systemstate 1
Statement processed.
SVRMGR>
```

---

1. $ORACLE_HOME/rdbms/admin/utlbstat.sql.

Try a level 1 dump (SYSTEMSTATE 1) to begin with, and then reconnect (to get a fresh tracefile) and try a level 2 dump. Send support anything that you get from this, which will appear as a standard tracefile in the user_dump_dest location.

Thankfully, memory leaks within the Oracle Server are rare. However, if you suspect a memory leak in the Oracle processes, support will be looking for the following information, at a minimum:

- The session pga memory and session pga memory max statistics from v$sesstat

- A heapdump of the PGA:

```
$ svrmgrl

Oracle Server Manager Release 3.0.4.0.0 - Production

(c) Copyright 1997, Oracle Corporation.  All Rights Reserved.

Oracle8 Enterprise Edition Release 8.0.4.2.1 - Production
With the Partitioning option
PL/SQL Release 8.0.4.2.1 - Production

SVRMGR> connect internal
Connected.
SVRMGR> oradebug setospid 17087
Oracle pid: 22, Unix process pid: 17087, image: oraclePRD1
SVRMGR> oradebug unlimit
Statement processed.
SVRMGR> oradebug dump heapdump 1
Statement processed.
SVRMGR>
```

This information may be only the beginning of a lengthy debugging session, but it will at least get support on the right track.

12.3.2 Oracle Parallel Server Problems

If the problem involves Oracle Parallel Server, different information will probably be required. In the case of an OPS hang, the following information will be required:

- DLM logfiles (lmon*, lmd* in background_dump_dest) *from each node*
- DLM tracefiles *from each node*

- `alert` files *from each node*
- `init.ora` *from each node*

The important theme to note here is that the same files are required from every node that has an OPS instance on it, because it only takes one node to misbehave, and the entire synchronization of Parallel Server could be disabled. Therefore, missing one node could mean that the required information is not present, even if that node still appears to be running normally.

In the case of a crash, the requirement is similar to that for a single-instance system, except that the tracefiles are required *from each node*. All tracefiles mentioned in the alert file on every node are required.

If you are still running OPS with Oracle7, the lock manager software is the responsibility of the hardware vendor. Things can get very difficult to diagnose in this instance, because the problem could lie anywhere in the Oracle or clusters code. When calling problems of this nature in to support, be sure to have the DLM version and the clusters version available.

OPS is particularly prone to hardware problems. Owing to its reliance on shared disk devices and the cluster interconnect, any errors in this area can cause OPS to have a problem. Therefore, if you experience a problem on an OPS system (or on a single-instance system, for that matter), make sure that you check the `syslog.log` for any hardware problems prior to calling Oracle support.

12.4   Chapter Summary

In an ideal world, you would not encounter any bugs. Reality, unfortunately, is very different, and bugs are a fact of life. The general trend has been toward fewer bugs, but as products get more and more complex, there is plenty of scope for bugs to be present.

Using the information in this chapter, you should be able to shortcut some of the burden of chasing down bugs by being ready with the answers before questions are asked.

Chapter 13

Internet Applications and the Future

13.1 E-Commerce Systems

The release of Oracle8i (or 8.1, if we dispense with the marketing terms) marks Oracle's biggest plunge into the world of the Internet. The standard RDBMS product has been supplemented with a variety of new features to allow it to integrate tightly with users of the Internet in addition to providing it with a significant boost in uptime through the online maintenance options. Combined, these changes make Oracle a powerful tool for deploying flexible Internet-based applications to millions of potential users.

Luckily, although the Internet has millions of potential users, only a small subset of these users access Internet applications at any one time. This means that the capacity requirements for Internet application are not as large as they may initially appear, although they are frequently very high.

This chapter will explain how Oracle fits into the Internet and e-commerce world and what this might mean for the evolution of the Oracle product.

13.1.1 The Implications

The widespread adoption of the Internet is now well underway. Although there are already many millions of Internet users, the user base is still growing at an enormous rate. Emerging services, such as free Internet service, are set to increase the Internet user base even more. Permanent connections are also on the horizon, through the adoption of home network services such as Digital Subscriber Line (DSL).

With a large base of potential customers, the Internet provides businesses with several advantages over traditional methods of trading:

- Increased exposure
- Reduced infrastructure costs
- Reduced head count

Along with these advantages, the Internet also presents the following challenges that must be overcome for project success:

- Increased user base
- Increased data volumes
- Network scalability issues

Increased Exposure

The size of the Internet population allows businesses to reach a large number of potential customers. Although the Internet is not yet a part of everybody's life, it has probably achieved significant penetration of the target market of many companies: Many people who regularly use the Internet are professionals with above-average disposable income. Therefore, traders of goods such as electronics, sports equipment, and computer equipment are already reaping the benefits of trading on the Internet.

Reduced Infrastructure Costs

The Internet is only a *virtual* shopping mall. It is not necessary to have store frontage in order to trade on the Web; it all takes place online. Therefore, tremendous cost savings are possible through having only office and machine room space instead of multiple, premium-priced shopfronts. In addition, the datacenter can be located anywhere in the country, not just where the target consumer is located.

Reduced Head Count

A reduction in locations also means that there is significantly reduced head count when transactions are performed directly between consumer and computer. While it is imperative to retain a strong customer service capability, the number of direct sales representatives need only be a token offering. This means that the idea of the large "call center" is shortly to become a thing of the past for many retailers.

Increased User Base

With increased exposure comes, arguably, a larger user base. Although the number of customers may not be a great deal more than that of a leading direct-mail catalog, the fact that all these customers also equate to users of the system means that there could be many more users working concurrently. This is particularly true during evenings, when many people have the time to go shopping on the Internet.

Increased Data Volumes

Alhough the number of customers does not necessarily imply that there is more data, the trend of e-commerce seems to be just that. One thing that online customers have grown accustomed to is a full order history, complete with tracking numbers and payment details. In addition, customers expect a very comprehensive inventory from an online retailer, along with distributed warehouses and probably some kind of customized look and feel to the site. The implication of all this is that the typical online retailer quickly amasses enormous amounts of data.

Network Scalability Issues

The biggest problem of the Internet is also its greatest strength—it is a globally shared network. This means that online retailers must factor this into their designs, and mitigate the problems of variable bandwidth and latency with good application design. The bottom line is that the application must

- Be compact (for fast downloads)
- Operate locally as much as possible

The first item clearly relates to the problem of low bandwidth. The second deals with both the scalability of the datacenter systems and, more importantly, reduction of the number of network round trips. This is done so that the network latency does not aggravate the user too much.

13.1.2   The Implication for Business Computing

As a result of all these issues, the industry had to overcome a variety of hurdles before e-commerce could become a viable option. Great progress has been made on these problems, and the Internet now works quite well as a trading platform. The side effect of this is that these problems all needed to be solved for internal applications too, and the online trading requirement has helped to accelerate the resolution of a variety of business computing problems. The same technology used for Internet applications is also very suitable for intranet (internal) applications and provides solutions for the following key problem areas:

- Wide-area rollouts
- Large user populations
- Customized content/presentation

Oracle8i and supporting application development tools incorporate several features that help to address these issues, improving both the Internet application and the more traditional multiuser business application.

13.2   Oracle8i Technology

Previous releases of Oracle already provided strong, scalable database services that made it an excellent platform for business applications. With the introduction of Oracle8i, Oracle has taken the next step in providing core support for emerging Internet technologies, and the emerging application development practices.

These additions can be grouped into two distinct areas: Java integration and new data services.

13.2.1   Java Integration

Perhaps the most crucial of the new features is the complete adoption of Java, including a fully integrated Java Virtual Machine (JVM) into the actual database server engine, known as JServer. For the first time, Oracle can execute the same code in any tier of the application, using Java. This has not been possible with any prior release or programming language; even PL/SQL has suffered from version mismatches between the client and the server implementations.

Java integration brings two important strengths to the Oracle product. First, it is the de facto standard for Internet application development. This makes the Oracle product more accessible to the Internet community, with no need to learn PL/SQL, OCI, and so on before useful application code can be constructed.

Second, it is a robust, portable, and diverse object-oriented programming language, taking many of the best practices from other OO languages and circumventing many of the common problems. Being object-based and multiplatform, Java is the ideal vehicle for multitier development, because the core logic can be insulated from the detail of the execution environment.

In order to allow simple relocation of Java code between tiers, Oracle has maintained the standard Java Database Connectivity (JDBC) method for accessing the database for every tier in the application. Whether the code runs on the end user's terminal, in the middle tier, or within an Oracle server process, it will always access the database through JDBC. The difference between the tiers is in the footprint of the JDBC interface and the subsequent performance.

There are now three different JDBC interfaces: Thin (pure Java), OCI, and Server. The Thin interface is used for distribution to the user's terminal/PC. It is small in size and consists of 100 percent portable binary code, but it is comparatively low in performance. The OCI driver is designed to be run in the middle tier, having a nonportable native binary, larger size, but significantly better performance. Finally there is the Server JDBC interface, which is simply a proxy straight into the RDBMS SQL layers. This interface is by far the fastest, but obviously can exist only in the server tier.

As JDBC is a standards-based database interface designed for all types of database access, it is subsequently a little cranky in usage. For this reason, Oracle supplies SQL, which is to JDBC what Pro*C is to C. It allows more simplistic embedding of Oracle SQL into Java programs, which are then preprocessed into standard JDBC code for compilation.

Starting with release 8.1.6, Oracle will be shipping the JServer Accelerator. This proves to be a very valuable addition to the product, addressing the single biggest problem with Java—performance. The accelerator does this by taking the Java byte code binaries and generating standard C code from them. This code is then compiled using the standard optimizing C compiler and made available for use. This promises to provide a significant performance uplift, although it is still unlikely to be as fast as native C code because of the language abstraction.

The final advantage of integrated Java is the ease of integration of ORB models into the application. In fact, Oracle has integrated an ORB with the product, written using JServer. Using this ORB, database-resident Java code can be invoked remotely with standard Internet Inter-ORB Protocol (IIOP) invocation.

The new suite of application development tools, JDeveloper 2.0, provides the development environment for the new language and moves Oracle out of the old days of SQL*Forms. JDeveloper allows the development of Enterprise Java Beans (EJB), client Java applications, Java stored procedures, and Java Servlet code, using a GUI Integrated Development Environment.

13.2.2   New Data Services

In addition to the Java integration, improvements in Oracle8i data services support large user populations and Internet programming practices.

For content handling, Oracle provides interMedia, a set of multimedia mangement services for various types of data. The services available immediately are those of audio, video, text (ConText), and GIS information (Spatial). The ConText and Spatial services were first introduced in releases of Oracle7.

These services allow for more intelligent handling of content, enabling the database to provide more dynamic content for the application. Standard services include intelligent searching within the data types and content-specific manipulation, such as cropping.

Other Internet additions include the iFS, or Internet File System. This is a more flexible way of accessing the content in the database, allowing access through ftp, SMB (Windows Networking), NFS, and standard Net8.

Perhaps of more interest to the large system builder are the improvements in how Oracle manages data. These changes include

- Online index maintenance
- Secondary indexes on index-organized tables (IOTs)
- Local space management
- Optimizer plan stability

Although some of these features are not strictly data services, they all relate to how data can be managed in a large database, and so are treated together.

Online Index Maintenance

First is the welcome arrival of online B-tree index rebuilds. When the ONLINE keyword is specified, an index can be rebuilt *without* taking a table lock (lock type TM). This means that the table can continue to be used for read and write while the index is built; any changes during this period are logged for later addition to the new index. Because IOTs constitute an extended B-tree index, this also means that an IOT can be rebuilt online.

Secondary Indexes on Index-Organized Tables

The provision for secondary indexes on an IOT means that an IOT can now be used in place of many standard tables. The advantage of this is that the indexes on the table and the table itself can all be rebuilt online, allowing online performance and space maintenance to take place.

The impact of this provision is a huge advance in system availability. Although it probably still makes sense to carry out these maintenance operations during quiet (and therefore unsociable) hours, the system does not need to be taken down in order to perform these changes. Most scheduled maintenance periods can therefore be carried out online, allowing the system to remain operational to the user for months at a time. In fact, it is likely that the UNIX operating system will need attention (with patches and other, similar measures) more often than Oracle will.

Local Space Management

Local space management addresses a different issue—the inefficiency of the dictionary cache at managing free and used extents in the database. In previous releases, Oracle used the SYS.FET$ and SYS.UET$ dictionary tables to store the free and used extent maps, respectively. In large databases, there could be many thousands of entries in each of these tables (and subsequently in the dictionary cache), making any operation on them a laborious exercise. This, in fact, is the reason that "database fragmentation" through many extents has been seen as a bad thing.

In Oracle8i, there is the option of having *locally managed* tablespaces. When locally managed, Oracle stores the extent information for a file in bitmap form in the file itself. Any time Oracle needs to work on the extents in a locally managed tablespace, it need only consult the series of *on/off* bits in the file-local extent map. Therefore, it is considerably faster than the previous method and is more scalable because there are many of these bitmaps in the database.

The impact of local space management is that yet another reason for database maintenance has been all but removed. Using the bitmaps for space management, the ST enqueue is no longer required, and it becomes far less important to keep the extent sizes optimized for performance.

Optimizer Plan Stability

Although the CBO has been around for some time, the process of ensuring that it is working from good statistics has been problematic. Where a database is growing dynamically, the danger of plans changing overnight presents an unacceptable level of risk for large systems. With 8i, Oracle has provided several facilities that make the management of the optimizer more predictable. All these changes relate to the same aspect—better control of statistics.

The most fundamental of these changes is the ability to *freeze plans,* ensuring that the CBO will not take a different approach to a given query once the plan has been frozen. This ensures that queries will respond in the same order of time, even if the data distributions were to change in the tables. Without frozen plans, query response times could change by many orders of magnitude.

Additionally, production CBO statistics can now be applied to development databases in a supported way, allowing developers to use EXPLAIN PLAN in a worthwhile way.

These features may not seem to be enhancements in data services, but the prior hit-or-miss CBO tuning could break as many things as it fixed. With this more controllable method, the execution profiles of the queries are repeatable, therefore ensuring reliable operation of the database.

13.3   Future Oracle Releases

Unlike release 8.0, it is likely that release 8.1 will have additional features released during its lifespan. A great many of these features will probably be associated with the JServer component, because this is the most radical addition and is such a dynamically changing landscape anyway.

In addition to this, however, is the roadmap for the database server itself, going toward release 8.2 and even Oracle9.

Oracle has been chasing Microsoft for some time, specifically seeking dominance in the Windows NT database market. One side effect of this effort is that Oracle has had to simplify the interfaces and management of the database in order to provide users with the kind of "wizard" interfaces they are used to on the Windows platform.

This simplification of mundane tasks has become one of Oracle's strategic goals, including better installers, wizards to help with database creation and configuration, and so on. In addition, Oracle is making the operation of the database server itself a more automatic task, starting with 8.1, where a whole range of sort parameters (SORT_READ_FAC, SORT_WRITE_BUFFERS, and so on) have been obsoleted in favor of automatic management.

It is likely that this trend will continue in the future. One potential target could be the management of rollback segments, allowing Oracle to self-manage a common pool of space for undo information. Other enhancements will include the removal of some initialization parameters, making their configuration automatic. Taking this one step further, Oracle is likely to adopt some kind of self-healing tuning, allowing the instance to reconfigure itself where necessary for better operation.

Of more interest to builders of very large systems, Oracle is *certain* to keep improving the scalability and performance of its product. As we discussed in Chapter 1, improving scalability and performance is a continuous task, and the product will continue to improve in this area from release to release.

Perhaps the most crucial part of this improvement will be the architectural "tweaks" that Oracle is starting to incorporate, in order to better support emerging hardware architectures such as NUMA. Through continued coengineering with hardware suppliers, Oracle is actively working at staying ahead of other database products in terms of performance.

Finally, Oracle has nearly cracked the availability nut. While Oracle has been successful in deposing mainframes from many sectors of the marketplace, most banks and financial institutions still have no alternative to the mainframe. Oracle and UNIX simply cannot provide the same degree of availability that a modern mainframe or fault-tolerant system can. However, the Oracle Server is rapidly getting to the point where this is no longer the case, and it will soon be viable as a true mainframe alternative.

The final hurdle is a tough one: Oracle and its hardware partners need to work together to provide seamless availability. It is no good pointing fingers—the system simply has to work, all the time, with no excuses. When this has been achieved, however, Oracle will be able to shift up another gear and enter into a whole new world of massively scalable and highly available applications.

13.4   Chapter Summary

While application architectures shift and the Internet grows in strength, Oracle covers all bases. By embracing the emerging technologies and continuing to develop and improve its core product, Oracle is keeping its flagship product—the Oracle Server—on top.

Oracle is quickly becoming the database platform of choice for large commercial Internet companies, providing the technology and scalability that will make their businesses work. At the same time, more traditional business applications are using the new features of Oracle to provide higher availability and greater performance.

The highly available application system is the real challenge, and when Oracle and the hardware vendors finally get all the pieces together, Oracle will become even more prevalent in the high-end marketplace. This means that highly scalable Oracle systems will be in demand more than ever, and those skilled in building them become yet more marketable by implication. Welcome aboard!

Index

CD-ROM Warranty

Addison Wesley Longman, Inc. warrants the enclosed disc to be free of defects in materials and faulty workmanship under normal use for a period of ninety days after purchase. If a defect is discovered in the disc during this warranty period, a replacement disc can be obtained at no charge by sending the defective disc, postage prepaid, with proof of purchase to:

Editorial Department
Computer and Engineering Publishing Group
Addison-Wesley
One Jacob Way
Reading, Massachusetts 01867-3999

After the ninety-day period, a replacement disc will be sent upon receipt of the defective disc and a check or money order for $10.00, payable to Addison Wesley Longman, Inc.

Addison Wesley Longman, Inc. makes no warranty or representation, either expressed or implied, with respect to this software, its quality, performance, merchantability, or fitness for a particular purpose. In no event will Addison Wesley Longman, Inc., its distributors, or dealers be liable for direct, indirect, special, incidental, or consequential damages arising out of the use or inability to use the software. The exclusion of implied warranties is not permitted in some states. Therefore, the above exclusion may not apply to you. This warranty provides you with specific legal rights. There may be other rights that you may have that vary from state to state. The contents of this CD-ROM are intended for personal use only.

More information and updates are available at:
http://www.awl.com/cseng/titles/0-201-32574-8